# Children's Well-Being: Indicators and Research

Volume 21

This series focuses on the subject of measurements and indicators of children's well being and their usage, within multiple domains and in diverse cultures. More specifically, the series seeks to present measures and data resources, analysis of data, exploration of theoretical issues, and information about the status of children, as well as the implementation of this information in policy and practice. By doing so it aims to explore how child indicators can be used to improve the development and the well being of children.

With an international perspective the series will provide a unique applied perspective, by bringing in a variety of analytical models, varied perspectives, and a variety of social policy regimes.

*Children's Well-Being: Indicators and Research* will be unique and exclusive in the field of measures and indicators of children's lives and will be a source of high quality, policy impact and rigorous scientific papers.

More information about this series at http://www.springer.com/series/8162

Riccardo Lucchini • Daniel Stoecklin

# Children in Street Situations

## A Concept in Search of an Object

Springer

Riccardo Lucchini
Professor Emeritus
University of Fribourg
Corminboeuf, Switzerland

Daniel Stoecklin
Centre for Children's Right Studies
University of Geneva
Bramois/Sion, Switzerland

ISSN 1879-5196 ISSN 1879-520X (electronic)
Children's Well-Being: Indicators and Research
ISBN 978-3-030-19039-2 ISBN 978-3-030-19040-8 (eBook)
https://doi.org/10.1007/978-3-030-19040-8



This Springer imprint is published by the registered company Springer Nature Switzerland AG.
The registered company address is: Gewerbestrasse 11, 6330 Cham, Switzerland

# Foreword

The United Nations Convention on the Rights of the Child (UNCRC) was adopted 30 years ago by the UN General Assembly, in 1989. Riccardo Lucchini's work on children in street situations started at the same time. This book presents his principal research findings, along with those of Daniel Stoecklin, who wrote his PhD thesis under Lucchini's supervision, in 1998.

I first came across Riccardo Lucchini's work while trawling through a dusty library in Jakarta in 1996. I happened upon three unpublished manuscripts, typed on A4 paper, written by Riccardo Lucchini and translated from French into English by Daniel Stoecklin. I have no idea how they ended up in the archives of a library in Jakarta, but I was supposed to find them. The manuscripts were a revelation to me and my 'light bulb moment' after a year of conducting research with 'street children' in the city of Yogyakarta, trying to make sense of their geographies and identities. I had spent endless hours reading the global literature on street children published at that time. Much of it categorised street children and youth as 'either victims or heroes', as the late Judith Ennew and Mark Connolly wrote in their introduction to the seminal special issue of *Childhood* on 'Children Out of Place' (Connolly and Ennew 1996). For me, the keystone paper in that special issue – among a long list of eminent authors – was Lucchini's unpretentiously named piece, 'The street and its image'. Building on the outstanding work of Lewis Aptekar's (1988) *Street Children of Cali* and Jill Swart-Kruger's (1990) *Malunde*, Lucchini was a pioneer in what Judith Ennew called a 'paradigm shift' in street child research. The paradigm shift signalled an acknowledgement that 'street children' are not victims or delinquents in a specific place but children with multiple identities who survive across different social domains and through a 'constellation of relationships' (Lucchini 1996, p. 169). This paradigm shift also developed the idea that children have "careers" on the street (Lucchini 1996). As a children's geographer, my research was significantly influenced by Lucchini's work, which considers issues of space and time to inform understandings of street-connected children's lives, including street girls. His work led me to interrogate children's lives and identities, in diverse street situations, through participatory approaches and the triangulation of data, in ways which had not yet been explored in Indonesia.

The last 30 years have seen enormous progress in the implementation of the UNCRC. During this time, governments, and nongovernment organisations, have grappled with the implications of their obligation to recognise street-connected children as citizens and participants in decisions that impact their lives. The UNCRC stresses that appropriate measures must be taken to address discrimination of vulnerable or marginalised groups of children and to ensure that they are encouraged and enabled to participate in decision-making on an equal basis with other children. In most societies, however, it remains the case that laws and discriminatory attitudes continue to exist towards street-connected children, undermining and placing severe limitations on their rights.

I first met Daniel Stoecklin at the International Consortium for Street Children (CSC) Conference at Amnesty International House in London in 2016, as we are both members of the Consortium's Research Forum. It is Daniel Stoecklin who coined the expression 'children in street situations' (Stoecklin 1998), a phrase which has become widespread in the literature and among NGOS and which is now the wording used in the *UN General Comment No. 21 on Children in Street Situations*. The emphasis of the CSC Conference was on the UN General Comment. The discussion focussed on how many government and civil society groups still regard street-connected children as a 'problem' that needs to be fixed. Discussants stressed the importance of hearing all children's voices in matters that affect them and the importance of sensitising and socialising government and other agencies – with very different agendas – to the rights of street-connected children.

The single most important and challenging (for governments and practitioners) aspect of the General Comment to the UNCRC is the assertion of street-connected children's right to be living and working on the street. Such a statement is an acknowledgement of the fact that children are often on the street as a solution to their own problems. This position challenges almost every norm and traditional form of intervention, including traditional community-based interventions, to stop children from going to the street. In many countries, Article 12 of the UNCRC (the right to be heard) is still a radical proposition, including for many NGOs, the government and the police – who believe that they know what is best for the child. The aim is consistently to take a child off the street and 'rehabilitate' and 'reintegrate' him or her back into the 'family'. As a result, legislation and policy exacerbates the situation, and children in street situations become increasingly stigmatised and marginalised. Is that in the best interests of the child?

This book is the result of a long collaboration between two scholars, Lucchini and Stoecklin, who have devoted the last few decades to exploring and understanding the lives of children in street situations. Their shared values of a true rights-based approach to research with street-connected children permeate each chapter. The book interrogates the concept of 'street children' by exposing the dominant social construction and systematic stigmatisation of this group of marginalised children. Crucially, their argument – one which they have consistently made over the decades – is that a focus on the rights of children in street situations is insufficient if we do not challenge the social processes which have led to their existence and which continue to marginalise them. This book takes us further on that journey.

University of the Sunshine Coast
Sunshine Coast, Australia

Harriot Beazley, PhD (ANU)

## References

Aptekar, L. (1988). *The street children of Cali*. London and Durham: Duke University Press.

Ennew, J., & Connolly, M. (1996). Introduction: Children out of place. *Childhood, 3*(2), 131–145.

Lucchini, R. (1996). The street and its image. *Childhood, 3*(2): 235–246.

Stoecklin, D. (1998). *Enfants des rues en Chine. Une exploration sociologique*. PhD Thesis. Fribourg: Université de Fribourg.

Swart-Kruger, J. (1990). *Malunde: Street children of Hillbrow*. Johannesburg: Witwatersrand University Press.

# Acknowledgements

We express our gratitude to the Fondation Boninchi and the Fonds Général de l'Université de Genève for their support regarding the translations of the texts from French to English. Translations were made by Jonathan Roux, Aurore Colin and Iain Campbell, whom we thank for their ability to reproduce all the nuances of the original French texts.

# Contents

# Acronyms

| | |
|---|---|
| ARVIM | Activities, relations, values, images of self, and motivations |
| CSS | Children in street situations |
| DRMC | Declaration of the Rights of Man and of the Citizen |
| GC on CSS | General Comment No. 21 on Children in Street Situations |
| GO | Governmental organisation |
| GSS | Girls in street situations |
| NGO | Nongovernmental organisation |
| SWOT | Strengths, weaknesses, opportunities, and threats |
| UN | United Nations |
| UNCHS | United Nations Centre for Human Settlements |
| UNCRC | United Nations Convention on the Rights of the Child |
| UNCRC | United Nations Committee on the Rights of the Child |
| UNESCO | United Nations Educational, Scientific and Cultural Organization |
| UNFDAC | United Nations Fund for Drug Abuse Control |
| UNICEF | United Nations Children's Fund |

# Chapter 1
# Introduction

**Daniel Stoecklin and Riccardo Lucchini**

This publication is the fruit of a long collaboration. It contributes to a renewed reflection on social processes that we must understand if we aim to link children's rights with their contexts of realisation. Failing this it is too easy to fall in the 'religion of the rights of the child' trap, with its churches and temples, whose followers recite texts out of contexts. Our approach concerns understanding the relationship to values (including children's rights) that govern observable behaviours. Illuminating the gap between claimed values and actual behaviours enables us to show the fundamental incompatibility between children's rights and the expression 'street child': this expression essentialises a human being whose situation in fact results from social processes that marginalise them. Access to their rights remains insufficient if we keep calling them 'street children', as this expression masks the very processes that must be changed to truly enable better access. This original intuition was confirmed throughout our work.

Who and what are we talking about? This remains far from easy to tell. The General Comment on Children in Street Situations (hereafter GC on CSS) starts with a definition of this population:

> In the present general comment, the term 'children in street situations' is used to comprise: (a) children who depend on the streets to live and/or work, whether alone, with peers or with family; and (b) a wider population of children who have formed strong connections with public spaces and for whom the street plays a vital role in their everyday lives and identities. This wider population includes children who periodically, but not always, live and/or work on the streets and children who do not live or work on the streets but who regularly accompany their peers, siblings or family in the streets (UNCRC 2017, p. 3).

This definition maintains a foundation in the modern ideology that centers on individuals:

> The individuals themselves become more and more responsible subjects, not only in relation to their group belongings (family, kinship, local community), but also towards the wider collectivity. The state must therefore guarantee children a harmonious development for them to become responsible citizens (Lucchini 1993, pp. 16–17).



R. Lucchini, D. Stoecklin, *Children in Street Situations*, Children's Well-Being: Indicators and Research 21, https://doi.org/10.1007/978-3-030-19040-8_1

We must therefore maintain a critical distance towards children's rights, by situating them within the context of a modernity "that makes childhood a distinct category, whose welfare is guaranteed by the state" (Lucchini 1993, p. 16). The conjoined and paradoxical dynamics of the protection and coercion of children by the state are both reinforced. When it legislates, the State requires greater individual responsibilities, but it must also consider the structural and material conditions that allow some to fulfil the requirements better than others. Such attention to local conditions is, however, incompatible with the overarching order instituted by the law. Consequently, legislation is always directed towards abstract individuals, which, as we can see with 'street children', partly misses the logic of action that it was written for.

Although the GC on CSS somewhat widens the focus by the inclusion of population (b), there is still a risk that intervention targets people and not processes, as processes involve many more people and there is therefore a political reluctance to target them. The very wide focus contained in the approach of "children in street situations" (Stoecklin 1998) is therefore somewhat "lost in translations" (Stoecklin 2017): while the GC on CSS gives a substantive definition of these children (population a and b), the expression 'children in street situations' remains for us 'a concept in search of an object'. Our approach is therefore not centred on individuals but rather on an 'object' (a social process) experienced by them. This displaces the focus from substantial characteristics of this population to processual experiences that they are exposed to and that they simultaneously construct.

The 'object' we study is therefore the 'forms' emerging from symbolic interactions that take place within the street space. We shall hence look at children's rights not just as a list of the rights that are most important for CSS, but at the 'forms' that children's rights actually take in the street space and in institutions that are supposed to provide these children with minimum standards regarding respect of their rights. The identification of specific configurations (Elias 1981, 1991; Heinich 1997; Ducret 2011) shall allow us to construct this broader object and hence contribute to a renewed sociological theory.

The expression 'children in street situations' disentangles children from their situations, stressing that the problem is not inherent to the children but to the situations in which they have to make a living. It obliges us to address the situations, and not just the children experiencing them. The plural form (situations) not only emphasises the diversity of these situations, it also stresses the evolutionary dynamics of the streets, as opposed to the static view that implicitly conveys the image of waves of uncontrolled children filling in dead-ends and submerging cities, as is especially portrayed by the Chinese words for 'street children' – *liulang ertong* – 'wandering children' (Stoecklin 2000; Aptekar and Stoecklin 2014). The expression 'children in street situations' therefore entails a change of perspective which looks valid cross-culturally: a widening of the focus. However, this change is difficult for various reasons: political reluctance, a cultural habit of individualized selves, and, last but not least, theoretical blindness. As researchers, our responsibility is to work on the latter. This is what this book is all about: a contribution to a theory of street life.

We approach this problem through the expression 'children in street situations'. Indeed, each child is situated in relation to the street in a specific manner. The reduction of such diversity within the single category of 'street children' is hence imprecise, and a cause of confusion. For some 'street children' concerns victims, whereas for others this denomination brings forth the image of delinquents from dangerous backgrounds. Who, then, are we speaking of? Is being on the streets for a certain amount of time enough to be a 'street child'? As we can see, merely objective criteria, such as length of time on the streets, age, gender, family contacts, and so on do not allow us to bring light to the subjective and psychosocial differences that make us consider a child as a subject. More generally, the diversification and adaptation of social work interventions is made possible when they are tightly connected with a differentiation of the perception of CSS. Conversely, censorship surrounding their reality, along with a reduction to a homogenous category, often comes with a strong tendency towards undifferentiated repression.

Our approach contributes to the efforts undertaken by social workers seeking to adapt their interventions to the nuances of the field, as it replaces the reductive definitions of 'street children' with a more fine-grained typology of children, drawing from an informed knowledge of their particular psychosocial dynamics. We challenge the claim that the common definitions of 'street children' are based on objective criteria, of the kind that produce synchronic cartographies of the population based on sociographic data: total number, gender percentage, age, origin, sanitary situation, and so on. Under the guise of a pseudo-objectivity enabled by the immediate comprehension of numbers, what is in fact constructed is a distorted abstraction. Populations are stratified according to criteria that do not correspond to the logics that form the basis of its concrete interactions. This distortion is due to the imposition of a quantitative grid of analysis on a reality which, because it is relational, is eminently qualitative. Such an abstraction is alienating, as it produces an image of the population image that is of no significance to the population itself.

The designation of a social problem becomes particularly ambiguous when a population is defined as a social category and the quantitative evaluations it is subjected to are multiplied. Indeed, the number of children in each country who can be situated within the highly flexible category of 'street children' will determine the media response to the phenomenon, influencing social reactions and the debates over advocated solutions. This has led to today's paradoxical situation: there is a profusion of misleading descriptions of the living conditions of 'street children', and a tendency to inflate their numbers. This in turn has led to passionate debates about what must be done, but there is no (perhaps *because* there is no) agreement on the very definition of the 'street child'.

The statistical approach is hence anything but neutral, and it is even misleading. It claims to measure the magnitude of a 'social problem', but in fact it contributes to its construction: it signals a population that does not correspond to the norms, without questioning the latter. Within this function of naturalising dominant social norms statistics are particularly effective, thanks to the nature of numbers: immediately graspable, but by the same token contributing to making the underlying stakes invisible. Their apparent neutrality establishes a vision of consensus about a social order that is in fact contested. We can see this process as a contemporary example of Plato's allegory of the cave: we are dazzled by our fascination with statistics to such a degree that we do not see the power that they incorporate. To shed light on this biopower (Foucault 2012) we must hence read ‘behind’ the statistic, and see its effects and its functions.

The standardising definition of ‘street children’ to a specific social construction of the notions of childhood and the street. Every discourse on ‘street children’ illuminates us on the social representations of childhood in a given context. Such representations are inscribed within discursive contexts, and, in turn, gradually transform them. We then witness changes in the institutional responses to a phenomenon that is apprehended from more or less conflictual perspectives. When this conflictuality is important, the polarisation between assistance and repression is increased. Numbers are then used by the media to reinforce their tendency to represent the world within spectacular and dramatic criteria. Suffice to say that this does not render any service to the fine knowledge of the phenomenon, nor to CSS themselves.

The general trend of public places in big cities is towards a dichotomy between a majority of people using them as transit spaces between their major integrative spheres, primarily the family and the workplace, and a minority constituted of marginalized people who tend to occupy these places for some time. The social visibility of marginal people in the heart of cities therefore becomes even more evident. Social reactions to such visibility raise debates about ‘policing’.

The evaluation of the street as a dangerous space stems from modernity, which, in its separation of private and public spheres, has reduced the street to the transitional function. Its differentiated use hence reveals social distinctions. This functional transformation of the street in countries of the Global South, via the middle classes, prompted a process stigmatisating the poor, as they cannot afford to make the street a mere transitional space. The simplest definition of ‘street children’, centred around their presence on the street, is also the most normative, because the spatial criterion by itself delineates the border between normality and marginality. The assumption that the street is depraved, and those who occupy therefore immoral, reinforces the perverse effect of the definition’s imprecision: the presence of children is explained in terms of poverty and family dislocation, their psychosocial diversity is reduced in one homogenous category. This, in turn, contributes to amalgams and alarming statistics. This is the vicious circle brought about by a lack of socio-historical hindsight.

## 1.1 A Nominalist Perspective

The title of this book deserves some explanation. It has two parts: the main title, ‘Children in street situations’, referring simultaneously to a population and to a conceptual device, and the subtitle, ‘A concept in search of an object’, insisting on the conceptual framing. It suggests that any labelling of any population embodies a specific frame, as there is no name or concept that does not stem from a social construction of reality. With this nominalist position, wherein concepts are considered as purely human constructions, we intend to uncover the social dynamics that lie behind expressions such as ‘street children’, ‘children of the street’, and so on, which are widely used when people refer to these children, and through which even people who have barely interacted with them seem to understand clearly what is being referred to.

Nominalism holds that there is absolutely no connection between the words we use and the essence of the things that these words refer to. Words are pure conventions, and therefore people who are named in any possible way do not intrinsically bear the characteristics that are infused in the names given to them. The process is actually the reverse: it is because they are named so and so that they begin to behave accordingly. This has been widely documented since interactionists began pointing at the process of secondary deviance (Lemert 1967; Becker 1963). The same is, of course, valid for ‘street children’: the children who are labelled ‘street children’ tend to behave like ‘street children’, by adjusting to the views that lie in the eyes of their beholders. ‘Street child’ is an oxymoron, an association of two names, street and child, which convey conflicting images, as each name is attached with specific historical constructions. Their encounter provokes clashes between supposedly opposed locations (public vs. private), qualities, or projections (dangerous and dirty vs. fragile and innocent), all of which are socially constructed. It is the encounter between these implicit images that leads to the stigmatization of these children. The children labelled ‘street children’ therefore have to bear a whole range of significations which they are not, in the first instance, responsible for. They ‘inherit’ cultural habits and views that they must live with, and they actively deal with these issues.

This active role is what we first highlight with the expression ‘children in street situations’, showing that these children have to face situations that actually exist not just because they are living on the streets, but because of specific reconstructions of ‘street life’. In other words, their behaviour is from the start enshrined in a complex symbolic world. Behaviours cannot be detached from the meaningful context attached to them, as it is through the social definition of context that behaviours acquire meaning. Like a text needs a context, individual behaviour can be meaningful only with reference to the social definition of reality. Situations are made of intersubjective appraisals of the issues at stake.

With the expression ‘children in street situations’ we therefore highlight the strategies of the population of children usually called ‘street children’. But we address their strategies as constituents of the social dynamics that stem from the specific interactions that can be observed on the streets. This goes beyond a phenomenological perspective. In the phenomenological tradition, the ‘object’ of interpretive sociology is the subject, as the bearer of meaningful intentions (Williame 1973, p, 18). In our approach, closer to symbolic interactionism and pragmatism, we consider that the object is neither the subject nor society, but the social process that links them together. In other words, there are no fixed entities (the known and the knower), but rather a flow of experience: “known and knower (the mind), object and subject, are merely the two sides of experience” (Kando 1977, p. 105). In Jamesian pragmatism dualisms such as the mind-matter and subject-object dichotomies are rejected. It views the human as simultaneously subject and object to him-or herself. This perspective was further specified by George Herbert Mead:

> Anything of which a human being is conscious is something which he is indicating to himself [...]. [...] to indicate something is to extricate it from its setting, to hold it apart, to give it a meaning or, in Mead's language, to make it into an object (Blumer 1986, p. 80).

This perspective supports the subtitle of our book: *A concept in search of an object*. With the concept 'children in street situations' we are in search of an object to study, to define, to explain, and so on. It is the heuristic property of this expression that interests us. 'Children in street situations' is not a customary expression, but rather one constructed by the researchers: it is indeed in Daniel Stoecklin's thesis (1998) that it appears for the first time.

As we have discussed, statistics can hide more than they reveal: this shared language is invested with different meanings and projects. The number signals the importance of the phenomenon, but important discrepancies appear as soon as interventions are discussed. These discrepancies concerning the 'object' of the intervention are very revealing regarding the insufficient knowledge of the phenomenon. It is precisely to reduce this ignorance, and to potentially enable more relevant interventions, that we have decided to seek out what 'object' is enlightened by the existence of 'children in street situations'. It is indeed essential to be understand the children's reality, from their point of view, to then adapt aid efforts towards them. Still today we too often see the opposite: the 'street child' is forced into the normative frame within which the aid programmes function.

Some figures crop up regularly. To give a certain weight to their statements, but also because they feel that without sensational numbers their pleas will not be heard, many NGOs talk of "100 million street children in the world", a figure voiced by UNICEF more than 30 years ago.[1] In fact, it is impossible to give an exact figure for CSS, as the literature uses different categories – 'children of the street', 'on the street', 'homeless', 'abandoned', 'in conflict with the law', 'in especially difficult circumstances', and so on – and such diverging yet overlapping categories cannot be compared or unified. In addition, it is practically impossible to draw up reliable statistics, as these children are highly mobile. CSS may be in institutions, in prisons, back with their families, involved in NGO programmes, then back on the streets again, in a circular way or just alternating between two places. Double or overcounting is therefore more than occasional, and sometimes brandishing huge figures may even be only for institutional reasons. One of the major features of the 'street situation' phenomenon is high mobility. Another one is the psychosocial diversity of 'street situations' themselves. Mobility is not just a problem for counting fixed 'categories' of children; it is an essential aspect transversal to many street situations. It is of prime importance to understand why millions of children pass from one type

[1] See J. Ennew (1994, p. 32). In the mid 1980s, J. Ennew and B. Milne (1989) arrived at a much lower estimate (23 million), and the NGO Childhope-UK (Strategy Plan 2001–2003) expressed the same reserve as ours regarding the possibility of giving a precise figure for children living on the street.

of social life (community, village) to another (slums, street), and how social solidarity evolves in this movement.

Quantitative clouding, in its quest for legitimate intervention proposals, often reduces the actors in question and their viewpoint to a mere 'opinion' on a problem, and both the problem's seriousness and the proposed solutions to resolve it are defined from the outside. This is prominent in the case of CSS, who are too often kept in the margins of any decision about them. This is also the case for their parents, as the ideal image of the responsible adult is often denied to parents from underprivileged backgrounds. Rationality is not attributed to them, as the practical nature of their survival behaviours and strategies break with the ideal image of childhood as 'carefree' and 'authentic' that the upper classes value.

Ultimately it is that those who were denied access to proper living conditions that are themselves made responsible for 'depriving' their children of their childhood. It is from this notion of responsibility, which is socially constructed and reserved for acts embodying the ethos of a culture, that actual behaviours are judged. Those with behaviours that respond to another rationality are designated as 'deviant', without any questioning of the structural and material obstacles that prevent individuals in the margins of a culture from corresponding to instituted ethical norms. They are simply constituted as an irrational 'out-group', deviant 'outsiders'. Being a 'street child' is therefore seen as the sign of a lack of good will, the symptom of the moral depravity of the poor.

There has, however, been gradual, if relative, change in this conception, since the adoption of the Convention on the Rights of the Child (UNCRC 1989). Until the early 1990s a logic that was prejudiced towards 'street children' prevailed. Such common sense definitions influenced practices and approaches. Little by little, the relation between practice and definition has shifted: empirical understanding of children, and most importantly of their own way of viewing their lives on the street, has taken precedence over prejudices. The proliferation of qualitative and phenomenological studies on this matter has greatly contributed to this shift. The adoption of the General Observation N°21 on Children in Street Situations in 2017 constituted a fundamental instrument in the transformation of approaches towards children's rights policies. In a way it sanctifies the long struggles of the NGOs, trade unions, social workers, and researchers who resisted a uniform and stigmatising treatment.

The sociologist can identify and describe what a street situation is by observing the social actor's strategies within their context. The elaboration of survival strategies will be dependent on a given context. Certain children will also better develop and practice their skills than others in the same context. There is hence an immense variety of street situations, depending on contexts and the children themselves. As researchers we also have an ethics, and in our opinion a better understanding of these varieties and variations is a condition for suggesting relevant measures to improve these situations. It is useless to condemn vaguely defined factors – poverty, family dysfunction, exploitation – as this invariably leads children towards marginal spaces. We must precisely specify each characteristic of these phenomena, from context to context. This is what we have attempted to achieve through our own studies in Latin America and in China. Many of our research results are set out in this publication.

What is most important to us, however, is proposing an 'object' that enables more systematic research on CSS in any context, in order for their reality to be better understood and therefore give means for public policy to be adapted in relevant ways. We must hence 'construct' this 'object' as far as possible from the haste that distorts the phenomenon when it is treated as an emergency. Attaining such a better understanding of the reality implies work conditions for the researcher devoid of outside pressure. In other words, as we highlight the dire fact that today researchers lack the practical conditions for the building of in-depth knowledge, we call for a necessary improvement of theoretical and practical resources for research. These will only be developed upstream, through better initial conditions of research: financing, independence of research and so on.

It is of the utmost importance to us to note that the stereotypical images of CSS, whether that of the young criminal or that of the passive victim, are not due the ignorance of the people who adopt these prejudiced views. This reduction rather reflects the intrinsic conflicts within social structures subjected to rapid modernisation. CSS are at once the 'object' of research and, by the same token, point towards something else: they signal the existence of a duality in the eyes of those who judge them. They spell out oppositions, divergences, and disagreements; in short, the normative conflictuality within all the groups or classes that claim to want the good of the child.

Such conflictuality increases along with the rise of social inequalities, and is inscribed within each of the principal spaces of socialisation: dwellings, schools, and workplaces. In a way, CSS are pointers towards these macrosocial changes. Yet it is of paramount importance to us that they are not only victims of this, but that they can become agents of change towards less conflictuality. There is much to be done still in this direction, and what we observed 20 years ago is still valid today.

The phenomenon of street life is multi-faceted and consequences are reciprocal, so it is difficult to pinpoint causes, and not expedient to attempt to isolate a single cause that would explain street life worldwide. Nevertheless, macroeconomic trends such as international dependency, neo-liberal policies, and structural adjustments imposed by the international creditors, as well as corruption and a lack of political will, are among the major factors affecting the lives of the poorest segments of the population.

Life on the streets is made up of various constraints affecting children and their survival strategies, and it therefore varies according to context. This requires that we also cast light on those who are in contact with CSS, because they are part of the problem, and hopefully also of the solution. Some exaggerate statistics, and this may increase feelings of insecurity, which, in turn, will be exploited to justify 'cleaning-up' the streets. Others underestimate the problem or simply censure the topic. A fascination with figures often corresponds to interests that are very distant from the legitimate expectations of those we want to help: these interests are those of institutions, politics, media, and international relations. By categorising children living on the street, we are not necessarily getting any closer to understanding them.

The tendency to define children as an object of attention and educational measures is made more prominent when they find themselves in supposedly marginal or deviant situations. This is particularly the case for 'children in street situations', namely children signalled as being out of place (Connolly and Ennew 1996). The stigmatisation of 'street children' is common to all cultural contexts, through which children are dispossessed of the right to apprehend their own lives (Ennew 1995). They are not, or no longer, seen as subjects, and their interpretation of their environment and their personal situations within it are not considered valid. These children are either reduced to an object of uncontrollable circumstances – victims – or designated as deviants that need to be reformed. In either case, child-victim or child-deviant, the children are not given the right to speak. Others speak in their place, and they are confined.

Chinese authors whose publications on this matter have been authorised speak of '*liulang ertong*'. Translated literally this means 'children of the wave', and is a reference to the mass of migrant populations designated as '*liudong renkou*', 'the floating population'. Such an amalgamation then legitimises a discriminatory treatment of individuals according to their membership of a social group to which stigmatising traits are assigned. Urban dwellers' prejudices about a drifting population that is considered to be dangerous thus enables and supports social discrimination. No psychosocial differentiation of children is proposed, not even according the length of time spent on the street or their everyday activities.

The presence of children on the street is usually explained in terms of poverty and family problems. Such elements of course exist, but they not sufficient to explain the behaviour of children on the streets in China, or their careers. Moreover, certain structural elements (such as political contradictions) are systematically disregarded from these analyses. We will see, however, that the presence of children on the streets in China is strongly connected to political, economic, and social factors. Like everywhere else, the Chinese definition of the 'street child' in terms of family disorganisation and poverty enables an evasion of these factors.

## 1.2 Approaching the 'Object'

In this publication, we propose to synthesise our works in order to better approach this 'object', as we believe a better understanding of it is still required for children's rights to make a genuine difference. Indeed, what now are the objects that bear the rights of 'children in street situations'? Is the focus on 'substantial' rights (such as education and healthcare) or on socio-historical perspectives? Children's rights are currently centred on the former, but such substantial rights will remain a 'text with no context' if they are not placed in the perspective of the social dynamics within they operate. An decontextualised reading of the Convention on the Rights of the Child and of the General Observation is simply insufficient. Rights only bear their full meaning as substantial objects if they are inscribed within social processes.

With the objective of a contextualisation of normative instruments, we propose throughout this publication a 'series of processual objects': we will, in each chapter, attempt to identify 'dynamic objects' through which sociological analysis can contribute to strengthening ethical interventions based on children's rights. Only contextualisation, and hence empirical work, can allow us to reconcile the academic demand for knowledge and the ethical demand for justice. Through this contextualisation work we have gone in search of 'processual objects', which we can here render.

Our perspective is therefore one of 'object collection': we have harvested objects, namely social realities, brought to light through the expression 'children in street situations'. Amongst these objects we find those constructed by CSS themselves. This is an essential feature of our study: the children who are the 'object' of the research are themselves reflexive beings who elaborate their own objects of reflection. To comprehend CSS therefore implies understanding how and why they develop specific objects rather than others. The leads us to the conclusion that when we study human subjects we must in fact study what they 'study' themselves – what they think, what they analyse – and try to understand why they think and analyse in such manner. The subject's reflexivity therefore constantly shifts the 'object' under scrutiny. We measure here how far we are from the sociology of the social fact, as advocated by Durkheim. From his perspective, each social fact is explained by preceding social facts. There is therefore an endless causal chain for the researcher to explore, with social facts being conceived as exterior to individuals and imposed upon them. In our approach, on the contrary, reality is seen as intersubjective and there are therefore no facts that imposes itself on all individuals in the same way. All phenomena are perceived, interpreted, and transformed in an intersubjective manner.

Subjective reconstructions are the bedrock of social facts; these do not exist outside of the consciousness of individuals. The example of human rights illustrates this process very well: what we call 'rights' only exist within our conscious mind's ability to conceptualise such abstract conventions. Animals don't agree on universal rights amongst themselves; they fight for their prerogatives rather than for rights. Only humans can fight for their rights, including, incidentally, what they have instituted as 'animal rights'. Each and every social phenomenon is thus carried out through the subjectivity of actors.

It could be argued in response that population density, for example, does not depend on subjectivity: there are more individuals on a given territory, full stop. But this 'objectivist' reasoning does not hold, as the notion of 'population density' itself comes precisely from the perceptions of individuals, in a given space, suddenly feel cramped. The concept emerges from experience. This can be said of all the sociological concepts that we elaborate. The 'children in street situations' concept also emerged from the experience, this time that of the researchers, that something crucial needed to be specified within children's lived 'situations' that the label 'street children' could not account for. We thus started to look for a word, a concept, that could render the existence of what we felt was missing. Only in a second phase did we attempt to describe this thing, our 'object', the existence of which remains somewhat vague and diffuse. There is a necessary back-and-forth between the concept and the object it is supposed to designate. These round trips are at the heart of the researcher's task, as they confront a concept with actors' lived realities. It is indeed the heuristic property of an open concept that allows it to collect elements of real, lived reality that it can embrace.

In their everyday experiences, human beings start from an observed phenomenon, and name it. When they do not find a name or a 'ready-made' concept, or rather one 'ready-to-be applied-on-others', they seek out a new term to designate it. Names thus stem from experience, rather than the opposite. But the names and concepts that we invent usually have a verifying purpose: we seek reinfornce and root the name or the concept within the significant universe of language by delineating the boundaries of what it names. This is precisely what we have done: we named an experience, or rather several experiences – 'street situations' – and we then attempted to comprehend what children placed in such situations perceived. This allows us to detail the object (or objects) of the actors' reflexivity within the 'situations' in which they are supposedly immersed. Starting from their representations we revisit our own conceptual tools, and hence always make 'discoveries' that enable us to specify or alter a theory. This process is dynamic and never ceases to evolve.

The expression 'children in street situations' must, however, also be comprehended from a nominalist point of view. Indeed, there is no more correspondence between the expression 'children in street situations' and the human beings it designates than between them and the expression 'street children'. What does it change then? The most important change is that with the expression 'children in street situations' we contextualise these children's behaviours within a symbolic world that is not merely confined to the street-space. Just like a text is only intelligible when it is situated within its context, it is a question of situating observed behaviours within their context. Our claim is that the street itself is too narrow a context to understand the behaviours that we observe; they must be reinserted into a much larger frame. We think that this context is the vast ensemble of conventions within which formal and informal social relations are regulated. This therefore includes formal instruments of a global scope, including international treaties such as the Convention on the Rights of the Child (UNCRC 1989).

We must emphasise here that the relevance of our approach is demonstrated by the social dynamics themselves. Indeed, as every naming has the potential to reconfigure its framing, we can notice today a relative popularisation of the expression 'children in street situations'. This is especially the case since it has become an official phrase used by the United Nations, through its GC on CSS. Our nominalist positioning, based on an unveiling of social constructions of reality, has hence been grounded by the empirical observation that our own analytical constructions have been (at least in part) integrated to the new questionings around CSS. This explains why some of the texts assembled in this publication are already quite old, such as Riccardo Lucchini's papers that were originally published in French and that English-speaking readers can now discover. Indeed, they are particularly interesting to read today when the expression 'children in street situations', which emerged from these texts, has since become official. Rather than seeing it as a form of consecration, our aspiration is to remain in a critical position, especially appropriate for researchers that see their constructions attain a level of success. We are researchers, not promoters.

The popularisation of the expression 'children in street situations' must therefore lead us to redouble our efforts with regards to keeping a critical attitude towards our work. For this reason, we will also critically examine the aforementioned United Nations GC on CSS (particularly in Chap. 10). But most importantly we seek to redeploy the questions we have been asking over the past decades of collaboration.

We will present to the reader our primary questions by progressively resituating them as contributions to a general theory of the 'street situation'. We will thus attempt to answer the following question: what are the factual objects that the expression 'children in street situations' enable to bring to light? In other words, our commitment is to unearthing what this new framing can illuminate.

To answer this question, we, at the end of this book, assemble a collection of all the 'objects' that we have brought to light. We are therefore collectors of social objects that the expression 'children in street situations' enables to discern.

The first 'object' that we have collected is the social actor, who, precisely to be an actor, must become an 'object' for him- or herself. There are indeed no social actors without interactions, and it is through these interactions that we observe the actor. Social interaction carries out identifications, because it has a mirror effect:

> The individual experiences himself as such, not directly, but only indirectly, from the particular standpoints of other individual members of the same social group, or from the generalized standpoint of the social group as a whole to which he belongs. For he enters his own experience as a self or individual, not directly or immediately, not by becoming a subject to himself, but only in so far as he first becomes an object to himself just as other individuals are objects to him or in his experience; and he becomes an object to himself only by taking the attitudes of other individuals toward himself within a social environment or context of experience and behavior in which both he and they are involved (Mead 1934, p. 138).

For James, the reflexive self is not a 'mind', looked at as an entity. It is, rather, an experience (the experience of thinking), a behavioural process, a stream of consciousness (Kando 1977, p. 106). Mead specifies this by stating that the conscious being is conscious of itself and is hence able to treat consciousness itself as an object: the subject can consider itself as an object and make observations on itself as if it were an other. If, in Meadian words, we are beings able to include ourselves in the list of the 'objects' we can in indicate to ourselves, then we are also able to build a 'theory' that foresees how 'objects', including ourselves, behave.

The analysis of social dynamics is itself proof and product of this auto-reflexive capacity. It grounds one's ability to foresee the attitudes of others, based on reflexive thinking about one's own behaviour, and to identify the 'meanings' or the 'reasons' attached to these attitudes and behaviours. This projective capacity – to think that others may have the same reasons that I have to do or to refrain from doing something – is foundational for the empathy that is necessarily involved in the interpretations of the behaviours and discourses of others.

This is how the 'new social psychology', also called 'pragmatic social psychology', was described in the late 1970s: "By taking social process as its point of departure, it is able to view both social structures and individual selves (which admittedly possess some permanence) as emergent products within that process" (Kando 1977, p. 89). What we must study is the emergence of 'products' (social and individual) that are shaped by intentions that are not there at once, but are 'emergent', always 'in the making'. Interaction is not, therefore, a product of intention: it is the process in which intention emerges and takes on specific forms that are reflexively interpreted by the interactants and reoriented accordingly. The object of study is therefore interaction as a (re)constructor of intentions.

Interaction is also something man is able to indicate to himself. This is what makes experience itself the precondition of meaning-making. There is no meaning *a priori* (unless we believe in the Platonic world of ideas): meaning is always constructed and reconstructed *a posteriori*. Experience is therefore both the means and the outcome of meaning. The situations experienced by specific individuals placed in specific conditions (forms or types of interactions) are reconstructed reflexively: social actors attach meanings to what they call a 'situation' by appreciating and qualifying the types of interactions they experience. Children 'in street situations', like any other actors, have an experience, that is, a specific kind of interaction, that they are able to indicate to themselves. Their reflexive capacity is shaped by specific configurations as well as shaping them in return. It's a process.

But CSS are not only a 'concept', they are also actors who are in search of an 'object'. They are actively trying to find the 'object' they can relate to, and thus trying to make sense of the 'society' they belong to. They try to find a point of view under which they can be recognised, and hence a certain definition of their situation. The definition of the situation is necessary to be able to experience a feeling of belonging. Attachment is precisely something experienced as problematic by CSS. This is not only because these children may have experienced traumatic events, broken relationships, violent reactions, everything that may lead to a sense of rejection, but also because they experience difficulty in relating to a 'society' that has no consistency, or not enough.

CSS often use the expression "no one cares for us". This is more than just a complaint. It reflects the feeling of having nothing in common, no 'object' to share with the rest of society. For them, 'society' is generally not a relevant 'object' that they can indicate to themselves, as it is too unpredictable. It does not become something one can count on, it cannot become a mirror of experience, something that can objectify one's own existence. The Chinese children experiencing street life used another expression that conveyed the same idea: "*meiyou banfa*" (which can be translated by "there's is nothing to do", or "there are no ways"). This expression reflects the feeling of helplessness that is linked to the impression that society is something one cannot grasp. It cannot be grasped; it escapes any attempt of locating oneself within it. CSS are children without a place. There are not just 'out of place', in the wrong place. They are 'placeless', without a place. They cannot constitute society as a place because of a fundamentally violent asymmetry: they are objectified by others in a way that makes it impossible for them to objectify these others (the 'society').

Being despised as 'street children', these children are deprived of the legitimacy to define others and hence to relate to them on equal footing. The subordinate status that is socially imposed on them makes it difficult, if not impossible, for them to relate to others through the mechanism of empathy. What is refused to them is the reciprocity of perspectives that is foundational of a common experience. These children can experience empathy only with other alike children. They tend to stay in a world of significant others and cannot construct a sense of the general other, and the sense of justice that goes along with this. Their loyalty tends to be marked by moral realism, seeing sanctions as directly attached to an act that can be justified by transcendental forces, and not as mediated by interpretations and hence power relations of the interpreters. This reinforces the vicious cycle of the unconsciousness of oppression.

The stigmatisation of 'street children' can therefore be alleviated only if we change the label we use (as they are not able to do it themselves, or are not heard in doing so): when we speak of 'children in street situations' we can begin to highlight something that the label 'street children' renders invisible, namely how these situations are defined. It is the definition of situations that makes them as they are, as is underlined in the Thomasian theorem:

> If men define situations as real, they are real in their consequences (Thomas and Thomas 1928, p. 571).

When children are defined as 'street children', this has different consequences than when they are defined as 'in street situations'. Once we acknowledge that 'street situations' are marked by an asymmetry in the power to define and hence relate to others, then we understand that the label 'street children', and not the children it is assigned to, is itself the problem, because it deprives the actors (the children) of the possibility of seeing themselves as participants in their own identity. The label is what impedes these children from building a sense of belonging, and, ironically, they become seen as 'detached', as they cannot recognise themselves in the image society gives them and hence they end with no attachment to this society. The lack of the possibility of reciprocity that lies in the unidirectional labelling process is the problem, and children whose deviant behaviour emerges from this problem are ironically considered as having in themselves some problematic features, or even being of a problematic 'nature'.

In the chapters of this book, we will highlight the social construction of 'street situations' by identifying different symbolic 'objects' that are negotiated in this complex social dynamic. What emerges in the observed behaviours and discourses of 'children in street situations' is linked to what these social actors integrate from their environment. Their strategies are reflections of the world they live in. They reveal 'emergent products' that must not be confused with a subtantialist view of either social systems or individual selves. These 'objects' are rather symbolic elements that filter and mediate the relationships between them.

This perspective allows us to situate even children's rights as a symbolic fiction, which affects relations between social actors. No right lives by itself: it exists in as much as human beings are able to designate together what it concerns. This designation itself constitutes the 'objects' that mediate the relationship between people and institutions. But these symbolic 'objects' are reductive with regards to experience. The word constrains the thing. Experience is indeed much wider than the concepts we use to describe things. In other words, 'what goes on' in our lives appears differently to us than the perceptions that we might render through socially consensual discourses. For example, to the question "what do you do in life", people usually simply designate their work. We then see that 'what goes on' is in fact a social construction: we select from the mass of available data that which constitutes relevant information (just like the media selects 'news'). We thus form a structure of pertinences, which we become so accustomed to that we completely miss the fact that other data and information is put to the side, or completely concealed. In this regard, children's rights also constitute a structure of pertinences. We must hence take some distance to better see what other structures they could possibly hide. The same goes for discourses collected on the streets:

> In general, all that pertains to survival on the street and to the representations of children belongs to an order of pertinence. The researcher must therefore discover the children's structures of pertinences. This enables the researcher to establish the roles and sometimes the norms associated with the children. It then becomes possible to study the social dimension of what is done and said by a child (Lucchini 1993, p. 27).

The 'objects' that are thus constructed by social actors are the result of an evolving structure of pertinences. According to this perspective, the study of CSS informs us about the 'objects' established by the actors for whom the street is the principal living environment. This is fundamental to comprehending if and how marginal structures of pertinences can have an impact on dominant structures of pertinences. The institutional vectors of such an influence must be analysed as structures of pertinences being translated from one social sphere to another. An example of this kind of translation is yet to be analysed in-depth.[2]

The identification of specific configurations (Elias 1981, 1991; Heinich 1997; Ducret 2011) will allow us to construct this broader 'object', and hence contribute to a renewed sociological theory. In this endeavour, the research will practically highlight translations within the 'children's rights agenda' – constituted of the UN Convention on the Rights of the Child (UNCRC 1989), the General Comments, the public policies of GOs and the operational strategies of NGOs – regarding CSS. As part of the guidance to state parties, the GC on CSS is both a recognition that these children face specific deprivations and a means to curb the discriminations denying them access to their rights. Observation of the factors transforming these norms into concrete realisations is therefore of primary importance for the sociology of children and childhood. It is our hope that this endeavour can be stimulated by the empirical evidence and the theoretical construction achieved in this book.

## References

Aptekar, L., & Stoecklin, D. (2014). *Street children and homeless youth: A cross-cultural perspective*. Dordrecht/Heidelberg/New York/London: Springer.

Becker, H. S. (1963). *Outsiders: Studies in the sociology of deviance*. New York: The Free Press.

Blumer, H. (1986). *Symbolic interactionism: Perspective and method*. Berkeley: University of California Press.

Connolly, M., & Ennew, J. (1996). Children out of place. *Childhood, 3*(2), 131–145.

[2] Research is ongoing at the time of writing, under the supervision of Daniel Stoecklin. It touches upon the participatory capability of children in street situations in Brasil and China (Research under SNFS Grant 10001A_179098/1).

Ducret, A. (2011). Le concept de « configuration » et ses implications empiriques: Elias avec et contre Weber., *SociologieS*, La recherche en actes, Régimes d'explication en sociologie, mis en ligne le 11 avril 2011, consulté le 01 octobre 2017. URL: http://sociologies.revues.org/3459
Elias, N. (1981). *Qu'est-ce que la sociologie?* Paris: Pocket.
Elias, N. (1991). *The society of individuals*. London/New York: Continuum.
Ennew, J. (1994). *Street and working children. A guide to planning*. (Save the children: development manual 4). London.
Ennew, J. (1995). Outside childhood: Street children's rights. In B. Franklin (Ed.), *The handbook of children's rights. Comparative policy and practice* (pp. 201–214). London/New York: Routledge.
Ennew, J., & Milne, B. (1989). *The next generation: Lives of third world children*. London/Philadelphia: Zed Books/New Society Publishers.
Foucault, M. (2012). *Du gouvernement des vivants – Cours au Collège de France. 1979–1980*. (Edition établie par M. Senellart, sous la direction de F. Ewald et A. Fontana). Paris: EHESS/Gallimard-Seuil.
Heinich, N. (1997). *La Sociologie de Norbert Elias*. Paris: Éditions La Découverte.
Kando, T. M. (1977). *Social interaction*. Saint Louis: The C.V. Mosby Company.
Lemert, E. M. (1967). *Human deviance. Social problems and social control*. Englewood Cliffs: Prentice Hall.
Lucchini, R. (1993). *Enfant de la rue. Identité, sociabilité, drogue*. Genève/Paris: Droz.
Mead, G. H. (1934). *Mind, self and society*. Chicago: University of Chicago Press.
Stoecklin, D. (1998). *Enfants des rues en Chine. Une exploration sociologique*. Ph.D. thesis. Fribourg: Université de Fribourg.
Stoecklin, D. (2000). *Enfants des rues en Chine*. Paris: Karthala.
Stoecklin, D. (2017). The general comment on children in street situations: Insights into the institutionalisation of children's rights. *The International Journal of Children's Rights, 25*(4), 817–869.
Thomas, W. I., & Thomas, D. S. (1928). *The child in America: Behavior problems*. New York: Knopf.
UNCRC. (1989). *Convention on the rights of the child (UN, 1989)*. https://www.ohchr.org/en/professionalinterest/pages/crc.aspx. Accessed 27 Oct 2018.
UNCRC. (2017). *General Comment No. 21 (2017) on children in street situations*. CRC/C/GC/21. https://www.crcasia.org/wp-content/uploads/2016/04/G1717034.pdf. Accessed 27 Oct 2018.
Williame, R. (1973). *Les Fondements phénoménologiques de la sociologie comprehensive: Alfred Schutz et Max Weber*. La Haye: Martinus Nijhoff.

# Chapter 2
# The *Street Child* as an Object

**Riccardo Lucchini and Daniel Stoecklin**

## 2.1 The Epistemological Question

The dominant rhetoric on 'street children' intended for the general public, politicians and funders is marked by an assurance that admits no doubt. We know who 'street children' are, where they come from and the reasons behind their presence on the street. 'Street children' are described as a perfectly identified social problem, and must then be treated as such. There are no major problems in targeting intervention, because 'street children', their families and the communities they come from constitute a population which is visible in terms of deviance and social disorganisation. According to the dominant rhetoric, visibility is therefore the main characteristic of 'street children', and it is this visibility that makes them a social problem. Yet it is by naming a child as a 'street child' that he or she becomes visible and takes on a new identity. The naming process is double. On one hand, there is the proclamation of the norms the child does not correspond to and the enumeration of the 'causes' behind this condition. These norms are what define the 'street child' as out of place. On the other hand, the naming process entails the quantification of these children. It means knowing how many children are on the streets, how many of them disappear, and how many get off the streets. It means making a quantified assessment of the situation in order to legitimise kinds of intervention and funding. But this quantification is destined to fail, for we can not add up qualities: identity, feelings, motivations, character, action, relations with others, and so on. We can add up individuals defined in advance by statistical categories (age, gender, schooling, etc.), but not people. The naming

This chapter is a translation of parts from Lucchini, R. (2008). L'enfant en situation de rue n'est pas un fait social. Entre détermination et indétermination. In: Jean Zermatten (Ed.). *Enfants en situations de rue. Prévention, intervention, respect des droits*. Sion: IUKB / IDE, pp. 31–41, with courtesy of IUKB/IDE, and a translation of parts from Stoecklin, D. (2000). *Enfants des rues en Chine*. Paris: Karthala, with courtesy of Karthala.



R. Lucchini, D. Stoecklin, *Children in Street Situations*, Children's Well-Being: Indicators and Research 21, https://doi.org/10.1007/978-3-030-19040-8_2

process of 'street children', then, is closely linked to the child's objectification. When a child is designated as a 'street child', this term becomes a concept which proves to be 'capable of existing in the absence of the object' (Jacquard 1997, p. 25).

The 'street child' becomes an object for intervention which can then be presented as the product of an instrumental rationality legitimised by science, social accountability (prevention) and kindness (charity). The reification of the child, like, for that matter, that of all those who are excluded from a social system based on quantifiable performances, is based, among other things, on what in the analysis of Michel Foucault has been named as biopower (Foucault 1972, 1975). Albert Jacquard reminds us of this quote by Jacques Lacan: 'the word is the murder of the thing' (Jacquard 1997, p. 25).

Biopower is a tool to manage the population, allowing society to intervene on itself. Applied to the excluded and to 'street children' in particular, biopower thrives above all on the logic of security. When this logic is combined with a charitable justification of the intervention it strengthens the alienating effects of biopower. The 'out of place' child is therefore perceived above all in terms of risks, both objective (violence and insecurity in the public space) and subjective (deviance and delinquency). The logic specific to biopower gives the impression of being able to calculate these risks and thus to choose the appropriate tools to limit them. The instrumentality of the intervention and its association with the process that designates the 'street child' as out of place makes it difficult to accept an alternative public discourse about the logic specific to biopower.

The process of designating 'street children' as out of place is therefore what defines them as a well-defined and visible social problem. Yet it is precisely this visibility that bothers and is criticised in public opinion. The postulate of visibility goes hand in hand with the postulate of simplicity: 'street children' are characterised by their presence on the street and by the absence of 'responsible' adults. The street is thought of as a merely a physical piece of data, a concrete space and not as a representation. The 'responsible' adult is a figure who is not precisely described but who is effectively identified as the child's mother. We will see later why this two-dimensional definition is ineffective, and why complexity is what characterises the world of children in street situations.

Those we call children in street situations (CSS) are not objects. They are not objects in the ontological sense, as they are subjects, but neither are objects in the sociological sense, as they do not embody, by themselves, the complexity of social dynamics. Yet it is these dynamics that are the sociologist's object of study. The expression 'street child', contrary to the expression 'child in a street situation', reduces these dynamics to a static thing. The child is then meant to embody a given problem. The expression 'street children' does not, then, account for social dynamics: it rather stigmatises a population and forever ties them to specific traits. This naturalisation is somewhat similar to ethnicisation and exoticisation. It 'objectifies' people, while the sociological object resides in the relationships between people.

This is why the expression 'street child' is ambiguous. It is a notion of a polysemous nature, for the 'street child' can not be defined as a social fact (in the terms of

Emile Durkheim) which would be given once and for all. A 'street child' cannot be identified, and much less easily defined, for he or she is a process, constantly evolving. A 'street child' is not simply an object located in space and time. The numerous mediations allowing us to reconstruct the environment that we study evolve, interfering with an unequivocal delimitation of the 'street child'. This is the case even though these children's lives are often marked by violence, precariousness, and suffering. We are not trying to deny or minimise this, but to show that, from a sociological point of view, it is impossible to build a theory on such elements. So based on what and whom should we define it? Which normality should we use to claim that a 'street child' is a child living outside the norm? When does a child become a 'street child'? What is the paradigm to which the researcher and the outreach worker (social workers, case workers, psychologists, and so on) are referring when they define their research 'object' or their 'client/consumer'? There are, of course, answers to these questions, but they differ depending on the 'unit of measurement' we choose to use to define normality.

For a long time, studies on children in street situations (CSS) were mostly of a descriptive nature and led to no theorisation. The accumulation of disparate data and the purely empirical description of the 'street child' did not lead to more knowledge. They were often narratives stating a succession of unconnected facts, and a discursive effort, a reconstruction of the research object based on explicit epistemological and theoretical premises, was then missing. Regarding Latin America, we could often find references to symbolic interactionism or Marxism, without these leading to a systematisation of the collected data. Broadly speaking, the 'street child' was seen and described by social science researchers as a victim of the socio-economic structure and of life circumstances. They were granted abilities for survival, but very few skills as social actors, as the subject of a story. This is in contrast, especially, to the rallying efforts of the young people integrated into the informal labour market, and that which was taking shape with the movements of the *protagonismo juvenil*. Here, the young person is, above all, perceived through his or her integration into a social movement which, in turn, is a constituent of a developing civil society. Outside of Brazil, no similar attempt at mobilisation has been made by children in a street situation.

The situation has changed, especially since the beginning of the 1990s, and many researchers now put an emphasis on the child as a social actor. Yet this research has barely influenced the public image of the 'street child', and, despite the discourse of numerous contributors highlighting the competence of the child as a subject, we have no proof of its real effects on practices of intervention. The epistemological debate in sociology is complex and we do not intend to take it up in detail now, but only to underline its main points. Indeed, the scholarly rhetoric on 'street children', much like the resulting practical suggestions of intervention, depends on the different epistemological positions that have been taken. Let us start by highlighting that the central issue of this debate is the question of the processes of mediation between the personal and the social, not their opposition. In other words, it is about knowing how the personal and the social are connected and reproduced in a constant logic of interaction. Thus, as Anthony Giddens writes, 'it is essential to recognize that structures only exist as the reproduced conduct of situated actors with definite intentions and interests' (Giddens 1977, p. 127). Yet, in the context of this approach, the 'recognition of the actors' reflective abilities and of their knowledge of the social mechanisms they have to face' (Watier 1966, p. 43) is one of the most debated questions. Indeed, the question is one of knowing how the actor becomes aware of his or her situation, and how this situation conditions this awareness. Here we are facing a dual conditioning specific to every interrelation between the individual and the collective. Anthony Giddens' theory of structuration and his concept of a 'duality of structure' are here an important response offered by contemporary sociology to the question of mediation (Giddens 1984).

There is no simple opposition between the individual and the collective, as here the structure is understood as a recursive set of 'generative rules and resources' (Giddens 1984, p. 127). These rules and resources are the property of communities, but also tools allowing social actors to influence the process of interaction. They develop in the context of these social actors' activities. The rules discussed by Giddens comprise two dimensions, namely normative rules and codes of signification. The resources are also made up of two types: 'authoritative resources, which derive from the co-ordination of the activity of human agents, and allocative resources, which stem from control of material products or of aspects of the material world' (Giddens 1984, p. XXXI). There is not here a simple, mechanical reproduction of practices.

According to Giddens, a structure is not, then, as the American sociologist Talcott Parsons has it, a 'group of relations crystallised in relatively stable models… a standardised system of the social relations between (social) agents' (Parsons 1947, p. 62). For Parsons, a social structure is a system of 'model relationships between agents capable of playing roles with each other' (Ibid.). The central aspect of the social structure is, then, a system of expectations defining the appropriate behaviour of the people playing roles. These systems of normative expectations are institutions, and they make up the structurally stable element of social systems. Institutions are essential references required for social action to take shape. In a manner of speaking, they light the way taken by social actors when they engage in interactions.

Giddens does not agree with this metaphor. For him, the weakness of structural functionalism is specifically that it does not look into the skills the actors must possess and 'mobilise' in order to create the 'junction' between the parts constituting the system of action. The sociologist, then, must then equip themselves with concepts which will allow him or her to '[analyse] what the actors know about why they act as they do, particularly … where they are not aware (discursively) that they know it' (Giddens 1984, p. XX). According to Giddens, any reproduction of structures is 'an active constituting process, accomplished by, and consisting in, the doings of active subjects' (Giddens 1977, p. 121). This indicates Gidden's criticisms of the Parsonian structural-functionalism, with its focus on the homeostatic nature of the relations between the individual and the collective. Indeed, this approach presupposes a 'static interdependence of parts', not a comprehension 'in terms of the internal self transformation of the system' (Ibid.). Through the theory of structuration, Giddens wants to avoid the pitfall 'which opposes subjectivism to objectivism, subject to structure', and to connect 'the action theory to the institutional theory' (Lazar 1992, p. 400). This theory must allow him to problematize the nature of social reproduction. Indeed, neither the voluntaristic theory of action (as found in Parsons), nor the determinism of a structure conceived as external to the social actors can give a full account of the nature of the social.

In his voluntaristic theory, Parsons presupposes a 'structural homology between the collective consciousness and the individual personality' (Dehier 1990, p. 246). Yet this homology is explained by the normative orientation of the actors who are internalising norms which pre-exist them and are external to them. It is this substantialization of culture that the authors criticising the voluntaristic option it implies are rejecting. Pierre Bourdieu reminds us that 'the collective can be found in *each individual* in the form of lasting dispositions such as mental structures' (Bourdieu 1980, p. 88). That is what we call the habitus. The habitus is a set of the acquired dispositions, the frameworks of perception, evaluation and action that the individual has acquired in various social contexts. Thus the habitus connects individual behaviours and the objective elements of contexts of action. On this topic, Bourdieu writes that 'between the system of objective regularities and the system of directly observable behaviours there is always introduced a mediation which is none other than the habitus' (Bourdieu 1984, p. 29). Yet this habitus is structured by the field, which is a 'network, or a configuration of objective relations between positions' (Bourdieu 1992, p. 72). These positions impose determinations on their occupants in terms of access to the different types of power. The position is in turn conditioned by the types of assets (social, cultural, symbolic, economic) available to the agents in a field. Capital allows the social actor to position himself or herself in different fields, and to influence their interactions. The field structure is defined by the state of the balance of power between agents, compared by Bourdieu to the players of a game. The field is then a 'structure of objective relations between positions of power' (Op. Cit., p. 72). It guides the agents' strategies and their interactions, and is, therefore, characterised by stakes. However, the social world cannot be reduced to a set of power relations, for it is 'to some extent recognised as legitimate… The subjective representation of the social world as legitimate is part of the complete truth of this world' (Bourdieu 1984, p. 25).

It is, therefore, the complex interactions between the habitus, the field and the different forms of capital which show that there is no dichotomy between the individual and the social. The theme of mediation is, then, the constant interaction between these three dimensions of the process of constituting society. According to Giddens, the consensus of values cannot be the foundation for both individual identity and the social system, as in functionalism. There is no 'regularized model' of the social relations (structure) explaining human action, nor is there an exteriority or interiority which could explain, on its own, the human world. Pretending so would be to indulge in the opposition between the individual subject and society. There is no determination of behaviours, nor indetermination, but rather a double character of the structuring and structured qualities of social relations, through which the structural is both 'constraining and enabling' (Giddens 1984). The reflexive nature of social interactions illustrates this duality of the structural. And yet, this reflexivity is the foundation on which reciprocal social orientations are built. Reflexivity and reciprocity make each other stronger, they enable society to exist. Any interaction can then be understood as a process of implementing reciprocal knowledge (Watier 1966, p. 123). The shaping of this knowledge translates into typifications which allow individuals to 'define' and 'position' themselves in relation to others and to make the world coherent. Thanks to these typifications, individuals can explain and make sense of what they are doing and of what others are doing. This is how individual and social identities, without which society would not exist, are built.

The study of typifications and identies is then a priority study object for sociology. There are two complementary approaches to this issue. The first approach emphasises what makes typification and identity possible. It focuses on the modalities and resources that govern their construction and implementation, but also on what enables the reproduction of the necessary knowledge for individuals to continue to perceive the world as taken for granted. This first approach focuses on the frameworks or interpretative procedures (Giddens, Aaron Cicourel) that enable us to make sense of the environment and which concern the communication of meaning between social actors. For Cicourel, the main properties of the interpretative procedures are: (1) the reciprocity of perspectives, (2) the et cetera assumption, (3) the presence of normal forms of interaction, (4) retrospective-prospective meaning, (5) talk itself as reflexive, (6) descriptive vocabularies as indexical expressions. These interpretative procedures allow for continuous feedback between individual and milieu. We then focus on 'the accumulation of practical knowledge of the conventions drawn upon in the production and reproduction of social interaction' (Giddens 1979, p. 128).

The second approach is primarily concerned with the contextualised manifestation of typifications and identities; on the way they express themselves and make sense. Here, the researcher's attention is drawn more to the instrumental character of typifications and identities than to the rules they are built on. This was illustrated by Anselm Strauss when he wrote that the 'establishment of one's own identity to oneself is as important in interaction as to establish it for the other. One's own identity in a situation is not absolutely given but is more or less problematic' (Strauss 1969, p. 47). Here, the researcher's interest is in what the speaker wants to communicate when he or she positions himself or herself in relation to different social contexts, past, present, and future. Identitary uncertainty is fundamental here, as it is at the core of the negotiation of identity which characterises social interactions when they contain stakes for the parties involved.

Both approaches look into the procedures of naming: the designation of others and the designation of difference by social actors. The researcher's focus is then on the dialectic between identification and differentiation in relation to the concrete and/or imaginary social situations which are at work in situations of interaction. Both approaches lead to the deconstruction of some important analytical categories, such as culture, social norm, social role, motivation, rationality, and adaptation, to name but a few. They also lead to criticism of the empirical categories used by individuals to talk about themselves or others. The notion of 'out of place child' is one of these empirical categories.

In both instances, induction takes precedence over deduction, and the field is prioritised over theory. Putting into perspective the different fields in relation to which social actors express themselves, as well as going back and forth between theories and fields, theories and practices, is a safeguard against an overly personal interpretation of the contents of research. This implies that the theory 'does not pre-exist the research but is produced by it: research is theorisation, generating theory, a progressive and continuous development of concepts, properties, and relations until the discovery of results that are judged convincing' (Demazière and Dubar 1997, p. 49).

In the world of intervention, several discourses about 'street children' are then possible, but most of them present the child as a product of the socio-economic and cultural environment, a product and thus an object. But they also perceive the child as being unable to control his or her urges and desires. The child is then doubly an object. In general, this discourse does not recognise the child as having skills, but technical and instrumental abilities which allow him or her to survive on the street. The epistemology of these discourses ignores both the reflexive nature of human interactions and institutional reflexivity. Yet those programs intervening with CSS are themselves institutions.

## 2.2 The Conformist Institutional Discourse: The Child-Victim

The discourse mentioned here is not the only possible one and there is no denying the existence of a certain plurality in the field of intervention with CSS. However, this discourse can be widely found in the world of assistance programs. We propose to call this the conformist institutional discourse (CID), as it adapts to the image of the 'street child' that is prevalent in national and international public opinion, as well as in the administration and the political world of countries that are concerned with these children (Lucchini 1993, pp. 9–22 and 227–233). This discourse presents the objectives of the intervention and proposes an image of CSS.[1] The CID is primarily intended for professionals working in intervention, potential donors, and the authorities.

One of the means often used by intervention programs to attract the attention of potential donors is the dramatisation of these children's living conditions. Such a dramatising discourse provokes pity, but also fear. It paints the child as an innocent

[1] For a more thorough analysis of the discourses discussed here, refer to: Antonella Invernizzi and Riccardo Lucchini, 'L'enfant, l'institution et les intervenants sociaux' in: Ricardo Lucchini (1996). *Sociologie de la survie. L'enfant dans la rue*. Paris: PUF; Abric, J.-C. and Campos, P. Les éducateurs et leur représentation sociale de l'enfant de la rue au Brésil, in: Jean-Claude Abric (Ed.), *Exclusion sociale, insertion et prévention*, érès, Saint-Agne 1996.

victim of domestic violence and poverty, and/or as a delinquent in the making. The intervention 'on' the child is then doubly legitimated. It creates, on one hand, the need to save an innocent victim, and, on the other, the need to protect society from what threatens it. The concrete interventions of the state in Latin America are often of a repressive nature. The primary discourse then becomes that of the delinquent-child. This dramatising discourse is reductive: it does not take into account the complexity and the diversity of life on the street. The street is not only a physical space but is, above all, a space which is symbolically invested by its users. Depending on the needs, interests, and biographies of its different users, one single street becomes plural. Nor does this dramatising discourse take into account the psycho-sociological heterogeneity that characterises 'street children'. One of the consequences of this discourse, and not the least, is, then, the legitimation of intervention in terms of the normalisation and integration of the child. The most extreme instances of this are those defending the institutionalisation and confinement of the child. As such, the financial requirements of assistance programs contribute to the homogeneity of the public discourse that they address to international public opinion and to the bodies likely to support them.

Other factors besides this influence the public discourse, and we do not claim to enumerate all of them, but we do want to point out the importance of religious beliefs when presenting intervention as a means of saving those who have strayed from the right path. Here, the child is portrayed as a victim of macroscopic determining factors which affect the poorest populations: social inequalities, injustice, bribery, poverty, and so on. The child is then the victim of his or her situation at home and at school. Finally, the child is a victim of the street. This discourse presents the 'street child' as belonging, on a psycho-sociological level, to a homogeneous category. This category is defined in terms of the street as a perverse environment, and in terms of risks. The street is then defined by negative characteristics and associated with a deviant subculture characterised by 'theft, prostitution, rape, violence, drug addiction, and disdain for life'. The instability of relationships and lack of solidarity are also important characteristics of life on the street.

The 'street child' is portrayed as the victim of an exclusively violent environment. This enables, among other things, the justification of a program of intervention without the need to explain the normative premises for its action. In other words, no explanation is offered for the behavioural expectations that the program has of the children. It is then tempting to simply use the norms of socially privileged groups (a part of the middle-class and the bourgeoisie) as a model of normality. The institutional discourse then implicitly describes poor people and outcasts as deviant. This is paradoxical enough for an approach denouncing the social inequalities the children are victims of! It is the consequence of an approach which is not interested, or not enough, in the issue of the reflexivity of the present social actors: children, parents, educators, and so on. This approach to the world of the 'street child', and the objectives pursued by the program, thus obey a functionalist logic.

Regarding the departure of the child from home, it is, most of the time, described in terms of expulsion (Lucchini 1997). According to the institutional discourse, some of the most important factors in explaining these expulsions are: (a) social disorganisation, namely the fragility or lack of relational fabric in underprivileged neighbourhoods; (b) family disorganisation, namely single-parent families; and (c) poverty. The child is then characterised by abandonment (although the issue of the definition of this notion and of the levels of abandonment is not discussed), poor self-esteem (there is no homogeneity among CSS in this matter) and the absence of responsible adults. The notion of responsibility is usually not discussed and certainly not contextualised.

This is not about questioning the necessity of protecting and guiding children in the process of building autonomy and responsibility. What can pose a problem, however, is the notion of 'responsible adult' itself. The notion of responsibility here is implicitly defined in relation to theories of the development of moral judgment in children, such as those of Jean Piaget (1932) and Lawrence Kohlberg (1981). Yet these 'only make sense within the question: How are we or how do we become individuals who are respectful or not of the rule?' (Debuyst 1985, p. 119). The definition of the responsible adult is then connected to discussions of the nature and origin of the rules they have to enforce and of the sanctions that they must apply in the case of non-compliance with these rules. We can see, therefore, that the notion of responsible adult is polysemous and that it requires discussion.

According to the CID, the child-victim simply reacts to the constraints of the environment. The child's capacities for working on and developing these constraints are weak or non-existent. On the other hand, his or her family and community environment is perceived as devoid of resources. As such the child can only develop limited skills and abilities which are seen from the outset as illegitimate. Consequently, the CID suggests that the necessary resources for a successful adjustment of the child are, inevitably, to be found elsewhere.

## 2.3 The Interactional Discourse: The Runaway Child

What we term the interactional discourse is that discourse which found in the field sheets and reports written by professionals – social workers, psychologists, educators – involved in a program. It is generated by the contact between the professionals and the children. Unlike the institutional image, which with a functionalist logic highlights the macrosocial factors creating different types of disorganisation and anomy, the interactional image states the individual motivations contributing to the child leaving to live on the street. Despite this, the child is perceived, above all, as an irrational, even deviant, being. Even if the interactional image of the child is more differentiated than the institutional image, here the child is nevertheless said to follow impulses and his or her abilities to express frustrations are limited.

Indeed, in the interactional discourse, we can note the absence of the notion of identitary mediation, as the child's individuality is defined not, first and foremost, in terms of identity, but rather in terms of personality traits. It is traits such as aggressiveness, lability, and selfishness, for example, that explain the child's violation of norms. The professionals' discourse almost never connects the violation of norms to an identity negotiation on the part of child. We can then presume that part of the conflict between 'street children' and outreach workers are the consequence of the children's strategies and of their stigmatisation by the outreach workers. This stigmatisation particularly concerns the immediatism that the children would be 'guilty' of, and the manipulation of the interpersonal relationships to which they dedicate themselves.

The interactional image is then built on register which is above all psychological in character. The outreach workers are particularly interested in the children's emotions and affectivity, in a psychodynamic and/or psychomedical perspective and in terms of frustration and aggressiveness. The family is present to the extent that it is the source – almost always hypothetical – of the psychological disorders and inappropriate behaviours of the child. In addition to leading to a therapeutic and sometimes pharmacological intervention, this approach leads to a form of education understood as a process of learning norms and appropriate behaviours. The educational intervention is then highly standardised.

On the other hand, the interactional discourse also uses notions like social disorganisation and family disorganisation. But these notions are built on a comparison with a social organisation which is perceived as unique. The idea of family disorganisation suggests a failure in the organisation of family roles, namely the roles suggested by the nuclear family model specific to the middle class, yet there are other possible roles than these. The social disorganisation affecting entire neighbourhoods in Latin American cities does not lead every child to live on the street. As we mentioned earlier, the notion of social disorganisation includes the stigmatisation of the single-parent family and of the woman as head of the household. As Leser de Mello writes, 'the available work on the populations of the suburbs and slums of large cities indicate that the families diverge from the normative organisational model. It would be unreasonable to talk about a lack of organisation, and we must talk about different modes of organisation. Free from models… it becomes possible to see the families as they are, not as they should be according to historical models of classes – abstract and generalising' (Leser de Mello 1989, p. 59).

On the other hand, the psychologising approach towards CSS contributes to the silencing of their rationality, as partial as it might be. It discredits their rationality when its traits are ascribed to pathologies or to imperfect learning processes. At best, it can be treated as an amoral and deviant rationality. The children's independence, their creativity on the street, and their survival abilities are hardly ever valued since, by definition, they must be protected by the adults. In turn, when children reject protection and care, in other words when they run away, it is perceived as a form of deviance. The child goes from being a victim to being an asocial person or even a deviant.

Both sides of the child's image, victim or deviant, find themselves combined in this approach. The evolutionary model could be understood as such: social disorganisation, social inequalities, and family disorganisation lead children to live on the street. Here, children internalise the deviant subculture specific to the street. They become victims of it at first, and then become deviant themselves.

## 2.4 The Child in a Street Situation Is a Subject

To go past the stereotypical images of 'street children' as victims or deviants, we need to give back to them their status as subject. The tendency to define children as objects of attention and of educational measures is emphasised when the children find themselves in situations considered as being non-conformist or deviant. This is particularly true for CSS, where being in a 'street situation' is signaled as being out of place (Connolly and Ennew 1996). The stigmatisation of 'street children' is a feature common to every cultural context, and children are then stripped of any right over themselves (Ennew 1995). They are not, or not any longer, seen as subjects, and their interpretation of the world around them and of their personal situation within it is not considered relevant. They are either reduced to objects of circumstances they do not understand, and hence to victims, or pointed out as deviants needing to be reformed. In both instances, the child-victim and the child-deviant do not even have the right to speech: someone speaks for them and they themselves are shut away.

Chinese authors whose articles on this topic have been authorised for publication speak of '*liulang ertong*', a phrase which literally translates as 'wandering children'. This phrase references the masses of migrants, themselves called '*liudong renkou*', or 'floating population' (Stoecklin 2000). This conflation legitimises a discriminatory treatment of individuals based on the fact that they belong to a social group to which certain stigmatising characteristics are attributed. Social discrimination thus rests upon popular prejudices nurtured by city-dwellers about a stray population presented as a danger. No psychosocial differentiation of the children is offered, not even based on the length of their time on the street, or on their daily activities.

In these articles, the children's presence on the street is generally explained in terms of poverty and family troubles. These elements genuinely exist, but they are not enough to explain the careers or the behaviours of the Chinese children living on the street. Most importantly, some structural elements are systematically removed from analyses. Yet, the presence of children in the streets of China is closely related to factors of economic and social policy. As elsewhere, the Chinese definition of 'street children' in terms of family disorganisation and poverty allows them to avoid this question. The corollary of such a political taboo, undoubtedly more obvious in China, is that CSS are above all designated as deviant.

Under these conditions, not enough literature is dedicated to the Chinese children's own perception of the street (Cheng 2006, 2008; Cheng and Lam 2010). The perspective of several researchers, which I share, is to not accept such a silencing. To reach a better understanding of the phenomenon, and thus to contribute to improving their situation, we need to give these children a voice. To describe life on the street, we must consider the street from the perspective of its users, and try to understand how the children themselves interpret their situation.

Understanding these children means, as for any individual, trying to grasp how they interpret their personal situation in relation to their environment. By following the comprehensive approach of Max Weber, I consider that it is only by understanding the normative criteria from which the actors interact that we can understand the social phenomenon in which they participate. Indeed, as any social actor does, CSS orientate their behaviours, and develop their strategies and their discourses, based on certain values with which they identify and on other values from which they keep their distance.

A first example[2] will allow us to illustrate this active detachment right away. Wei, a 9 year old boy who has been on the street for a year, justifies his begging by his lack of choice. In order to do so, he says about the women and girls he sees on the street: '*They are not real beggars; they are too lazy to work so they come here to beg. But I have to beg, I don't have a choice*'. According to Wei, they are lazy because they have the possibility of staying at home and working. Wei therefore makes use of popular prejudices about begging which are normatively part of Chinese culture. He positions himself in relation to these values and puts them into perspective: they do not apply to him, since he is an orphan and does not have a choice. This way, he contests the stigmatisation he is subjected to: he refuses to be mixed up with the 'lazy people'. Wei thus distances himself from this social category, making use of the disapproval that is commonly directed towards him.

Wei spends his days begging and living off leftovers with Sun, a 15 year old boy who ran away from home a week before, '*to avoid having to go to school*' where his results are bad. Unlike Sun, who says he does not have a goal, Wei states he wants to become a truck or bus driver (*kai qiche*). But for Sun, '*driving doesn't make sense either. I might go home when I'm older*'. Sun's indecision encourages Wei to draw a line between them, again in terms of his lack of choice: '*I don't have any other option but to be on the street. If I could, I would go home; even if your family is poor it is more welcoming. Here, begging is always hard*'. Wei tries to convince Sun to go home: '*Family is the best thing. You are very lucky to have your parents. In your family, there is only you, an only son. If you don't go home, your parents will be very sad. Don't you know how valuable having a son is?!*'.

Wei refers to the importance of the son, fundamental in the patrilineal structure and in Chinese culture. His argument for warning Sun that the street has nothing to offer him is based on one of the strongest institutions in China: the family. This leads him to protest against the social reactions, of passers-by: '*People think that children without parents are bad. They look down on me (*renmen kan bu qi wo*). I already have no parents but I also have no friends or money to get by*'. By alluding to the institution of family and a social norm like working hard to distinguish himself from the 'lazy people', Wei can not accept that people would '*look down*' on him, since it is not by choice that he has had to turn his back on such institutions and norms.

It is through this relation to values, then, that we can understand how Wei positions himself in the street-space. His relation to the environment is mediated by

[2] All examples taken hereafter come from Stoecklin's dissertation: Stoecklin, D. (2000). *Enfants des rues en Chine*. Paris: Karthala.

cultural values which he actively interprets. He takes a stance, and thus he rejects the stigmatisation against him – '*they judge me badly*' – while identifying with a virtual group of CSS – '*But, actually, we are not bad*'. Moreover, it is significant that Wei never uses the phrase 'street children' (*liulang ertong*). Such a distancing from this categorisation can also be found in other fields: many CSS have a tendency to identify with a concrete group of children while denying belonging to the stigmatised category of 'street children'.

This strategy of defence from stigmatisation is, however, reversible: at times, children will claim a collective identity as 'street children'. In these instances, children assume their deviant identities partly because it gives them a certain satisfaction linked to a feeling of belonging and a certain prestige in the eyes of their peers. We will see that, unlike in other fields, in China this happens very rarely. But for now let us note that, in every context, cultural representations of childhood are a key factor in the treatment of children living on the street. And the strategies adopted by children to deny others the right to stigmatise them use this same normative framework.

This ability to interpret norms in order to use them in one's favour is precisely what characterises the social actor. This shows that even though we can consider Wei as a victim of circumstances, he is also a social actor. What we observe is that some actors can perform with greater flexibility than others, and that what we need to understand are the reasons for this difference. Our perspective considers that these reasons can be found not in the personal characteristics of individuals, but in the nature of the social relations which can establish themselves in the street space. The structuration of the street-space is a crucial element in reflecting the diversity of the situations that CSS experience all over the world. Understanding the level of complexity of social interactions on the street thus becomes important for the sociologist.

CSS who, when possible, form groups, can be seen as developing a defense strategy suitable to face the structural constraints and popular prejudices that associate them with a danger to the social order. In China, children are not able to form such groups in a durable way. We must try to understand why this is. In order to do so, it is essential to use what the children tell us about life on the street, as the relevant structural constraints and cultural values are not self-evident. These actors do not orientate themselves only in relation to values but also depending on constraints, and it is only them who can tell us which, among these, may be influencing their behaviours.

In this specific case, Wei is the one to reveal the existence of 'bosses' (*laoda*) who take advantage of CSS in exchange for some form of protection from the police: '*The other children, when they give money, they receive their protection and can keep begging. (...)* 'Laoda' *doesn't do anything, he doesn't work. He lets the children go to different places to beg and steal, and if the older children behave badly, they are taken by the police and sent to the deportation centre (*qiansong-zhan*)*'. This means that, in the informal urban sector, practices of exploitation emerge thanks to police extortion. The conversation with Wei and Sun thus highlights the challenges that newcomers and isolated children must face when they arrive in Shanghai: submission to or independence from the bosses (*laoda*) is, for them, a choice between two forms of violence: clandestine exploitation or police repression. The price to pay for a desire for independence is exclusion from the street: '*I don't have their support and so I'm in danger. I don't want to give them money so they hit me. When I have no money for them, then they beat me up and tell me to leave the station area*'.

This is an example of how, without the discourse of these actors who are generally never listened to, we can not be aware of this essential aspect of the structuration of the informal sector in Shanghai. It is precisely from this conversation, and from paying more attention to individuals who, without this, would have undoubtedly escaped observation, that we can observe the street in a new light. Without this attention to the relations of protection-victimisation any study of the behaviour of the children could not be relevant, since this behaviour can only be understood by knowing that the children are part of this relatively restrictive structural setting. These elements also allow us to understand why Wei does not want to go back to Changsha, in the Hunan province where he is from: '*I spent six months on the street in Changsha. In Changsha, there are also bad young people on the street. They hit the youngest children if they don't want to beg for them and give them money. If I want to go back to Changsha, things won't be good either. In Changsha, I would also have to beg to eat. I don't know what to do*'.

We can only make sense of the fact that Wei stays on the street in Shanghai even though he paints the street in a negative light if we understand the pros and cons he has to weigh before orientating his behaviour. There is, in all likelihood, an element which does not show through in his speech but which could be motivating his path: the desire for independence. Indeed, Wei says he does not want to go to the orphanage of Shanghai, because he would not be free there.[3] With Wei saying that he does not want to give money to the *laoda*, and that his dream is to become a bus driver, we can not come to the conclusion that Wei is simply a passive victim without skills or projects. We must try to understand his ambivalent motivations for staying in a space which, nevertheless, seems to give him some autonomy. We can find these expectations in Sun's attitude. He is experiencing an initial phase of contact with the street, where it is seen as a space of opportunities containing resources that he judges superior to the ones he can find at home. For his part Wei, despite the fact that he is only 9 years old, is already in a later phase of his career on the street, in which he thinks it has nothing to offer. Wei does not protest against the search for autonomy, but against the attitude of others towards him: he yearns to get out of the condition he faces the street-space, which is, however, the only space he can be in.[4]

For Wei, family, which he does not have, is a guarantee for the future: '*If you don't go home, then you won't be able to make your hopes come true either, because*

[3] This interview with Wei was done 2 months before the scandal caused by the BBC broadcast of the documentary 'The Dying Rooms', following the revelations of the paediatrician, Dr. Zhang: 'Death by default. A policy of fatal neglect in China's State orphanages', London: Human Rights Watch/Asia, 1995.

[4] 'I don't have a choice' (*wo meiyou banfa*).

*there is no one to help you out here. Why don't you want to go home?'*. Sun replies that '*it doesn't make sense*'. It seems that Sun thinks there is something on the street that he can not find at home. It could be fewer constraints: the street seems to victimise him less than his family. Like Wei, he assesses the situation. Objectively, it is highly probable that the street does not have as many opportunities to offer as Sun is hoping for, and that this is what Wei is warning him about. However, Sun's behaviour – the fact that he does not contact his parents, that he wants to experience the street, that he does not listen to Wei's orders to go home – all this derives in part from his subjective judgement of reality. Sun sees his situation on the street as full of hope, expectations, and courage, while Wei sees it as synonymous with indecisiveness, disillusionment, and the desire to leave. This subjectivity greatly guides the path and the behaviours of these children.

We thus notice that, by having access to the subjective meaning that children give to their presence on the street, we can understand the street situation as a situation of an evolutionary and transitory nature. It depends not only on the circumstances motivating the child to leave home and on the opportunities and material, social, and identitary rewards that the child can find on the street, but also on the image that the child has of the street. But the creation of this image is connected to cultural representations of and to the social reactions to the prolonged presence of the child in that space. We then need to think of children's paths on the street as being the result of the multiple influences that these objective and subjective elements have on each other and that the children actively organise.

The child is then not this passive being, roaming as circumstances change, a 'wandering child', a *liulang*: he or she interprets his or her situation as well as the social norms surrounding him or her. As such the street situation can not be assimilated into a clear, objective and unequivocal social status, recognised by all, but must be viewed in terms of a flexible positioning of the child in relation to the street environment, and so with a changing involvement in this environment. For Sun and Wei, for example, one of the concrete questions brought about by their integration into the street is the one of the involvement in the mafia environment of the *laoda* (bosses) who exploit them in exchange for a degree of protection. The future of their path on the street depends on their choice.

The forms of more or less forced integration onto the street vary according to context, and the children can be confronted with a considerable number of alternatives in relation to which they must position themselves explicitly in the eyes of others who are concerned with this situation. It can be the integration into a group of peers, the sharing of food, the search for territories to sleep in, the organisation of thefts, the way to use drugs, and so on. It involves negotiations and thus requires skills. Yet it is clear that the development of these skills influences the image of the self and the self-esteem, and we can then understand that the motivation to stay on the street depends in a large part on the way the child sees himself or herself, as a person with more or less skill on the street. As such, we can not talk about the 'street situation' without taking into consideration these subjective and identitary elements.

The child's experience of the street is the result of his or her subjective assessment of the actions and social reactions that prevail there. These assessments are highly influenced by the social representations of childhood. The 'street child' is typically represented as an 'object'. This is no different from other iconic images of childhood: like every child, these children are put in a category that is more or less distant from the ideal image of childhood. This discrepancy is actualised by institutional actors (the media, politicians, NGOs, etc.), who use these iconic images of childhood for their own purposes. Thus we can observe an important variability of the figures of marginalised childhood.

In the iconography of victimhood, the 'street child' has been replaced by the 'child victim of violence' during the last two decades (Poretti et al. 2014). Children, in particular marginalised children, are objectified by social representations. We will therefore, in the last part of this chapter, examine social representations because they mediate the subjective relationship that children in street situations (CSS) have with their environment. Social representations paint an idealised picture of childhood – in other words a picture in accordance with the Ought, rather than the Is, is allocated to the child. These role expectations constitute what George Herbert Mead calls the 'Me', where the individual perceives himself or herself from the point of view of others. Individuals perceive the object they are to others, and thus become an object to themselves. They refer to this object by saying 'Me'. But they also say 'Me, I…' (Me, I do this and that): The 'I' is 'the response of the individual to the attitude of the community as this appears in his own experience' (Mead 1963, p. 167). From this tension between 'Me' and 'I' results in the compromise of a 'Self'. Throughout this work we will hence analyse this 'compromise', the 'Self', in terms of agency (in Chap. 9). For now, we must dwell on the 'Me' formed through social representations, especially the ideal image of childhood, in a given context, because it is this 'objectification' which transforms the child into an object we call the 'street child'. The Chinese context presents a striking example of how social representations function, and we will now address it in detail in order to highlight the theoretical considerations, developed by other authors, which are of great relevance in understanding the situation of marginalised children.

## 2.5 Representation as a Mediation Between the Individual and the Social

Children's skills and the more-or-less forced forms of integration onto the street depend on larger sociocultural factors. It is therefore necessary to study the social representations through which these factors operate. On what symbolic order on which the ideal image of childhood in China based? The primary difficulty is in identifying the elements that make up the ideal image of childhood. It would have been invaluable to be able to look into it through a study of the representations of childhood expressed in the different layers of the Chinese population. But such a project would obviously exceed my means, and I had to settle for extracting this image from exiting analytical documents. They are texts written by Sinologists about family in China, texts about socialisation written by Chinese sociologists, and empirical studies by sociologists, anthropologists and social psychologists, not necessarily Chinese, most of them about Chinese communities living outside China. I only analysed a small sample of this diverse work, but one idea can be found in all of them: in China, the ideal image of childhood is the image of a disciplined, productive, and respectful child. This image differs considerably from the ideal, widespread in the West, of a child who is, above all, playful, innocent and genuine. This conception of childhood, corresponding to the Western model of the nuclear family providing 'a carefree, safe, secure and happy phase in human existence', has been extensively propagated in the South, which is not without problems.

As social facts and discourses on facts are inseparable, our main purpose here is to try to clarify the connections between the representations of childhood and social practices. Yet the ideal image of childhood is a discourse about childhood that sinology and Chinese sociology have helped shaping. The culturalist focus of sinology and the functionalist perspective that dominates Chinese sociology have created an image, more ideal than empirical, of a Chinese child full of Confucian values such as discipline, obedience, filial piety, persistence in effort, productivity, respect, collectivism, and so on. But such an ideal image most likely cannot make sense of the diversity of representations in the different regions and social classes. The goal here is apparently not social representativeness, but rather an instrumental function, or the use of this ideal image as an instrument of social control – in particular through the media, but also through academic legitimisation. This is why an analysis of the theories of socialisation offered by Chinese sociologists seemed particularly interesting to me. I see these theories as emblematic of the will to standardise society through the definition of ideal childhood, among other things. The people in power are not interested in knowing whether this image truly emanates from a consensus in the population, but rather in its instrumental value, what it enables them to do. The labelling and repression of CSS then appears to be one of the most efficient applications of what I consider to be a 'political' definition of ideal childhood.

Every social definition of childhood conveys a particular understanding of society: what the child should be is a socially constructed ideal that shows a specific representation of the social order. 'Street children' are then judged as more or less divergent from the ideal child as it is represented in various cultural contexts. It appears as if the bigger the discrepancy between the ideal representation of childhood and the genuine situation of children is, the more violent the actions taken to reduce this discrepancy for the children designated as maladjusted are. Everything happens as if it were easier to change 'street children' than to meddle with the image of ideal childhood. This shows just how much this ideal image is constitutive of the legitimisation of the social order. It then has an ideological function. Indeed, the representation of ideal childhood is part of the expected behaviours specific to social groups which, in a given society, are able to assert their way of life as self-evident, as the norm. By highlighting the fact that this normality is not accessible to everyone, the presence of children on the street questions the symbolic order through which this definition of normality emerged.

As a result, 'street children' are mediatised: they are filmed, photographed, articles are written about them and studies done concerning them. This has happened to such an extent that in several countries it is difficult to determine whether the number of 'street children' has truly increased or if they simply have more social visibility. It is therefore impossible to compare the evolution of the number of CSS internationally, since, on one hand, their 'visibilisation' is extremely diverse, and, on the other hand, there are different definitions for these children. The role of the sociologist is not to try to unify these definitions but rather to observe this diversity and to understand what it refers to.

CSS are not primarily defined on the basis of their intimate knowledge of their own world, but rather simply by criteria that are deemed objective, yet are actually characteristics that are seen as opposites to the ones we use to define the ideal childhood. But these representations of ideal childhood vary depending on cultural context and social hierarchy. Consequently, the definitions of the 'street child' are diverse because the ideal images of childhood to which they are being compared, implicitly or explicitly, are not identical. It is therefore essential to identify these social representations (by identifying the actors who express them) for each context, since it is from them, or against them, that a child gives meaning to their situation on the street. It is in accordance with this 'structure of pertinences', or through it, that children devise their sense of agency (we will return to this in Chap. 9).

Representations and social practices interpenetrate. These representations are not enough to explain the situations these children are in, but those situations would be different if the representations were also different. In other words, a CSS is always a 'street child' to someone. It is therefore not enough to shed light on the children: we also need to shed light on the main actors, individual and collective, for whom these children are 'street children'. It is this reversal of perspective, from children to society, which, when it occurs, provokes the most passionate debates. As such, most of the discourse around 'street children' sheds more light on the normative presuppositions or prejudices of the authors of these discourses more than it reflects the situation as it is experienced by CSS. Debates on 'street children' are actually debates on the social order, in which the children themselves are often only objects of evaluation, more or less utopian projections, and not subjects.

In daily life, representations of childhood are normalised to the extent that we do not think about them. They only become problematic when a 'different' child 'barges in', so to speak, into the daily routine, and changes the field of representations that enables individuals to categorise reality: 'Society establishes the means of categorizing persons and the complement of attributes felt to be ordinary and natural for members of each of these categories. Social settings establish the categories of persons likely to be encountered there (...) We lean on these anticipations that we have, transforming them into normative expectations, into righteously presented demands. Typically, we do not become aware that we have made these demands or aware of what they are until an active question arises as to whether or not they will be fulfilled'. By listening to Erving Goffman, we can understand that the labelling of 'street children' stems from the presence of depreciatory attributes (dirty clothes and so on) and from the absence of other characteristics that one expects to find in someone in order to be able to recognise them as members of a 'category of persons available for [them] to be'. One of the primary expectations for children, as a social category, is their confinement to certain spaces deemed legitimate. The presence of children in a space that is not part of those usually reserved to them is judged as 'out-of-place'.

Labelling thus proceeds via linkage: it highlights a discrepancy between the reality of 'street children' and the ideal representation of childhood, or rather the living conditions we use to characterise a 'normal' childhood. This non-conformity to expectations is what makes us say that the 'street child' is not really a child any more. By giving those on the street the image of children who are no longer really children, the idealised understanding of childhood works as a stigma: "He [the 'street child'] is thus reduced in our minds from a whole and usual person to a tainted, discounted one. Such an attribute is a stigma, especially when its discrediting effect is very extensive; sometimes it is also called a failing, a shortcoming, a handicap. It constitutes a special discrepancy between virtual and actual social identity". The 'street child' appears as a discounted child, a child missing part of the 'complement of attributes' that makes up what Goffman calls 'virtual social identity', and that we associate with the ideal image of childhood.

What is thus decisive is how people explain this discrepancy, in other words who they deem responsible. Some judge 'street children' as being maladjusted, others condemn society as being dominated by injustice. The debate thus classifies 'street children' either as pathological individuals or as beings passively enduring outside constraints: if some children cannot meet the behavioural expectations addressed to them, is it because they are morally deficient, or, on the contrary, because these expectations are too high compared to the means at their disposal? Should we lower these expectations? Or extend their means? Which expectations, which means? And so on. This debate thus focuses on the question: 'who should change'? Children or society?

The answer to this question in China is almost entirely aimed towards rehabilitating children, and practically forbids any critical stance. This case is an example that sheds light on numerous different contexts. It appears, indeed, as an extreme case, but one that is not fundamentally different from the others. Simply because of its ideal-typical character, this case the advantage of highlighting the political dimension of the stigmatisation of 'street children', a dimension that can be found to varying degrees in all contexts.

Social representations have a functional aspect, in other words a practical ambition: 'Social representations describe, explain and stipulate. They offer a manual on how to understand reality, master our environment and behave in society'. Their normative character thus influences daily interactions, the way of presenting oneself and behaving, of evaluating others and relating to them. Understanding a social interaction thus implies being able to identify the representations that social actors negotiate in their face to face meetings. In order to do so, it is necessary to problematise the question of social structure, and therefore the groups and institutions playing a specific role in the creation and propagation of these representations.

In common debates on 'street children', the fundamental issue is the attribution of responsibility for a situation which is judged as deficient. We should consider that the behavioural expectations to which the attitudes of CSS are compared are expectations expressed by actors, individual or collective: we are always an 'object' to someone else. Knowing if and how these actors succeed in imposing their representations as legitimate is a complex matter. In order to describe such an imposition, Pierre Bourdieu uses the notion of 'symbolic violence', which he assumes to be based on the ignorance, by the dominated, of the processes that make invisible the 'naturalisation' of representations that dominate in favour of an asymmetry of power (Bourdieu 1977). Despite what this 'ignorance' postulated by Bourdieu says about his vision of the social actor (which has been widely criticised), we can nevertheless, alongside the understanding of the ideal image of childhood, identify the instances of it being used as an instrument for social control. This is necessary in order to better understand the room for manoeuvre available to the children. The connections between the social actor and the social system depend, indeed, on a symbolic normative order that mediates the relations between social actors. A more functional analysis of social representations must then enable us to specify this symbolic order before, if necessary, attributing it to a specific class or group, as theories of conflict, including that of Bourdieu, suppose.

## 2.6 Social Representations of Childhood: The Mechanisms of Reduction and Inversion

In the West, several authors note the progressive awareness of a personality specific to the child. This movement seems to accompany the decline of 'the instrumental value of children [which] has been largely replaced by their expressive value'. Marie-José Chombart de Lauwe (1983) ascribes the change of the system of values, shifting from the idea of a child associated to 'sin' to the idea of a natural child impersonating 'authenticity', to the fact that every society compensates for its tensions by creating an imaginary world. Non-industrial societies used to live their myths through ritual practices. Today, the imaginary is translated and produced by machines that allow for mass diffusion. The means of communication thus use certain social categories to produce dreams. Thereby, the 'Woman', the 'Child', and the 'Primitive' have become symbolic, mythical characters, showing 'other' ways of living, in an imaginary, compensatory world. They are the objects of emotional projections from the corresponding dominant category: in industrial societies, men and adults. The mythification of the child thus enables us to imagine an idealised world: authentic, genuine, not altered by conventions, norms and rules, while 'society' appears as codified and suffocating. The discourse on children in the West is then based on a way of thinking that opposes the 'authentic child', being of nature, to 'society': in other words an image of the normative adult or of the moulded child that is already 'damaged'. The influence of Rousseau is clear here.

As such the dominated categories of Western countries (children, teenagers, and women) are both used and marginalised in reality, and support desires in the social imaginary. For Chombart de Lauwe, the representation of the dominated is carried out through two modes:

(a) Reduction: individuals are presented as having the same attributes as the referent (man, woman, child) but with a lesser intensity.
(b) Inversion: the attributes of the dominated are opposed to those of the dominant category. Most of the time they have negative connotations, or they are subjected to unrealistic idealisation that gives prestige to the dominated category in the imaginary, but not in real society.

As we have seen, the mode of reduction can also be found in the common definition of 'street children': they are 'already no longer children'. Reduction means seeing them as deprived of the attributes qualifying 'normal' childhood. As for inversion, the mechanism of unrealistic idealisation can also be found in the phenomenon of 'street children', when we picture them as more free and autonomous than other children. This idealisation does not so much highlight the reality of 'street children' as it shows the romantic projection of individuals who are not in direct contact with these children, and who use them as a substitute for their own anti-establishment commitments.

Yet 'street children' themselves partly integrate these representations and conform to the different images we have of them: "No one who has ever watched street children for any length of time would miss the fact that they often break into spontaneous bursts of fun and recreation. It is often this engagingly playful behaviour that gets them photographed". Collective representations thus generate common practices which, in return, modify these representations. We should thus focus our attention on the matter of interpretation: without interpretation there is no social transformation. Social representation is then not the simple reflection of a subjective feeling, but a social creation. Culture does not command our relation to things, it mediates it: social actors interpret and negotiate the normative elements. The perspective offered by Marie-José Chombart de Lauwe is certainly close to this interpretative approach, since the key element is the interaction (interface) between the psychological and the social. However, this greater share of interpretation held by the social actors is not enough to create *de facto* a fundamental social change: indeed, Chombart de Lauwe (1983) shows that real behaviours are caused by conflicting social representations, valuing on the one hand rationality and work, symbolised by men, on the other hand idealising dreams, the escape symbolised by women and children. The decline of dominant values and the compensation in the face of constraints reflect a crisis of modernity, but idealisation keeps the dominated categories (women and children) in their place and thus reinforces inequalities. This is leading towards theses concerning the subjectification of domination.

Representation therefore has a mediating role within interactions: it can be a mechanism of adaptation, of communication with others. It is also a cultural product, attached to objects-vehicles, especially thanks to the media, translating or creating a social imaginary. In opposition to the deterministic approach, Chombart de

Lauwe (1986) brings to light the actors' ability to transform values and highlights how important the concept of representation is to identifying times, places, objects, and mechanisms of social transmission. According to her, the social transmission of ways of life, systems of representation, and values does not happen directly from one generation of adults to the next; the passage through the melting-pot of childhood and adolescence is likely to bring transformations in knowledge and in these ways of life and values. There is a 'dialectics of psycho-social processes': young people integrate and select the experiences of previous generations, gain new knowledge, and reflect it back to the adults. These new experiences are likely to modify practices, representations, and values (Chombart de Lauwe 1986).

If social representations and common practices produce each other, this means that there is always a more or less important discrepancy between representations and practices: we have seen this with the mode of inversion, in which there is ideal validation but real devaluation. As a consequence, despite the fact that social representations are highly normative, they are not always followed by corresponding practices. Actors can resist them or not, which suggests the highly important role of reflexivity, but also the fact that the observed behaviours are always and already interpretations of norms – we will get back to this in Chap. 9 with the subject of agency. Thus, Chombart de Lauwe (1983) even alludes to the possibility of a reverse relation between representation and behaviour, at least with regards to the dominated categories (of children and women). The modes of representation of the dominated categories, reduction and inversion, can then explain that, despite there being changes in representation (from reduction to idealised inversion), the associated behaviours remain practices of domination. There can thus be a change in the representation of childhood without it necessarily being accompanied by a corresponding change in behaviours: positive representations of childhood can sometimes hide sordid realities, since representations do not guarantee corresponding practices. Representations of the ideal childhood as authentic, innocent, and carefree can thus also contribute to dehumanising 'street children'.

The pathologisation, even demonisation, of children who do not conform to the normative expectations defined by the upper classes seems widespread in contexts where the ideal child is an 'authentic' being, a being 'naturally' innocent. What about in the Chinese context, in which the ideal child is a 'disciplined' child? From explorers like Marco Polo, who recounted his expedition from 1277 to 1294 in the *Book of the Marvels of the World*, to Max Weber, the most intrigued by China amongst the founding fathers of sociology, empirical descriptions and secondary analysis subordinate, when they do not completely erase, the Chinese child to topics such as the organisation of the state and its historical creation, the relation between type of society and political system, the economy, philosophy, archaeology and Chinese rituals. Chinese children do not appear as a subject of description in themselves.

On the face of it, this would strengthen Philippe Ariès' argument that childhood as a specific reality is a recent Western invention (Ariès 1960). According to his theory, and based on representations such as icons and historical texts, what Ariès calls 'a feeling of childhood' only appeared in the eighteenth century. Before this pivotal period, these texts confirm, childhood did not have any particular meaning. Childhood was not perceived as being made up of differentiated stages, and children did not receive any special affection or education and they would not have known games or specific modes of sociability. However, before Ariès' publication, sinology already informed us about educational goals and prescriptive images of childhood that could be found in texts, often ancient ones, and thus, indirectly, about the social environments in which children could have been socialised. More recently, historians and anthropologists have attacked what has become the theory of the 'invention of childhood', observing that the specific status of child already existed before, namely in Rome and medieval Europe, but also in other cultures, including Egypt, Greece, Africa, India, Japan, and in China. These authors point out that people in China clearly differentiated childhood in several stages: the mother was a protector and breastfed the child until he or she was 3 years old or older, and there was a distinct separation between the age of four and the age of seven, after which strict obedience was demanded of the child. In texts as ancient as Confucius' *Book of Rites* we can already find phases of learning and the development of the child connected with types of interpersonal relations. The Chinese imperial examinations, advanced examinations through which students would become state officials, implied teachings, by a private tutor, from a young age. This form of social recognition based on knowledge instead of simply social rank at birth sparked interest throughout the world, and Ariès could not ignore it. Yet it is impossible to build such an education system without a precise image in mind of what children are and what we must lead them to.

In this case, Confucianism leads children towards a discipline acquired through tireless efforts; the *Sanzijing* (Three Character Classic) was the book that countless generations of Chinese children, spanning more than a millennium through to the mid-twentieth century, had to learn by heart. Today, Chinese authors compare its teachings to forms of torture in prisons: "When reading, you should tie your head with a string to the beam overhead, and sit on a chair with pinpoints on its back. When you fall asleep, the string will straighten you up, and when you lean against the chair, the pinpoints will pierce you in the back". Ariès' dichotomous theory must then be put into perspective: on one hand, the rarity of pictorial or handwritten representations of childhood is a matter of access to sources, on the other hand, these representations actually represent just one one vision of childhood amongst others. As suggested by Chombart de Lauwe, behaviours towards an object are not always in-keeping with the dominant representation of this object: there are, indeed, numerous practices contradicting the representation. We can therefore not linearly match the dominant representation of an object with the importance given to it by the different actors.

With Ariès (1960), representation and feeling are confused. The social character of representation is not problematised; it does not take into consideration the fact that culture 'filters' representation, which is a construction produced and shared socially. Thus, between the 'feeling' and 'consciousness' of a phenomenon – here, childhood – and its representation, an entire series of cultural and structural elements will form a filter: the access to means of expression, the social status of painters and writers, the goals pursued, the recipients of the messages, literary and pictorial techniques, social norms, religion, and especially the place of painted and written representations in a given cultural context. It is thus not because images, icons, and representations of children in texts become more and more numerous from the eighteenth century that this conveys the apparition of a 'feeling of childhood' (Ariès 1960, p.177), which would not have existed before.

Yet this correspondence between representation and reality is precisely one of the main characteristics of sinology: we use the representation of an 'object' (rites, dictates, thinking) in ancient canonical texts in order to deduce the social reality. Ariès is, then, an example of an approach that we could qualify as 'reflectivist', in which representation is meant to reflect feeling. There have been arguments made against Ariès that were based on historical and intercultural research on attitudes towards children: it is real behaviours that reflect the feeling, the subjective value linked to the child. Yet these behaviours have always expressed the fact that, historically, a great importance has always been given to childhood. However, the linear correspondence established between representation and feeling by Ariès – the theory of the recent apparition of 'childhood' – is based on the assumption of a linear correspondence between facts and ethnographic documents. This assumption leaves behind the interpretative dimension suggested by Chombart de Lauwe, which seems to be more realistic and even central, for it makes it possible to depart from determinism and better understand the connections of co-determination between objects and their perceptions, and thus to shed light on the resulting social dynamics.

## 2.7 Children as Subjects of Their Own Representation

The ideal image of childhood constitutes, in every context, a must that the child in street situation who is able to recognise this image knows how to use. The case of children who on certain occasions present themselves as victims to obtain special favours is the most obvious demonstration of it. At other times, the same children can be aggressive towards the adults who judge them, make fun of them by imitating them, or taunt them and provoke them. What is observable here is behaviours that are the result of an interpenetration between the situation of 'street children' and the ideal image of childhood. The children actively, and on a daily basis, participate in a negotiation of the place that is attributed to them in society. The symbolic order is actualised through daily behaviours: interactions between 'street children' and those around them are mediated by fluctuating ideal and normative references. Between the 'street child', the passer-by, the police officer, the trader, the employer, the social worker, the journalist, the politician, and so on, it is a system of values, norms and specific interests, including the ideal image of childhood, which are constantly negotiated.

However, the social actor does not exist outside of the structure in which he or she interacts, and some social structures are more open than others to the negotiation of social roles and statuses. For negotiation to happen the different actors need to share a minimum of common representations of reality, but, simultaneously, the representation of childhood to which the protagonists refer is a conflicting symbolic creation. Not every social group shares the same ideals. A culturalist perspective sees the univocality of an ideal image of childhood as the reflection of a great cultural integration. On the contrary, according to a conflictual perspective, this univocality is the result of the domination of certain social groups. To answer this question case-by-case, rather than in a dogmatic way, we must identify the collective actors who have the power to evaluate, denounce, and stigmatise deviations from the ideal, for it is in the differential power of repression that lies the ability to impose an ideal image of childhood.

This attention to discourses on childhood and to their authors is necessary to understand the behaviours of the children that we observe. Indeed, it is essential to know the ideal image of childhood at stake in a specific cultural context, as well as the authorities that developed it, in order to be able to give meaning to the concrete interactions observed on the street between the children and the other actors who stigmatise and use them, or, on the contrary, help them and cooperate with them. The 'street child' seen as an 'object' on which we have to act is thus an 'objectification' of the individuals, which it is then a question of deconstructing. We will do so in the next chapter (Chap. 3) by giving a voice to these child 'objects' who are often deprived of it, and we will see later on (in Chap. 9) how the agency of CSS adapts to this 'objectification' or tries to overcome it.

## References

Abric, J.-C., & Campos, P. (1996). Les éducateurs et leur représentation sociale de l'enfant de la rue au Brésil. In J.-C. Abric (Ed.), *Exclusion sociale, insertion et prévention*. Saint-Agne: Érès.

Ariès, P. (1960). *L'enfant et la vie familiale sous l'ancien régime*. Paris: Plon.

Bourdieu, P. (1977). Sur le pouvoir symbolique. *Annales, 3*, 405–411.

Bourdieu, P. (1980). *Le sens pratique*. Paris: Editions de Minuit.

Bourdieu, P. (1984). *Questions de sociologie*. Paris: Editions de Minuit.

Bourdieu, P. (1992). *Réponses*. Paris: Seuil.

Cheng, F. (2006). The street children's street life and the victimizations against them: An ethnographic study. *Youth Studies, 9*, 1–9. (in Chinese).

Cheng, F. (2008). *Negotiating exclusion: An ethnographic study of the street children in Shanghai, China*. Unpublished doctoral dissertation. Hong-Kong: University of Hong-Kong.

Cheng, F., & Lam, D. (2010). How is street life? An examination of the subjective wellbeing of street children in China. *International Social Work, 53*(3), 353–365.

Chombart de Lauwe, M.-J. (1983). La représentation des catégories sociales dominées. Rôle social, intériorisation. *Bulletin de Psychologie, Tome, XXXVII*(366), 877–886.

Chombart de Lauwe, M.-J. (1986). Liens entre les représentations véhiculées sur l'enfant et les représentations intériorisées par les enfants. In W. Doise & A. Palmonari (Eds.), *L'étude des représentations sociales*. Paris: Delachaux & Niestlé.

Connolly, M., & Ennew, J. (1996). Children out of place. *Childhood, 3*(2), 131–145.

Debuyst, C. (1985). Jugement moral et délinquance. Les diverses théories et opérationnalisation. Kohlberg – ses études comparatives. *Déviance et société, 9*(2), 119–132.

Dehier, G. (1990). Individu et société: détermination et indétermination. In J.-P. Durand & R. Weil (Eds.), *Sociologie contemporaine*. Paris: Editions Vigot.
Demazière, D., & Dubar, C. (1997). A propos des travaux de A. Strauss. In D. Demazière & C. Dubar (Eds.), *Analyser les entretiens biographiques*. Paris: Nathan.
Ennew, J. (1995). Outside childhood: Street children's rights. In B. Franklin (Ed.), *The handbook of children's rights. Comparative policy and practice* (pp. 201–214). London/New York: Routledge.
Foucault, M. (1972). *Histoire de la folie à l'âge classique*. Paris: Gallimard.
Foucault, M. (1975). *Surveiller et punir. Naissance de la prison*. Paris: Gallimard.
Giddens, A. (1977). *New rules of sociological methods*. London: Hutchinson University Library.
Giddens, A. (1979). *Central problems in social theory*. London: Macmillan.
Giddens, A. (1984). *The constitution of society*. Cambridge: Polity Press.
Invernizzi, A., & Lucchini, R. (1996). L'enfant, l'institution et les intervenants sociaux. In R. Lucchini (Ed.), *Sociologie de la survie. L'enfant dans la rue* (pp. 221–286). Paris: PUF.
Jacquard, A. (1997). *La légende de demain*. Paris: Flammarion.
Kohlberg, L. (1981). *The philosophy of moral development: Moral stages and the idea of justice*. San Francisco: Harper & Row.
Lazar, J. (1992). La compétence des acteurs dans la théorie de la structuration de Giddens. *Cahiers Internationaux de Sociologie, XCIII*, 399–416.
Leser de Mello, S. (1989). Un barrio y sus familias. In *Medio ambiente y urbanizacion*. London: IIED.
Lucchini, R. (1993). *Enfant de la rue. Identité, sociabilité, drogue*. Genève/Paris: Droz.
Lucchini, R. (1996). *Sociologie de la survie. L'enfant dans la rue*. Paris: Presses Universitaires de France.
Lucchini, R. (1997). *Between running away and eviction: The child leaving for the street*. Working Paper, Institut des Sciences Economiques et Sociales, Université de Fribourg.
Mead, G.H. (1963). *L'esprit, le soi et la société*. Paris: PUF.
Parsons, T. (1947). Programme d'une théorie structuro-fonctionnelle des systèmes sociaux. In G. Gurvitch (Ed.), *La sociologie au XXème siècle*. Paris: PUF.
Piaget, J. (1932). *The moral judgement of the child*. New York: Harcourt, Brace Jovanovich.
Poretti, M., Hanson, K., Darbellay, F., & Berchtold, A. (2014). The rise and fall of icons of 'stolen childhood' since the adoption of the UN Convention on the Rights of the Child. *Childhood, 21*(1), 22–38.
Stoecklin, D. (2000). *Enfants des rues en Chine*. Paris: Karthala.
Strauss, A. (1969). *Mirrors and masks: The search for identity*. San Francisco: The Sociology Press.
Watier, P. (1966). *La sociologie et les représentations de l'activité sociale*. Paris: Meridiens.

# Chapter 3
# Children in Street Situations: A Complex Reality

**Riccardo Lucchini**

## 3.1 About Complexity

One of the major difficulties in constructing a typology children in street situations (hereafter CSS), even a partial one, stems from the absence of a precise definition of what a CSS is. As J.G. Cosgrove writes, "the term 'street children' says little more about the members of the population it purports to describe than where they tend to congregate rather than denoting a common set of characteristics of a unique group of abused, neglected and exploited young people" (Cosgrove 1990, p. 185). The 'street child' is one of the categories that, in the system of classification adopted by UNICEF, considers the child as being in a situation of risk. In this case, the key variable of the classification is the degree of contact between the child and the family. While it is not easy to define what is understood by family contact, what this expression means appears to be globally understood. But difficulties appear as soon as we try to define precisely the nature of this contact, as well as what is understood by its degree. In fact, degree does not mean the number of meetings between the child and the parents, but its quality. This refers to affective and material expectations as well as those regarding the identification of the child, in respect to the relationship between parent and child and the responses that are given to the child. When these expectations meet adequate responses, we can be sure of the quality of the family relationship. If many CSS suffer from a lack in the affective and material realms as well as with regards to their identification, they cannot be affected with the same intensity.

There are important differences between children, especially in relation to their family's socio-economic situation. On the other hand, children similarly lacking in affective and material resources do not all go to the streets, and no explanation has

---

This chapter is adapted from Lucchini, R. (2007). « Street children »: Deconstruction of a category. In Irene Rizzini, Udi Mandel Butler and Daniel Stoecklin (Eds.): *Life on the streets. Children and Adolescents on the Streets: Inevitable Trajectories?* (pp. 49–75) Sion: International institute for the rights of the child. Reprinted with courtesy of International institute for the rights of the child.



R. Lucchini, D. Stoecklin, *Children in Street Situations*, Children's Well-Being: Indicators and Research 21, https://doi.org/10.1007/978-3-030-19040-8_3

been given for this phenomenon. We can even say that the great majority of such children do not go to the streets, for if they did the streets of the large Latin American cities would be flooded with children. All this suggests that there is a 'choice' between children who leave and those who stay. This depends on factors that have not yet been isolated nor studied in a comparative and systematic way.

This gap, however, does not prevent the recognition that, from a psycho-sociological point of view, children in street situations form a heterogeneous category (Fischer Ferreira 1979; Aptekar 1988; Glauser 1990; Visano 1990; Roggenbuck 1993; Lucchini 1993). This heterogeneity asks for the development of a typology of children in street situations, being of not only scientific interest but also of practical concern. As such, intervention and prevention on the street, and together with the family, cannot be universally effective by only knowing empirically the phenomenon upon which we wish to act. Since we are led to believe that CSS will not disappear in the near future, our efforts must be oriented towards the constant support and accompaniment for the child. There are measures which have a positive effect on children, security and material assistance in particular, but the greater part of interventions are concerned with individuals or small groups of children, each with their own histories and personal identities. If the effectiveness of intervention depends on its duration and with this the level of follow-up it can receive, its success also depends on the degree of personalization that can be achieved. All this, of course, depends upon the available material and human resources, but even more on the image that we have of the CSS as a personality type of the urban scene. On the other hand, those helping almost always dedicate themselves to urgent interventions, such as illnesses, injuries, imprisonment, or physical threats, not leaving them much time to work in a long-term collaboration with children. In this way, intervention becomes fragile and loses its effectiveness.

We know that CSS cannot be singularly defined from criteria such as their presence on the street or the absence of relationships with family members. On the other hand, the notion of 'career' developed by the sociology of marginality proves useful in this case. This career is – as we shall see – a constitutive element of the psycho-sociological heterogeneity characteristic of CSS. A child does not become a CSS overnight, even when they are suddenly expelled from home or when they abandon home. The fact of being on the street for a prolonged period is an important criterion for distinguishing 'street chidren' from other children, but this alone is not sufficient to identify CSS as a particular social category. As such, many institutions working with children said to be in a situation of risk propose a two-dimensional definition, as Fig. 3.1. indicates.

The CSS is here defined by two dimensions: the physical and the social. The first has to do with the time the child has spent on the street, the second, with the relations or non-relations with parents or other responsible adults.

In this diagram we see that the position A is defined by the existence of frequent contact with responsible adults, as well as by the short existence on the street, for the child regularly returns home. While children categorized in position A are also

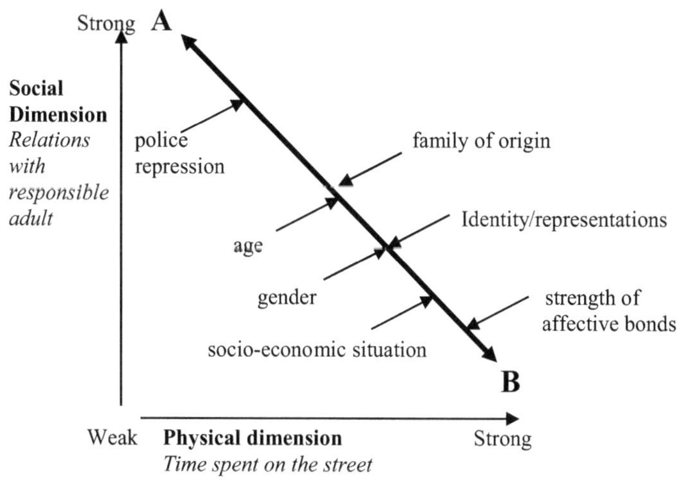


**Fig. 3.1** The two-dimensional definition of the 'street child' (Lucchini 2007, p. 50)

defined as 'children on the street', the notion of the 'responsible adult' implies the existence – in the identity of the child – of a reference to this adult. On the other hand, this responsibility is of a gradual nature and can be divided between various people who do not necessarily live in the same place. It can also be temporary, as when the child moves from one domestic unit to another,[1] going back home daily and yet without necessarily maintaining a relationship with a responsible adult. The two-dimensional model is not adequate in these cases. Position B in the diagram is defined by the absence of responsible adults. It is also defined by the use of the street, which becomes the primary residence of the child. Children in position B are categorized as 'children of the street', or sometimes also as 'real street children'.

The on/off distinction (Taçon 1985) has become widespread in recent years. However, this categorization, corresponding to the A/B positions in our diagram, is only seemingly operational. Between A and B, there exists a space for a series of intermediary situations which raise important problems of classification. Most definitions of 'street children' emphasize the time that they spend on the street, but this criterion is insufficient to define who the 'street child is', since it relates to a gradual, evolving condition. In this way, the child who moves on the axis from A to B progressively actualises their status as 'street child', or 'child of the street'. But the reverse is also true: the child who goes from B to A would not be a real 'street child' any longer, but rather a 'child on the street'. Then, one may rightly ask: when does a child become or cease to be a 'street child'? The criterion of duration of stay on

[1] The precariousness of the material existence of the poorest means that they seek out varied support outside of the domestic sphere. This is how the institution of *compadres* (godfathers) who assist the children and young adults in their various steps. It is often the children themselves who takes the initiative to look for a *compadre*.

the street is insufficient to answer this question. Certain careers are very long and intense, others are very short and unengaged.[2]

In fact, the position that the child occupies in the continuum between A and B depends on numerous other factors that can be grouped under five different categories:

(a) Biological factors like age and gender.
(b) Factors directly linked to the family, such as family composition and organization, the strength of family ties, the economic situation of the family and the degree to which the family is rooted in the city (bringing up questions of migration).
(c) Factors directly connected to the street: the representation (the image) that the child has of the street, the contacts the child has had with persons who already have experience of the street, the presence of the child within a group or network of other children, the profitability of activities, police repression and violence between children.
(d) Factors connected to urban spaces: the significance of the distance which the child would have to cover from home to the street in which they practice their money-making activities, the speed of moving between these two spaces, the nature of the urban space which the child has to cross to reach this place. This last issue has to do with the survival opportunities that the child encounters in moving within or towards the city centre.
(e) Factors that we can term macroscopic, referring to the social, political and economic situation of the country.

These different factors are interdependent and offer the possibility of multiple combinations. These combinations, like the factors that make them up, accelerate or slow the career of the 'street child'. There are also other influences that need to be mentioned, such as: the partial insertion of the child in the informal economy, the shifting movements between the street, home (with responsible adults) and institutions, the circumstances that provoke these movements, the initiation rituals for life on the street and for the world of crime. The two-dimensional definition of the 'street child' is surpassed by the psycho-social and cultural complexity of this phenomenon. It is preferable to operate in terms of models than in terms of definitions. This has become necessary because of what we have come to term the Child-Street System**:** all typology related to CSS should bear in mind the constitutive dimensions of the Child-Street System.[3]

The Child-Street System is comprised of nine interactive dimensions. The whole system can be visualized in Fig. 3.2.

The spatial (1) and temporal (2) dimensions are concerned with questions such as the existence of territories on the street, the child's departure to the street and the progressive character of this distancing, and the dislocation between the street and

[2] There are also children who, more and more, live in the street with their family. Some are second and even third generation. Are they street children? Such cases illustrate perfectly the difficulties encountered by the application of the two-dimensional schema.

[3] The number of dimensions in the Child-Street System has evolved along empirical findings.

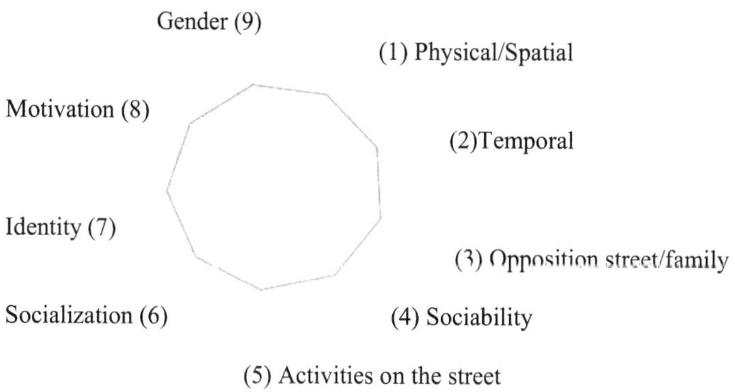


**Fig. 3.2** The nine dimensions of the Child-Street System (Lucchini 2007, p. 52)

**Fig. 3.3** Continuum of ways of leaving home

other places (family, relatives, friends, institutions). This mobility occurs not only by chance nor on the child's whim but because of particular choices and pressures of life on the street. CSS do not always have a well-delineated territory. Important differences can exist between one group and another, between groups in one district and another and, even more so, between groups found in one city and another. The progressive movement to the street does not only depend upon the occurrences and circumstances that led to the departure, but moreso reveal the existence of a complex process that includes, amongst other things, the child's representation of the world of the street (Lucchini 1997). The progressive character of the movement is not only about a material relocation to the street and a distancing from the home. It also involves a symbolic appropriation of the street and a distancing in relation to the place of origin. The degree of symbolic appropriation (representation) of the street and of the distancing in relation to the place of origin (family home, institution, etc.) greatly varies from one child to the next. This increases the diversity of the personal situations of the children who go to the street.

The process of symbolic appropriation of the street space is incorporated into the identification system of the child, and the spatial and temporal dimensions are connected to the dimension of identification in the Child-Street System. It is true that some children are expelled from home by a violent incident, such as an accident or death of a parent, or by the degradation of the economic situation of the family. We then have a continuum of concrete cases between two poles representing ideal types, as shown in Fig. 3.3.

Some children leave home without an apparent cause threatening their position within the family. The child here does not leave the home because of initial difficulties or violent situations. On top of this, there are significant differences between boys and girls. For girls, the conditions of access to the street are not the same, and in the same family conditions boys tend leave the family home more quickly. This is what we refer to as the different access for girls into the world of the street (Lucchini 1995).

Neither poverty nor violence, then, is a sufficient explanation for the child's departure to the street. We must consider other factors. Firstly, there is the subjective perception of violence by the child, and this varies from individual to individual. No simple formula is capable of explaining why, living under similar conditions, only a minority of children leave for the street. To explain the child's departure, it is too easy to evoke poverty, violence, promiscuity, instability of family relations and possible conflicts with parents, the absence of responsible adults, the high spatial mobility of the family group, the precarious work in the informal sector by the child, the lack of functional spatial division characteristic of many *favela* settlements, being expelled from school, and so on. Considered in isolation, a single factor, even if important, does not explain anything. On the other hand, the simple addition of the effects of each factor does not make sense. What connects the factors together, what makes a factor into an occurrence, what produces a rupture, all this depends on the meaning given to it by the child and their context. The identification of these ruptures is indispensable in order to begin reconstructing the biography of the child who leaves home.[4] The complexity and progressive nature of the movement to the street is the consequence of a subtle mixture between the limiting effects of the social and spatial context, the experience of the child, and their available resources (affective, social, physical, and in terms of identity). These latter aspects are always very different from one child to the next, with age and gender also being important differentiating factors. This explains why similar disturbances in a child's environment do not produce standard reactions. On the contrary, we can see important differences in how the child departs the home, in the degree of distance to the family home, the number of departures, the frequency in the periods between departing and returning home, and the choice of destination, which is not always the street.

The majority of children oppose the world of the family to the world of the street. This is the third dimension of the Child-Street System. Three cases present themselves. The first is of a child who values the image of an ideal family. The street is here perceived and lived as a state of emergency. In the second case we find the opposite, where the street is valued, whereas the family is presented as a space that is momentarily closed. Finally, some children ambivalently adopt both of these attitudes – variously valuing and devaluing both the street and the family. This is most often the case. In all three cases the street is also a subculture, even if all the children do not identify in the same way. This in turn depends on the child's history and resources, on the circumstances that took them to the street and on the image they have of the street.

The fourth dimension, forms of sociability, has to do with the forms of social organization of CSS. There are many variations of such forms, with a network of subgroups, dyads and triads being the most common arrangements of these. The highly organized and hierarchical group is, however, the exception. This arrange-

[4] For the concept of biographical rupture, see: Francisco J. Varela, *Quel savoir pour l'éthique. Action, sagesse et cognition*, La Découverte, Paris, 1996, pp. 25–38; Norman K. Denzin., *Interpretive Interactionism*, Sage, London, 1990, pp. 18 ss.; Abraham Moles, *Micropsychologie et vie quotidienne*, Denoël/Gonthier, Paris, 1976, pp. 17 ss.; Anthony Giddens, *Modernity and Self-Identity*, Polity Press, Cambridge, 1991, pp. 35–70.

a place where the survival of the fittest is the rule, there is no reason to affirm that the children are deprived of a moral sensibility. Many other authors have shown the importance of this dimension (Fischer Ferreira 1979; Dallape 1987; Aptekar 1988; Rubén 1990; Larvie 1992; Cussianovich 1997; Lucchini 1993, 1996; Ennew 1994; Parazelli 1995).

The seventh dimension, the dimension of identification, is one of the central dimensions of the Child-Street System. Amongst the components that constitute the identification system of the child, the most important are their references (to place, group, category, people) and the image of the self. In relation to the references, we found identifications, or distancing, that differed among the children. These are directly linked to the time spent on the street. Here it is the experience of the child on the street, as well as their material and symbolic resources, that, in an evolving manner, changes their relationship to the street. The children have many ways of talking about the street. There exist different ways of being on the street, as well as many modalities or types of street. The system of identification is by its very nature dynamic: the references change their objects and value, and the relationships shift. Besides this, the self-presentation or the presentation of the public or social self, and the phenomenon of identity negotiation and of the maintenance of self-image, influence the dynamics of the system. The social, emotional, and linguistic resources of the child also influence their performance of identity. On the other hand, these performances do not only depend upon the context in which the interaction occurs, but also on the way in which the children feel themselves to be perceived by those with whom they are interacting. The comparison of different performances of identity by children in different contexts of interaction is imperative in order to understand their behaviour.

The eighth aspect of the Child-Street system, the aspect of motivation, concerns the way in which the child perceives the street: that is, as a means of resolving the problems, in terms of family, school, or identity, with which they are faced. Going onto the street is also connected to playful and practical motivations. For some children, the pleasure in breaking prohibitions is a significant motivating factor. It is necessary, therefore, to consider the relationship that the child has with risk and adventure. This component is almost always an important incentive, not only for the child to go to the street but also to remain there. Chance is also relevant. Here the child stays on the street without the initial intention of not returning home. It is the circumstances of the moment that prevail. It is the occasion of remaining on the street that becomes the determining factor. Following this, the child rationalises their behaviour and builds their motivation. Imitation is almost always an important element that motivates the child to go to the street and remain there for a prolonged period of time, but generally it is a combination of different aspects that come to make up a motivational dynamic. The street cannot be presented as simply a means used by the children to resolve their problems or realize their aspirations. Motivation does not reduce itself to a simple rational choice in which the children consciously combine an objective (such as solving a family problem) with a means (going to the street). Motivation is only one of the constitutive elements of the identification system of the child. The structure of this system is influenced by the combination of components of this identity and by factors of an affective nature. According to John

P. Hewitt, the components of identity are: (a) motivations, (b) roles and the knowledge that allows individuals to interpret them, (c) norms and values, (d) cognitive competencies, and (e) self-image. Identity is then a combination of predispositions and potentialities related to possible behaviours (Hewitt 1970).

The last dimension is that of gender. Access to the street as a living space differs between boys and girls. We have seen that it is necessary to speak about the differential access to the street and about the invisibility of girls on the street. This question, like many other dimensions of the Child-Street System, is still ignored by the scholarly literature. It has been primarily boys who have been the objects of studies on CSS. We know very little about the different modalities that guide the girl's departure from home and her relation with the world of the street, nor about her career as a CSS or about her eventual departure from the street. We know nothing about her insertion in networks or groups of boys, nor about the nature of the relationships that exist between girls. This ignorance has consequences: the 'street girl' is often associated with prostitution. Because of this we highlight all that distinguishes 'street girls' from professional prostitutes. Not only is this assumption false, but it also creates prejudices that stigmatise street girls. Even if some girls sometimes sell their bodies, this does not mean they are prostitutes.

The Child-Street System shows that the reality of the child on the street is a complex one and that its study is delicate matter. This has consequences for social interventions on the street or in institutions, and for the evaluation of such interventions. This complex reality highlights that we cannot under any circumstance reduce the children in question to statistics. There are no trustworthy indicators to 'measure' in an objective way the impact of interventions. This applies even more when the intervention occurs directly on the street: the histories of children in a street situation (CSS) imply all the dimensions of the Child-Street System. These dimensions allow for the reconstruction of the experience the child has of the street as a spatial and social environment. They also permit us to understand their relationship with other social environments, such as family, neighbourhoods, school, other institutions, and work. The dimensions of the system are interlinked and a variation in any of them will influence all the others. This explains the diversity of the personal circumstances of children in a street situation, even if the children share similar life-histories. Amongst the factors that explain this diversity there are:

(a) the modalities of the departure to the street;
(b) references and models of identification;
(c) symbolic and instrumental competencies;
(d) the degree of insertion/participation of life on the street;
(e) movements between different fields (street, family, parents, school, institutions, etc.);
(f) necessities and motivations;
(g) the modalities of the departure from the street;
(h) institutional experiences (NGO, police, courts, media, education system, work).

These factors make up the stages of what I have described as the career of the child in a street situation. The combination of these factors is variable and any modification in any one of them has repercussions for the whole. The career, however, is a central element that defines the position that the child occupies on the street. This position is almost always different from one child to the next because of the stage of their life on the street, as well as the stages they have already passed through. Knowing at what stage a child finds themselves in, and of their career in general, is vital for any intervention that seeks to improve the situation of the child while on the street, or of distancing them from this space. With this knowledge we can begin to understand the relation that a child has with the street as a living space. An example with five stages illustrates the notion of career:

(a) Progressive distancing: the child gets closer to the street through successive stages; they explores the urban space found between their house and the streets of the city centre;
(b) The observed and the playful street: the child still maintains a distance from the street;
(c) The alternating street: here the child takes on the world of the street with all its contradictions and almost always claims the status of 'street child'. For the child at this point, the street is neither good nor bad, it is ambivalent;
(d) The denied street: the child recognizes that the street no longer meets their needs;
(e) Leaving the street, which includes many forms (Lucchini 2001).

Not all children pass through these stages in the same way. The stages are not static, they are the result of a combination of many variables among the factors that we mentioned above. A systematic approach shows that the children 'of the street' is not a homogeneous category and, therefore, that it is preferable to speak of children in a street situation. Intervention, therefore, can no longer restrict itself to the child; it must encompass the collection of social interactions of the children on the street and in other social environments or fields.

## 3.2 Mobility Among Several 'Fields'

The children studied here show a high degree of institutionalisation (State institutions, social work programmes), but they also remained on the street for long periods of time. As we shall see, these children are not CSS, as the street did not become an autonomous space of survival in relation to the family home or the institution. These children are found in many fields, without one being necessarily more important than the other, and without one complementing another. They tend to enter into opposition with each other.

A field does not only define itself by the positions that it contains, but also by its specific challenges and interests (Bourdieu 1984). The challenges and interests of a field are not reducible to those of other fields, and as such the children will oppose one field to another. The limits of the field "are situated at the point where the effects of the field cease" (Bourdieu 1992, p. 76). These limits are not precise, as the actors – in this case, children – have different representations of the fields that they inhabit. The collection of these representations is part of the identification system and follows the actor in their movement from one field to the next. The limit, however, does not only have an objective aspect comprised of the influence of those who exercise positions of power within a field, but is also of a subjective nature. In this case, the actor elaborates on the symbolic and emotive realms of the particular forces active in a field and the positions that come to make it up. The limits of the different fields touch and overlap with one another. The actor who finds themselves in a field resorts to the resources and representations that correspond to the challenges and interests of the field. Here, the actor is characterised by an instrumental approach to the field, whose limits they tend to delineate.

Each of the fields (family, assistance programme, school, street) is in itself conflictual. The child takes advantage of this double tension – internal conflict and a lack of integration between the fields – to justify their periodic abandonment of a given field. In this way the child leaves the street to return home but runs away from home to the street or to an assistance program. Or, they run away from the program to return home or to the street. The child is imprisoned between the influences of the different fields and cannot choose between them. The family, dominated by the maternal figure, is the organising pole of the relationships that the child establishes between the different fields. However, because of material reasons and reasons of identification, the child does not have the capacity to establish a stable and lasting position in this field, despite the importance awarded to the affective relationship with the mother, who has a central position. Almost always it is the figure of the stepmother or stepfather who structures the family field and conditions the type of adjustment that the child will encounter within it.

We can speak about the emotional priority of the family field above other fields, but this priority is not demonstrated in the evidence. The child has access to a position that, even within this field, is itself unique. There are material obstacles (housing conditions and the economic situation, amongst others), but these are not the most important ones. The symbolic and identification dimensions, the emotional dimension, as well as the search for autonomy, are elements that prevent the stabilisation of a child in a field. There is also a playful component in the movements of a child from one field to the next. All these elements influence the process of distancing the child from the family sphere. Institutionalised children are characterised by an incessant mobility between different fields, with the street as the organising pole. The child, integrated in the social, family and school levels, passes from one field to the next, following the paths traced by adults. These movements are legitimated by precise practices and rituals. In most cases the child alternates between two fields: family and school. The institutionalised child, on the other had, regularly abandons a plurality of fields for only one of them, for instance temporarily abandoning an assistance program to go back home or to the street. Almost always this is done in an abrupt way. The rhythm of the passage from one field to the next is more intense than that of the 'street children'. For the latter, the street is the main field, even if there are significant differences between the different categories of children (Lucchini 1993).

The child tends to fix themselves to a field that allows for the best investment of their emotional, cognitive, social and identity resources. There is also the case of those who use psychotropic drugs (almost always glue or other inhalants) and who have developed an addiction to these products. It is this addiction which, to a large degree, serves to explain their permanent place on the street. The conflictual character of the fields, the absence of integration, and the vague nature of their limits influences not only the rhythm of the movements from one field to another, but also the distancing from the home as well as the return home. The CSS alternates between the family and the street, but always has the street as their main field. They determine the rhythms of their own activities. This does not occur with the institutionalised child, who runs along a circuit that is more or less the same for all who are part of it. Some CSS who go to the street go through such a circuit rather than alternating between different fields, but not as a matter of choice. Their condition is similar to that of institutionalised children. However, work on the street stabilises for a certain time and in certain conditions the relationship that the child maintains with this field.

It is therefore difficult to distinguish clearly between the different fields in the process of distancing. For most institutionalised children everything is mixed up: running away from home to an assistance programme, from the programme to the street or back home, abandoning school for the street. There is a kind of equivalence between these movements so that the child remains constantly in movement without there being clearly marked stages. There are also children who leave the family home to find a parent who lives in another locality. All this makes studying the process of distancing from the family home more complicated, since there is no definitive pattern. Escape and distancing are not the same phenomenon. The first implies the improvised and short-term character of the departure, leading to a new set of changes. Distancing, however, suggests a longer process; the existence, if not of preparation, at least of an apprenticeship. It follows from the exit of the child from the family field, even if this occurs briefly. As a general rule, from the moment that a relation of relief is established in a particular field in detriment to another, we can speak of distancing. It is not about a rational choice, as understood by the theory of that name, in which a scale of preferences is clearly established and leads to strategies of a utilitarian nature. The child seeks, preferably, to satisfy their necessity in relation to their past and to the circumstances that lead to their departure. When the motivation that led to the departure is, above all, of a playful nature, and the need for experimentation in the child is strong, escape takes priority over distancing. Repeated escapes end up as distancing when they imply a project, and/or when the child enters a field which for a time meets their needs. Distancing does not imply a definitive separation. In the case of the institutionalised child, distancing is short term and coexists with repeated returns to the family. The normal form of leaving is the escape, distancing being more exceptional.

However, in the case of CSS, leaving home through distancing is more frequent. This occurs even when there are returns home. In this case it is the centrality of the street for the child that explains the difference in relation to the institutionalised child: the street becomes the organising pole for the daily life of the child. This is why it is important to highlight its importance. As mentioned previously (Lucchini 1993, p. 134), children produce different discourses about the street. As a result, there are many different ways of being on the street, and many different kinds of street. These differences are not of a physical kind but of a social and symbolic kind. In fact, when there is a change in the way of life on the street and the child has access to new networks, we can speak of a new modality of the street, in which the child offers a new definition of it. When the evaluation offered by a child changes, their relation to the street changes: they becomes another person. In this way we can say that there is an evolution in the children and in the way they participate in life on the street.

It is in this evolution that we find the origin of the significant diversity of living conditions on the street. This diversity is the base of what we call the psycho-social heterogeneity of CSS. The passage of the child from one modality of the street to another constitutes a stage in the career of the CSS. In this way their career is defined, among other things, by the combined stages that they experienced on the street. The combination of these stages constitutes a continuum that children undergo with different rhythms and in different ways. Some children stop in a stage, or skip another. These different routes comprise an important component of the psycho-social heterogeneity of CSS. This heterogeneity prevents us from affirming the existence of a unique departure to the street. This means that even for CSS, distancing occurs in different ways.

Institutionalised children also do not comprise a homogeneous category in the psycho-social field. However, it is plausible that their departure organises itself differently because of certain parameters. But it is not sufficient to isolate these parameters in order to build a typology. It is necessary to obtain information about the uses that children make of the street and the place of this in relation to other fields that they frequent (Lucchini 1996). The departure cannot be explained exclusively by economic conditions, nor by precarious housing conditions. Children who leave the family home live under very different material conditions that are not always unsatisfactory. Instead, what characterises the majority of these cases is the dissolution of the union of the parents, a frequent movement of the domestic unit, and premature institutionalisation. All this leads to instability in terms of the references of the child, who, at regular intervals, seeks to reconstitute their relations in the affective and social levels. Far too early, then, the child is faced with the provisional and fragile character of social bonds.

Institutionalised children who work on the street comprise yet another category. If they run away, their escapes are less frequent and their movements from one field to another are less disorganized. Money-making activities on the street confer a certain organization to the daily activities of these children (Lucchini 1996). The income-generating and other regular activities the child takes part in have an effect on the self-esteem of the child, at least for a time. In the more favourable cases, self-esteem and the gratification of work lead to a positive self-image, and, therefore, a positive identification system. In such cases their daily activities and perception of time become more stable. This stability is a result of a greater integration between the different fields: school, family, assistance programmes, street-work. However, the problem is the precarious nature of the child's informal work. At any moment they can lose this work, or become a victim of abuse. It is necessary, therefore, to have some kind of protection or control over this work so that it can be, over time, integrated to the other fields. The commercial areas of the urban peripheries are almost always the places that allow the child their first apprenticeship of the street. In these spaces the street holds many sources of gratification. It allows the child to be in a group, to experience the excitement produced by places where there is an abundance of objects, the presence of money, and the possibility of escaping parental control and pressure. Progressively the child then moves towards the city centre. Leaving home takes place when they discover that the street can be a place of new gratifications and an antidote to boredom.

What collectively characterizes institutionalised children is the precocity of the first escapes. These first experiences comprise an initiation into the world of the street. But this initiation is not the end, for in each new incursion the child remains on the street for only a short time. This initiation is never finished and in the absence of a structured field, the activities of the child have a double effect. On the one hand, the child multiplies their exits in the hope of gaining a position in a given field. For this same reason they return to where they had left. Because of this, we would rather speak of a *circuit* between different places rather than a distancing. In this way, unfinished initiation is not only about the street, but also about all the other fields. This is with the exception of the closed institution which, in general, the child refuses. The movement towards the moment when the child manages an initiation into one of the fields is subjectively important for them. Children, however, differ in terms of the degree of initiation and in the fields involved in this initiation. The initiation consists in the progressive appropriation in a field of all that allows them to secure this position.

It would be imprudent to suggest a causal relation between an event (such as physical violence, or a parent leaving) and the departure of the child to the street. Many factors are in play, such as the age of the child at the time that the parent leaves the family, the make-up of the group, the example of siblings or friends who frequent the street or an assistance program, the sudden arrival of a partner for the mother, a change of house which coincides with the departure of the father, the placing of the child in the house of relatives or in an institution, the economic conditions of the family and the work of the mother, as well as the support network of neighbours. But these characteristics, belonging to the social environment of the child, do not explain why only certain children regularly leave the home and move onto the circuit between the different fields.[5] The factors that filter the influence of the environment are of a personal nature, concerning the identity of the child as well as with the social, cognitive, and emotional resources available to them. It is not the episode retold by the child (punishment, conflict with a member of the group, violence by the stepfather, poverty, etc.) that explains the logic of the departure and of the circuit

[5] Actually, the number of families in which various members of the group were or are runaways is very low. This is also the case in the situation of the children in the street that we studied in Rio de Janeiro.

**Fig. 3.4** Continuum of integration of the fields

between different fields. The majority of children from the more impoverished social groups are not runaways. The episode that apparently leads to the departure of the child does not offer much explanation if it is not connected to a combination of other factors that influence the adjustment between the identification system of the child and of the different fields that they cross.

It is almost always enough that the fields become integrated (for example, the family and the assistance programme) for the frequency of departures to diminish. This interdependence of the fields explains why it is not sufficient to reinforce in an isolated manner the integration of the child to a particular field to reduce the number of their departures. We can also speak of a continuum in which different children are found. One of the poles of this continuum is marked by the total absence of integration between the fields, and the other by a perfect integration, as shown in Fig. 3.4.

Institutionalised children are close to pole (1) and experience a large number of departures. They are very susceptible, and their departure almost always depends on a chance encounter or a small eventuality. In this case their departure is more the result of a succession of events that fit together than a reflexive choice. The child can leave at any moment. This depends on small events and on encounters with other children and adolescents who influence their decision. These children are regarded as runaways. However, the further a child moves from pole (1) in direction of pole (2), the less their departures depend on chance and on the unfolding of small events. The frequency of departures is reduced, and they occur because of significant events, such as the worsening of a conflict, and because of the need to find a solution to a certain problem.

## References

Aptekar, L. (1988). *The street children of Cali*. Durham/London: Duke University Press.
Bourdieu, P. (1984). *Questions de sociologie*. Paris: Editions de Minuit.
Bourdieu, P. (1992). *Réponses*. Paris: Seuil.
Cosgrove, J. G. (1990). Towards a working definition of street children. *International Social Work, 33*(2), 185–192.
Cussianovich, A. (1997). *Some premises for reflection and social practices with working children*. Lima: Rädda Barnen.
Dallape, F. (1987). *An experience with street children*. Nairobi: Undugu.
Ennew, J. (1994). Parentless friends: A cross-cultural examination of networks among street children and street youth. In F. Nestmann & K. Hurrelmann (Eds.), *Social network and social support in childhood and adolescence* (pp. 409–426). New York: de Gruyter.
Fischer Ferreira, R. M. (1979). *Meninos da rua*. São Paulo: Ibrex.
Glauser, B. (1990). Street children: Deconstructing a construct. In A. James & A. Prout (Eds.), *Constructing and reconstructing childhood. Contemporary issues on the sociological study of childhood*. London: The Falmer Press.

Hewitt, J. P. (1970). *Social stratification and deviant behaviour*. New York: Random House.
Houchon, G. (1990). Pratiques et réseaux: éloges de l'ambiguïté. *Déviance et Société, 14*(2), 213–221.
Larvie, P. (1992). *A construção cultural dos meninos de rua no Rio de Janeiro: implicações para a prevenção do HIV/AIDS*. Chicago: Ed. Universitária de Chicago.
Lucchini, R. (1993). *Enfant de la rue. Identité, sociabilité, drogue*. Genève/Paris: Droz.
Lucchini, R. (1995). Femme et deviance ou le débat sur la spécificité de la délinquance feminine. *Revue européenne des sciences sociales, 33*(102), 127–168.
Lucchini, R. (1996). *Sociologie de la survie. L'enfant dans la rue*. Paris: Presses Universitaires de France.
Lucchini, R. (1997). *Between running away and eviction: The child leaving for the street*. Working paper, Institut des Sciences Economiques et Sociales, Université de Fribourg.
Lucchini, R. (2001). Carrière, identité et sortie de la rue: le cas de l'enfant de la rue. *Déviance et Société, 25*(1), 75–97.
Lucchini, R. (2007). "Street children": Deconstruction of a category. In I. Rizzini, U. M. Butler, & D. Stoecklin (Eds.), *Life on the streets. Children and adolescents on the streets: Inevitable trajectories?* (pp. 49–75). Sion: Institut International des Droits de l'enfant.
Parazelli, M. (1995). L'espace dans la formation d'un potentiel de socialisation chez les jeunes de la rue: assises théoriques. *Cahiers de géographie du Québec, 39*(107), 287–308. https://doi.org/10.7202/022500ar.
Roggenbuck, S. (1993). *Strassenkinder in Lateinamerika*, Frankfurt-am-Main.
Rubén, E. R. (1990). *Cuando el lugar no es la casa* (unpublished manuscript). Mendoza.
Taçon, P. (1985). *A Unicef response to the needs of abandonned and street children*. Geneva: UNICEF.
Visano, L. (1990). The socialization of street children: The development and transformation of identities. *Sociological Studies of Child Development, 3*, 139–161.
Yablonsky, L. (1979). The delinquent gang as a near-group. In D. H. Kelly (Ed.), *Deviant behavior* (pp. 464–477). New York: St Martin's Press.

# Chapter 4
# Leaving for the Street

**Riccardo Lucchini**

## 4.1 General Considerations

The streets to which the child leaves for are neither those of the slums nor those of the urbanised city's suburbs. They correspond to areas that are endowed with numerous commercial activities and public transports. They are the hotspots of the towns, though not necessarily town centres. Neither domestic violence nor destitution are sufficient to explain why the child leaves home for the street.[1] Domestic violence directed towards children is not the preserve of the most underprivileged classes of southern countries. It is found everywhere, and among the people of every walk of life. Most of the time, it does not lead the 'child-victim' to the street. Other factors have to intervene. There is first the question of the child's subjective perception of violence and the question of the ability they have to develop it. This varies from one individual to another, as is shown by numerous studies (Ferguson et al. 1993; Corby 1994; Werner and Smith 1992; Calam and Franchi 1987).[2]

But it varies also according to sociocultural and affective parameters specific to different societies, and which influence the child's socialization process. The cultural definition of childhood is quite indebted to psychological models developed in northern countries, and since those models have been considered to be universally implementable and have been adopted by aid and development programmes, "there

This chapter is updated from Lucchini, R. (1997). *Between runaway and eviction : the child leaving for the street.* (Working Paper, Institut des Sciences Economiques et Sociales, Université de Fribourg).

[1] One of my interlocutors told me that in the dynamics of leaving home, familial culture is more important than economic situation. The image of man and woman, the child's place in relation to the parental couple, and the quality of affective links are the elements which are most influential to the child's attitude toward leaving home for the street.

[2] These studies focus above all on Europe and the United States. There is as yet no reason to claim that this diversity of reactions toward violence is not to be found elsewhere.

 
R. Lucchini, D. Stoecklin, *Children in Street Situations*, Children's Well-Being: Indicators and Research 21, https://doi.org/10.1007/978-3-030-19040-8_4

is an easy movement from naturalization of child development to its abstraction" (Burman 1996, p. 60). For Erica Burman, it is at least careless to postulate the existence of a child development model that would be natural, uniform and invariant. In fact, from one society to another, one must take into account "differential profiles of socialization-enculturation". With this logic, it is important to consider the "variable degree of solicitation of the child, fixed by the model which determines their 'distance' from the adults [...] So, in western societies, culture institutes a discontinuity which goes up to the opposition between the roles of a child and those of the adult in at least three domains: irresponsibility/responsibility, submission/domination, and sexual avoidance/assertiveness" (Camilleri and Vinsonneu 1996, p. 20).[3] But this discontinuity is found neither in every culture nor in all social stratas of any society. It is thus prudent to question the development models on their degree of adequacy to local conditions of socialization: this cultural relativism is necessary in order to avoid the excesses of a universalism which loses its ethical justification when transforming into an imperialism. But this relativism is with no solution when it maintains that cultures are completely irreducible to one another. No ethical dimension can emerge and relativism becomes absolute. One must account for the different cultural rationalities at play in order to find the conditions ensuring the dignity of the person in a specific sociocultural context.

We have shown elsewhere that the move from the home to the street is influenced by a series of factors which are linked with one another and which form a system (Lucchini 1993, 1996). Yet none of these factors is determining. No determinism can explain why only a tiny minority of children living in similar material and familial conditions leave home for the street for a significant period. It is too simple to invoke destitution, violence, lack of privacy, instability of familial relationships and of the parental couple, absence of responsible adults, high spatial mobility of the family group, the precocious work of children in the street and in the informal sector, the lack of functional differentiation of built space typical of numerous slums, expulsion from school and so on in order to explain why the child leaves home. Considered in itself, a single factor, even if important, does not explain anything. In turn, the simple addition of the specific effects of each factor is no more satisfying. What links the factors one with another, what makes a factor become an event which can eventually turn into a break, depends on the meaning the child attributes to this factor. However, this meaning is hardly accessible to others. The researcher cannot just question the child *a posteriori*, even if the information collected in this way is precious and essential. In fact, the attributed meaning cannot be reconstituted on the sole basis of the child's verbal testimony. In order to access to this meaning, one must accompany and 'observe' the child in their different life contexts. These contexts are numerous: activities in the street, episodic returns to home, temporary work in the informal sector, or integration into an institution, for instance. The child's practices in these different contexts are what makes it possible to interpret the meaning of their speech. The child's immediate comments and their

[3] Translation by the author.

behavior in particular contexts are what give the most interesting information to understand the specific characteristics of their act of leaving home. As Anselm Strauss writes, only a comparative and continuous method allows us to reconstitute the framework of leaving (Strauss 1992, p. 283) and hence to elaborate on the 'street-child' system.

But this is no simple task. In fact, like everyone else, the child has "a readiness-for-action proper to every specific situation. Moreover, we are constantly moving from one readiness-for-action to another. Often these transitions or punctuations are slight and virtually imperceptible. Sometimes they are overwhelming, as when we experience a sudden shock or come face-to-face with unexpected danger" (Varela 1999, p. 9). The identification of these breaks is essential to be able to reconstitute the biographic frame of the child who is leaving home. As Norman K. Denzin (1990, p. 4) writes, "troubles are always biographical [...]. Strategically, the researcher locates epiphanies in those interactional situations where personal troubles became public issues". The notion of public applies in our case also to the neighborhood, to its young gangs or to the extended family. As we will see, when a break has a public dimension, it generally concerns an issue of identity. "It is at the moments of breakdown, that is, when we are not experts of our microworld anymore, that we deliberate and analyze" (Varela 1999, p. 18).

These breaks are critical events in individual biographies. Their identification allows the researcher to give consistency to the discourses and practices of the subjects they observing. The distinction between micro-level and macro-level breaks is not simple, because it depends among others on the personal sensibilities of the concerned individuals and on the specific stakes at play. As such, important differences do exist between the children on this question. What may be only a micro-break for the one may become a macro-break for the other. In fact, the break is felt differently according to individual character and the individual's socio-affective surrounding. As C. Wright Mills puts it (1959, p. 8), the break is linked to the personal Self as well as to "those limited areas of social life of which he (she) is directly and personally aware". Yet each of the "limited areas of social life" is composed of several micro-worlds and their routines. Regarding these dispositions to act for each of the specific situations encountered by the individuals, Francisco Varela speaks of "a *micro-identity* and its corresponding lived situation a *micro-world*. Thus, 'who we are' at any moment cannot be divorced from what other things and who other people are to us [...] 'who we are' – the pervasive mode of living – consists of *already* constituted microworlds" (Varela 1999, p. 10).[4] This is why, for Aaron

[4] Varela is not the inventor of the concept of micro-world, as used to stress that in daily life nothing is strictly determined. Anselm Strauss uses the concept in reference to the segmentation of social worlds in which individuals evolve. By using this concept, Strauss also wants to raise attention on the extreme fluidity of the set of social worlds (or fields of activities) which constitutes a society (Strauss 1992, pp. 273–274). Others, like Abraham Moles, stress the importance of micro-actions, of micro-events associated to daily routines. This means that when one considers the detail of the elements in the situation where an individual is placed, "behavior in fact results from a range of micro-decisions, largely located under the threshold of the conceived, but perfectly explainable by the observer" (Moles 1976, pp. 17–18).

Cicourel, daily experience "is for the actor always compartmentalized in different fields of meaning in which they use categories of typification stemming from common sense and considered as taken for granted" (Cicourel 1979, p. 50). One sees how strong the correspondence is between the micro-world, as defined by Varela, and Cicourel's fields of meaning. The break occurs when the routines currently used no longer produce the expected results. What ensues is a situation of insecurity and of tension which demands solutions. As Anthony Giddens writes: "Ordinary day-to-day life [...] involves an *ontological security* expressing an *autonomy of bodily control* within *predictable routines*" (Giddens 1984, p. 50). When this security is in trouble, the actor is driven to make choices which may modify their personal career.

It is therefore important to locate in the child's life the events they consider breaks. This allows us to rebuild a personal history or one of its components, the progressive distancing from home being one such component. In this respect, the researcher must appeal to the child's memory, and therefore to their discursive consciousness, but also to their practical consciousness as manifested in contextualized action. Key is to ensure that the child is "recapitulating past experiences in such a way as to focus them upon the continuity of action" (Giddens 1984, p. 49). The distinction made by Anthony Giddens between discursive consciousness and practical consciousness is not original, having been expressed before by John Dewey (1922). Dewey makes a distinction between know-how and knowledge. The first is largely unconscious and is at play in the multiple practices of everyday life. It corresponds to dispositions toward action in specific experienced situations, relating to Varela's micro-identities and micro-worlds. Meanwhile, knowledge implies reflection and conscious evaluation. Yet only a part of know-how is expressed in knowledge, and thus in the discursive consciousness. It is therefore essential for the researcher to have access to the child's diverse know-how and to the contexts in which it may be expressed. Thanks to the observation of the child in different contexts and to the triangulation of their testimonies, the researcher is then able to correctly interpret the knowledge expressed by the child.

Most of the children invoke domestic violence, neglect from the father or the mother, or their family's poverty to explain why they left for the street. This applies in Rio as well as in Mexico, Montevideo, and elsewhere. To anyone asking them, the child answers that they are on the street reluctantly. In the first instance, they always presents themselves as victims of circumstance. Little by little their speech differentiates, and the researcher is led to put the first testimonies into perspective. It is true that violence, often linked to alcoholism, to destitution, to lack of privacy, to lack of affection, to neglect, or to the death of a responsible adult (mother, father, grandmother, aunt, or other form of guardian) affect the stability of familial relationships and have an 'expelling' effect on children. There is no question of denying this side of things. However, we have shown that leaving home cannot be considered as simply the product of factors like those that have just been mentioned (Lucchini 1993, 1996). Causal attributions are insufficient to understand the complexity of the move towards the street and its progressive character. This complexity, we repeat, is the consequence of a subtle combination of environmental constraining effects (social and spatial) and the child's experience and their own resources (affective, social, physical, and in terms of identity). The latter are often very different from one child to another, age and gender being important distinguishing factors. This explains why similar environmental constraints do not produce standardized reactions. We observe, on the contrary, important differences in the modes of leaving home, in the degrees of distanciation from home, in the numbers of departures, in the frequency and alternation between leaving home and coming back home, and in the choice of the destination, which is not always the street.

The act of leaving home for the street is also frequently associated with survival. But survival is not an easy concept to define. This notion refers to living conditions and to a personal and collective experience which has multiple dimensions: economical, cultural, social, mental, environmental, and ethical. These dimensions form a whole, and it is impossible to define a threshold below which the life conditions of the individual and/or the group would be of a survival type that would be universally valid. This notion implies also a 'must be', that is, norms and a definition of what constitutes 'normal' life conditions. There are always references to normality, alongside ethical references. The whole difficulty lies here. One can simply say that survival is when the superfluous is impossible, or that survival corresponds to a limit under which the individual is at risk to disappear physically and the group (family, community) to break up. One can also define survival as a set of living conditions that do not respect human rights. In this case, one considers survival as being incompatible with human dignity, as comprising a considerable symbolic and physical violence. But it is also a question of degree, because destitution and poverty do not have the monopoly on violence. Far from it! Such a definition of survival is inseparable from the stigmatization of those who experience it. There is therefore no satisfying definition of survival outside of concrete life contexts. The only possibility is to contextualize the living conditions of an individual or a group in order to study the needs (felt and/or expressed) to what extent they are satisfied. One will then find a threshold beyond which the absence of a positive response to a need is judged intolerable by the individual themselves and by the community of which they are a member. This threshold will then be a survival threshold which is expressed in a given sociocultural context and at a given time in the life of the individual and of the group. The survival threshold of children who leave home for the street, then, is variable. This explains why, as we will see, children who live in similar life conditions do not all leave home.

The children who leave their family do not always directly go to the street, but may pass through a relay, such as a family in the neighborhood, a parent, or the family of a friend. The child sometimes already knows these places on account of having previously been placed there by their parents or, in the case of single-parent families, by their mother. On the other hand, proportionally more girls than boys are held back from leaving home for the street by these relays (Lucchini 1995). Leaving for a relay can be considered a very short-term 'refuge-departure', in which the intention of going onto the street is not yet present. Often, this type of runaway postpones for some time the act of leaving home for the street, because the latter requires the child to have more competencies and resources. As a consequence, these 'refuge-departures' may occur several times before the child leaves home for the street.

## 4.2 The Dynamics of Leaving Home and Its Causes

One may also see the child's departure from home as part of a progressive break-up of some taboos. We will see that it would be imprudent not to consider the playful motivation as well as the search for autonomy in the process leading the child towards the street. Imitation and initiation by a friend who already knows the street also play a definite role. Besides, many children know the street because they have been working there with an adult or on their own. The precariousness of this job, the often high expectations of the employer, and the daily contact with the street world and its attractions drive certain children to escape from adult guardianship. Yet only a tiny minority of children working in the informal sector become children in street situations (hereafter CSS).

Regarding taboos, their intensity is variable and the break with them does not have an identical effect on all children. The consequences of a break vary according to the type of relationship the child has with their familial environment, as well as according to their knowledge and practice of the street world. Moreover, the image of the street and accounts of it also exert an important attraction on the child. Yet the narrative concerns above all the identity and history of the population living in the street. This narrative is collective in nature, because the adults, like the children, use it commonly. It justifies and at the same time judges those who have left home for the street. Everyone can therefore draw from this narrative the elements that suit them in giving a meaning to events. Despite appearances, there is a consensus around this narrative and it varies little from one individual to another.

The child who leaves knows that they are not the only one to leave the family home, and that they share a narrative with many others. This feeling of sharing a common adventure is an element that facilitates the movement towards the street. On the other hand, the narrative presents the street as a space entirely opposed to the domestic sphere. The child perceives the possibility of acquiring new resources and to find solutions to domestic problems. The collective narrative thus confers on the street a reputation which gives rise to the child's interest and reinforces its attraction. But the image of the street produced by the narrative is not free of ambiguities. In fact, the street appears as simultaneously good and bad. It is dangerous, because it is unpredictable and arbitrary: one can die there. But it also promises rewards (Lucchini 1993).[5]

There is also the case of children who leave home for the street at certain periods of the year: during festivals or school holidays, for instance. In this case the street is not ambivalent, but above all playful and utilitarian. There is no running away, and the departure to the street is not undetermined in time. The street is not opposed to family or to school, but integrated as a natural component of the child's life. One thus sees that there is no sole type of leaving, but several.

---

[5] Not all of the children have the necessary competencies to go to the street and to stay there. However, this does not mean that the child who does not possess the required competencies leaves the street sooner that the one who successfully adapts to it. In fact, the social control exerted by the group and the child's concern for their reputation often delay their exit from the street.

In the movement conducting the child to the street, we find thresholds, or stages of no return. The number and type of thresholds differ from one child to another because they depend on the biography as well as on the personality and identity of the child. The way to cross a threshold is therefore not the same for all the children. An example of a stage of no return concerns the emergence of pleasures brought by new sensations and competencies developed by the child who progressively appropriates the street. An important element of the stage of non-return is the subjective impression to have surpassed the limit beyond which turning back is no longer permitted. It implies a break with the familial environment, as well as modifications in the child's perception of the self. The spatial distance separating the child from the family home and the properties of this space – in terms of social, economic and playful resources – influence the establishment of the stage of no return. This distance is not only physical, but also symbolic. In fact, when the child takes the initiative and dares to leave the family home, they become someone else.[6] This transformation drives the child to go on further and to delay their return. This change of identity is a critical event, a biographical break orienting the child's behavior. It is true that such a break occurs only if the child can count on a reference adult within the family they are leaving. It is also true that the child must be able to feel solicitude. The word solicitude "expresses the fact that the individual feels concerned and involved, and that, at the same time, they feel and accept a responsibility" (Winnicott 1994, p. 121).[7] The degree of concern varies from one individual to the next and explains in part why one child will interrupt their movement towards the street while another one goes forward.

When the child goes to the street accompanied by another child who play the role of a guardian, and who is already well inserted into a group of CSS, the interruption of the movement towards the street is less frequent than when the child leaves home alone. In this case, there is often something at stake for the child who leaves home: consisting of not being judged incapable by the other children. In addition, the child's insertion into a group of CSS holds them back from returning home. When the child begins to develop survival competencies in the street, they feel the need to

[6] This is not the case if some other children in the family have already left for the street. These cases are relatively frequent, and the child has not anymore the feeling of breaking a taboo, because they are not the first one to leave home.

[7] The birth of the feeling of solicitude finds its roots in early childhood, even if it develops or on the contrary diminishes in later experiences. Winnicott tells us also that in order for this feeling to be expressed and to be strengthened, the small child must "feel that the mother or the maternal substitute is a total person". Yet, this requires, among other things, not only the material presence of the mother, but also attentive listening on her part. However, the personal history of children is often characterised by the absence or the extreme weakness of such a readiness to listen to the child. By analysing the child's familial relationships, we will see that they are characterised by a certain coolness and the lack of appreciation of the child by responsible adults and especially by the mother. Despite individual histories marked by a relative absence of the mother, we have observed the presence of solicitude with most of the children. This implies that despite appearances, the child has a reference adult at home. This reference is often strongly idealized by the child. This explains why we find with many children the presence of a claim for autonomy and at the same time a feeling of guilt toward the reference adult, in most cases the mother.

have these competencies recognized elsewhere, notably by the reference adult of the family. But this generally does not happen, and the child is confronted with the impossibility of having their new competencies appreciated. As one of them says: "I don't want to go back home because I am proud". In fact, the most independent children claim such recognition even if they know that it will not be valued by the adults. Having overcome ordeals, the child has advantages – material and symbolic – which they do not want to give up.

An important component of leaving home is the diffuse responsibility of the adults toward the child. The child is often placed with relatives, and this placement is rarely final. Most of the time the duration of these stays is not defined, but they are generally short-term or middle-term (several months to one-to-two years). The parental couple's instability or the premature death of one of the parents can also disturb the child's familial references. It is therefore not surprising that for the child the social bond is above all marked by its provisional and unpredictable character. The child's feeling of solicitude is not annulled by such conditions of socialization, but it is weakened. However, their need for identity and affection remains intact, and conditions the child's experience while leaving home. The departure is often an attempt to test the mother's response to the child's challenge.[8]

It is important to bear in mind that, in most of the cases, reference adults are women –biological mother, adoptive mother, aunt, grand-mother, neighbor – who, in the absence of a stable male support, must take material and affective responsibilities that are often overwhelming.[9] They thus often turn to placing children with a parent or an acquaintance. These placements are a survival strategy which splits the costs of bringing up the child among the members of the parenthood system. Indeed, not all children can contribute to the family's survival, as work opportunities in the street are limited. Yet these placements, above all when they repeatedly concern the same child, are felt by the child as a neglect, and as a biographical macro-break. The probability that the child will leave home becomes high.[10]

After one year, Augusto's grandmother wants the child to return to his 'real mother'. When the child comes back home he is not alone, but finds himself in the

[8] Girls do not react to breaks as boys do. In fact, under equal conditions, girls leave home less quickly that boys. We can then speak of a differential access to the street for girls. This is not applicable to girls who work in the street's informal sector and who are accompanied by an adult – mother, father, sister, brother. One also finds them in groups of children coming from the same neighborhood or linked by parental ties. These children come back home on a daily basis. See: Riccardo Lucchini, op. cit., 1995. We will also see that for the girl the relationship with the mother represents a stake which is as concerned with identity as it is affective. For the boy, the stake is above all affective, even if the dimension of identity is not absent. This is one of the reasons why the girl does not go directly in the street, but 'wants to show' to her mother that she is also able to be a woman. She therefore leaves home for some time in order to form a couple with an older boy or a man. These couples are unstable and it is only after they break up that certain girls will go to the street or return home.

[9] See especially: Latin American Perspectives, Women in Latin America, Issue 85, Vol. 22, No. 2, 1995; and Latin American Perspectives, Women in Latin America 2, Issue 88, Vol. 23, No. 1, 1996.

[10] There is also the phenomenon of children being placed according to the logic of gift and counter-gift. This is a circulation of children. See Fonseca 1985, 1991.

company of other children. So he must fit in with his siblings, and this poses him some problems of adaptation and membership. In fact, with his biological mother, the child finds some half-brothers and half-sisters. He is not the only one, as he may wish secretly. He is in competition with other children. The more the child's expectation is centered on the unique character of his encounter with his mother, the more the 'expulsion' effect of this experience is important. This experience constitutes a new macro-break in the child's biography. This break is more important when the various siblings are treated differently by the mother. For instance, a child speaks of how his biological mother, with whom he has resided only recently, forces him to do the cleaning. He feels this as an unjust punishment and attributes it to the fact that he is not on good terms with the other siblings. He illustrates that his interpretation is well founded by describing his mother's behavior when his elder sister gets married. The child says that he has a very great affection for this sister. When the invitation to the wedding arrives, the mother tears it up without informing her son about it. The child feels discriminated against. The accumulation of episodes of this kind transforms into a macro-break and drives the child to leave home. The child thus gives accounts of episodes which appear to be details, but which in fact are not. For the child, these episodes are important signs for the construction of the image of self and of the feeling of membership. When the child cannot evaluate what he represents for his mother, it becomes easier to leaves home for the street. Leaving becomes a means to test maternal reactions. It is therefore a procedure of identitary verification.[11]

Juan is a ten-year-old child whose departure from home for the street illustrates the importance of the question of identity. He leaves because he feels 'he is in the way' at home. In fact, he has been put in the care of a host family and has not found his place in the siblinghood. He believes that his adoptive parents do not treat him like they treat their own children. To prove this, he says that they did not allow him to enroll in school as he had wished. He uses the term 'abandonment' to describe his placement in this situation.

Such denominations as 'mama from here' (*mamà de aqui*), 'mama from there' (*mamà de allà*), 'mama who raised me' (*mamà que me criò*) are regularly used by the children. Yet these expressions involve conflicting references. The maternal figure is multiple, and the child is unable to give it consistency in terms of parental responsibilities. The conflict between this multiplicity of maternal figures and the child's need for a unique maternal reference intervenes in the dynamics of leaving home in a significant way. This conflict manifests itself especially when the child lives with one of these 'mothers' who is not the biological mother. And this even if the 'current mother' is not object of major grievances expressed by the child. However, in order for this conflict to drive the child into the street, there must be a

[11]All this occurs without any explicit plan and most of the time remains unconscious. The part of identitary provocation in the dynamics of a child leaving home must not be underestimated. We have observed that this component of leaving home is weakly influenced by the economic situation of the family. It concerns families living in total destitution as well as families whose income allow the purchase of durable commodity goods: TVs, video players, cookers, or washing machines, for instance.

catalyst event and some favorable opportunities. Two typical situations are observed: on the one hand, the chain of encounters and micro-break which lead to distanciation, and on the other hand the voluntary and planned leaving home. The first situation is by far the most frequent, while the second is more theoretical than real.

But one of the crucial elements in the dynamics of leaving home remains the child's perception of the place they have in the siblinghood. Successive placements in the care of different members of the parenthood system disturb this perception. The differential treatment of the siblings by the mother or the father produce an 'expelling' effect, because it is perceived by the child as arbitrary. The child will evoke, for instance, their mother's reaction to the violent acts the father or stepfather subjects them to. The case of Alda, twenty-one years old, is such an example. Her stepfather tried to rape her, and she told her mother everything in the hope that she would stand up for her.[12] The mother must choose between her daughter and her companion. In the dynamics of leaving home the mother's choice is more important than the violent act itself. In the case of Alda, her mother's choice is in favor of her companion. Not only does she not stand up for her daughter, but she even accuses Alda of being responsible for the act she is denouncing. She tells Alda, "I have no daughter". The child then answers her, "I have nothing more to do in *your* house". Alda hopes that her mother will give her the chance to feel like her daughter. In all her accounts, she insistently expresses this need for recognition. Alda now feels she has become a stranger to her mother. Her account expresses this feeling: she says that her mother does not allow her to enroll at school, because only allows this of 'her own children', that is, Alda's half-brothers and half-sisters.

The expelling effect of these breaks is important. Everything happens very quickly. This account shows the speed at which the actor perceives events happening: "I took my small suitcase with my clothes, the few clothes I had, and I left". This happened when the child was nine years old.[13] Alda also says that her mother used to place her with her grandmother, because neither her mother nor her companion loved her. Those put in this kind of care felt themselves to be abandoned. On the other hand, the reference to the father is very strong: "I have been his only daughter".[14] Alda says: "my mother abandoned me for a long time (between the age of seven and nine) [...] she left me in the hands of my grandmother". We have here a first configuration of factors which ends in Alda's departure from home: (1) placement in care is experienced as abandonment, (2) the differential treatment of siblings, (3) conflict with the other siblings, (4) the stepfather's rape attempt, (5) her mother's negative reaction, (6) her mother's prostitution. Among the siblings, Alda is the only child of a former companion of the mother. This reinforces the child's feeling of isolation and of helplessness towards the events of which she is the victim.

---

[12] Alda also speaks of another rape attempt by one of her uncles whose care she was in. Rape or attempt of rape is the violence most often mentioned by the girls who talk about their leaving home.

[13] Alda's account has been confirmed by one of her aunts and by her grandmother.

[14] The Spanish expression is heavier. Alda says: "*Yo fui la unica de el*".

One of the major difficulties in the analysis of the dynamics of leaving home that they are not linear. The movements between the family home and the street are constant and numerous, and the total break between child and family remains exceptional. In most of the cases, leaving home is a means and not a goal. The case of Fabrice illustrates this. This sixteen-year-old child says that he left home because his father treats him like a little child. He demands a new identity and running away is the means that allows him to express this need. Here, the act of leaving home for the street is first of all an act of identitary protest more than an identitary quest. In the street, the child does not search for the male role models who are absent in the female-dominated single-parent family. Fabrice wants to have his new competencies, like responsibility and independence, recognized. But leaving home is not only linked to an identity claim of which the child would know all the stakes. On the contrary, Fabrice presents three contradictory claims, and these claims preside over the repeated acts of leaving home. First, the child claims more liberty. This liberty is of practical nature, because it concerns places as well as things intended for use and consumption. Second, he claims for an autonomy concerning his identity system, and more precisely the image of self. In the terminology of Erving Goffman, the child presents a new face.[15] The third claim concerns the demand for affection. Fabrice had health problems as a young child and he regularly had to give up what was allowed to children of his age. This dependency explains in part why he so vehemently claims for more autonomy and at the same time more affection. This demand for affection opposes to the two first requests and explains why Fabrice will never feel at ease in the street. This conflict is essential to understand the repetitive character of Fabrice's acts of leaving home.

Augusto is fifteen years old. He says that he left home knowing that his mother would come to look for him on the street. This information is true: his mother tells us that she regularly looks for her son when he leaves home. We have observed that this is the case for many other children. Here, leaving home for the street is closely linked to the affective dimension of the identity system. It is above all the identity as a son and not gender identity that is part of the dynamics of leaving home. The father is present and, after his departure, he is replaced by a stepfather who is appreciated by the child. However, the child also tells us that he had to go to school with broken shoes and that his mother had to work in order to buy him another pair. This is not only a detail, as the child talks about it despite many years having passed since. In fact, he was ashamed, and preferred not to go to school. The child then more and more frequented the suburban streets and more and more often he strayed from his neighborhood. This is one of the first steps towards the locations frequented by CSS: city centres, railway stations, metro and bus stations, parks, important crossroads, markets, vacant lots near areas highly frequented by adults. The episode of the broken shoes is also a way for the child to criticize the father he takes to be responsible for the prolonged absence of his mother.

[15] The face is the image the person has of themselves and that they wants to be recognised by others. With the child, leaving home for the street is an act of protest against the parental non-recognition of this ideal image they has of themselves.

This episode and the child's subsequent dropping out of school do not yet represent a major break in the child's biography. However, they coincide with an event that is constitutes a macroscopic break which deprives the child from his social competence. He is no longer an expert, because the event places him in a situation that he no longer masters (see Strauss 1992 and Denzin 1990). This event occurred when the child's father placed him with his paternal grandmother. The child perceives being put in this care as a sudden and unexpected event. In fact, he comments: "my father talked with my mother and suddenly said: pack your bag, we're off!". The child was not prepared to face this change and no longer masters the relationship with his parents. To put him in the care of his grandmother is to insert him in a network of multiple dependencies toward different members of the system of parenthood. The child experiences this as a rejection from his mother, attributing the responsibility for this rejection to his father. One can thus better understand the meaning the child gives to the episode of the broken shoes, and the related feeling of shame. Having been put in the care of his grandmother gives this minor episode an significance that, taken on its own, it could not have. This all the more because his grandmother lives with one of her sons, whose wife enrolled him in a school. The child is thus well treated, and adults take care of him. But, when speaking of put in this care, Augusto does not talk about this woman, but only about his grandmother. While at his grandmother's home, Augusto began to run away. At the time he was twelve years old.

Remo is fourteen years old. He explains that when he was five years old his parents put him in the care of a woman, who he stayed with and believed to be his mother. It was when she told him that he was actually a 'given child' (*regalado*) that he left her for the street. Even if other factors intervene in Remo's departure from home, it is interesting to note that he focuses his attention on what he considers to be an abandonment. When the child learns that the woman he believed to be his mother is in fact not, his identity changes. The maternal reference is no longer the same and his place in the siblinghood is modified. Doubt becomes pervasive.

Leaving home for the street is also connected to an overload of domestic work and to family responsibilities that the child does not feel able to take on. For certain boys, this overloading takes on an identitary dimension, a dimension which generally does not concern girls. The family tasks are understood to be their lot, and do not bring their identity into question. These tasks keep the girls from going onto the street and keep them under the control of their mothers and of their neighborhoods. This is not the case for boys who from a young age frequent the neighborhood streets and integrate into groups of children. This participation goes hand in hand with a progressive and rapid emancipation from maternal control.[16] This control is

[16] One must not forget that we talk of single parent families, or families in which the father is present only during the night hours because his job keeps him away from home during the day. The mothers of CSS often express their helplessness in the process that takes their boy away from home. They say that the attraction of the street and of gangs is stronger than any of their attempts to forbid this behavior. Moreover, these mothers often work all day long and cannot take all of their children to their workplaces.

felt by the boy as contradicting the expectations of his friends on the street (of the suburbs and of the centre). His reputation as a boy is at stake.

The case of David is exemplary. His mother works all day long and charges him with important family responsibilities: he has to do the cleaning and to look after his two little sisters. In David's account, his overloading in terms of family responsibilities is doubled by what can be referred to as a statutory and identitary overloading. This overloading constitutes a macro-break, leading David to leave home for the street. His relationship with his mother – his father left when he was small – are excellent. He is eight years old when he leaves home for the first time. He first stays on the street for four to five days, leaving when his mother comes to pick him up. David's mother's behavior pleases him, as it marks the affection she has for him.[17] This demonstrates that the affective component is an important dimension in David's episodes of running away. However, it is subordinated to dynamics of identity. It is these dynamics that transform the running away into a leaving home.

The identitary overloading affecting David is expressed in the following statement: "going to school and being the housewife". The child cannot reconcile these two activities. There is a conflict between the role of friend and the role of son. This conflict is conditioned by his status as a boy: David must defend this identity with his friends. As he lacks time, he cannot participate in his friends' activities, and he cannot justify his absence by invoking the domestic work he has to do. This would attract sarcastic remarks, and put his identity as a boy into doubt. In order to counter her son's running away, David's mother brings in new recreational activities – visiting the cinema, going for walks – for him. But this has no effect: David is leaving home for ever longer periods and going and further and further away. The conflict of roles, the problem of identity, and the need for fun and games take priority over the pleasure of being found by his mother when she looks for him in the street. He is also hiding now.

When doubts about the identity of his biological parents appeared, David experienced a macro-break in his life. This doubt is appropriate, because the instability of the parental couple favors mix siblings. When one child suffers discrimination in comparison to other siblings, or has the impression of doing so, they feel the need to understand. They often search for an explanation by questioning their biological filiation, and the many times the child is put in the care of others from a young age encourage this doubt. When the parental couple breaks up, children feel their own responsibility, and feel guilty. The case of Morro illustrates this process. The father abandons his mother for another woman. Following this, Morro's mother has to work all day long in order to make ends meet, and the maternal grandmother cares for the children. Morro experiences this as a double abandonment, because, as he says, he has simultaneously lost his mother too. Regarding his father, Morro says he hopes that he has not left them because of Morro himself, but because of his mother. He does not want to be responsible for this abandonment, but he is not certain about it.

[17] Many CSS describe this maternal behavior. Even if they hide in order not to have to go back home, they want to stress their mother's affection for them. To the child, this behavior from their mother is valorizing. With certain children, it brings with a feeling of guilt that they express by justifying their strategy of evasion.

Leaving home for the street is a process that varies in timespan. The idea of a continuum with one pole marking brutal and immediate expulsion and the other a nurtured and chosen departure from home allows us to express this diversity. The progressive introduction into the street world by other children, while temporarily running away from home, first sporadically and then more regularly, is the most frequent form (Lucchini 1993, 1996). The rise in the frequency of episodes of running away, of the length of stays on the street, and the distance from parental home progressively leads the child to leave 'definitively'. This departure from home is the result of a process of learning the street, during which the child acquires knowledge and competencies that are necessary to be able to live on the street. In fact, with similar family and economic conditions – with regards to violence, care situations, abandonment, poverty, and so on – only a small minority of children definitively leave the familial home for the street, as we have seen. So, a macro biographical break is itself not enough to explain why a child leaves home for the street 'definitively'.[18]

Many children leave their home for places other than the city centre. Some integrate into delinquent gangs, others find refuge in institutions, while some others yet go to relatives or acquaintances – this is especially the case for girls. It is not rare that a girl will leave her family home in order to live with a companion. There is also the informal economy that can allow a child to become autonomous. In this case, they are often part of a group of children with whom they share the accommodation expense. Children frequently circulate between these different locations. Yet this circulation is a way to avoid going onto the street, a kind of alternative to the street. We have seen how the great majority of children living in similar family conditions do not leave home, or they alternate between a set of locations which do not involve the street as a living environment.

Different sets of factors allow us to understand why the child leaves home for the street. These factors variously macro-, meso- and microscopic in character (Lucchini 1993), and can be grouped into six categories: (1) economic, (2) social, (3) familial, (4) identitary, (5) psychological, and (6) spatial. The effects of these factors are in large part determined by the meaning the actors – children, parents, educators, politicians – give to the events in which they are involved.

To conclude this chapter, we would like to make some supplementary remarks about the role of familial and spatial factors in the child's act of leaving home. Among the first ones we find are:

(a) Important care-giving responsibilities: for instance, caring for the youngest siblings when the mother is absent – at work, for example. The impact of this fac-

[18] In this respect, the case of Axel is interesting. He is eighteen years old and has been mistreated by his mother since he was small. The woman in whose care he is entrusted for a significant even forces him to eat his own excrement. Despite of this, Axel does not stay in the street, and comes back home quite quickly. He is completely subjected to a sadistic mother who has even risked killing him by practicing witchcraft on him. This youth does not stay in the street, because his subjection to his mother is too strong. Besides, he does not have the minimal competences – instrumental, symbolic, social, motivational – to stay on the street. The case of Axel is a limit case, because the mistreatments that he has suffered for so long have put him in a situation of complete dependency. It is therefore no longer possible to speak of a biographical break.

tor notably depends on the age and the sex of the child, but also on the sharing of tasks with others, such as neighbors, relatives, or educators. Girls are more involved in these care-giving tasks, but it is boys who are incline to leave home when they are confronted with an overloading of such responsibility. The familial responsibilities become an overloading when they imply a statutory and identitary conflict. This is also the case when these responsibilities separate the child from his friends, and from their requests of him in terms of his emancipation from maternal control.

(b) Responsibilities regarding the child's contribution to the family budget. These responsibilities must be separated from the first set, because they concern economic activities. One speaks of an overloading here when the child is not capable of responding to parental expectations regarding income, and is punished when they fail to bring home the amount that was expected. By their work, the child has money and opportunities to spend it, and they will stay in the street more readily if they consider that the money they have earned belongs to them.

(c) The maternal reaction to violence exerted on the child by the father or the stepfather. The effect of male violence on the child with regards to leaving the home is not direct as such, but is mediated by the maternal reaction to the behavior of her husband or companion. The child, in large part, experiences this violence according to what the mother does or says when they are attacked by the father or stepfather. This means that the expulsion effect of the mother's behavior is as important as the one contained in the violent act itself. Three possible cases illustrate the importance of the mother's reaction. In the first case, the mother makes the child feel guilty by making them feel responsible for the violence they have suffered. This notably concerns girls who are victims of sexual abuse. The mother fears losing her companion and being left alone if she defends her daughter. The status of a single woman is devalued where the woman is culturally subject to the man. Boys are just as sensitive regarding their mother's behavior, and will point out her lack of reaction toward the stepfather's violence. In the second case, the mother trivializes or relativizes the acts of violence by systematically excusing her companion. In the last case, the mother is passive and does not express herself: in other words, she resigns herself to the inevitability of the violent behavior.

These three attitudes of culpability, trivialization, and resignation, as well as the self-guilt of the actors involved, have an important effect of expulsion. On the other hand, when the mother defends the child, the expulsion effect of the violent act is strongly reduced, even if the mother's reaction is not sufficient to change the behavior of the violent person. In some cases a coalition is set up between the mother and the children, marginalizing the man within the family.[19]

---

[19] Survival is characterized by, among other things, a devaluation of the statuses of father and of husband, and of the identities attaches to them. Male violence within the family is linked to a conflict of identity, and to the stress resulting from it. The woman takes on most of the family's economic and educational responsibilities. This *de facto* independence is not recognized in a society

(d) The composite siblinghood. This siblinghood is one that unites under the same roof children who are of different fathers or mothers. It is not necessarily any more conflictual than those composed of children who have the same biological parents: it becomes conflictual when one or both parents discriminate against the children that are not their biological children. This is most often the case with the stepfather. It often happens that the violence of the stepfather is accompanied by the added violence of a half-brother or half-sister. The mother is then confronted with a conflict which has no simple resolution. She finds, on the one hand, her child demanding her help and, on the other, her fear of losing her present companion. In such a situation, the child easily becomes an issue for the couple. With this issue comes a strong expulsive charge.[20] The child is searching for an explanation for discrimination they have experienced, an explanation that would allow them to preserve a positive image of the self. So Alda, says of her biological father: "I have been his only daughter (*yo fui la unica de el*)". She pretends to look like him. This is the reason why she thinks that the other members of the family do not like her.

(e) Diffuse responsibilities in the system of parenthood. The child is placed in the care of others several times and their identity references become blurred. This is true only when being placed in care is experienced by the child as an abandonment.

Regarding spatial factors, two appear immediately significant. First, there is housing conditions. The dimensions of the home are too small to allow family members any privacy. This lack of privacy is the rule, and it provokes animosity and conflict. Construction materials are often weak and generally do not guarantee sound isolation. Moreover, these homes offer little safety against external aggressions, especially against theft. This results in a great insecurity results, added to by the presence of multiple gangs of teenagers, who at night control the streets of the neighborhood. The streets of the slums naturally become the place that allow children, especially boys, to escape the familial lack of privacy. Secondly, we have the neighborhood as a constructed space. In most cases it has no infrastructure to accommodate teenagers or community life. It is a matter for local communities themselves, often assisted by NGO's, to work towards this aim, but most of the neighborhoods have nothing or are under-equipped.[21]

in which the man is still perceived as the guarantor of family honor. A growing responsibilization of the woman and a growing marginalization of the man in familial concerns constitute conditions favoring male violence. The conflict between the traditional image of man and his real situation in survival is inevitable. This shakes the man's self-esteem and entails violence. This is related to the man's statutory aspirations and the absence of a means to concretize them. Furthermore, the woman takes herself to be responsible for this situation and is subject to male violence. There are many women who work seven days a week on the markets, and for whom the workplace and the relationships they can constitute there are the most important positive references they have.

[20] One must recall that only a minority of children who leave their family are then found among CSS.

[21] The housing conditions of the slums are not homogeneous. The circumstances of their beginnings, their growth, and the struggle of their inhabitants to obtain the legalization of their occupa-

Children sometimes compare their neighborhood to a desert, as there is nothing that attracts the eye and it is incapable of stimulating the senses. The attraction of the city centre is therefore even greater.

## 4.3 The Child's Leaving Home in the Words of the Mother[22]

The mother of seventeen-year-old Roberto and fifteen-year-old Axel says that it is her own fault that her children have left home for the street. Her account is representative of the complexity of familial relationships that is common among children who go out on the street. From their earliest childhood, Roberto and Axel have experienced difficult life conditions. There was first their mother's divorce, provoked by her mother-in-law's accusation of adultery.[23] Their mother tells us that at that she then went to live with her own parents, who mistreated her sons. She cannot care for them, because she has to work all day. She leaves her parents and gives birth to a girl who is the result of a short-term relationship. Then, she meets her present companion, who already has four children from two previous relationships. Over time he becomes violent towards the three children of his new partner, and demands that the boys to work. The mother also specifies that her daughter had to act as servant for the sons of her partner. In her account, Roberto and Axel are presented as victims. They left home for the street as a consequence of these events and their mother's inability to find solutions to the family's conflicts. In addition, we learn that Roberto leaves home in order to not have to give his stepfather the money he has earned by working. This information is important, because it reveals the existence of factors that, by adding to the child's biography, provoke his leaving home for the street. Their effect is thus mediated by the breaks contained in this biography. One thus can understand why, starting from a same event, some children leave home for the street while others stay at home or choose to go to an institution, a friend's home, a relative's, an acquaintance's, or an assistance centre.

---

tion of the land have led to quite diverse urban forms. Nor is the socio-economic status of the slum population homogeneous. There are important differences among the inhabitants, and this is especially true for the oldest neighborhoods.

[22] We have analysed elsewhere the maternal discourse about their children leaving home for the street (Riccardo Lucchini, op. cit., 1996, pp. 57–62). Four discourses have emerged from this analysis. In the first, leaving home is imposed by familial and material circumstances; the second discourse invokes the child's character; the third stresses the behavior of certain members of the family; the fourth points out the role the child plays in the organization of the family as a financial support. Most of the mothers of the children we have studied in Brazil, Uruguay and Mexico have experience an early placement in care, abandonment, the death of one of their parents, or parental violence. The information collected in other contexts (Honduras, Nicaragua, Peru, and Argentina) confirm this.

[23] It seems that this kind of accusation is not rare, as we have noticed it in several accounts made by mothers of CSS.

The instability of the couples and the practice of children being placed in care within the network of the parents (or outside of it) are reflected not only in the speech of the children, but also in that of the adults. The adoptive mother of sixteen-year-old Amigo tells us that when he is at home, he prays for "his mother, for his mother who gave him life, for his mother who has raised him ('*crio*'), for his brothers he doesn't know, for the whole family".[24] This double reference to the two mothers presents a dilemma for the adoptive mother. She does not know where her place is in the child's references, and cannot estimate her part of the responsibility in his episodes of running away. The identitary uncertainty linked to her role as an adoptive mother interacts with the identitary questioning of the child, who is not sure about his own place in relation to his two mothers. If the child finds no answer to this need for belonging, the probability that he will leave home for the street rises. The existence of these different mothers does not necessarily constitute a problem for the child. However, it becomes a problem when none of these women respond to the child's emotional needs, or when this becomes an issue for the women. The search for the 'real mother' also becomes a question of identitary survival. In these cases, the repeated episodes of running away and leaving for the street may be linked to this search.

The familial situation of women belonging to the most deprived social stratas is characterized by an overloading in terms of multiple responsibilities: health, education, nutrition, accommodation, affection, clothes, and so on. The mother often takes on these responsibilities with a man who is present only sporadically, and in a passive and repressive way. Moreover, she is caught between the contradictory expectations of her family members: those of the partner or husband, father, or stepfather on the one hand, and those of the children of several partners on the other. This situation is often complicated by the accusation or suspicion of adultery raised by a member of the family. We have seen this. The paternal grandmother of Roberto and Axel tells them that her own son is not their real father. According to their mother, this is an attempt to influence her sons and to turn them away from her. Conflicts of this nature are very destabilizing for the child, as they question their identity and the image of the parental couple. The feeling of security that the child develops in their relationships with their parents is then strongly affected by these conflicts. This lack of security conditions also the quality of social relationships that the child will have with others. In fact, "the attachment bond with the parent is incorporated in an internal working model that is applied to any subsequent closer relationship" (Schneider and Younger 1996, p. 98).

[24] Amigo was ten years old when he seriously ran away from home for the first time, but since he was four years old he had often left home for the streets of the neighborhood. He is a child who alternates between periods in institutions and periods at home. The street is an intermediary space between these two. While his school results are fairly good, he often drops out. The child's biological mother put him in the care with a woman who had no parental ties with him when he was born. The father is unknown. His adoptive mother left her partner and the man who had replaced him died in a road accident when Amigo was thirteen years old. He has a brother who is four years old, from his adoptive mother and his second stepfather. The adoptive mother is very affectionate with the child, but she is likely to be depressed.

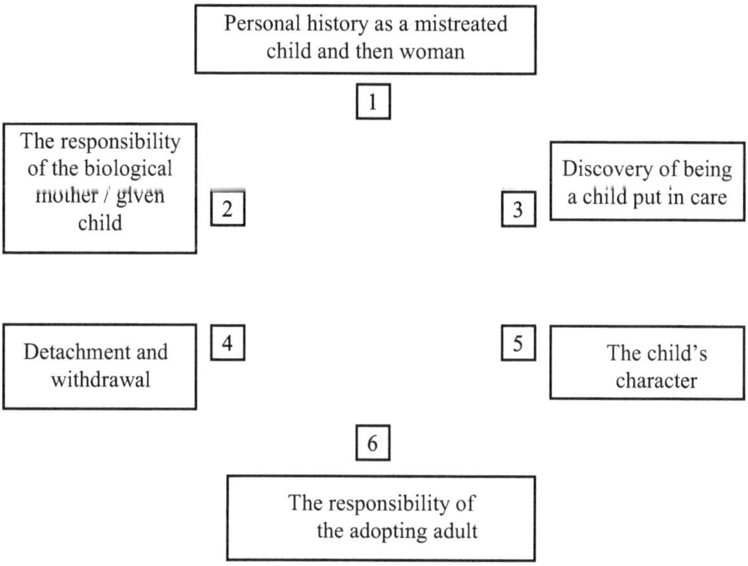


**Fig. 4.1** The maternal themes of the child leaving home

There are several themes which repeatedly arise mothers and stepmothers talk about episodes of children running away (see Fig. 4.1).

These episodes include:

1. First, their own history of abuse and a lack of affection in childhood. This history often concerns several generations, as in the case of the mother of fourteen-year-old Mario. Here four generations are concerned. The great-grandmother, the maternal grandmother, and the mother have been abandoned by their respective husbands, while Mario's seventeen-year-old sister has a two-year-old daughter, but does not live with the child's father. The mother of Alda tells us that her mother beat her when she was informed that she was pregnant. She says, "I believe it is because of this that she (Alda) is bad".[25] These histories evoke a fatalist perspective on a story that repeats itself.
2. Amigo's stepmother says that the biological mother gave her the child ('*regalaron*') when they were neighbors. This is the second theme.[26] The theme of the gift involves the abandonment of the child by their biological mother as well as an explanation for the child's episodes of running away.
3. The third theme concerns the discovery by the child of their status of having been adopted, given away, placed in care, or abandoned. The adoptive mother says

[25] "*Yo creo que tambien por eso salio mala*".

[26] Placement in care and circulation of children is a common practice which should not be assimilated to abandonment. Some of these practices are close to the logic of gift and counter-gift (*don et contre-don*). Some others are free and are part of a logic of mutual aid. Care placements may be definitive, temporary or unspecified in time. For a detailed analysis (see Fonseca 1985, 1991).

that this discovery coincides with the child's leaving home. They can becomes aggressive towards their adoptive mother, and accuse her of preventing them from finding their real mother again.

4. The ordeals of life wear down the affective resources and motivations of the adult who is responsible for the child. Alda's grandmother is an example of this. When she is informed that her granddaughter has lost the child she gave birth to on the street, she says, "May God be on her side [...] because I can no longer give her courage. I have no more strength to encourage her. I cannot go on anymore".[27] She has given everything and has nothing left. Moreover, when she meets Alda after some long months apart, she does not show any particular affection. One finds here again the theme of detachment.
5. A fifth theme is that of the difficult character of the runaway child. This has always been the case and the mother cannot change it.
6. The sixth theme is that of the responsibility of the person who the runaway child has been put in the care of. The child has become what they are because they did not get to stay with their biological mother.

## 4.4 The Alternation Between Street and Home

When they just started to running away, some children return home when staying in the street becomes uncomfortable and dangerous: as a result of the cold, police, conflicts with other street users, and other factors. The case of Rafael is also a common one. His mother has a fixed vending post in a metro station, but the family resides in the suburbs of the city. According to Rafael, it is too far away to go back home daily. On the other hand, he regularly visits his mother at her workplace. Arguments regarding the distance between the familial home and the streets on which the child lives are often invoked to justify non-return.

The child who returns to the street after he has been back home for some time often compares the boredom he has suffered and how he longed for the street by referring to the diversified activities and the friendly relationships of the street. Membership of a group and identification with a place – markets, squares, parks, crossroads, vacant lots, metro stations, big stores, and so on – are opposed to the unattractive character of life at home. The children who have had a regular job for some time compare the constraints of this activity with the liberty they experience on the street.[28] The case of fifteen-year-old Augusto illustrates this aspect. He is the

[27] "*Dios lo acompañe [...] porque yo ya no puedo estar haciendo coraje. Yo ya estoi acabada para coraje. Yo no soporto*".

[28] Regarding this, one must recall that CSS generally have more money than if they had regular jobs. They can also use it as they please. However, it is not really the average income the child has that pleases them, but rather the possibility of occasionally obtaining significant amounts of money, such as through thefts. In order to understand the relationship CSS have to money, one should not simply consider the amounts they have at their disposal. One must also know through

companion of Carine, a girl of twenty-one who has a leading role in this group of children they belong to. By coming back to the street, Augusto enjoys gratification he does not find at home: (1) a romantic relationship, (2) a delegation of power over the other children, (3) diversified social and environmental stimulation, (4) autonomy from his family. But the case of Augusto illustrates the situation of the child who is caught between two opposed and irreconcilable references: the street towards which he is attracted and the family, and in particular the mother, that he does not want to see suffer. The tension between these two poles is, strong and the child suffers from a feeling of intense guilt. This is the reason why he regularly feels the need to justify his decision to not stay at home.

The case of Augusto informs us that one of the mechanisms that is at the foundation of the alternation between home and the street is precisely the existence of opposed references, and the identitary and affective tension that this provokes. The alternation is not only the result of this conflict, but also an attempt made by the child in to diminish its effects. CSS are constantly moving from one place to another in the urban space, and they circulate between several fields: family, the street, institutions, aid programmes, work among them.[29] This is even if each child has a privileged place and sense of socio-spatial belonging. Yet temporary return to the home is part of this movement. The length of this return is variable: it can span from several hours to several weeks. This depends on the reasons that have driven the child to go back home, and on the way he is welcomed at home. When the child goes back home in order to benefit from a service – to take some clothes, wash their clothes, wash themselves, or simply have a rest – they only stay for the time necessary to satisfy this momentary need.

This type of return is very frequent and does not imply that the child is following a project of renouncing the street as a way of life. However, these visits are not just simple routines, as they allow the child to maintain contact with their family and, in particular, with their mother or another reference adult: grandmother, grandfather, aunt, or elder sister, for example. In fact, contrary to appearances and to the official discourse of assistance programmes, governments, and the media, most of the children have among their relatives or other adult acquaintances some people who they refer to and who they may contact. In addition, the children will often go to one another's homes. This is a way to protect against the feared severity of parental reactions.

The great majority of mothers accept these visits, because it is a way for them to keep in touch with their children. While they accept this presence, knowing it will only be temporary, they will lay down conditions that the child has to respect if they want to come back home definitively. As one mother told us regarding her fifteen-year-old son, home is not a hotel, and the child must respect certain rules in order to have the right to stay. These rules concern obligations like looking for a job, going back to school, giving up street life and the associations it entails, the respect of

---

what means they have obtained this money, and what they intend to do with it. In fact, the modes of acquisition are linked to the child's competencies, and thus to their reputation in the eyes of their peers.

[29] See Riccardo Lucchini, op. cit., 1996.

domestic discipline, and drug abstinence (namely from inhalants). Giving up drugs and the association with friends on the street are the two requests most regularly mentioned. These conditions are demanding, and explain why children will return to the street – or, less often, to institutions managed by assistance programmes – many times.

The acceptance of the mother is conditioned by the nature of this return to home. When this return is practical and/or only out of politeness, the mother will not lay down conditions for her child, but she will bring to their attention on the conditions they should meet in order to be accepted again at home.[30] The case of fourteen-year-old Mario illustrates a mode of 'visit-return' that is frequent with CSS. He goes to the home of an aunt, where he stays for one week. He enjoys speaking about this visit, because he had a lot of fun with his cousin. They spent a whole day roller-skating in the streets of the neighborhood and annoying the passers-by. Once back home again, he feels bored because, as he says, there is nothing to do. His mother – who works as a secretary in the public administration – lives with Mario's older sister and the daughter of this sister latter. At weekends, Mario's younger sister comes to join the family. Mario's parents split up before the birth of this child. The house is small, but two stories high and recently built. Mario's mother is the owner. The house is well furnished, with domestic appliances (microwave oven, washing machine, cooker), a television, a video player, a games console, and so on. The house has five rooms. The houses of the neighborhood are all the same, and the population are largely state and private employees belonging to the lower-middle classes. It is a sleepy community, and the streets are empty. There is no sign here of the stereotypical image of the highly populated slum devastated by destitution and bad weather. From a material point of view, the child is lacking nothing. But Mario feels no attraction to the neighborhood, because nothing happens in it. One better understands why he went to his aunt's and not to his mother's, who works elsewhere all day. He then returns to the street he had left just one week before. To explain his return in the street, Mario invokes boredom, nostalgia for the street as a lifestyle, and the consumption of inhalants.

When returning home goes beyond the simple visit and reflects a project of staying at home, the child adopts another behavior. Most children who are in this situation give signs of nervousness, and the idea of changing their lifestyle so radically makes them anxious. Indeed, it involves a commitment towards the family and a break with the street world. For the child who has spent several months or years on the street, it is difficult to undertake such a change because they fear to find themselves alone in front of their mother or their parents. These children will therefore look for the help of an adult – educators, researchers, or friends among them – who can play the role of a mediator between them and their family. When this is impossible, these children will adopt other strategies. One of the most frequent is to first go

[30] It is possible to differentiate between two types of attitude in the mother when their child 'visit-returns'. The first one contains no moral blackmail. In this case, the mother limits herself to explaining the child how anxious she is about their life on the street. She raises their attention to their responsibilities rather than on their guilt. The second type concerns the mother who makes her child feel guilty by taking them to be responsible for the moral suffering imposed on her.

to another family member – perhaps an older sister, aunt, or grandmother – in order to have this person play the role of mediator between the child and their parents.

Sixteen-year-old Fabrice wishes to go back home, and asks us to accompany him. At the same time he asks to have three days before returning home to wash his clothes and to collect some money. Another child asks him for some time to earn the money that will allow him to buy the return ticket. These requests are significant and do not represent isolated cases. Children who go back home with the intention of staying there are very sensitive to the image their parents or their mother has of them. But this attitude – quite widespread among the children – is also a strategy that allows the child to delay a decision they fear making. In fact, the request for a definitive return is often induced by the speech of the adult (educator, researcher or any other reference adult), by a traumatizing experience (the illness of a family member, an accident in the street, a threat to physical integrity), by the example of a friend, or by the feeling that life on the street is ultimately without a real outcome. It is frequent that the child expresses their intention of returning home without yet concretizing it.

Fabrice's situation is uncomfortable. He finds himself between two worlds that he rejects: the street and the family. He looks for an alternative, because his self-conception has become irreconcilable with both the street world and with the family. He has now a girlfriend in the neighborhood where his parents live, and he wants to become independent. He reacts by intensively consuming inhalants. Then, he recovers: he gives up inhalant use and starts to take care of his clothes and his physical appearance. He alternates between depression and hope. Fabrice expresses the doubt that affects the children for whom the street has lost its attractiveness. He goes to Acapulco – the famous Mexican tourism location – to look for distractions. It is not rare for children to leave their adopted street for some time to live in another place. Fabrice finds himself alone in Acapulco. He works as gardener for a family, but he feels isolated. His friends from Tasqueña are not around and he feels bad: "I think it is at this time that I felt all the distance separating me from my parents. As I was alone and had nothing to do, I began thinking about what had happened to me". Fabrice says that the street dazes those who live on it. He adds that when he is with his friends he does not have such doubts. It is the presence of friends that makes the street bearable. Yet the dazedness he refers to signals an affective and identitary survival strategy for some children, particularly children for whom the street is no longer the pivotal field capable of giving meaning to their existence, present or future, and is no more able to monopolize their energy and competencies. These children now feel in danger on the street, and this frightens them. At this point, motivation to leave the street reaches its peak.

The alternation between street and home is a phenomenon that concerns most CSS. The frequency of the movement varies according to the situation in which the children finds themselves. It is particularly important in two cases. The first is that of the child who comes back home for practical reasons, who has no major problems on the street and for whom returning home is part of a routine that simplifies their survival conditions. These are generally children who do not fear significant parental sanctions. The street remains a positive reference and the child does not state major conflicts with their parents. Here, the return is similar to a visit, with no intention of returning home definitively.

The second case is that of the child at the end of their career on the street, for whom the street has become a dead end and who is now looking for an alternative. The returns of these children are not simple practical visits, because they include a hope to be able to stay at home. The child has a project, even if it remains unformulated – by means such as finding a job or returning to school. This project also includes the restoration of confidence in the relationship with their mother or their parents. This element is central in the explanation that the child gives about their new departure. It is also true that as time passes the parental relationship becomes more demanding. It poses some conditions the child must meet in order to be accepted at home. Here, there is a contract between the two sets of actors that is not found in the case of the 'visit-return'. Any new departure from the home will then be felt as failure by the child and parents alike. The child fears the project of a definitive return, because it holds an important risk of failure and requires a promise to completely renounce the street world. Yet this world is never totally rejected, as there are always some activities and contacts that are the child will continue to value. This explains why the child fears less the parental sanctions than they do the failure of their project of definitively return to home. This is the reason why the child often looks for solutions allowing them to leave the street while staying there at the same time. To do this, they can work for a time for a merchant, in a small office, or perhaps on a construction site. They thus delay the test and do not definitively break the ties they has with the street world.[31]

## 4.5 A Complex Process

We have shown that leaving home for the street is a process, the length of which varies according to different parameters. We may group theses parameters in the following way:

1. Material conditions: family and community resources
2. Identitary conditions: image of the self, possibilities of identity negotiation, etc.

[31] There are moments in the life of a group of CSS characterized by the beginning of a new cycle of contacts with the family. Such a cycle is characterized by the temporary return home of several children belonging to the same network. Generally, the cycle begins when a child who has a certain prestige among his peers takes the initiative of going back home, or when a group of children in the same network leave the street together. A number of factors can lead to such returns: (a) the presence of a charismatic mediator between the children and their families; (b) the existence of an institutional initiative from an assistance programme; (c) a crisis of the leadership in the group; (d) an important change in the survival ecology, such as police repression or a change of the space the children occupy; (e) the effect of imitation.

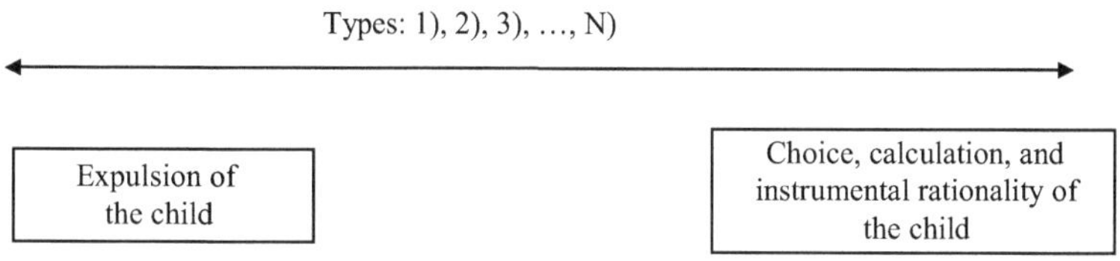


**Fig. 4.2** Types of leaving home

3. Affective conditions, quality of social relationships
4. The child's personal resources (symbolic, social, cognitive, and physical)
5. Family structure and organization
6. Mediation of family violence and solution to conflicts
7. Presence or absence of accessible extra-familial fields (the system of parenthood, institutions, the informal economy, pairings, the street, etc.)
8. Gender: differential accessibility of the street for the girl
9. Urban structure: location of suburbs, layout of city center streets, means of transportation, etc.
10. Welfare policy: assistance programmes, NGO's
11. Repression from the police and judicial system

These parameters interact with each other and the balance between them may vary according to the children. It is therefore necessary to speak of plural modes of leaving home, and not of a single way of leaving home. In this respect, it is possible to use the idea of a continuum (see Fig. 4.2).

The types of leaving home are comprised between two poles. It is of course clear that these two poles are never found as such in reality. The position of a particular type of leaving home on the continuum depends on the specific combination of the above-mentioned parameters. At the currents stage in our research, it is possible to group two sets of parameters by order of importance. The first set of parameters are directly affecting CSS on the microsocial level (see Fig. 4.3).

The second set of parameters (see Fig. 4.4) are on the macrosocial level and they are indirectly affecting CSS, by the mediation of the first set of parameters (see Fig. 4.3).

Indeed, we have observed the importance of logics of identity – including the claim for autonomy – to explain the process of leaving home for the street. The degree of accessibility of the street and the personal competencies of the child are the factors that most condition the impact of identitary logic on this process. Nevertheless, all of the identified parameters are important, but the importance of each one is relative and differs according to the individual child who leaves home for the street. Besides, the combination of parameters influences their respective impact on the process of leaving home. It is thus necessary to study the different possible combinations according to the children we are observing.

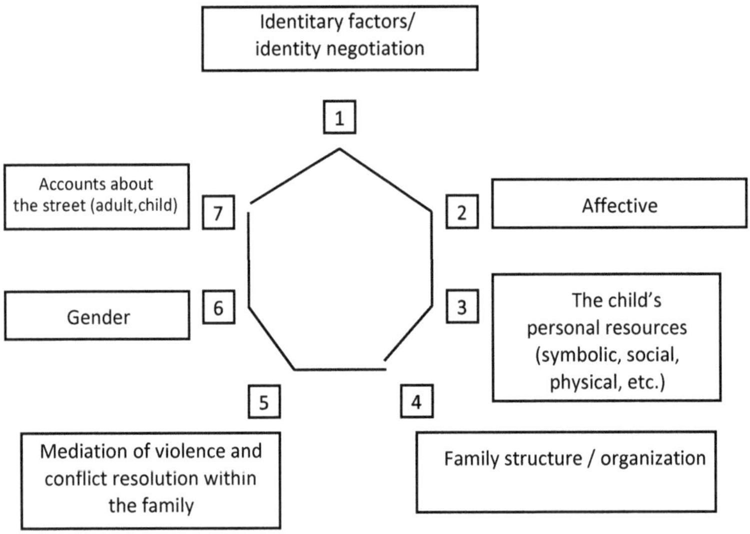


**Fig. 4.3** Parameters on the microsocial level directly affecting CSS

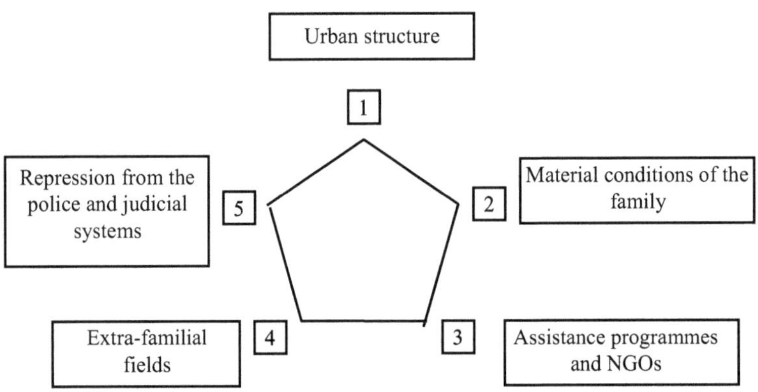


**Fig. 4.4** Parameters on the macrosocial level indirectly affecting CSS

## References

Burman, E. (1996). Local, global or globalized? Child development and international child rights legislation. *Childhood, 3*(1), 45–66.

Calam, R., & Franchi, C. (1987). *Child abuse and its consequences*. Cambridge: Cambridge University Press.

Camilleri, C., & Vinsonneu, G. (1996). *Psychologie et culture: concepts et méthodes*. Paris: Colin.

Cicourel, A. V. (1979). *La sociologie cognitive*. Paris: PUF.

Corby, B. (1994). *Child abuse: Towards a knowledge base*. Buckingham: Open University Press.

Denzin, N. K. (1990). *Interpretive interactionism*. London: Sage.
Dewey, J. (1922). *Human nature and conduct: An introduction to social psychology*. London: Allen and Unwin.
Ferguson, H., Gilligan, R., & Torode, R. (1993). *Surviving childhood adversity*. Dublin: Social Studies Press.
Fonseca, C. (1985). Valeur marchande, amour maternel et survie: aspects de la circulation des enfants dans un bidonville brésilien. *Annales, 40*(5), 991–1022.
Fonseca, C. (1991). Menores carentes. In B. Trillat (Ed.), *Abandon et adoption* (pp. 49–54). Paris: Autrement Revue.
Giddens, A. (1984). *The constitution of society: Outline of the theory of structuration*. Berkeley: University of California Press.
Lucchini, R. (1993). *Enfant de la rue. Identité, sociabilité, drogue*. Genève/Paris: Droz.
Lucchini, R. (1995). Femme et deviance ou le débat sur la spécificité de la délinquance feminine. *Revue européenne des sciences sociales, 33*(102), 127–168.
Lucchini, R. (1996). *Sociologie de la survie. L'enfant dans la rue*. Paris: PUF.
Mills, W. C. (1959). *The sociological imagination*. Oxford: Oxford University Press.
Moles, A. (1976). *Micropsychologie et vie quotidienne*. Paris: Denoël/Gonthier.
Schneider, B. H., & Younger, A. J. (1996). Adolescent-parent attachment and adolescents relations with their peers: A closer look. *Youth & Society, 28*(1), 95–108.
Strauss, A. (1992). *La trame de la négociation. Sociologie qualitative et interactionnisme*. Paris: L'Harmattan.
Varela, F. J. (1999). *Ethical know-how: Action, wisdom, and cognition*. Stanford: Stanford University Press.
Werner, E. E., & Smith, R. S. (1992). *Overcoming the odds*. Ithaca: Cornell University Press.
Winnicott, D. W. (1994). *Déprivation et délinquance*. Paris: Payot.

# Chapter 5
# Survival Strategies

**Riccardo Lucchini**

## 5.1 Innumerable Strategies

Children in street situations (hereafter CSS) employ innumerable strategies to overcome their everyday challenges. The objective of this chapter is not to describe each of them comprehensively, as this alone would necessitate an entire field-based study. We have not chosen an ethnographic approach: our aim instead is to highlight the symbolic and social skills of children in street situations (hereafter CSS). Investigating these skills allows us to show the children's capacity to draw on their available symbolic resources in order to adapt to the conditions of street life – resources which are no less important than their physical resources. Symbolic resources may even turn out to be more important for the well-being of CSS than physical resources, for they enable them to build and deliberately convey meaning that they can use to their advantage. This we will see in the case of Paulo, who does not let himself get dragged into confrontations with those stronger than he is, but rather uses verbal jousting to affirm himself. Verbal competences are indeed very often favoured by children as defence strategies. On this topic, Y. Riaño-Alcalá (1990, p. 12) explains that a good sense of humour, the ability to criticise in a sarcastic tone and to 'talk about people' are skills that characterise a leader.

Well-being concerns all the needs of a child, and in particular his or her identity needs. Social gratification and the need to be valued are amongst the most important of needs. Indeed, they directly affect the child's self-image.[1] Studying the symbolic aspect of the child's strategies, then, allows us to show how he or she uses the street. In other words, he or she is not defenceless facing the constraints of the street: he or she is a social actor, who makes choices and who creates opportunities that he or she

This chapter is translated from Lucchini, R. (1993). Les stratégies de survie, in: Riccardo Lucchini. *Enfant de la rue. Identité, sociabilité, drogue* (pp. 58–73). Genève/Paris: Droz. It is translated and published in English with permission.

[1] See Chap. 7.



R. Lucchini, D. Stoecklin, *Children in Street Situations*, Children's Well-Being: Indicators and Research 21, https://doi.org/10.1007/978-3-030-19040-8_5

knows how to exploit. We will also see that there are significant differences in skills from child to child. It will be pivotal to study how these differences are articulated.

## 5.2 Rationality and Strategy

Survival strategies make an appeal to the child's rationality. As is the case for everyone, this rationality is limited. It depends on the child's knowledge of the street world, on the control he or she can exercise on his or her emotions, on his or her cognitive skills and on his or her social integration: that is, his or her groups or networks. This rationality is therefore subject to the information available to the child and to his or her capacity to use it. A child cannot be deemed to have a strategy if, despite possessing relevant information, he or she is unable to use it to achieve a goal. The absence of a goal is of course an insurmountable obstacle for the laying out of a strategy.

The level of strategy development amongst CSS can vary wildly. It depends on the kind of goal, on the context in which this goal is situated and on the skills (means) available to the child. The simplest strategies are those employed to escape danger that arose suddenly: for example, police raids or physical aggression. The most elaborate strategies generally concern the search for protection and self-affirmation.

We must differentiate, in the search for protection, between that which pertains to what happens on the street and that which is directed to what happens in life more generally speaking. The former concerns first of all the younger children and is linked to survival on the street: food, clothing, washing, money, shelter, affection, comfort. Its function is to improve living conditions on the street. The latter concerns older children (teenagers) who are seeking ways to leave the street, and its function is to ensure a form of continuity after life on the street. In this case, the search for protection goes hand in hand with a long-term project. It is often associated with the search for a '*compadre*' (godfather) who can introduce the child to the adult world. It is usually during this phase that some adolescents enter the world of crime. We will not study this second kind of search for protection.

Self-affirmation equates to claiming forms of social recognition from those with whom we interact. Yet on the street, self-affirmation is constantly subjected to challenges which jeopardise it. By addressing this challenge, we will see that children use it as a tool for self-affirmation.

Survival strategies are behaviours. To be of a strategic nature, these behaviours must be 'oriented towards results, and have their own rationality which considers the opportunities available to the actor and the behaviour of his/her opponents' (Cusson 1981, p. 64). A strategy, however, does not only address itself to opponents. In fact most strategies of searches for protection are non-confrontational. Here the child presents him/herself as a vulnerable person, often in the role of a victim. There is nothing at stake for the person the child is addressing, perhaps other than what it will be possible to demand from the requesting child. On the other hand, a child who asks for a favour from another child will often be offered, in addition, a form of protection. The offer of protection is a strategy aimed at creating a relationship of dependency between two or more children. We see, therefore, that there are several types of strategies. While they are drawing from H. Touzard, E. Marc and D. Picard (1989, pp. 206–207) distinguish four types of strategies found amongst CSS. First, there is coercion: for example, threat, bluff, overbidding or aggressive behaviour. Then there is concealment: manipulation and the retention of information. After this we find the strategy of persuasion: to show one's own resoluteness, to use seduction. And finally there is accommodation: interacting parties looking for common ground, and making use of bargaining techniques. These strategies are all situated within contexts of negotiation. Depending on the circumstances, children use one or another strategy.

These strategies, however, do not apply to what we will call emergency situations: exploiting a favourable situation which suddenly comes up, such as the snatching of a handbag, or the avoidance of an unforeseen danger. When there is no negotiation, the child resorts to other strategies. We will see that he or she also uses these other strategies to open up favourable situations.

The notion of proper rationality should be further clarified, as it is important within an intercultural perspective. What characterises this type of rationality is that it is on the one hand limited, and on the other culturally conditioned. It is limited by the nature of the information available to the deciding actor, as information is never comprehensive.

Rationality is also a function of the freedom enjoyed by the social actor. Within the classical model, the social actor is free if he or she is able to define his or her preference order (Flamm 1990, p. 40). The rational man must not be limited by contradictory desires or beliefs, and his choices must be consistent. Yet all of these choices are conditioned by the pursuit of personal interest. The main problem facing the rational man is therefore the choice of means, this choice being itself influenced by a cost-benefit comparison. However, this model of rationality does not allow us to incorporate what is particular to the proper rationality of social actors. This specificity comes from the normative conditioning of rationality: that is, Max Weber's normative rationality (*Wertrationalität*). The actor's point of reference is not solely his own interest anymore, but is also guided by others. When he seeks to satisfy a desire, the actor is limited not only by his resources, but also by the values of society, of the group to which he belongs (op.cit., p. 42).

As rationality is conditioned by culture, considerable differences can exist between the proper rationalities specific to different societies and social groups. Thus, for example, in Brazilian favelas, the practice of placing small children in other families is part of a complex strategy that allows for the creation of an interwoven network of rights and obligations. This is often linked to the survival necessities of single-parent families. But this circulation of children is often perceived as depraved by the middle classes, and no rationality is attributed to it. The strategies adopted by CSS therefore imply specific rationalities, which are culturally and emotionally conditioned.

## 5.3 The System of Opportunity

It is now pertinent to address the concept of opportunity. We will then apply this notion to the problem of how the child is conditioned by the street environment. Exploring this concept will enable us to tackle the issue of the child's autonomy in relation to their social situation. In this context, children are principally defined either as active subjects (who have an effect on their environment), or as objects (who are 'acted upon' by their environment). This brings us to the theme of the child's degree of autonomy in relation to the constraints of the world of the street.

Opportunity is defined by M. Cusson (1981) as a triad, consisting of:

(a) the resources of the actors (affective, cognitive, cultural, social, physical)
(b) the occasions to act they encounter
(c) their intentions or goals

An opportunity occurs 'when, thanks to his resources, an actor can take advantage of given circumstances to achieve his ends.' It is the 'encounter between a situation and one's ability to exploit it.' (Cusson 1981, p. 64). Opportunity and occasion, then, refer to two distinct phenomena. An occasion occurs within an actor's environment without their personal intervention. It is only one of the elements of the system of opportunity. More precisely, an occasion is the 'raw' component of a system of opportunity. It is perceived and elaborated upon – for example, categorised as favourable or unfavourable – in accordance with the actor's skills (resources), interests and social affiliation. The presence in the field of other actors also greatly affects the perception and elaboration of an occasion. Some of these actors belong to the original actor's network of resources, while other actors, on the contrary, determine his or her boundaries.

The system of opportunity enables actors to situate themselves in the social space. As a general rule, the more developed a system is, the more autonomy the actor possesses with regards to the social environment in which an opportunity arises. The degree of elaboration of an opportunity is determined by the quality of the actor's resources along with their ability to set adequate and achievable goals, corresponding to their resources and interests. However, it is the combination of resources and goals which constitutes the motivation of the actor.

As this motivation becomes more structured, so does the system of opportunity. On the other hand, the system of opportunity is bound to the social structure within which the actor participates: that is, to their relations of role and hierarchy within the group. On the streets, the system of opportunity is a particularly important survival tool. It allows the child to anticipate events instead of only experiencing them when they occur. Thus, the more a child's opportunity is structured, the better they will adapt to life on the street. In other words, they use the street to the best of their abilities. For the children to whom such a system is available, the streets are experienced in a positive manner. They can find a balance between the challenges posed by the streets and their response capacities. However, children who don't enjoy a solid system of opportunity experience the streets in a negative manner. Their self-evaluation of street life is characterised by a constant need to explain their failures. These children are continually searching for protection (Emilio). Children found in the first category, on the contrary, assert their independence (Paulo, Gordo). As we have already signalled, we find this distinction in Aptekar (1988), when he differentiates '*kids*' from '*chupagruesos*' in his study conducted in Cali, Colombia. They are satisfied with their life on the street and often adopt a provocative attitude in their relations with others. They revel in their life on the street and affirm it as a lifestyle. In the section on identity we will show how this is exteriorised by children in Rio de Janeiro. The group of children who suffer on the street and wish to leave it readily blame themselves, and look to others for protection. Still, they admire the 'kids' and take them as models (Aptekar 1988, p. 54).

The importance of the system of opportunity for survival on the street increases with the child's age. Indeed, adults' perception of CSS changes according to their age: the physical appearance of children conditions attitudes of acceptance or rejection from adults. The presence on the streets of younger children, of five to ten years old (but in fact physical appearance is more important than age), is widely accepted by adults. However, as early as pre-puberty, and certainly during adolescence, rejection is preponderant. Younger children arouse compassion, but slightly older ones trigger fear. Adolescents provoke repulsion. Relations between adults and children are mediated through these feelings. When a child starts inspiring fear in adults, he needs to reinforce his system of opportunity to compensate for this change in attitude. This system becomes a determining factor for self-preservation, but also for the quality of the connections that the child forms in the world of the street. Hence, the more developed the system of opportunity, the more a child will feel in tune with and independent within his environment. Deficiencies in the system of opportunity bring the child, however, to seek out situations where others – adults or groups of children – can protect him. We will see that the success of this transition into later childhood will condition the later development of a CSS.

## 5.4 The Different Strategies

The youngest children from our research body – spanning the ages of nine to twelve – have all spoken of security issues at night. Night time is a continual concern, as one must find shelter from harsh weather, and, more importantly, from assaults. It is significant that all of these children have, at one point or another, sought and obtained protection from the police. For the younger children, the police booths spread out over the city centre constitute secure spaces. None of the older children or adolescents, on the other hand, have sought such protection. Going to the police is the undertaking of a child who has yet to integrate into the streets and is still relatively isolated. It is an individual approach that does not yet involve a significant counterpart for the child. From the moment a child is part of a network, such an approach loses its *raison d'être*. It is therefore reserved for street novices, or for children who have been excluded from a group to which they belonged. This individual approach is not comparable to the protection offered by the police to certain older children and adolescents: in the latter case, it is always a form of protection given to the children in exchange for remuneration, be it monetary or with stolen goods.

In the case of an individual approach, the child must negotiate their protection with the police officers on duty. In general, children adopt the strategy of persuasion. In order to attract the adult, they present themselves as vulnerable and harmless. Their aim is to be perceived by the police as a potential victim of night-time assault. They know that physical appearance is an asset, and even a type of life insurance. The child also knows that they can do small favours for the police officer with whom they interact: for example, buying cigarettes or newspapers, or shoe shining. If they have no negotiating power, still they know how to take advantage of how younger CSS are perceived by adults in general, and by police officers in particular. Indeed, this is one of the main reasons why this category of children prefers to seek out adult protection. Another important element that determines a child's approach is the presence of a small, recognisable team of police officers. If police officers are assigned to the same post it is favourable for the children, who are ensured, for a certain time, stability and security in their protection.

Pirulito, eleven years old, tells us – in the form of a dialogue – how he obtained protection from officers from the nearby police station. This form of direct discourse is widespread amongst CSS and, more generally, within working class Brazilian society. The child re-enacts the events that he is referring to through a series of dialogues which make the episode tangible. He stages the scenes that he is recounting, giving voice to the protagonists and speaking himself in the first person. It feels more real as it brings us closer to the narrated scenes. Direct discourse appears to abolish time and to reformulate the past. It indeed seems to be a form of language that facilitates an updating of what is stored in memory.

CSS tend to use narrated dialogues when they want to emphasise events which have a particularly strong importance to them. Direct discourse allows for the meaning of an event to stand out in its own right, and the speaker does not need to comment or explain any further. Non-dialogical forms of narration are not as self-evident. We can also assume that the dialogue is a form of language that adapts to the socio-cognitive mechanisms of CSS. These mechanisms have not been studied in depth, so it is impossible here to derive any kind of solid hypothesis. Nevertheless, it is safe to assume that dialogic discourse is an instrument at the child's disposal which they can use to convey the meaning of narrated episodes. As U. Windisch has explained (1985, p. 33), signification entails a situated meaning. If dialogic discourse directly presents the characters who performed an event, then this staging situates the actors – it gives a context which itself carries meanings. Words acquire for the child a correspondence to the situation that the child is recounting.

Narrated dialogue carries out a quadruple function:

(a) It is used as proof or illustration of what the child says. In this case we are mostly describing children with well-developed verbal skills, who are capable of recounting events and commenting on them. We are therefore referring to the older children from our research group.

(b) Narrated dialogue is also a means to abolish time, as it includes 'a rhetoric of spectacle (...) within which time also eludes its determinations' (Pulcinelli Orlandi 1988, p. 56).
(c) Narrated dialogue enables children with limited verbal skills to describe an event without the need for a more complicated analysis of the facts.
(d) The didactical aspect of dialogic discourse seems obvious to us. It is itself a strategy which serves to convince the interlocutor of the account's truth. We find here a fourth function of this kind of discourse. The use of dialogic discourse is therefore not, by any means, always the sign of deficiency in verbalisation and abstraction from the speaker.

We can however assume that, sometimes, dialogic discourse is the consequence of weaknesses in syntax and vocabulary, and thus of a difficulty in making use of abstract language. When a speaker is unable to give an account of an event or a complex idea, they use the dialogic form.

Coming back to Pirulito, we find him cautiously approaching a police station. He does not address the police officers straight away. Instead he chooses to sleep near the police station for a while first because, he says: 'nobody was looking for a fight.'[2] He pronounces this sentence with a definite pride and emphasis, as this protection is a privilege. Indeed, it is uncommon for children to benefit from such respite. Then Pirulito took a further step as he asked for a police officer to protect him: 'watch over me, don't let anybody bother me!'[3] His approach is gradual, and he waits for a suitable occasion to finalise it. This occasion presents itself when, to shelter himself from the rain, Pirulito runs to the police cabin. Events then take a very quick turn as the child tells us that the police officer lets him come inside the police station, without any transition in his account. He is allowed to sleep inside. He can even sleep in the police car. With a very solemn voice, Pirulito explains that the police officers watch over his sleep and respect it. Indeed, not only do they not wake him up, but when an officer arrives at the station, he even asks about the child. He feels valued by the police officers. The tone of Pirulito's account, along with conversations amongst police officers he recounts, illustrate their consideration for him. He tells us of three verbal exchanges between police officers in which they were speaking about him. In all three, they discuss the quality his sleep. Pirulito is defenceless when he is asleep, so the policemen's attitude is particularly credible.

The streets as a living environment conditions survival strategies. They are not lived in the same manner, however, by all children. Yet the manner in which they do experience the streets influences their strategies. By definition, the streets are ambivalent, presenting a combination of constraints and liberties, of violence and complicity, of dangers and survival opportunities. This mixture alternately produces pleasure and suffering, alliances and separations. With some children, this leads to a condition of constant excitement which has repercussions on their system of opportunity. In these cases, the system of opportunity is not very elaborate, as these

[2] '*Ninguem mexia comigo.*'

[3] '*Moço toma conta de mim, nao diexa ninguem mexer nao*!'

children tend to react to events rather than anticipating, exploiting or even creating them. They are subjected to events, and their strategies are often characterised by a deficiency in goals and personal resources, particularly affective and cognitive resources.

Yet the uncertainties of the streets are not incompatible with more elaborate strategies. The situation of children who specialise in stealing from passers-by illustrates a strategy of average complexity.[4] It is also common for children to not reveal their real name. Some go as far as to take another child's identity, in some cases even using their identity certificate. This is a precious document as it gives them proof of legal existence – and a certain degree of protection when confronted with police violence. For the older children, such certificates serve to prove that they are still minors, as is the case with Gordo, who holds a dead child's certificate. This paper provides him with a relative – but nevertheless real – security in his contact with the police. A child who does not divulge his name, but probably uses that of another child who actually exists, tells us that 'every truth is there to be discovered, but only up to a certain point.'[5]

Camouflage is a strategy employed by all children. It does not consist solely of simple forms of strategy, such as changes of identity, manipulation of nicknames, or of age. It can grow into other dimensions, as Silvano shows us. He is a twelve-year-old boy who expresses the art of camouflage in a caricatural manner: 'I fled from my house, I am eleven years old, I am twelve, I am three, I am four, I am sixteen years old, I am twelve, I am fourteen. I live in Belford Roxo, I live in Itaipu, I live in São Cristovão, I live in São Gonçalo, I am fifteen years old.' He finishes by telling us that his mother would beat him and burn him with hot water. As we consider the playfulness of his account and his verbal behaviour, there seem to be two messages that we can decipher from his words. The first is a warning for the adult: CSS never reveal everything. If it suits them they can decide to remain elusive and indiscernible. They can become anyone, at any time. If their context and needs call for it, they can invent an entirely new identity in a matter of seconds. In this manner, they claim a degree of respect towards their personal sphere, which they can keep control over. They do not give themselves up unless they want to, it is a decision that belongs to them. They remain the sole judge of when, how, why, and to who they will confide. Thus, the camouflage strategy concerns not only the personal safety of children, but also their identity.

This is the second message we can read in this child's account. Indeed, matters of security and claims of autonomy on the one hand, and identity on the other, are closely related. What Silvano says illustrates a precise type of relationship between himself and events. He can have any age, depending on circumstances. It's like time becomes extendable and reversible. He can also choose to live anywhere, or decide on where he wants to say he lives. He does not allow for himself to be defined once and for all. He is child, adolescent and adult at one and the same time.

---

[4] The average retail price of objects stolen and sold by children in our case study is between 1000 and 2000 cruseiros ($3.20 and $6.40)

[5] 'Toda realidade é pra ser dita até um certo ponto.'

In the streets, the need for safety is the priority, and most children's survival strategies are conditioned by it. During our first interviews Gordo told us he was fourteen years old, when he was in fact eighteen. The identity certificate he carries belonged to a child murdered by a gang. Thanks to this document, Gordo can prove that he is still a minor. He explains how he conceived his general safety strategy. This strategy rests on two necessary conditions. The first is the code of silence. This law is paramount in the streets. However, if a child determines that someone is trustworthy, and that the person doesn't belong to the street world, they can circumvent this code. On the other hand, silence can also be bought. We see Gordo buy silence by protecting certain children from stronger ones: 'in exchange, they never speak.' The code of silence is all the more important as it is 'easy to meet a new friend, but difficult to realise it': that is, to realise the friendship. An encounter is merely about the short term, the moment, the occasion. But realisation is about the long term, an investment in time. Yet survival on the streets offers little space for such an investment. For Gordo this is felt very deeply, as 'even his shadow could betray him.'[6] Furthermore, money can change any situation, disrupt every equilibrium. Gordo tells us that everything can be bought: people, feelings, goods, happiness. Social relations become things, become 'objectified', to be bought and sold like commodities. It is hence particularly difficult to 'realise a friendship'.

The second condition for safety on the streets pertains to what we will call the controlled visibility of children in the streets. Children need to manage this visibility themselves. Gordo feels safe from attacks because 'many people around here know me'. Danger and death occur when there is no one to bear witness: 'they [vulnerable children] don't have any witnesses, people to see [what happens]'. By definition, the witness is the person who sees and thus exercises social control. It is therefore critical to ensure the presence of witnesses. It is a survival rule. One must be seen, and, better still, be known. Gordo seems to practice this strategy as, when he is strolling in the city centre, numerous people come to greet him. In his account, Gordo does not specify whether witnesses must be close relations or if this is not necessary.

Regarding visibility, it can be defined in a threefold manner: 'to be seen' – 'to know' – 'to be known'. The first and the last terms designate very distinct attributes. 'To be seen' means to be physically perceived by others: to have potential witnesses around. It is not necessary for anyone to personally know the child, as the physical presence is sufficient. 'To be known' entails, however, an identification process. The child is recognized by certain people: they are somebody. They occupy a place in a certain social space, and their absence is noticed. CSS who are simply seen but not recognized by others are isolated children. The control of their visibility is the single most important element of any survival strategy that is not only a short-term strategy. To achieve it, children must be able intervene in the three components of the visibility triad in order to modify each to their advantage. Thus, a child who is in possession of a lot of personal information about many people, and who at the same time is well known in an area, will enjoy a high degree of visibility and therefore security. A general safety strategy is not available to all children. Indeed, it requires

[6] 'Meu inimigo é minha sombra'

that children have significant social and cognitive resources. For the most part, children who know how to use a comprehensive general safety strategy are also the leaders of a group or a network.

The code of silence and controlled visibility are interdependent, because children know everything that goes on in the streets. They know what each of them is doing and has done in the past. Between them there are no secrets, but rather an intricate interlacing of unspoken matters. All of our interviews and observations show that the implementation and success of a general safety strategy is dependent upon the social influence that a child is able to exert on others.[7]

Amongst the most frequent survival strategies are those that enable children to take on a protective identity. Children carrying around a shoeshine box exemplify such protection. Thanks to the box a child is identified with a job, and their presence in the streets is recognised as legitimate. The risk of police harassment diminishes. Children who deliberately harm themselves are also looking for a way to escape aggression. The best-known example is that of the child prostitutes from Recife (in Nordeste), who cut their forearms with razor blades to escape aggressors, such as police officers or thieves. Some strategies are grounded in popular sayings. As Paulo, a seventeen-year-old, once told us: 'The one who is hit remembers. The one who hits forgets!'.[8]

The use of force alone does not guarantee survival on the streets. It engenders respect only if this strength comes with other skills: if the children can use their strength to accompany their resources. Brute force does not bring about any long-term results. It is chiefly the symbolic skillset that conveys power, and the more a child's skills are developed, the easier it is for the child to impose themselves. Indeed, when children make use of their entire persona, and not just their physical strength, they value themselves more highly and allow their resources to expand. The use of symbolic skills contributes to constructing and fine-tuning children's survival strategies. Thus, the hardships of such conditions do not prevent children from developing better living environments: the more a strategy makes use of the child's symbolic resources, the more they are able to free themselves from their adversaries and from daily contingencies. The survival strategy then becomes a general course of action, which children apply to the different incidents that they must tackle.

But the street is also strongly characterised by the specific rhythm of its events. As Paulo says about a child who is new to the streets, 'he gets used to it, he gets to know the rhythm, he ends up taking on the fast pace of street life.' However, the 'street-rhythm' does not always allow for the adequate use of symbolic skills. Sometimes children have to make do in urgent situations, where speed of action takes precedence over all else. Every child has told us that to live on the streets, one must know when to run, and to run fast![9]The reality of everyday life on the streets does not always enable children to choose a complex strategy that combines physical and symbolic resources.

[7] See Chap. 7.

[8] 'Quem apanha lembra. Quem bate esquece!'

[9] In Chap. 7 we will see how children talk about violence on the street.

## 5.5 Symbolic Resources

By symbolic resources we mean everything which relates to social representations and significations. Without them, social interaction would be unthinkable: communication would simply be impossible. Indeed, symbolic resources enable us to classify and give order to the events and people in our environment, whether close or distant.

The hermeneutic approach in social sciences, along with research on the moral development of children, has shown the importance of the symbolic in human communication, and in the identity formation of both individuals and groups. Socio-cognitive structures filter the outside world and give it meaning. Such structures are defined by "cognitive and social elements pertaining to a certain manner of knowing" (Windisch 1985, p. 24). There is thus a correlation between an individual's symbolic resources and their perception and evaluation of social reality: the more abundant these resources, the better an individual can relate to their environment in diverse ways. The resulting behaviour is differentiated, and allows for a greater adaptability. We can then speak of a de-centred socio-cognitive structure, as the categories through which it classifies persons and events are subtle and numerous (op. cit., p. 50). Within this type of structure an individual will be more active, they will innovate and take initiative. Their social, cognitive and linguistic practices will be more elaborate. They will also be able to take more distance from their environment as they tap in to these wider resources. As Uli Windisch writes: 'any given form of thought is more or less centred or de-centred. It is a matter of degree' (op. cit., p. 51). Such a de-centring can never be absolute, as the individual would lose all normative references.

The symbolic skills of CSS are therefore a function of their socio-cognitive structure. There is no empirical data available on this matter. The rare studies on affective and emotional performances of CSS engage with other questions. Moreover, these studies are too disparate in their methodologies for it to be possible to compare the results they reach.[10] But nevertheless we can say that symbolic resources give diverse perspectives to CSS in their analysis of the reality around them. They are able to change viewpoints, or relativise, when they put themselves in the place of those with whom they interact. This is always only partially possible, and there are thus degrees of relativisation.

Children must indeed 'reflect' on the motivations, interests, strength and authority of the person they interact with. In this manner, they determine their interlocutor's attitude and intentions. They thus possess an image of the other, and through this can assess their own prospects within the interaction. The more that is at stake in an interaction – for example, authority, honour, defence of a territory, goods to

[10] See L. Aptekar's critique in: op. cit. pp. 17–37. This interesting work on underprivileged children's language skills in Rio treats the question of cognitive skills in an indirect manner. It does not, however, only relate to street children. See also: Monica Rebello de Castro, *O Avesso la Logica: Aspectos da relaçào eniso-aprendizagem na escola da Tia Ciata*, unpublished document, Rio de Janeiro, 1990.

share – the more symbolic skills become necessary. To those who possess them, such resources grant a greater quality of survival in the street, and a greater flexibility in how they can act. Indeed, as we have seen, the more elaborate a child's system of opportunity is, the more fulfilment they can get from street life. We can therefore understand why certain children prefer to stay on the streets rather than return to a home where it is much more difficult to exercise their skills.

Paulo's story provides a remarkable example of an elaborate strategy. At a young age, he was detained in a facility for young offenders. These institutions are all but real prisons, where the rule of force trumps any other order (Arruda 1983; De Souza Campos 1984; Violante 1985; Junqueira 1986; Sadir et al. 1987; Passetti 1987). Like all CSS, Paulo knows about the living conditions in such establishments. He knows what to expect and adapts his behaviour to the circumstances. To ensure his position in the institution, he must show his skills straight away. He proceeds in three stages.

The first objective is to make others understand that he does not fear them. To malicious glances he responds in kind, and he accompanies this look with provocative questions, such as, 'what do you know of me?'[11] Paulo presents this question and this look to someone who he designates as a 'guy' ('*nego*'). It means that he accepts the challenge the 'guy' poses, and that he is capable of fighting back at any time.

This face-off, however, is not enough to guarantee his security. Paulo must still call out to the other children and move on to the second phase. He begins to talk with 'a whole bunch of children',[12] without specifying what they talked about. Paulo, we learn, is gifted with a valuable asset: he is an expert in *capoeira*, the traditional dance-martial art of Black Brazilians. All Brazilian children, especially those coming from poorer social backgrounds, admire anyone who can master this art. Paulo knows this, and makes the most of this admiration. He teaches *capoeira* to children in the establishment: '*I introduced capoeira over there.*'[13]

These two first stages illustrate a strategy of adaptation to a violent environment. It is necessary, from the start, to display certain skills without, however, revealing all. In Paulo's case, we can note a strategy of 'de-escalation'. To start, he indicates to his opponent that he is the measure of any provocation. Then, he makes himself known to many children. Finally, he displays his skills in the prestigious domain of *capoeira*. This is where another character comes into Paulo's account: a *capoeira* master nicknamed '*Mentrinha*' ('Little Liar'), who gives lessons to children in the institution. A confrontation with Paulo becomes inevitable.

Here begins the third phase of Paulo's strategy, which reveals important symbolic resources. The child identifies the master as a formidable opponent, undoubtedly superior to him in their common art. He must deal with the situation promptly in order to keep hold of the benefits he gained from his initial strategy. This is all the more important as the master provokes him by using prohibited strikes in a *capoeira* face-off. The instructor then asks Paulo who his master was outside. When the master hears the name, he promises Paolo to do all he can to get him of the institution.

---

[11] '*O que tà sabendo?*'

[12] '*Conversei com um monte de moleque*'

[13] '*Botei capoeira là dentro.*'

This promise is highly suspicious to Paulo, as it clearly contradicts the master's obvious desire to humiliate him. To Paulo there is no doubt that the *capoeira* master is setting some kind of trap. He must therefore neutralise this threat, without using physical strength nor *capoeira*. His prestige with the other children – and hence his security within the institution – is at stake.

Paulo chooses two courses of action. Firstly, he grabs a *birimbao* – a traditional musical instrument associated with *capoeira* – and starts singing a song (*xumba*) for the master. The master responds with a *xumba* of his own. They then play the instrument for a good half-hour. Paulo therefore brings the confrontation onto a less risky battleground, but one which nevertheless remains within the realm of *capoeira*. Paulo relies on his skills in this field to preserve his status in the institution. Through the musical exchange, he shows that he is the equal of the master. The master then proposes that Paolo also teach *capoeira* to the other children. This proposal is a turning point. If the master offers this to Paolo, it is to show that he is still at the top of the hierarchy. Had he accepted, Paulo would have merely complied, and would have been poorly rewarded. He refuses. This refusal is the second course of action chosen by the child in order to win the challenge he faces in confronting the master. This is an issue of great importance as the master is not only a competitor who is superior to him, but an adversary who can destroy his prestige with the other children. Paulo's whole strategy can be boiled down to shifting his confrontation with the master from the physical realm to the symbolic.

He thus knows that he can hold on to his status. By refusing, Paulo achieves several goals: a) he signifies to the master than they are not competing in the field of *capoeira*; b) he does this without losing face in the view of the other children; c) he preserves his prestige within the institution.

Certain CSS know how to systematically create situations which they can subsequently exploit. These are the children who have the most developed and strongly-structured system of opportunity. Such situations can be created in cases where: a) symbolic resources are more important than physical resources, and b) these resources can be invested into achieving pre-established goals.

A child we talked to illustrates this situation. He was looking for food. In a bar, he recognised a prostitute, accompanied by a client. He knew that this situation was more favourable to him than if the woman was alone: even if she refused to offer food, she may ask her companion to do so. Indeed, the child said of this man that he seemed very proud to be in the company of such a striking woman.[14] This pride felt by the man is then the best guarantee for the boy to get something: he knows that the man cannot refuse without losing face in front of his companion and the other customers in the bar. The child knew that the request immediately created a new situation, as something new was at stake for the man. By exploiting the situation, the boy got what he wanted.

This example is an illustration of a well-structured system of opportunity. The presence of the couple in a public space is the occasion. The objective is to obtain food. The child quickly evaluates this presence as potentially favourable to him. He can then make use of an important range of symbolic resources – cognitive norms

[14] '*Se sentira machào, com maior mulherào do lado dele.*'

and norms of evaluation – because he can precisely identify the nature of the social interaction he has come across.

Survival strategies also concern the network of relations that children build with adults who work on or around the streets: taxi drivers, police officers, street peddlers, night guards, doormen, managers of cheap hotels, prostitutes, hustlers, drug dealers… Children create relational webs of variable duration and consistency, but which are in general precarious in nature. Unfortunately, these networks have never been systematically studied, and for the most part remain unknown. On the other hand, we do know somewhat better the relations of CSS with the drug scene. The social networks of CSS also encompass families who live on the streets, even if they have no family ties with one another.

We have already underlined the important distinction between the streets of the city centre and those of the favelas. Going on the street is a process of conquering the street, an act of taking partial and temporal ownership of the space. Street learning may well start at a very young age in the favela, but no child in our research group ever talks about time spent in these streets. This is striking, as these streets were and are inevitably important in the lives of children from such poor neighbourhoods. But for CSS, it is the experience of the streets of the city centre that is extraordinary. Only the downtown streets compose and frame their identity as CSS. The streets of their original neighbourhood still belong to the local community – and to gangs. The careers of CSS only start when they arrive in the city centre. This career and the gradual conquest of the streets are closely connected to each other, along with the identity of the CSS. As they integrate into the street's social system, children acquire instrumental and symbolic skills, skills which in turn regulate the relations the children have with the street world and with their home alike.

The pendulum movement between the poles of street and home characterises most careers of CSS. By studying children' points of reference, we can more precisely determine what we mean when we speak of a 'career'[15] of CSS. Indeed, children's references are conditioned by a progressive estrangement from home, and by the back and forth between home and street life. The career of a child and their identity are hence closely related. The careers of CSS are therefore systems, comprised of:

(a) The manner in which they left home
(b) The development of their references and representations
(c) The development of their instrumental and symbolic skills
(d) The development of their social integration into the streets
(e) The occurrences and reasons for their returns home
(f) Exiting the streets

The careers of CSS can be seen as a system constituted by the set of relationships between all of the above dimensions. With the exception of a very few biographies and autobiographies (Herzer 1982; Collen 1987), there are no rigorous studies of the careers of children in street situations that are available. We can nevertheless

[15] See Chap. 6.

observe a certain diversity amongst these careers, which attests to the psycho-social diversity of those who we designate as children in street situations.[16] In the long term, research on these children should eventually lead towards the constitution of a typology built to accommodate and account for the variety of their respective careers.

In general, CSS accept work if it is offered to them. They therefore often alternate between periods where they carry out legal odd jobs, and others where they 'do nothing'. However most CSS fail to sustain long-term regular employment, as they often fail to fulfil their commitments. This is usually for two reasons:

(a) Regular work is not compatible with belonging to a group of CSS.
(b) Survival strategies enable children to have a higher income than the wages paid for a job would offer.

One must differentiate the data on this matter according to age groups. We must also, furthermore, distinguish between children themselves, according to their identity, in the different relationships they maintain with the street world.

As for collective survival strategies, they are affected by social relations and sociability on the streets. These primarily entail criminal activity, such as the organisation of thefts, the purchase of drugs, and the organisation of the 'workplace', or '*ponto*'.

## References


Aptekar, L. (1988). *The street children of Cali*. Durham/London: Duke University Press.
Arruda, R. S. V. (1983). *Pequenos Banditos*. São Paulo: Global.
Collen, P. (1987). *Mais que a Realidade*. São Paulo: Cortez.
Cusson, M. (1981). *Délinquants pourquoi?* Paris: Colin.
De Souza Campos, A. (1984). *O Menor Institucionalizado*. Um desafio para a sociedade: atitudes, aspirações e problemas para sua reintegração na sociedade. Petropolis: Vozes.
Flamm, H. (1990). Emotional 'man': I. the emotional 'man' and the problem of collective action. In: *International sociology*, Vol. 5, n°1.
Herzer, A. (1982). *Queda para O Alto*. Petropolis: Vozes.
Junqueira, L. (1986). *Abandonados*. São Paulo: Icone.
Lucchini, R. (1993). *Enfant de la rue. Identité, sociabilité, drogue*. Genève/Paris: Droz.
Marc, E., & Picard, D. (1989). *L'intéraction sociale*. Paris: PUF.
Passetti, E., et al. (1987). *O Mondo do Menor Infrator*. São Paulo: Cortez.
Pulcinelli Orlandi, E. (1988). Une confrontation dans le langage. *Langage et Société*, n° 46, Paris.
Rebello de Castro, M. (1990). *O Avesso la Logica: Aspectos da relaçào eniso-aprendizagem na escola da Tia Ciata*, (unpublished document), Rio de Janeiro.
Riaño-Alcalá, Y. (1990). Las Galladas: Street youth and cultural identity in the barrios of Bogota. York University, (unpublished manuscript).
Sadir, E., Birrenbach, M. I., & Figueiredo, C. P. (1987). *Fogo no pavilhào*. São Paulo: Brasiliense.
Violante, M. L. V. (1985). *O dilema do decente malandro*. São Paulo: Cortez.
Windisch, U. (1985). *Le raisonnement et le parler quotidien*. Lausanne.


[16] See Chap. 7.

# Chapter 6
# The Street Career

**Riccardo Lucchini**

## 6.1 A Question of Identification

Leaving the street is the final stage of a complex process that is not always progressive and linear. It brings to the child numerous challenges and questionings. The connection of the child with the world of the street is real and must be interrupted – at least partially – in order for him to begin the process of leaving. In fact, this connection and the feeling of belonging to the world of the street are important components of the identification system of the child. Leaving the street represents therefore, a modification of this system. It implies a change in the components that constitute the system. According to Hewitt, these components are the following: (1) motivations, (2) norms and values, (3) social roles, (4) cognitive competencies and (5) self-image (Hewitt 1970). These elements interact when the social actor is positioned in relation to their close and distant environment. The resulting combination of this interaction allows the actor to create meaning, to situate themselves in relation to other actors and to find a place. They categorise things, people and events. This process of mediation is not always gratifying for the actor. In the case of children in street situations, the connection and feeling of belonging to the world of the street are strong when they find themselves in a place that satisfy their different needs: affective, social, material and in terms of identification. The need for consistency among identifications is one of the most significant, and leaving the street implies an important shift in this dynamic.

The children examined in this chapter live in Ciudad de Mexico, San José (Costa Rica) and Tegucigalpa (Honduras). The triangulation of research fields – between the street, institutions and families – as well as our further research carried out in Brazil and Uruguay (Lucchini 1993, 1996) together form the groundwork for the

This chapter is the translation of Lucchini, R. (2001). Carrière, identité et sorties de la rue, in : Déviance et société, 25(1), 75–97. It is published here with courtesy of Déviance et Société.



R. Lucchini, D. Stoecklin, *Children in Street Situations*, Children's Well-Being: Indicators and Research 21, https://doi.org/10.1007/978-3-030-19040-8_6

study that is presented here. The interviews with children and young adults presented in this chapter have been conducted by the author and his collaborators (S. Chanfon and L. Alvarado), between 1992 and 1997. They took place in different places, depending on the youths' availabilities (on the street, within support centres, in bars or restaurants). The examined population can be divided into two categories of children: (a) those for whom we had detailed, personal information (face-to-face interviews, written reports from social workers, home visits, drawings, photographs). This population included 150 children. The second category (b) includes children with whom contact was less personal and systematic (observation, notes of behaviour in public spaces, improvised conversations). This population includes about 300 children and young adults living in street situations. It is usually impossible to give the precise age of these young people, as this information is often unreliable. The widest range goes from 8 to 23 years-old, with an average of 15 or 16 years-old. Girls constitute 6% of the corpus. To study the street exit process we retained a limited amount of cases. We made this choice as we were comparing the different cases amongst our corpus, in order to present in a contextualised manner the most characteristic cases. For further details about methodology and research techniques regarding children and youth in street situations (Lucchini 1993, pp. 23–29; 1996, pp. 1–8).

## 6.2 Language as a Form of Sociability

For Ricardo, formerly a child in a street situation (CSS), 'the street is also a school of life, because we learn to mature even if we're still children. With this maturity we gain skills that go further than simple day-to-day know-how. It also enables us to recognise the people we can trust. The child is mature when he knows to value someone who can help'. We see that a child's maturity is defined by their cognitive skills and ability to empathise. The child is then able to anticipate what is expected of them, and consequently decide whether they want or need to meet these expectations. Ricardo explains that the street taught him 'to smell out many things'.

To the question 'what do you give the most value to?', Ricardo answers: 'to ourselves'. This unequivocal response comes despite the fact that between themselves children seem to insult each other readily, 'son of a bitch' and 'poorly born' amongst the examples. 'But these words must not be taken literally,' Ricardo explains, 'because they express of form of affection.' He continues: 'it is embarrassing to tell someone that we love them and that we care for them. In the relationships they have with each other, children carefully avoid any words that relate to caring and affection, as it makes them uncomfortable. Being mistreated and abused is not embarrassing, but telling someone I love them or that they're important to me is.' There is, Ricardo says, a form of modesty with regards to expressing care with words, but also the inability to use words which simply aren't part of the child's cognitive universe. The child does not know how to express their feelings with the appropriate words, and caring words are not part of their vocabulary.

From a very young age Ricardo was designated with derogatory names that signified to him that he was nothing and useless.[1] On the other hand, his socialisation included only a very limited learning of the verbalisation that allows for the expression of differentiated feelings and sensations. This verbal insufficiency is reflected in compensatory behaviours that seems to express only violence and aggression, but in fact these behaviours are often an oddly adapted means to signify the need to establish a relation within which the child finds a place. When Ricardo says that in the street you learn 'to smell out many things', he points to the gap between the intensity of feelings and the difficulty in translating them into appropriate words and even behaviours.

Furthermore, young boys are influenced by a culture in which the verbal and physical expression of affection is perceived as a weakness. The boy is afraid to be labelled as a girl and to be mocked by other children. This is of course not a mechanism unique to Latin America. This deficiency in verbal expression, combined with the experience of a childhood marked by systematic devaluing, produces low levels of self-esteem. Moreover, it leads towards a feeling of vulnerability and humiliation, which favours the adoption of violent conduct towards people seen as weak. This same culture imposes the image of the man – and therefore of the boy – who must act dominant in both domestic and public situations. The perverse effect of an imposed masculine identity is in fact enhanced when the context (family or socio-economic) calls it into question. What follows is a situation that promotes the spirit of competition by all means, including violent means, and the effect is also stronger when the competition for scarce resources (material, symbolic and affective) increases. The verbal aggression of CSS is therefore explained by a combination of cognitive deficiencies, such as the inability to express feelings and sensations in a differentiated manner, and by cultural influences that impose a masculine identity, of which an important component is the representation of domination.

Yet, for the most part, acts of verbal aggression are used amongst children as jokes. They are not to be understood literally, as the intention is rarely to offend but on the contrary to signify attention and interest. It is also customary to address each other in a very coarse manner without this questioning the identity of the addressee. Crudeness, presented in a joking tone, often goes together with a certain form of humour and self-mockery. It thus becomes a mechanism for regulating the interactions amongst children, serving to decrease violent confrontations. It is closer to a form of verbal jousting, where there are often neither winners nor losers. When there is a winner it is because of the competitive nature of such jousts, where the rules of the rhetorical game are understood and accepted, so that the loser generally accepts defeat and does not try to compensate for his failure in a violent manner. Banter and profanity also enable the children to unwind, and are therefore a path to deescalate hostility in a non-violent manner. Words then take on a different connotation and lose part of their crude and derogatory content. The use of coarse language can, quite to the contrary of its immediate meaning, defuse its own negative charge and even invert its meaning.

---

[1] *no sirves para nada.*

This helps us to understand the association Ricardo makes between coarse language and the symbolic value it carries. When children use depreciative qualifiers in the tone of a joke, they also indirectly address those who use these words literally, with the intention to humiliate them. It is a way to show that they do not feel concerned by this verbal aggression. Sometimes it is also a matter of a 'linguistic counter-legitimacy' (Lepoutre 1997) which expresses the opposition of CSS to so-called 'normal' language. In this case the identity function of coarse language is obvious: it also expresses the children's protest against the stigmatisation they suffer. Crudeness and obscenities then enter the secondary deviance process analysed by E.M. Lemert (1975, pp. 167–172). This type of deviance does not exclude a permanent attitude of protest against stigmatisation by adults and in public opinion. More often both coexist. Secondary deviance occurs when the stigmatised person undertakes the deviant roles and stereotypes ascribed to them by the stigmatising agent. The stigmatised person takes on a modification of identity that corresponds to their new role, entailing specific ways to act and, of course, speak.

In the case of habitual, daily use of coarse words, however, they lose their positive or negative connotation and become neutral expressions. They then become a way to punctuate and give rhythm to sentences, without any specific meaning. These words are uttered without being directed to anyone in particular. Furthermore, coarse language also serves as a support for social relations within a peer group (Lepoutre 1997, p. 120). According to Lepoutre (op. cit., p. 125), coarse language and obscenities occur in narrative statements as well as in ritual verbal exchanges (banter, insults, addresses, thanks, greetings), and just as much in friendly interactions as in formal ones. It must be noted that language skills are highly valued by CSS. Such skills are in fact seen as one of the most efficient ways to sustain oneself on the street, more important than physical strength. The latter only has a weak symbolic weight, whereas the strength of language resides within the symbols that it conveys. We can go as far as to claim that conversation skills are amongst the most important skills for CSS. They bestow respect and admiration.

A CSS shows a very strong need to express the feelings they experience on a daily basis. But these feelings are numerous and contradictory – hope, resignation, fear, freedom, constraints, etc. – and the child does not know how to represent and articulate them. From this situation emerges an impression of confusion. The child has difficulties in delineating the space they occupy in their social relations, and likewise in their interactions with street educators and social workers. These latter encounters are even more complex, due to the fact that there is competition between children to benefit from these professionals.

For a long time, the CSS has been characterised as someone who does not know how to control their emotions on account of their experience of deprivation. If their street survival knowhow is acknowledged, it is in no way valued. Not only is this resourcefulness perceived as something close to delinquency, it is also associated with character deficiencies. The first of these deficiencies is the inability to postpone gratification. They are seen as *presentist* because they are solely oriented towards the present time and immediate rewards. It is true that CSS often adopt behaviours that can seem excessive, such as provocation and aggression on the one hand, and forceful demands for affection on the other. Moreover, they alternate frequently between these two kinds of behaviours, switching very quickly from one to the other. The use of coarse language is pivotal in this dynamic.

The behaviour of CSS is perfectly adapted to their world, because they obey cultural logics and have identity needs that are always going to favour negotiation. The child in street situations (hereafter CSS) is in fact a seasoned negotiator! Coarse language, within the alternation of apparent or real hostility and the bullish demonstration of affection, are all part of a negotiating logic, the rules and codes of which are often difficult to decipher.

With regard to girls, Ricardo asserts that there is no difference between them and boys. It is not their gender that distinguishes between girls and boys, but indeed their skills and competences. Respect and recognition depend on skills, with gender being a subordinate dimension. Ricardo explains that on the street it is very difficult to tell a girl from a boy (*muy dificilmente se diferenciaba, mujer de hombre*) when the latter manages to earn respect. This is also imperative for the boys. On equal terms of skill or, at the opposite pole, incompetence, there is no difference in the way boys and girls are treated by their peers on the street. Girls are, however, constantly threatened by the violence of adult men who do not belong to the same world but are also present on the street: policemen, criminals, and passers-by, for example.

We can therefore say that sexist prejudices are less strong on the street than in the families or communities where the children come from. Indeed, each is given the opportunity to demonstrate his or her skills. As Ricardo says, girls take their place on the street, and this place is respected by boys because it is defined by a competence. Boys can come to the defence of girls when they are assaulted. This protection is not given to all girls, but only to those who 'deserve it' (*una chamaca que es muy querida*). The right to respect is not a natural right but one that is earned. The brave girls (*valientes*) are those know how they want to be treated on the street, says Ricardo.[2]

The weaker ones are not, however, left entirely at the mercy of events and situations. Even if cases of systematic victimization occur, it is very rare for an 'omega child' at the bottom of the reputational hierarchy to be physically assaulted by other children. A child at the bottom of the hierarchy will be the object of constant jeers, mockery and jokes, they may sometimes be bullied and exploited by a dominant child to obtain food, wash clothes or give up their inhalants, but yet the weak child is somewhat protected from threats to their physical integrity.

In general, CSS are not structured in strictly organised and hierarchical gangs. There is no strong and defined leadership (Fischer-Ferreira 1979; Aptekar 1988a, b; Riaño-Alcalá 1990; Connoly 1990; Visano 1990; Lucchini 1993, 1998; Ennew 1994; Fernández 1995; Taracena 1995; Taracena and Tavera 1998; Parazelli 2000). Nevertheless, the children constitute networks and subgroups, which enable them to

[2] What Ricardo tells us about girls on the street is very representative of what boys have told us in the different countries where we have conducted this research (Mexico, Honduras, Costa Rica, Brazil, Uruguay).

deal with the daily challenges posed by street life. Children of one same network have a meeting place towards which they converge at certain times of the day or night. This place is first and foremost where information is exchanged and commented on. There is no territory where children of one network would be the exclusive user-owner, as is seen in certain cities in the United States or in the shanty towns of Latin America. In the case of North America, territory is often defined in terms of ethnic belonging and material interests, such as drug trafficking or prostitution, which will be defended by the use of firearms. The imbrication with adult criminality is more frequent than with the CSS we observed. The CSS we encountered were more in contact with adults involved in petty crime, theft or receiving stolen goods for example, than organised crime. With regards to the street gangs of Latin American shanty towns, these are always organised around drug trafficking and the control of territories. The average age of these gang members is significantly higher than that within the networks constituted by CSS.

The reputation of a child within their network is a function of the skills and abilities with which they are recognised. There is therefore a hierarchy of reputations, which is functionally the equivalent of the hierarchical organisations of gangs with a centralised leadership. It is indeed this differentiated distribution of reputations that ensures structure within the network, and not relations regulated by the compliance to a leader. This mode of functioning is particularly well adapted to the street context, as it is characterised by the change and spatial mobility of children. The street world consequently requires very flexible forms of sociability, which also respect the individual trajectories of each child: for instance, in terms of entry to the street, exit from the street, and repeated returns to the street. Membership of a network is not nearly as constraining as belonging to gangs in North American ghettos or South American shantytowns. A child does not need to ask for anyone's permission to exit a network. There are notable exceptions, for the most part when a child heavily depends on another. In these cases, however, we can speak more of a particular dependency relationship pertaining to a dyad or a small group of children. In other words, there is no general rule within the larger network preventing a child from leaving the street. The street does not belong to the network in the same way that it can belong to a gang. Even if they rely on the network for certain aspects of their life, CSS are not the simple corollary of their networks.

## 6.3 About the Career

The question of leaving the street can be put from a theoretical and empirical point of view: how to define it, but also how to verify it? This, then, has as much to do with the researcher as with the mediator, be they educators, social workers, psychologists, or NGO workers. In this way the notion of leaving is directly connected to the career, with its characteristic of passing through stages. The definition of the stages is no easy task. For each stage it is necessary to locate an event that marks, in a different way, the person in relation to an anterior or preceding stage. This mark modifies the status of certain roles of each individual and, therefore, their identity. We consider such modifications to be related to a stage in their career if they influence the way in which the person perceives themselves and is perceived by others, and by the place they occupy in the group. It is also possible, but not necessary, that the individual changes their reference group. There can be a clear rupture between two successive stages, or a progressive passage from one to another. A career does not correspond to a linear trajectory, for it has returns and periods of rest in the progression from one stage to another (Ogien 1995).

The career of a CSS is composed of several elements, which together compose its different phases. These phases can be framed by the modification of specific areas of activity, such as remunerative activities of a child working on the street. A simple example of a career consisting of three phases is the case of a child who starts with begging to gain money, then works for the owner of a newspaper stall by selling newspapers for him, and finally sets up their own business by selling objects such as holy images or flowers that they can buy in bulk for cheap (Lucchini 1996, pp. 70–71). We see here that the child's career is a function of their remunerative activity, and the passage from one phase to another depends on a change in these activities. Such a career is that of a child who does not live on the street, but rather comes to work there.

Another example of a career would be one that is primarily determined by the relationship between a child and the street as their living space. In such case we can broadly break the career up into five stages. The first (a) corresponds to a child's gradual distancing from home. The child arrives to the street in small steps, first by exploring the urban space in the centre of town or around their neighbourhood. The second (b) is the street as an observed and playful space, the child keeping a certain distance from the street. The third (c) is the alternating street: here the child starts to embrace the street and its contradictions, often claiming the status of "street child". The street is neither good or bad, rather it is ambiguous. The fourth (d) is the rejected street, when the child recognises that the street offers no way out. Finally the fifth (e) is the exit from the street. The pattern presented here constitutes the ideal-typical model of the career of a CSS. Not all children go through all the stages, nor do they do so in the same way. This can be explained by the fact that such stages are not static. They are rather the result of a combination of factors.

Figure 6.1 gives us an idea of the 'production' of the career of the child in a street situation.

All these factors are interdependent, and the modification of one of them has repercussions for all the others. In this way, the career becomes the central element that defines the place that the child occupies on the street. This place differs from one child to the next because of the stage that each one occupies at a given moment, as well as because of the stages already passed. We see that, on the socio-psychological level, CSS do not constitute a homogenous category. Even if they often share similar life stories, these can translate into very different identities, skills, levels of insertion within the network, skills and lived experiences.

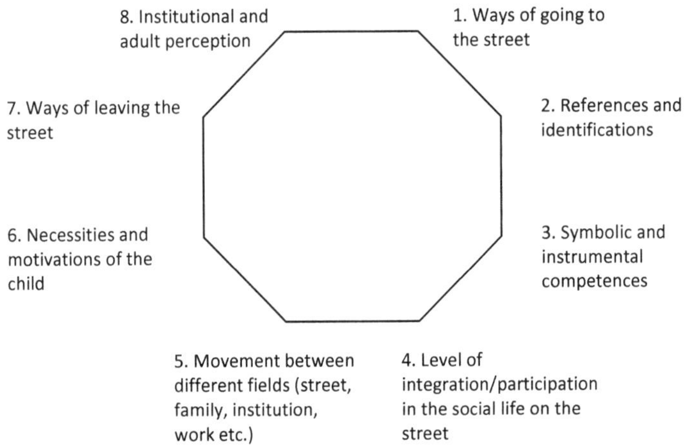


**Fig. 6.1** Factors in which the combined variables 'produce' the different stages of the career of the child in a street situation

## 6.4 The Relation to the Street and Exiting the Street

Leaving the street is influenced by the career of the child and depends on the combination of all these factors. From a theoretical point of view, leaving the street does not require that they cut all ties with the world of the street. We have a number of examples of children who left the street and placed themselves in a field of new activities (school, work, or the military, for instance), and that for a certain time they kept in touch with old friends. However, in order for us to be able to speak about an exit from the street, it is necessary that there is a change in the dominant biographical line of the child. The child begins leaving the street when the desired or ideal image of themselves becomes irreconcilable with their way of life on the street. This image is often built through a positive reference. This reference is usually someone whose respect the child is trying to gain, who does not live in the street, and who does not appreciate the fact that the child lives there.

A change in the biographical line takes time and greatly varies from one child to the next,[3] As Albert Ogien (1995) writes, the notion of the biographical line "refuses the idea of the uniqueness of the biography, admitting the postulate: the life of an individual can rarely be understood as a linear, homogenous, and definitive history". And, according to Robert Castel (1998, p. 26), "a normal individual can represent his life as being organized around some key lines of investment: the history of his childhood, of his loves, his professional career". Each one of these lines of investment "remains relatively independent, and imposes its own kinds of demands". The child in a street situation is, therefore, a child whose daily life is organized according to only one reference: life on the street and its demands. Their line of investment is exclusively organized in terms of life on the street. As such, leaving the street can

[3] For the concept of the 'dominant biographical line', see Castel (1998) and Ogien (1995).

begin when the child is still physically residing on the street. This exit can begin as soon as there is a change in the factors of the scheme. In order for this to truly occur, these changes must harness the first manifestations of a new line of investment which would be able to replace the line that is organized around life on the street. According to the children, this process can be short or long. Meeting an adult who is a point of reference (educators, parents, street hawkers, passers-by and so on) is almost always an event that begins this process of leaving. We therefore see that leaving the street has many dimensions that can evolve with different rhythms.

The complexity of the process of leaving becomes evident. This has to do with the fact that the street is a plural space, permitting many uses and forms of belonging. This belonging can be 'measured' by the resources (material, social, affective, symbolic and in terms of identification) that the child has access to on the street or that they attribute to the street. The relationship to the street-space is therefore complex, in the sense that it contains different ways and degrees of appropriating the space. This appropriation as well as the integration into the space allows for behaviours that express concrete forms of action, allowing at the same time a dominance over places and the production of cultural symbols. This appropriation establishes itself through an essential dialectic, between the existence of control and the introduction of freedom. Appropriation is projection of human conduct over space. It affirms a control that can be expressed in many ways (Fischer 1984, p. 88).

Fischer distinguishes different types of appropriation of space, going from the gaze, the minimal form of domination over the exterior world, to the freedom of marking a place and performing certain acts within it that differentiate it from other places. The transformation of space into territory is the strongest degree of appropriation of space. We can say that the greater the degree of appropriation of the space of the street, the longest the process of leaving. The appropriation of the street is high when the child dominates the dialectic that is established between control and freedom. This domination is very gratifying, for it refers to the power that the child exercises over the risks that make up life on the street and over access to the different resources of this space, benefiting from the freedom but also from the obligation that this situation endows.[4]

There are also children who go to the street for limited periods of time, perhaps a few days or a week, and then return home. They generally do this because of the adventure, to 'have a party', consume inhalants, or steal. These children are 'visitors' for whom the street is primarily about fun, a field that does not monopolize either all their competencies or their energies. The street is a parenthesis, a place to 'hang out'. It is not opposed to family, school, work or the institution, but something that complements them. The relevance of the street and the child's identification with it are limited and are part of a project whose beginning and end the child them-

[4]This domination is always partial and temporary and, in most cases, occurs in a specific field of activities that are limited in time and space – thefts, diverse income making activities, conflict resolution between children, distribution of food or inhalants, negotiations with professionals from assistance programmes, etc. – and in the sphere of subgroups or partnerships that make up a broader and unstructured network.

selves have defined. It is the existence of this project that distinguishes between the child-visitor and other CSS. This project is essentially of a playful nature, and does not meet material necessities or those related to identification. However, the child-visitor lays claim to the importance of meeting their friends and of living with them, for a time, the adventure of the street. For this kind of child there is no exit from the street as such for the world of the street is not her/his main reference point.

Let us examine the case of Mamo, a child from Ciudad de Mexico. Mamo's story illustrates the fine balance that is established between the street, family and school. This child spends time on the street during school holidays, has a good relationship with his mother, and goes back to school when it reopens. Each of these three fields responds to the child's different needs, and importantly they do not contradict each other. His mother's attitude is the central component that allows Mamo to construct non-exclusive relations between these spaces. Other factors also explain this situation: (i) the absence of a dominating father figure and of domestic violence, (ii) the financial independence of the mother, (iii) a relationship of trust between mother and son, (iv) a limited number of brothers and sisters, from the same father and not in conflict, (v) the street as a space of encounter, reunion and leisure, (vi) the street as a source of pride for the child, as he feels as though he leads a double life between school and street without it hindering him. We can add to these factors a non-repressive boarding school. All of these factors allow a complementarity between family, institution and street. The child finds in these three fields responses to his identity, affective and material needs. Such complementarity therefore springs from the complementarity of responses to the child's needs. This balanced relation is the result of the cognitive activity of the child, who finds positive references in all three fields. The references are positive, as these fields are interaction configurations (Elias 1994) in which the child finds his place as a subject. The relation between the positions occupied by individuals who constitute the field (Bourdieu 1984) – or configuration – enable the child to become a social actor himself.

However, from the age of 14, Mamo exits the street because of a decrease in the complementarity between fields. Indeed, the street becomes more dangerous for the child as he grows and his physical appearance changes. He is gradually perceived more like an adult by the street users and the police, and becomes more visible. He is also entering the age when people start to stigmatise older CSS: 'they look at you with an evil eye',[5] Mamo tells us. This change in perception, added to the fact that Mamo changes schools and starts to work, brings about his final exit from the street. This example relates only to a minority of CSS, as it entails the positive insertion into at least one of the two fields valued by society: school and family. Even if they represent only a fraction of the children, such cases are far from exceptional. Moreover, these children exit the street without any adult intervention.

For most children, the street experience is overarching, in that it tends to nullify the screens – family, home, school – that usually separate children from the adult world. There is no more mediation between them and the street world as a whole,

[5] *te quedan mirando feo.*

and the child is directly confronted with the other users of the street space.[6] The intensity of the experience often implies a total commitment for the child, a mobilisation of all of their physical, affective and symbolic resources.

The idea of life on the street having a high degree of intensity implies a reference to a state of dependency towards this way of life. It is difficult to break this relation of dependency by oneself. It requires an encounter with someone, or an event. But it is such encounters, according to Ricardo, that allow accumulated street experiences to be made fruitful. Such an evaluation of the street is not rare – quite the contrary.[7]

The street, with its dangers and uncertainties, also includes the paradoxical interspersing of the same and the unprecedented. The alternation between one and the other is an important element of the conditioning of a child by the street world. Exiting the street entails a strong uncertainty that is difficult to overcome alone.[8] It can be said that this conditioning, and the uncertainty of 'after-the-street', contribute to keeping children on the street.

Ricardo's exit from the street was kickstarted by a double encounter and an event, and it holds a paradigmatic value. The encounter with one or several people and the event that is associated with them leads to the construction of the motivation necessary for a child to contemplate leaving the street. The child can then imagine a credible option for the future other than the street. Importantly, the richest and most promising encounters will only have a positive follow-up if they occur at the 'right time', when the child is in a receptive situation and therefore looking for plausible alternatives to their situation. For this right time to happen, a child must first evaluate the price they pay for staying on the street, and this price must be deemed higher than the value of the benefits they receive from the street. This equation is difficult for a child to pose, as it requires them to imagine a different future, yet one that they think is credible. This is when encounters with one or several people and a key event are crucial. The thought process started by the child is not only instrumental and practical, but also has an identitary and affective dimension.

---

[6] It is true that in favelas, children are also very much involved in the adult world. The mediation and filtering effect of families and schools towards the surrounding environment is often very weak. Work and the lack of personal space (with much mingling between different age groups and genders) lead to a very early confrontation with the adult world. This early confrontation is not necessarily bad for the child. It becomes so when it includes an emotional and identitary excess that the child is not able to control.

[7] A constant and systematic devaluation of life on the street by interveners and aid programmes therefore does not match reality as children live it. Rather it is necessary to re-organise a child's street experiences towards a longer term project, which includes their insertion into the community. Such an inclusive policy implies long-term programmes by organisations that work with CSS. Indeed, it necessitates collaboration between NGOs, community organisations, city authorities and services, as well as potential employers on the labour market.

[8] This is not the case for children who are on the street for short time periods, and for whom the main motivation to be there is leisure. Neither is it the case for children who systematically alternate between street, home and institutions. In such cases we can speak of a complementary relation between different fields, as we have seen.

When the street exit is solely motivated by practical reasons, it will be questioned and often dismissed as soon as the child slightly changes their calculation.

Ricardo's case is particularly interesting, as it shows the progressive nature of the exit from the street, and the necessary presence of an event that acts as a catalyst. Ricardo remembers the precise date – the 3rd of December – of his first encounter with the person who offered help. He was 14 years old and during this meeting he and his friend earned some money by helping a merchant from the fair. This person behaved well towards him,[9] and Ricardo even suspected foul intentions, as there were rumours that foreigners (*gringos*) kidnapped children to sell them. One month later he sees this person again, as she is the leader of a community-based welfare programme in a deprived neighbourhood. Ricardo then agrees to go to her house with his friend, where they shower, get new clothes, and have a meal. All of this surprises them greatly,[10] but they like it. They then both start to attend the community centre, still living on the street. This will last two years.[11]

During this time, Ricardo alternates between the street and the community centre, but without abandoning the former. He does not exit, as it is still the streets that provide him with the most rewards: money, adventures, social recognition amongst his peers and hence a social status, a feeling of freedom due to an absence of institutional obligations, freedom of movement, etc. However, the most important thing keeping the child on the street is the opportunity to benefit both from both the advantages offered by the street and those offered by the community. There is therefore a practical logic, a calculation from Ricardo. The intervener (educator or social worker) must take into account this rationale when they seek to motivate a child towards an exit from the street.

For such a dynamic to be brought to an end an event must happen that modifies a child's life and narrative, in this case by altering the relation they have with the street but also with the community centre and society at large. For Ricardo this event was his arrest on vandalism charges (he and a friend were accused of burning a judge's car), his detention in an institution for underage offenders, and, most importantly, contact with his mother. He was almost seventeen years old, the age at which CSS most often start seeing the street as a dead end. Physically he indeed looks more and more like an adult, becoming more visible and therefore attracting more attention from repressive forces and other street users. The child struggles to negotiate with this new visibility, as it imposes an identity that does not attract much legitimacy on the street. This visibility is primarily the result of the new stigma, that of the child who has become physically mature. He now projects an image that

[9] *fue tan especial conmigo.*

[10] *nos extrano bastante.*

[11] When children claim to want to exit the street, it is very difficult to know their true intention. As Turnbull Plaza writes: 'Whether they really want to leave the streets and the drug is never clear. But they know that we want to hear it. In a normal visit, more than one of them will talk about rehabilitation without any prompt from the outsider. The naive visitor would believe that many of them are on the verge of leaving the street and quitting drugs' (Turnbull Plaza 1998, p. 115).

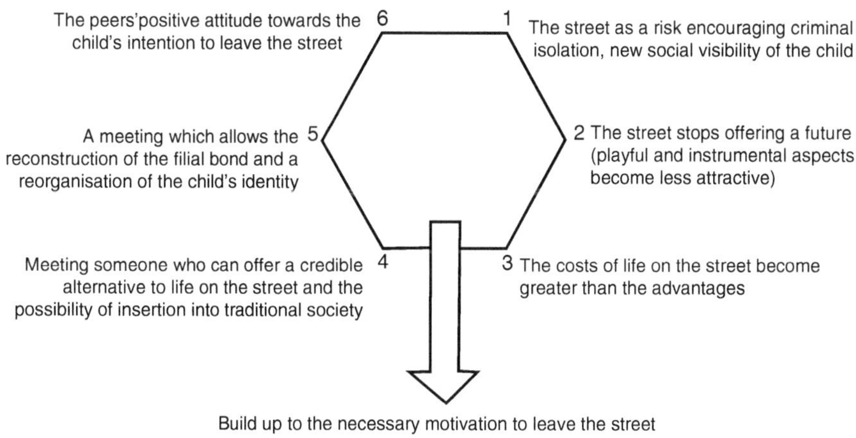


**Fig. 6.2** Process of exiting the street

implies a form of deviance. The child therefore becomes much more receptive to calls to the abandon the street as a way of life.

For Ricardo, meeting his mother again after several years was of the utmost importance. He saw her on Mother's Day, while he was still incarcerated. In tears, she told him she wanted to do everything possible to get him out. These tears his mother cries for him[12] are decisive, as they reconstitute the connection between mother and son. They are the proof that he exists in her life. Ricardo's arrest was not the event that, by itself, enabled his biographical break, but it was the occasion for mother and son to reunite. The core of his biographical break is constituted by this newfound connection, and all that it entails for him in terms of identity (re)construction. The attitude of the members of the Ricardo's group also pushes him to seize the occasion to exit the street. But the final decision is nevertheless very difficult to make. Ricardo tells us that it required a huge effort.

It is thus possible to schematically reconstitute Ricardo's street exit as the outcome of a process encompassing several elements (Fig. 6.2).

We see that the street exit can only happen through time, and this time varies from child to child. Indeed, each child is a unique case with their own personal story and sensibilities.

The most important element for a child who starts to engage with the exiting process is the re-organisation of their identity system. This means they must find, or find again, personal references that enable them to mentally project a future outside of the street. It does not mean, however, that a child must make a clean slate of everything they have learned on the street, nor must they disavow what they used to value, such as skills acquired on the street, friendships and solidarity, and the pride of knowing how to live in a dangerous environment, for example. They therefore value at least part of their street experience. For the children who have a strong

[12] *yo vi a mi mama derramar una lacrima por mi.*

identity claim bound to this experience, having lived on the street was not only a way of life due to circumstances, but also a choice.[13]

Exiting the street therefore depends on the type of complementarity that exists between the street world and other fields. This complementarity will itself be a influenced by the child's references and representations (activities or cognitive skills), along with more structural elements such as the place occupied within different fields. A child will use this place as a resource to position himself according to the different stakes – material, identitary, and affective – at play in each field at a specific time. When given the choice, a child will stay in the field that offers them the most rewarding place. This choice is not always final however, as each field's structure can change over time, and a child moves from one field to another; hence the frequent return to the street that we have observed.

The cases of Donald (16 years old) and Carine (21 years old) from Mexico City illustrate a situation in which the street in fact offers the most rewarding place. The former left his family to escape an authoritarian father, for whom he retains a lot of respect. On the street, he discovers the influence he seems to naturally exert on the children around him. This discovery is crucial to understand why Donald stayed on the street despite the affection he keeps for both of his parents, and despite the worry that his father's heart condition gives him. Indeed, it is on the street that he became conscious of his influence upon others, rather than being constantly subject to his father's authority. He did not use this influence to gain any leadership power; rather he used it to act as an arbitrator when conflict arose between other children. This bestowed on him a very rewarding identity, especially in contrast with his family situation. It was therefore out of question for Donald to exit the street and come back home. School was equally out of the question: Donald did not refuse school as such, but only insofar as it implied coming back home, and with this submission to his father. He was simply against any exit that involved living at home. Two attempts to come back were in fact unsuccessful. Donald nevertheless recognised that the street, for all it gives him – autonomy, prestige, money, leisure – does not hold any future for him. He worked for about three months in a restaurant, washing the dishes for around $100 per month. He could easily have earned more on the street, through odd jobs or petty crime, and over less time. Income was therefore not the main reason for this first exit attempt. It was rather because of the influence of an educator. Donald eventually quit his job because he could not change or wash his clothes. He was embarrassed to come to work looking dirty, he explains, because he was already

[13] It must be said that not all children express such a discourse about life on the street. Indeed, children who experience the street almost only as a suffering does not valorise it, and will usually present themself as victims. We find here the difference between children who have an active rapport with the street and those for whom it is only a fatality. L. Aptekar has differentiated these two categories of children (Aptekar 1988a, b, pp. 55–78). He distinguishes between *gamines* and *chupagruesos*. About this he writes: 'Where the *gamine* defines himself independent of others, the *chupagrueso* sees himself in relation to others.' The former claim to have chosen to leave their original home, whereas the latter explain they were chased away. They define themselves as victims and do not like the street. I have noted this broad difference between children myself during my fieldwork in Rio de Janeiro (Lucchini 1993).

seen as a 'street child'. As he was no longer completely living on the street at that time, he found this look particularly unfair and stigmatising. As long as the street was more rewarding, even if only in the short term, the child prefers it to other ways of life. He permanently exited the street when he was accepted by a military boarding school. This allowed him to see his father without living with him. A rehabilitation programme enabled the exit.

The street was also the most rewarding space for Carine. This young mother of two children who live with their grandmother chose to remain on the street, despite the possibilities offered to her – housing financed by an assistance programme, a home return with paid work opportunities – to exit and live with her children. The street remained attractive to her because of the dominant position she occupied amongst her small group. She acted as mother for certain children, and as wife for others. She would be the mediator for any conflict, and be in charge of the distribution of food, inhalants or money placed under her care. Furthermore, she would shop for the group of children, find buyers for their stolen goods and cook warm meals. This made them feel more like a family, which suited everyone.

Carine was hence able to control a large part of the group's resources, without this position requiring great effort or investment from her. It was enough to navigate between different registers – mother, lover, arbitrator, supervisor – to maintain a great deal of influence on all of the group's children. For the children the cost of disputes between each other was deemed greater than Carine's arbitration and the fees she would charge. Therefore her influence relied on her specific roles rather than on any kind of natural authority. Her presence also provided a relative security to the location occupied by the group, as it was possible to store goods (clothes, food, inhalants, money, stolen objects) under her supervision. We see a complementarity between the children's needs and Carine's, and this enabled her to retain her power. It is also important to note that the children negotiated and haggled with each other very often in order to secure a positive decision from Carine. This competition for Carine's backing not only strengthened her influence, but was also a factor in the stability and order of the group. Her leadership was fragile, as it relied on the children's changing needs and the competition she managed to establish between them.

Carine exited the street only when the territory occupied by the group was definitively lost.[14] This loss did not change the group's composition, but immediately modified its functioning and organisation. Carine's authority drastically decreased, as she could not control a territory used for the children's private needs anymore. The wasteland (*baldio*) was a place of meeting and rest, protected from the gaze of an otherwise very busy neighbourhood. It offered a degree of privacy to the children, of which Carine was the guarantor. The street therefore ceased to be rewarding for her, but also became less safe as a living space. She would likely have had to become a sex worker or a beggar, and, as she categorically refused both, exiting became the only solution. Carine then returned to her father's home, and he made

[14]This territory was wasteland surrounded by a high wall, which was eventually transformed into a parking lot by the city council. This space was situated in a zone that included metro and bus stations, supermarkets, stores, restaurants, kiosks, open-air markets, parking lots and two parks.

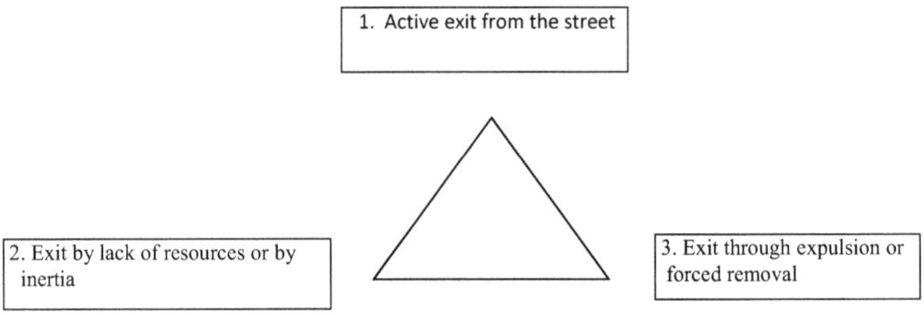


**Fig. 6.3** Types of exit from the street

space available for her and her children.[15] Carine's street exit occurred, then, because of the exhaustion of resources on the street.[16]

Both Donald and Carine illustrate cases of children for whom the street offered the possibility of social rewards and important contributions to identity formation. Psychoactive drugs played a rather minor role in the street's appeal for these children. The street exit process begins as soon as the street's rewards start to decline. This is evident for Carine, but Donald's case is slightly different. Indeed, he does not have a much of a plan when he starts entering the street. It is a kind of challenge for him to gradually pull away from his family, and in the end completely leave them. He discovers the influence he holds over other children and soon enjoys live on the street, in terms of the independence, money, surprises, friendships, and risk it offers. Life on the street allows him to rebuild his self-esteem, so much that it enables him to construct the project to finish his secondary schooling within the army. As soon as this occasion presents itself, he exits the street, for he has also exhausted its resources.[17]

It is possible to differentiate three types of exit from the street (see Fig. 6.3 hereunder): active exit from the street; exit because of the exhaustion of resources or because of inertia; exit because of expulsion or forced relocation.

The active exiting of the street is connected to a choice and to a project that is elaborated during the process of leaving the street. In order for there to be a project, it is necessary that the child imagine their future out of the street. It is also necessary that they have a tangible and desired future. For this category of children, the street

[15] This exiting process lasted several months, first supported by workers from an assistance programme, then by my research assistants (S. Chanfon and L. Alvarado), who tried to look for viable alternatives for Carine outside of the street. At first the exit process failed because the assistance programme's condition was that Carine undertake a tubal ligation, which she refused. Then she went to live in a temporary room financed by the programme, but came back onto the street because she hated living alone. The final exit only happened after the clearing of the *baldio*, though Carine then often came back to the street to visit her old friends. This exit was therefore prepared and facilitated by third parties.

[16] We will discuss this type of street exit further.

[17] It must be noted that this this project was prepared with the support of my research assistants, who not only helped out with some practical elements, but also extensively discussed with Donald the necessity of undertaking such a move.

becomes a laboratory in which they experiment with an identity connected to a post-street project. This child contributes to the creation of opportunities that allow them to leave the street. The active exit of the street has several modalities:

1. The first modality is when life on the street, from the beginning, is part of a project that connects three fields: the street, school and the family. The three fields form a system whose coherence is secured by their integration in terms of meeting the material, affective, and symbolic necessities of the child, as well as their needs in terms of identification. Exiting takes place with the rupture of this integration. The obstacles that impede an exit from the street are considerably reduced and it is the child who decides to abandon it. External influence, such as assistance programmes or other professional interventions, is normally absent. It is a self-controlled exit (Castel 1998). This type of exit from the street does not require any modification of the biographical line of the child. It is also one that has the fewest temporary returns to the street.
2. A second modality is when there is no integration between the three fields of street, family, and assistance programme or institution prior to leaving the street. This exit begins when a first meeting provokes integration between the street and an intervention programme or another place outside the street. This weakens the street's centrality in the child's reference system. However, words alone are not sufficient and it is necessary that an event takes place that questions the biographical line of the child: for instance, a death threat, the risk of being institutionalised for a long period of time, or the valuing of the identification with a person who is affectively important for the child. It is also necessary that they can benefit from that which is offered as an alternative to life on the street. Leaving the street, therefore, organises itself around a new reference of identification, of a real alternative to the street and a new self-image. This kind of exit demands a radical change in the biographical line of the child, for life on the street comprises an exclusive way of life. The exit is partially controlled.[18] The main component of the leaving process concerns identification.[19]
3. A third modality is also characterized by the absence of integration between the different fields and the street, but the street is experienced by the child as an all-encompassing life environment which is at the same time temporary: the street is a parenthesis that contains the development of a post-street project. The gratifying character of the street, in the material field and in the field of identification, gives it an essentially playful and hedonistic connotation. Leaving the street occurs without there being any integration between the street and another field, which is always the case in the second aspect of exiting the street. Leaving the

[18] Here we do not find full attention on the part of an institution but only the support of someone who the child trusts.

[19] Other factors also interfere, such as the child's resilience. Despite the criticism levelled at this concept, as it implies a normative dimension that is not made sufficiently explicit, there is no doubt that among children there are different ways of living through events that are hazardous to their development. Here I do not touch on the necessarily contentious use of this concept of development and of the stages that comprise it. This would be beyond the scope of this chapter.

street does not contain an initial phase in which the child alternates or circulates between the street and other fields. This leaving the street only requires a partial biographical rupture. Indeed, the child always considers life on the street as a parenthesis that they can close and move beyond at any moment. It is not sufficient that an occasion appears for the child to seize it or want it. For this to happen they must still rely on external support. As in the previous modality the exit here is partially controlled.

4. A fourth modality of leaving the street is characterised by the impact of a transformation in the child's identification to the adults who they meet on the street. The refusal of a *marginalizing identity* by the child is at the centre of this process of exiting.[20] For this modality we can take the example of Samuel, a child from Tegucigalpa, Honduras, who exited the streets at 17 years old. For this child, the street consists of diverse activities that allow them to meet many needs: material, playful, social and in terms of identification. For a long time, this street is not propitious to the implementation of a process of leaving, as the Samuel's biographical line is determined by his way of living in the world of the street. This excludes any insertion of the child into another configuration: family, school, work, or institution. His exit process is initiated when he acknowledges a change in the behaviour of passers-by in relation to him. He speaks of the hostile gaze of others ("everyone saw me as bad"), observing that they will do anything to avoid him on the street. He is profoundly shocked by the attitude of women who cross over the street in order to avoid passing him by. At first he does not understand these actions: they imply a new learning about life on the street. When he understands that he is perceived as a potential aggressor, he feels very angry.[21] Samuel refuses this identity and begins his exit from the street in two periods.

First he tries to remain on the street by adopting a strategy in which his presence may be more acceptable to others. In order to do this, he becomes a shoeshine again, and afterwards a chewing gum and cigarette salesman. Someone still helps him in this. But this does not last very long, because he uses his earnings to buy inhalants. Then he and a friend find jobs as security guards at a car park in the city centre. Both stop using inhalants at the same time and use the money to buy clothes and food. Samuel is then not alone when he leaves the street, and this exit with a friend is strengthened by their sharing of the task of the job at the car park. This change of behaviour is important because it allows a connection between the child's exit and the question of the frames of references that orient his actions.[22]

---

[20] It is not, however, a change of identification that is induced by a meeting with the mother and the person responsible for an intervention programme. However, for the two children the changes in identity are connected to changes in their physical appearance. They are both perceived by others as young adults and as a potential threat by other people on the street (passers-by, shopkeepers, police).

[21] Other children, at different places, have also spoken to me about this same feeling.

[22] The concept of a frame is not the same as that of the field. The latter refers to a collection of relations between social positions that contain phenomena referring to power, influence and the negotiation between things. The concept of the frame of reference or reference group has to do with the

In Samuel's case, there are four different frames of reference that each gradually led him away from the street. The first corresponds to the looks he received from passers-by, whose stigmatisation he refused to accept. The second concerns the other children's attitude; those who stayed on the street became hostile towards Samuel when he started leaving, which was seen as a form of treason. The third is people's gaze towards his former companions who stayed on the street (*la gente los quedaba viendo*); while not affecting him directly, Samuel nevertheless feels the stigma. The fourth frame of reference concerns inhalants, which Samuel progressively stopped using.

Samuel's street exit therefore begins when he realises that his street presence is incompatible with the image he has of himself. He has no intention of attacking people who seemed diffident towards him. He could take on, like many other children, an attitude of protest, and adopt the behaviours that adults come to expect from CSS: ostentatious public consumption of inhalants and aggressive actions among them. If Samuel acted in this manner he would not have effectively started his street exit. Rather it would have been delayed in favour of a passage towards adult criminality. Indeed, the connection between stigmatisation and the behaviour it induces has been analysed by E. M. Lemert (1975) as a 'secondary deviance'. In such a case, an individual regarded as deviant takes on this attribute and starts incorporating it into their identity. They end up seeing themselves as deviant, and behave accordingly. As Lemert (1975, p. 170) writes: 'when a person begins to employ his deviant behaviour or a role based upon it as a means of defence, attack, or adjustment to the overt and covert problems created by the consequent societal reaction to him, his deviation is secondary'. Secondary deviance is more easily constructed when the social visibility of a person perceived as deviant is significant, when behaviours and attitudes considered deviant are frequent, and when they are subject to much public response. As we see, there was a high chance of Samuel experiencing secondary deviance and staying on the street.

The existence of an alternative project to the street and of a dynamic of identification is what all four kinds of exit of the street have in common. In terms of the differences, there are four aspects that are immediately apparent: (1) the absence of a biographical rupture in the first case, the radical rupture on the second and fourth cases and a partial rupture in the third case; (2) the rupture of the integration between the three fields leads to an abandonment of the street in the first case, while in the second it is the establishing of an integration between the street and the field of the adult of reference who is outside the street, who is crucial for initiating the exit from the street and supporting them; in the third and fourth cases, exiting the street occurs without the need of any integration; (3) in the first and fourth cases leaving the street

mechanisms that "serve to link men to groups and their values". This concept applies, therefore, to questions that have to do with the normative orientation of individuals and the structuring of their expectations in relation to their environment. This environment can be near or distant, or both at the same time. Often, individuals orient themselves through groups to which they do not belong to or through individuals who they do not know. The structuring of expectations can also occur through mythical or dreamed characters. Often individuals have multiple references, which are, at times, very diverse (Merton 1965).

is self-regulated, while in the other two cases it is in part the result of what Soulet (1997) terms spontaneous control[23]; (4) life on the street is considered by the child as a parenthesis in the first and third cases, while in the second and fourth it is totally undetermined by time.

The second type of exit from the street, exiting because of expulsion or forced removal from the street, is concerned with cases of the prolonged institutionalisation or imprisonment of the child. Here, rupture with the world of the street almost always means the insertion of the child into the world of adult delinquency. In any case, the youngster who leaves prison or an institution after some years can no longer find their place on the street. For these youngsters, as well as for other children who have had a long existence on the street, family does not constitute a real alternative. As Bernardo Turnbull Plaza writes (1998, p. 164), "the obvious difference between the institution's agenda and that of the youngster has to do with the reintegration into the family: they no longer see this as an alternative to the street. There is also the additional discrepancy between the superiority of our point of view over theirs". We will see this in leaving the street because of the exhaustion of resources and in the aborted attempts at exiting.

The third type of exit from the street, leaving because of exhaustion of resources (material, symbolic, affective, and social), differs from the active exit because the child does not have a project or a real alternative to the street. Sources of gratification are exhausted and the child remains on the street through lack of choice and inertia. The exhaustion of resources has a subjective and objective aspect. The first is cognitive and concerns the child's perception of the street and its associated images. The second has to do with changes in the configurations that structure life on the street, such as networks of children, networks of adults and children, police repression, assistance programmes, and the informal economy. The exhaustion of subjective resources can manifest itself without there being any change in the objective resources.

In this kind of exit the motivation to leave the street is not absent but it is above all reactionary. In leaving the street the child reacts rather than acts. Normally the only options that they have are to return home or to go to an institution. This is a very unstable exit and often has many returns to the street. It occurs in children for whom the street no longer has any specific attraction but whose biographical line is not changed in any significant way. The exhaustion of the resources of the street means that the street becomes a place in which the child can no longer make choices in terms of survival strategies, spatial mobility and sociability, even if they belong to a network or group. The pleasure of living on the street has gone. Even the excitement in the risk connected to certain activities has lost its attraction. The exit because of the exhaustion of resources is more fragile than the active exit because it is improvised and occurs because of "a lack of better things". This exit is marked by resignation and the anticipation of probable failure. It is for this reason that the exit

[23] This means that the exit is connected to a project of intervention by an adult – professional or researcher. As Soulet writes, the process "of managing an alternation between relational distance and proximity is particularly difficult in some types of social work such as that of working on the street".

because of the exhaustion of resources is very close to the aborted attempts at leaving the street.

From the affective point of view, leaving the street because of the exhaustion of resources seems more painful than the active exit of the street. It brings with it the reestablishment of family ties, with all that this implies in terms of rethinking and questioning that which "is not said". For the children, as well as for the parents, the responsibility for failure cannot be attributed to a third party or outside causes. The actors are placed before themselves. It is one of the reasons that explains the hesitations and questionings of the children who wish to leave the street.

Let us take the example of Alda. Alda is a 22-year-old woman from Ciudad de Mexico who ran away from home for the first time aged six.[24] Alda has stayed in institutions several times, but she always comes back to the street. She never completely lost touch with her mother, calling her sporadically and even coming back to her home on a handful of occasions, but again without the intention of leaving the street. When discussing her mother with a social worker Alda seemed very tense, repeating a lot of questions rather than answering them, even anticipating the social worker's words. Alda also learns that her mother lives with a man she did not know (Alda did not know her father, who disappeared before she was born). This led Alda to conclude that her mother behaved exactly like her, with multiple partners. She did not, however, want to be like her mother, and claimed that she had changed. Their relationship seemed very strained. In the first encounter that we witnessed, the mother said to the daughter: "I curse the day you were born, you're are a bad daughter". Alda replied: "I'm not the girl you knew any more […] I know how to defend myself if you try to beat me like you used to at home".

A neighbour confirmed to us the abuse that Alda suffered as a child. She was even placed in an institution to escape the violence of her half-brothers, her mother's partner, her uncle, and her mother herself. It was from institution that she ran away from to go to the street for the first time.[25] Many years later, a meeting between the now-adult Alda and her mother was organised. After such a long time without seeing each other Alda was extremely nervous, first of all worrying that her mother would simply not recognise her. Her grandmother had previously told her to forget about her mother, and to not count on her. The meeting nevertheless happened, in the company of Alda's partner and two social workers. Not only was her mother distant towards her daughter, but she also spoke hurtfully. For example, when Alda asked for her birth certificate in order to legally register her own child's birth, her

[24] Alda has been through four pregnancies. The first time a policeman raped her at the age of 12. She was living with a violent man who during an argument violently beat her, causing a miscarriage. With another partner she gave birth to a girl who died of heart problems within two weeks. She later had another two children: a boy who was taken by his father's uncle, and from whom she lost all trace, and a toddler with whom she was living when we met her on the street. She was looking unhealthy, and her daughter was evidently not taken care of. For eight years Alda had been the partner of a man who wasn't the father of either of these children. She had performed a wide range of survival practices during that time, from prostitution and petty theft to street tricks.

[25] Alda's family story is similar to Ricardo's, and both children were heavily reliant on the street for the reasons we have seen. Their street exits, however, are completely different. Ricardo had an active exit, whereas Alda left following an exhaustion of resources.

mother replied: "I registered my daughter Carmela, but not her". Carmela is one of Alda's half-sisters, and the message was very clear: Alda has no mother any longer. Alda was born out of wedlock and for this she suffered violence at the hands of her own mother, and indeed Alda's mother's story contains much violence, at the centre of which is several rapes. She also practiced prostitution.

After this visit, Alda returned to the street with her partner and child. She was pregnant again. Shortly after, the couple exited the street with the help of a charity that managed to contact the young man's family. They went back to a town in the south of the country, where his family homed them. A few months later, however, Alda went back to Mexico City with her child, and we lost track of her.

## 6.5 Exit Attempts

Attempts at leaving the street have to do first and foremost with the family, and, to a lesser extent, with institutions (like assistance programmes). The latter constitute a stage in the process that takes the child out of the street, or else they are simply used by the children as an easy way of obtaining shelter and food. The child regularly leaves the assistance programmes when these no longer meet their expectations and when their needs are met. In these cases, the child does not have the intention of leaving the street, and staying in the institution is for "taking some time out". The narratives of children and adolescents about this are very revealing.

The attempts at leaving the street must not be confused with the visits that children make to their families without any intention of staying. It is not always easy to make this distinction, as they frequently alternate between home and the street. In order for us to speak about an attempt at leaving, it is necessary that the child show a wish to leave the street through concrete actions. Amongst these actions we find repetitive returns home with the intention of staying, repeated requests through an intermediary or an adult of reference to be taken back home, and the search for a stable job outside the street. The changes in behaviour of children and adolescents reflect a wish to leave the street. A decrease in the consumption of inhalants, the refusal to participate in risky activities like robbing and stealing, the direct criticism of friends who behave like "street children", the growing anxiety to return home, and the wish to live with a woman outside the street are examples that show such a change in behaviour. The intention to leave the street is also seen in unprecedented behaviour such as buying clothes or school material for later use. This sort of behaviour shows that a significant change is taking place: the capacity of postponing gratification. The child already begins to identify with roles and practices that do not belong to the world of the street. However, these changes remain fragile, for returning home requires preparation. It must be made real and, therefore, be more than a simple wish to leave the street.

The aborted attempt of returning home is essentially connected to two factors. There is, first of all, the refusal of parental authority and the hostility of an adult – normally the stepfather or stepmother – in relation to the child. The child is also incapable of finding a place in a group whose members are no longer those who were there when the child left for the street. Next there is the discrepancy between what the street offers in terms of entertainment and sociability and the reality of the district where the family home is found. Nostalgia for the street and idleness make the child easily bored. In this way a return to the street is planned.

Exiting the street cannot be build only through a perspective of a return home. The child and in particular the adolescent aspire to the status of the adult, with all that defines this status. They aspire to "the reconstitution of their place in the world" and, therefore, to an "insertion in the universe of normality" (Castel 1998, p. 210). We have here an important reason that explains the failure of leaving the street. The presence of this aspiration distinguishes an attempt at leaving from a mere alternation between the world of the street, the home and the institution. Almost always the same child chronologically goes through a logic of alternation to one of repeated attempts of leaving the street. In the case of the alternation, the child does not have the intention of leaving the street and balances between the two worlds, between which they cannot choose. In this way when a child leaves home to return once again to the street we are not seeing an aborted exit but a new instance of alternation. We find here the integration of the fields. It is only when this integration is weakened that alternation is substituted by the attempt to leave the street.

Returns to the street can be numerous. The story of Morro, from Ciudad de Mexico, illustrates such cases. At 17 years old, Morro returned to the street for the eighth time. On average, his home returns lasted about four months. His longest spell at home was thirteen months and the second longest ten months, while the shortest stay lasted only two weeks. His home stays therefore have very different meanings. The shorter ones – from two to six weeks – fit the logic of alternation, whereas the longer stays constitute attempts to exit the street. Morro said he wanted to build a solid room on a piece of land his parents had bought, although he also declared at the same time that he was in a phase in which he felt neither child nor adult. When we visited him at his parents' home, where he had been living for several weeks, he told us that the street allowed him to become a child again. We see that Morro was torn between two aspirations, neither of which family life offered an appropriate frame for. Indeed, he is unable to become an adult at home – he has a strong relationship of dependence with his mother, and one of submission to her partner – but neither does it correspond to the image of childhood he can links with the street. Added to this is the attraction of inhalants, which he cannot use at home. These movements back and forth between home and street lasted five years, during which he spent more time at home than on the street. This case shows a child who is searching for a plausible alternative to the street, but fails to find one. We do not merely see an alternation, but a series of exit attempts.

After a failed exit attempt, the intention of a CSS to change lifestyles can be expressed, paradoxically, through an exaggeration of 'street child' attitudes and behaviours: the child uses inhalants more, becomes more aggressive towards other children and intervening parties, and no longer seems to care about the image they present of themselves.

For many children, failed exit attempts are the counterpart of what happened when they left their family home. Indeed, their departure often happened in stages: stays on the street interspersed by returns home. These situations indicate that a child is neither completely at home nor on the street. It must also be noted again that a child who has been placed in an institution – most often by their mother – is likely to show the strongest desire to return home. However, these children are often the least active when it comes to concrete return planning.

We have shown that a child's career, identity, and the nature of relationships between fields all condition the manner in which the child exits the street. The existence of a plausible project for after the street, along with events and encounters between the child and an adult, also influence the process of exiting the street. The length of this process varies greatly between children, and often depends on the number of failed exit attempts. In general, when a child approaches the age of legal adulthood, they become more active in their search for an alternative to the street. They know that from a criminal perspective they will not be considered as children, and are hence at greater risk. Furthermore, access to assistance programmes will become more difficult. This influences a child's decision to exit the street.

We have seen that it is possible to differentiate between three types of street exit, and between different modalities of implementing these exits. This diversity is key in order to apprehend the psycho-sociological heterogeneity that characterises CSS. It is a factor that any intervening party must take into account, as it concerns a child's attachment both to the street and to elements outside the street. Furthermore, the street exit does not always follow a linear process, gradually leading a child from the street to the non-street. Indeed, the process incorporates many returns to the street. A child must not only be able to exit the street for a time and have the option to return, but also be able to bring to mind this possibility. Often children mention their intention to exit the street without actually believing in the prospect. They merely anticipate an exit that they know is inevitable, and respond to what they know adults expect from them. In actuality, the street exit itself is a learning process, made of a succession of trials and errors. The length and the progress of this process varies widely, as children have the challenge of coming to question their way of life and the habitus that accompanies it. We have shown that the street exit is never improvised, but must on the contrary be prepared as the last stage of a career in the street. Its execution therefore depends on all the previous stages of this career. Any intervening party must hence take into consideration the child's street career if they wish to successfully accompany them through the street exit process.

## References

Aptekar, L. (1988a). *Street children of Cali*. Durham: Duke University Press.
Aptekar, L. (1988b). Street children of Colombia. *Journal of Early Adolescence, 8*(3), 225–241.
Bourdieu, P. (1984). *Questions de sociologie*. Paris: Editions de Minuit.
Castel, R. (1998). *Les sorties de la toxicomanie*. Fribourg: Éditions Universitaires de Fribourg.

Connoly, M. (1990). Adrift in the city: A comparative study of the street children in Bogotá, Colombia and Guatemala city. In N. A. Boxill (Ed.), *Homeless children, the watchers and waiters* (pp. 129–149). New York: The Haworth Press.

Elias, N. (1994). *The civilizing process*. Oxford: Blackwell.

Ennew, J. (1994). Parentless friends: A cross-cultural examination of networks among street children and street youth. In F. Nestmann & K. Hurrelmann (Eds.), *Social networks and social support in childhood and adolescence* (pp. 409–426). Berlin/New York: de Gruyter.

Fernández, D. (1995). *Mulumbureando. La cultura de los niños de la calle*. Ciudad de México: CRT.

Fischer, G. N. (1984). *La psychosociologie de l'espace*. Paris: PUF.

Fischer-Ferreira, M. (1979). *Meninos da rua*. São Paulo: IBREX.

Hewitt, J. P. (1970). *Social stratification and deviant behavior*. New York: Random House.

Lemert, E. M. (1975). Primary and secundary deviation. In S. H. Traub & C. B. Little (Eds.), *Theories of deviance* (pp. 167–172). Itasca: Peacock Publishers.

Lepoutre, D. (1997). *Coeur de banlieue. Codes, rites et langages*. Paris: Odile Jacob.

Lucchini, R. (1993). *L'enfant de la rue. Identité, sociabilité, drogue*. Paris/Genève: Droz.

Lucchini, R. (1996). *Sociologie de la survie: l'enfant dans la rue*. Paris: PUF.

Lucchini, R. (1998). L'enfant de la rue: réalité complexe et discours réducteurs. *Déviance et Société, 22*(4), 347–366.

Merton, R. K. (1965). *Éléments de théorie et de méthode sociologique*. Paris: Plon.

Ogien, A. (1995). *Sociologie de la déviance*. Paris: Colin.

Parazelli, M. (2000). L'appropriation de l'espace et les jeunes de la rue: un enjeu identitaire. In D. Laberge (Ed.), *L'errance urbaine* (pp. 193–220). Sainte-Foy: Éditions Multi Mondes.

Riaño-Alcalá, Y. (1990). *Las Galladas: Street youth and cultural identity in the barrios of Bogota*. York University (unpublished manuscript).

Soulet, M.-H. (1997). *Petit précis de grammaire indigène du travail social*. Fribourg: Editions universitaires de Fribourg.

Taracena, E. (1995). Enfants de la rue et enfants dans la rue à Mexico, Lien social et politique. In *Revue internationale d'action communautaire* (Vol. 34, pp. 101–118).

Taracena, E., & Tavera, M. (1998). La fonction du groupe chez les enfants de la rue à Mexico. In S. Tessier (Ed.), *A la recherche des enfants de la rue* (pp. 70–87). Paris: Karthala.

Turnbull Plaza, B. E. (1998). Street children and their helpers. A social interface analysis. PHD, University of Sussex.

Visano, L. (1990). The socialisation of street children: The development and transformation of identities. *Sociological Studies of Child Development, 3*, 139–161.

# Chapter 7
# The Social Bond and Sociability on the Street

**Riccardo Lucchini**

## 7.1 Gang, Network, "near-Group": Collective Sociability

Children in street situations (hereafter CSS) are characterised by a high spatial mobility and the short duration of their social relationships. These relationships can be intense and immerse the children completely, or can be intermittent and superficial. A relationship being short term, then, does not imply a lack of intensity or personal involvement.

Survival on the streets is made up of conflicts and complicities, and these make it difficult for the child to maintain a distance from the events that affect him or her. All the children in our study are deeply involved and embedded in their daily lives, lives which are intense and allow only brief moments of respite. Yet this emotional intensity is an obstacle to the establishment of lasting and stable social bonds. Spatial, social and material constraints, as well as emotional constraints, mark the social relations of CSS. Individual spatial mobility is in itself a survival strategy that limits the creation of stable and important groups. Furthermore, the children of Praça Carioca do not have to defend a particular territory, as they share the urban space with the other city dwellers. This sharing is one of the conditions of their survival. The absence of assigned and exclusive territories that need defending has a great influence on the relationships between the children themselves, and on the creation of groups in particular. Indeed, a sense of territory or of the space occupied by the members of a group is an essential component of their social and cultural identity.

This chapter is translated from Lucchini, R. (1993). Le lien social et la sociabilité dans la rue, in: Riccardo Lucchini. *Enfant de la rue. Identité, sociabilité, drogue* (pp. 75–105). Genève/Paris: Droz. It is translated and published in English with permission.



R. Lucchini, D. Stoecklin, *Children in Street Situations*, Children's Well-Being: Indicators and Research 21, https://doi.org/10.1007/978-3-030-19040-8_7

That said, the street as a living space is likewise an important component of the individual identity of the child in street situations (hereafter CSS). However, as far as the group is concerned, it must be stressed that the absence of territory makes it harder for a group to form and persist. For this reason, we do not find amongst the CSS of Praça Carioca any gang that is similar to the ones studied by Thrasher (1927), Whyte (1943), or Short and Strodtbeck (1965). In the American cases, the neighbourhood where the gang lives is the territory that they occupy (Whyte 1943). This space is therefore an important component of the identity of the gang and conditions its organisation, making the defence of their territory an imperative the gang cannot ignore. Each member of the gang identifies with the territory it occupies, and defending it adds value to both the group as a whole and to each member individually. The same goes for the gangs (*galladas*) studied by Pilar Riaño-Alcalá (1990) in the *barrios populares* (slums) of Bogotá. An analogous phenomenon can be found in the suburbs of Brazilian cities that have a basic structure formed by a block of individual dwellings. This basic structure, made up of concrete single-storey homes, is called *quadra*. Often, each *quadra* is controlled by a *quadrilha*: a gang of teenagers and young adults. Each *quadrilha* jealously controls its territory, and conflicts between *quadrilhas* are numerous and violent.

The situation of the *quadrilhas* is, however, quite different from that of the *galladas*, or of the younger teenage gangs that live in the *quadras*. Indeed, the activities of the *quadrilhas* are, first and foremost, delinquent: drug trafficking, property crime, and prostitution among them. The *quadrilhas* are therefore closer to organised crime than we would find with a gang of young people whose delinquent activities are not their primary activity. This does not mean that there is no contact or cooperation between a gang of youths and a *quadrilha* that controls the *quadra* it inhabits. *Quadrilhas* often draw new recruits from the gangs and smaller groups that live in their sphere of influence. Moreover, members of *quadrilhas* are on average older than members of gangs, the gangs being made up exclusively of teenagers. With these factors combined, we find a tendency in the suburbs of Brazilian cities for *quadrilhas* and teenage gangs to enter into alliances, yet with the gangs remaining subordinates in these situations.

In the case of CSS, the situation is different. They prefer to use spaces where people congregate and activities take place: city centres with their squares and plazas, stations and markets. But these children do not dislike wastelands or crumbling houses, and parks bring them joy. They do know, however, that these spaces do not belong to them. We noticed that they move from one area of the urban space to another with great ease. They cannot be said to inhabit this space, even if they live in it for a brief period of time. There are cases of settling in urban spaces, but they never involve the 'street' as a public space. More often than not, they are small shelters for night-time: worksite huts, bits of pipes stored on a construction site or a wasteland, abandoned buildings …

If they do use the street, they cannot afford to make it theirs for long, but they know every corner of it and how to make the most of its resources. CSS tend not to identify with a territory as such, and rather take advantage of it only for survival and recreational activities. Their relationship with the street is above all functional and instrumental. The street-space does not have the same meaning for all children, and that it differs across different categories of children in street situations. Yet the fact that this functional approach is predominant in the relationship of CSS with the street does not mean that they find no rewarding aspects to it. It simply implies a fragmentation of the space into several temporary territories. This fragmentation is a function of the child's needs in terms of survival and play, and of the activities that result from them. But yet these territories cannot be compared to the territories defended by gangs in the suburbs.

The presence of the police and a large number of adults using the space does not permit the children to permanently occupy and claim a part of it. The very public character of the city centre, and of Praça Carioca in particular, is an insurmountable obstacle. There is, however, an exception: the monastery's stairs are occupied by children sniffing shoemakers' glue. As we have seen before, this space is a dead end that overlooks Praça Carioca, and so there are no adult passers-by and the children have no competition to face. These stairs are the only territory in our study to have been claimed by a specific group of CSS.

And yet while there are no permanent territories like the ones found in the suburbs, we can, however, speak of partial territories, occupied temporarily and fleetingly. These territories are located in public space and do not fundamentally change its public character. The fear that the presence of CSS provokes in adults is not enough for us to talk about the transformation of public space into private space. The situation is no different when it comes to children who work on the street shining shoes, washing or watching cars, or selling newspapers or other miscellaneous objects. The only distinction is that their presence on the street is perceived by the adults as legitimate, as long as their physical appearance passes for that of a young child or preteen. Rosa Maria Fischer-Ferreira (1979) reports on the transformation of the public space into private space by the children's activities. In this case, it is preferable to speak of a private use of a public space for profit.

The categories of public and private are in fact unsuited to the living conditions of the marginalised social classes from which CSS come. The categories of public and private sphere are a product of the modernisation that industrialised 'northern' societies have undergone since the Industrial Revolution. These categories became more relevant with the emerging formation of the middle class and, as such, are not valid for the social classes excluded from the modernisation process, like those living in high density neighbourhoods. This density manifests itself in two different ways. The first at the spatial level, where we find a very high land use index. Every square metre is used to build shelters, and homes are often built with unsound materials. All this leads to a physical proximity which is a hindrance to the existence of a private space away from the scrutiny of others. The inhabitants use the Spanish phrase '*vecinidad*', meaning neighbourhood, but also proximity, to refer to dwellings which are arranged in a square shape, with all the doors looking out onto a central space (as seen, for example, in Mexico City, in the Colonia Benito Juarez). This high density, added to the layout of the homes, does not facilitate the intimate social relationships that make up the private sphere. The social aspect is therefore characterised by a high visibility of people's behaviours, which naturally leads to a high level of social control. Furthermore, when neighbours need to help each other in order to survive, the formation of a private sphere is impossible. It seems that this lack of intimacy, and most importantly the visibility of others' behaviours, is a crucial part of what drives these children to the street. Regarding underprivileged populations, it is more accurate to oppose the public space to communal space, rather than the private space; and in fact, these categories are a better fit for the study of the function of space in social relationships.

The formation of partial and fleeting territories is - as we will see later on - dependent on the children's activities. The CSS of Praça Carioca do not have a territory comparable to those of gangs from the suburbs, and, with the exception of the monastery's stairs, they do not have a monopoly on the use of the street. During the day, they share the space with many others making use of it, but when it comes to their nocturnal activities, information is almost non existent. This shortcoming is a general one, and there are no studies on the night life of CSS.[1] We can, however, note a difference between the night-time and daytime use of the street: night-time is mostly used for delinquent activities and settling vendettas. Most of the children in our study group are not involved in this use of the street and are, on the contrary, often victims of attacks at night.

A territory is created from daily practices on an individual as well as on a collective level, and is a function of the representations of its users. From "the superposition of individual socio-spatial experiences emerges a 'collective imagination', a true territory" (Di Méo 1991, p. 150). The relative absence of a shared territory similar to the situations in the suburbs does not imply that, if studied individually, children in street situations do not develop a sense of territory. But this is a sense of territory which leads to relationships of varying intensity (op. cit., p. 266). Remaining on the subject of their individual relationships with the street, the children are at a crossroads between, in Di Méo's terms, the endogenous actor and the allogenic actor (op. cit. p. 267). For the allogenic actor, the practical and recreational dimension is primary in their relationship with a space. The endogenous actor, on the other hand, "is deeply rooted within a socio-spatial formation". We will return to this topic when we address the matter of the child's image of the street, where we will see a very differentiated reality appear.

The question of shared territory is also linked to the ecological density that characterises a given urban area. This type of density refers to the relation between the physical and social resources of an area and the number of people depending on them for their survival. An 'artificial' reduction of resources (such as through police repression or bans on children spending time in some places), accompanied by a rise in the number of children in street situations, help to increase the ecological density. A high density is an extra obstacle to the constitution of a territory that is reserved exclusively for the activities of a group of children.

[1]The only data we have on the whereabouts of CSS at night are the nocturnal tallies of children sleeping on the streets in the centre of some Brazilian cities. These tallies are unreliable and only allow for a rough estimate of the children present on public thoroughfares at a given time of the night.

There are many obstacles to the formation of organised gangs of CSS in Praça Carioca as well as other areas in its vicinity (for example Cinelàndia and Lapa): in addition to heavy policing, there is a role played by spatial mobility, the lack of their own shared territory, and the fleeting character of the children's presence in the city centre.

The relatively diffuse nature of social roles under conditions of survival also influences the forms of these children's collective sociability. Instead of a hierarchical, strongly-organised gang which maintains stability over time, what seems to exist is rather networks, near-groups and dyads. The idea of network "refers to a group of connections between actors (individual or collective) that constitute a mobilisable resource base for the achievement of goals specific to particular conditions." Networks concern "light, timely and dissolvable structures which allow for a limited advance on a largely undefined territory" (Houchon 1990, p. 213).

A near-group is a group which is characterised by the following factors:

1. a diffuse definition of roles[2]
2. limited cohesion
3. a transitory nature
4. minimal normative consensus
5. unstable group membership[3]
6. limited expectations of the group from its members[4]

We have not mentioned the factor of 'disturbed leadership' because nothing proves its existence amongst CSS. This characteristic of gangs is also noted by Roger Mucchielli (1965, pp. 183–193). Indeed, the activities of CSS are mostly related to survival activities and to the street as a living environment as a whole. It is not centred on delinquent activity as a primary activity to which all others are subordinated.

As Yablonsky (1979, p. 476) writes, in order to satisfy momentary needs the members of a near-group often give a highly personal definition of their role. This means that the young person adopts a practical attitude towards the near-group. We can also find the same attitude in CSS, because they cannot survive alone on the street. This practical attitude poses the problem of the existence of the network's identitary function. In fact, this function responds above all to needs related to the children's material security and not to their identity needs. When these needs are pressing, the expression of their identity needs is pushed into the background.

The network's identitary function does not seem to be its primary function. Indeed, when speaking of identity, the children prefer referring to 'street children' as a whole, rather than to the particular group they associate with. They know that this association is only temporary and that it could be challenged at any time by

[2] However, when a network member has to perform a specific task (purchasing drugs, stealing, looking for food, scouting for a safe place, hunting for information, contacting a police officer, etc.), his role becomes consistent and precisely delimitated.

[3] See notion of "shifting membership" (Yablonsky 1979).

[4] See Yablonsky (1979).

unexpected events. Moreover, the intensity of these associations can be extremely variable, not only in terms of time but with regards to the children themselves. Children often leave the street for varying lengths of time without any apparent reason or explanation, an occurrence which does not raise questions or surprise anyone.

The running and organisation of networks and near-groups are specific to them, and adapted to this mobility of their most peripheral 'members'. When we refer to these children it is therefore more accurate to speak of association with the network instead of membership to the network. We have observed, in the children of Praça Carioca, the existence of different levels of membership within a network. On this subject, Yablonsky (1979, p. 479) speaks of a "decrease of cohesiveness as one moves from the center of the collectivity to the periphery". As such we will use the notion of membership of a network for the children who form its core (such as Xavier, Ricardo, Cesar, Marco, and Bruno), and the notion of association with a network for the others. Let us remind you again that an in-depth study of a network is made extremely difficult by the children's mobility.

In this way, children in street situations' collective sociability is not related to delinquent subculture as studied by Albert Cohen (1955), or to the 'undesirable' young people studied by François Dubet (1987). In the first case, delinquent subculture is perceived as the product of a process of acculturation and deculturation of young people from underprivileged classes. The origin of this subculture could be found in the conflict of identities that these young people feel when they are confronted with the middle class culture delivered to them by schools. Gangs would then be a way to resolve this conflict. Nothing like this is visible in children in street situations. Their presence on the street owes nothing to a confrontation with the culture and ethos of the middle classes. There is no identity claim in CSS caused by an opposition to a specific out-group.

In France, young people described (and stigmatized) as coming from the « banlieue » live in the low-income housing, and their situation cannot be compared to that of CSS. Their daily lives are characterised by disorganisation, exclusion, and rage (Dubet 1987, pp. 67–93). Disorganisation because of the lack of activities and relational structures, and the absence of the sense of a daily life. Exclusion because of the nature of their relationship with the environment outside of their « banlieue »: they feel excluded by unemployment and poverty. Rage because of the feeling of rebellion and violence produced by a domination that is felt to be faceless and without principle (op. cit., p. 80). Boredom and lack of activities mark the daily lives of these struggling young people, but these are not found in the lives of CSS (types of streets and relationships to the street need to be differentiated). They are not confined to a peripheral space but can move freely through the city, and even from one city to another.

Amongst children in street situations, the existence of networks, near-groups and dyads is predominant, but it does not rule out the existence of more integrated groups. The networks that children are part of do not have a monopoly on their activities. What seems to exist is a mobile and evolving organisation which is, in itself, a function of the activities and problems to be solved: pickpocketing, stealing from a shop or a supermarket, buying and using inhalants, playing, looking for adult support, wandering the streets (which takes up a large part of their day), looking for a job and a way to get off the streets, looking for night-time protection to be able to sleep. It is this mobile organisation which characterises the order of the network, near-group and dyad. Activities shape the mode of association, and not the opposite way around. This kind of flexible organisation is better suited to life on the street than a highly organised and hierarchical gang would be.

The street is a multifaceted environment which requires a great capacity for adaptation from the children. The flexibility of the types of partnership between the children offers such adaptability, and it is from this adaptability that the strategies derive (see Chap. 5). Some of the children (for example, Fabio, Daniel, or Julio) admit that they prefer to be alone rather than be part of a group. But, depending on the circumstances and on their needs, they can be part of a network. It is not so much a refusal to partner with others that motivates this preference, but rather a desire to maintain a certain distance. There is, on the street, a subtle balance between, on one hand, temporary, relative isolation, and, on the other, membership of a network or near-group. The nature of networks and near-groups is compatible with such a balance. The children switch between these two poles according to their needs and the constraints that are exerted on them. Moreover, relative isolation does not imply loneliness, since the children often form dyads or triads. The frequency with which they alternate is conditioned by the street's constraints and the children's activities. Alternating is, in itself, a survival strategy.

If a child is not introduced to a group by another child, he or she is often recruited. Paulo recounts an instance of how he and a friend recruit children: "We walked past and saw a young child[5] who was alone. We took[6] him because we know how to speak."[7]

Recall the importance of at least five factors that foster 'alternating movement'. The first concerns the relatively open structure of networks and near-groups. The second refers to the actions of the children themselves: everyone knows what the others are doing.

This means that there is no room for secrets and that social visibility between children is very high. The third factor concerns the absence of any territory that would be under the exclusive control of the members of a network. There is no claim on the exclusive collective use of a given space, and any such use of space would be a major obstacle to alternating movement. The fourth factor that stimulates the flexible nature of the relationships between the CSS of Praça Carioca is the social reaction of adults. Indeed, repression and, above all, a prevailing stigmatisation encourage the creation of a collective identity through which a degree of recognition can be developed between the children. This incites the children to cooperate and, on some levels, accept others, which would not happen without such a constraint.

---

[5] "*Moleque*".

[6] "*Pegava*".

[7] "*A gente tem um papo forte*."

Finally, alternation is influenced by the activity of social workers on the streets and by the amenities available to them (for instance, refectories, health centres, night shelters, schools, workshops, and so on). The influence of this presence depends on its frequency and on the personal commitment of the social worker.

Alternation is therefore a process made up of numerous and changing personal partnerships, and of membership of a network. The network remains a point of reference, but not of exclusive membership. The intensity of this membership varies depending on the careers of CSS, and the stage of their life in the street that they are in. The membership is more intense when the child is still learning about life on the street, or when delinquent activities take priority over other activities. Membership of a network is not the result of a choice that the child makes, but rather the consequence of a number of factors; integration into a network depends on the children's social mobility, the degree of autonomy or self-sufficiency of their dyad or triad, their personal resources, the support they find off the street (assistance programs, part-time work, adults of reference) and on the street (parents living on the street, police officers, street workers, shopkeepers). The strength and nature of the constraints of their environment also have an influence on how strongly integrated into their networks children are. The search for identity and the feeling of belonging to a specific subculture do not seem to be important factors in the integration into a network. This belonging is rather based on the playful and practical contribution of the network, as well as on the constraints it puts on individuals.[8]

The group of twelve to fifteen regular inhalant users belonging to the CSS of Praça Carioca, the *cheira cola*, make up a network with denser relationships. There are two main reasons for this: the search for and distribution of the product, and the use of a space reserved for collective drug use. Yet this network does not have a single leader or centralised organisation. The network is divided into subsections of two or three children (dyads and triads). Cesar (13 years old), Cicero (14), and Marco (15) are an example of this.

Cesar and Cicero are half-brothers and left their family home together, at the same time as Marco left his own home. They all come from the same neighbourhood. When asked about whether or not the drug-sniffing children form a group, Cesar answers: 'Sometimes'.[9] This intermittent and temporary existence of the network as a group is produced by external constraints and the children's activities and needs. In other words, there is not a feeling of belonging specific to the network as an in-group. This confirms the mostly practical character of the network. Marco speaks of 'loads of people' being part of the network.[10] At night, they split into small groups or even sleep alone. They do not always sleep in the same place.

Quarrels and conflicts between the children are frequent. Most of the time, they are about matters related to inhalants. One member of the network was even killed

[8] In the network made up of children who use inhalants, namely shoemaker's glue, the identitary aspect should not be underestimated.

[9] '*De vez em quando*'.

[10] '*Um montào de gente*'.

by others after he claimed some of their drugs as his own when he did not have enough for himself.[11] The network of drug-sniffing children is therefore characterised by the flexibility of its organisation. These children partnered to resolve their need for drugs. In other words, their activities do not always take place within the network, even if glue-sniffing is one of their most common activities. Inhalant use is important for it is a criterion that allows the children to distinguish themselves within the network. Those who use it every day are identified as *cheira cola* by the others. Among the children of Praça Carioca, this identification also has an important spatial dimension which is caused by their habit of using the monastery's stairs as a space for communal drug use. This medium is part of their collective identity.

We can then note that the structure of the network is not incompatible with the existence of an in-group. This in-group is characterised by the following attributes:

(a) Its members develop a specific feeling of belonging to the group
(b) It is a significant component in the personal identity of its members
(c) It has a specific culture
(d) It allows them to justify specific behaviours and conducts.
(e) It enables its members to identify strangers
(f) It creates meaning, for it is a place that organises and links meanings.

An interesting incident illustrates the existence of the in-group amongst the drug-sniffing children of Praça Carioca.

Research assistant Susana Chanfòn was in Praça Carioca at around 5 pm one evening when she noticed twelve-year-old Pedro sniffing glue on the hill, at the bottom of the monastery's stairs (the territory of the *cheira cola*).[12] Chanfòn then met him at the top of the hill, although, as she wrote, 'I usually do not walk up "their" hill'. The other children who were down in Praça Carioca were watching them. Suddenly:

> there were about ten children around us, all of them with their packet of glue. It was impossible for me to speak with all of them or to keep control of the situation by myself. I had an idea: distracting them by taking pictures. It helped a little. Suddenly, I noticed that everyone on the plaza was looking at us: me surrounded by these children.

Then, the children also noticed that people were watching them. So 'they got up to insult everyone and throw stones at all these curious people'. The simple fact of being the object of what was perceived as hostile attention prompts the children's collective response.

---

[11] Every child on Praça Carioca knows the perpetrator of this murder. The versions they tell vary in the way the teenager was killed (stoned to death or attacked an iron bar) as well as in who was the perpetrator or perpetrators of this deed.

[12] Pedro has been on the street since he was around seven or eight years old, but he went home for short periods of time many times. He lost contact with his mother, who left the family neighbourhood without leaving an address. Social workers found one of Pedro's sisters who was prepared to take him in, but he refuses to leave the street. He does not want to be far from the city centre where he made a home. He hangs out with a group of *cheira cola*. It is not the group from Praça Carioca, but it does not keep him from hanging out with them as well. Pedro's case is a good example of the mobility that allows children to be part of several groups at the same time.

Chanfòn continues:

> I got scared but I took a stand. I shouted, asking everyone to stop throwing stones and to walk down the hill immediately. I think that the children were so surprised by my authority and firmness that they did as I asked. I walked down with the children behind me. In the square, several young people, tall and strong, asked me if I was all right, if I needed help. The children surrounding me were furious and wanted to attack them, but I managed to calm them down. It was clear that people wanted to help because they thought the children were attacking me, but the children got offended as they did not find anything exceptional about my presence among them. We went to sit on the stairs of Praça Carioca and I took out paper and pencils to draw with. Younger children then came to join us. As I expected, five minutes later, a military police car was in the square and driving slowly towards us. The children saw it from afar and sat on top of their packets of glue. The police officers stayed in front of us for approximately five minutes … which felt like an eternity. We kept drawing and they left. As it turned out, the children did not draw anything. They were only pretending, for - just like me - they were waiting for the police. It is for the same reason that they remained close to me. After a while, one of the children threw away his packet of glue. He then took the pencils and left, saying that he was going to sell them in order to buy glue. I then asked the other children to run after him, but nobody moved. I got really mad and left. The reason no one tried to get the pencils back from him was because the children stuck together and because they understood it was a game.

This episode is significant as it shows at least three things: the open nature of the network, the existence of a 'We are street children and we are entitled to be' type of identity, and the combination of playfulness and aggressiveness in these children's behaviour. The episode is also interesting as it reveals the improvised character of the daily lives of CSS. The children are very resourceful. Their daily lives are a combination of improvisation and short-term projections, surprises and routines. They can turn anything into an event.

A child's spatial mobility and irregular presence are not incompatible with their participation in the network. The following episode also shows that the adaptability of the network satisfies a dual need: finding a way to get inhalants, and having fun by challenging a child or adults on the street. This episode also illustrates the central role of play among the children of a transitional age (13–15):

Juvenal is a twelve- or thirteen-year-old child who proudly claims his talent for theft, particularly since he lost two fingers on his right hand in an accident. The other children know him as a highly efficient thief. All of this influences the sequence of events and its double meaning: playful and practical. This episode shows as well that delinquency among children of this age group is mostly associated with play and a need for excitement – a need for a kick. Other children complain about Juvenal's aggressiveness[13] and temporarily reject him. He has a high inhalant intake, and does not spend a lot of time in Praça Carioca and its vicinity. He is often alone, but also spends time with a group of children from a different neighbourhood. He sometimes disappears for a few weeks. It is difficult to understand him as he stutters and speaks very quickly. He gesticulates a lot and speaks with a very low voice. To a certain extent, the other children admire him for his strength and talent for theft,

[13] Let us underline that he also threatened a social worker with an iron bar.

and this despite his multiple disabilities. He suffers from an eye disease and his eyesight is greatly affected. He seems to have close relations with a woman who works and sleeps in Praça Carioca during the week.

The group of children that Juvenal associates with is made up of regular users of shoemaker’s glue. These children do not have enough drugs and, in order to get some, they ask Juvenal to steal a blazer in one of the smartest shops in the area. They are not allowed entry to this shop, and the entrance is safely guarded. The desire to break this prohibition becomes a need, and the operation turns into a game. They then challenge Juvenal, who cares deeply about his reputation as a brave and expert thief. By shying away from this challenge he would risk his reputation, which he uses to compensate his disabilities. They put together a plan. The children let off a big firecracker in front of the shop entrance. The explosion is extremely loud, and draws the security team to the site of the explosion. It is then that Juvenal, taking advantage of the general confusion, enters the shop, steals a blazer, and leaves without problem. The stolen item is quickly sold, and the money raised is used to buy drugs.

This episode is an example of the children’s abilities to innovate, abilities which are enhanced by the flexibility of the network’s structure, and therefore the types of partnerships specific to children. The absence of hierarchy as well as the lack of an unquestioned leader are important factors of this flexibility. The challenge given to Juvenal allows him to confirm his reputation, and therefore to feel empowered, but it also enables the group to satisfy their need for drugs and entertainment. This demonstrates well the flexibility of the network’s structure and the improvisational abilities that come from it.

Playful and practical motivations are once again the cause of action, and the challenge given to Juvenal is only a pretext. The network also allows for the existence of temporary and low commitment memberships, as well as the child’s isolation and the formation of dyads. However, it does not rule out the creation of more homogeneous groups. Speaking of a group of twelve children (between ten and fifteen years old) to which he belonged for four years, Paolo said ‘We had a meeting place for all the group members. At a specific time, we would all meet and everyone would go looking for money.’[14] Children meet to undertake a precise activity: theft. This example illustrates the network as a superficial, flexible and temporary structure which allows them to reach specific goals (Houchon). Yet the children in this group shared food, cigarettes, and drugs, and slept together.

When talking about leadership, Paulo contradicts himself between interviews. He once claimed that there is no leader: every decision would be taken unanimously and thus made mandatory for all of them. But in a different interview, Paulo claimed that he was, alongside another child, acting as a leader in two specific areas: organising theft and arbitrating conflicts.[15]

[14] ‘*Arrumar dinheiro*’.

[15] This latter version is the most probable. Indeed, his powerful personality and his mastery in *capoeira* seem to give Paulo great authority over the other children. As for the second leader, he is Paulo’s childhood friend.

The group that fifteen-year-old Emilio belongs to is made up of fourteen children. The life of the group is organised around inhalant use and by trips to the *morros* to get glue. Despite being part of the group, Emilio does not look for night shelters with them. He plays with the young children of a woman who has been living in Praça Carioca for a long time so that he can enjoy her protection at night. When he cannot find a safe shelter for the night, he sleeps during the day in order to be able to face the dangers of the night. This example, just like the other individual strategies, illustrates how relatively independent children are from their networks. A flexible network is also a consequence of the high number of children who only spend time on the street temporarily.

Indeed, the high turnover of children on the street is a widespread phenomenon. It is also common for children to disappear from the street for a while and to reappear later on. This mobility is incompatible with a strict hierarchical organisation of the social group formed by children in street situations. Here, there is an important difference with the stability and constant presence of teenagers and young adults making up the 'Street Corner Societies', and the delinquent gangs of the suburbs and slums. There are very few similarities between these groups and the networks made up of CSS.[16]

Despite this flexibility, the network does not exclude certain activities that require a high level of group integration. But in this case the integration is irregular and instrumental, and does not concern every aspect of the child's activities. This polymorphic and polyvalent form is more suitable for the challenges that CSS have to face. The network is organised in dyads and subgroups living in relative independence from each other. Children belonging to these subgroups meet regularly, and it is during these meetings that the phenomenon of leadership can be seen. The networks discussed by the children of Praça Carioca comprise on average thirteen children.

There are several ways for a new member to be admitted in the network. First of these, a new member can be admitted via *funçào*. The *funçào* is made up of two children: 'the street father' and 'the street son' (Carlini 1986, pp. 10–12). The street father introduces the street son to the street and to the network. In return, he demands obedience and small favours. The *funçào* coexists with the network and evolves as the newcomer gains independence (Ibid.). Then, the newcomer is introduced to the network by a child they knew before they left their home for the streets. This child is often a relative or a friend. There is also the case of children asking younger chil-

[16] Jorge Amado's novel 'Captains of the Sands' (2013) tells the story of a gang of street children which is highly organised and hierarchical. They occupied an abandoned warehouse near the port of Salvador in Bahia and made it their territory. It is from this territory that gang members go to the city streets, moving by dyads or triads. Now, this territory is the essential ground without which the children would not have been able to form a gang. Moreover, these children no longer have parents or relatives. They, therefore, cannot go home, and the gang is truly built as a functional replacement for family. This is, however, never a topic of discussion when the children in our study group talk about the network they belong to. Thus, the absence of parents or adults of reference, as well as the absence of a territory, stimulate the creation of networks rather than gangs.

dren for favours[17] and giving them a form of protection in return. This type of structure turns into a network when other children become involved.

In the network and the near-group, the relationships of dependence alternate in line with the independence of the children who are part of it. In this case, the factors at play are combined with the ones conditioning the child's movement. This movement alternates between a situation in which all the members of the network are present and act together, and a situation in which the same children act alone or in independent subgroups. The following factors influence this alternation:

(a) the nature and degree of autonomy of the child and of the subgroup they participate in (survival strategies)
(b) the frequency at which they return home
(c) partial integration into the 'non-street': organised crime, assistance programs (home, temporary work)
(d) the detention of the child in a state institution. In these institutions, children build relationships which give them access to other networks.

Alternation is what characterises the lives of CSS, at least among pre-teens (11–14). For younger children, as well as for teenagers, the situation is different.

## 7.2 The Victim and the Group

Life on the street is violent, and violence produces victims. In this regard, we must note the distinction between these four different situations related to children in street situations (CSS):

(a) a child who is a victim of the police and adult violence in general
(b) a child who is a victim of an isolated attack by other children
(c) an adult who is a victim of an attack by children
(d) a child who is 'victimised' by the members of the group they belong to

The last situation is the only one we will take into consideration here.

We have consciously used the phrase 'victimised' to emphasise the difference between this and a situation in which the child is 'simply' the victim of an isolated attack. By using this phrase, we want to draw attention to an important component of the act itself. Indeed, when there is 'victimisation' of a child inside a group, we are in the presence of a continuous and ritualised process. This process is also defined by a certain number of functions. However, the child who has to do favours (for example finding food, getting money, washing clothes) for another child within a *funçào*, or in the case of a hierarchical relationship within a group, is not considered a victim. For such a distinction to be accurate, a rule of reciprocity needs to be observed by the parties affected. In other words, the favours a child provides create

[17] '*Manda fazer serviço*'.

one or more obligations for their partner, while the child gains one or several rights.[18] This rule of reciprocity then engenders a trade which, while being unequal, respects the interests and therefore the needs of both parties affected.

When the interests and needs of the subordinate child are altered without change in the conditions of the trade, then there is 'victimisation' of this child. Such an alteration of the child's interests and needs occurs gradually when the subordinate child accumulates street experiences, and thus progressively becomes less dependent on their partner for survival. From this moment on the partnership between the two children faces a crisis, and tends to dissolve. If the subordinate child is held against his will, then he becomes a victim, as there is no suitable compensation for the favours he does. In this reasoning, we have deliberately disregarded the means dominant children have to obtain the favours of the children subordinated to them.

We are also disregarding how subordinate children live their dependence. Most *funçòes* disintegrate with the gradual emancipation of the subordinate child. This process is usually of a conflictual nature. Indeed, by freeing themselves from their protectors, children make them their opponents, which means that they usually must leave the urban area they used to stay in for a while. If they do not follow this rule, they risk not being able to find a new means of integration among the other children (Carlini, op. cit., p. 10). We must note, however, that the emancipation process does not always have such dramatic consequences. Indeed, it depends, among other things, on the quality of the relationship the two children used to have. Some *funçòes* are made up of brothers, half-brothers, cousins, or friends who knew each other before either of them left home, and in these cases their partnership on the street is based on bonds which usually make any evolution less conflictual.

Life on the street is hard! Daniel is a fifteen-year-old who works as a shoe-shine boy. At night, he sleeps with the *cheira cola*, but he does not belong to their group. He is often alone and sleeps until noon because he works late at night, taking advantage of the customers coming out of the neighbourhood cinemas and nightclubs. For a while, he was part of a cooperative of shoe-shine boys. This child - who will definitely leave the street for good to go home – speaks of the difficulty of living conditions on the street: 'To learn how to live on the street, I think you need to be a hero.' You need to be a hero to face the deprivations and dangers of life on the street.

Paulo uses the word hero to describe a status which keeps him from being attacked. Learning *capoeira* enabled him to gain that status. In the case of Daniel, the child-hero is the one who suffers and who resignedly accepts the attacks on the street. Being a hero and a victim at the same time is not a contradiction. For Paulo, on the other hand, the child-hero is dominant and self-confident, and will never become a victim.

These two children thus have completely different meanings for the word hero. Paulo notices that the other children fear him because, as he says, 'they think I could beat them.' He seizes this opportunity because, he adds, 'I am going to use them.'[19]

---

[18] Introducing newcomers to the street, or protecting them from attacks, are common illustrations of such obligations.

[19] '*Entào eu vou usar eles*'.

This use has a double function here. The first one concerns the small favours that these children can do for Paulo. The second is related to the prestige conferred by the children's obedience onto the one benefiting from it. This latter function is the most important one, corresponding to the importance of competition for supremacy between the members of a group. Paulo clearly links these when he says: 'I am going to use them because there are a lot of "big eyes"[20] in the group who want to be above everyone else.' He must then protect himself from this excessive appetite for power. The 'victimisation' of a child can take roots in such a context without excluding, as we will see, the mixture of playful and practical elements.

We will also see later that children use challenges as a strategy to try to control, at least partly, the constraints they have to face. We will additionally talk about how the 'victimisation' process is linked to the strategy of the challenge. Children who do not pay attention to everything that is happening on the street become victims of their environment. This is what Gordo (seventeen years old) means when he says that 'The wave sweeps away the prawn that sleeps too much.'[21] It is a warning against routines and habits, for every child is a potential victim. This raises the question of the nature of the social bond between CSS, a matter which we will also discuss later.

We will analyse the victim's position in the group and the 'victimisation' process through two examples. Additionally, we will see what the functions of the 'victimisation' process are. In the first example (recounted by Colen), the victim has to bring food to the leader of the group in the evenings. He does not, however, get any money from it. He also has to supply the group with cardboard boxes and newspapers, or steal blankets, items which are useful to protect oneself against the cold at night.[22] The whole group makes fun of this child and turns him into their scapegoat because he is physically weak and clumsy, a position intensified by his facial appearance, which is read as that of a fool, a naïve person.[23] 'The group made him the weakest,' says Colen.[24] The group picks its victim and keeps them that way, because the victim fulfils certain functions. Here, the victim is not the youngest child in the group. The child-victim cannot leave the group because he is the weakest.[25] The group keeps its victim captive, plays cat and mouse with him: for example, giving him a task they know he cannot execute only to give it instead to another child at the last minute. But the group also knows how to spare its victim. For this reason, they sometimes pick tasks that the victim is able to perform. At other times, the child-victim is not called upon, such as when the group is undertaking something which is beyond the victim's abilities.[26] It is the group, not the leader, that picks the child who will be the victim, and that runs the 'victimisation' process.

---

[20] '*Olho grande*'.

[21] '*Camarào que dorme muito, a onda leva.*'

[22] Stealing blankets from those sleeping on the street is a common occurrence among street children.

[23] '*Cara de bobo.*'

[24] 'A gente botava ele pra ser o mais fraco.'

[25] 'A gente ficava com aquele mais fraco.'

[26] 'A gente via que dava pra ele, a gente botava ele também. Quando via que nào dava, a gente ia.'

The fact that the child-victim has to bring back food is less important than the way he has to do it. What we see is a gesture of a mainly symbolic nature. Not only does the child have to serve the group and its leader, but he has to do so under difficult circumstances. He has to devote himself and show initiative. The daily duty this child submits himself to confirms the leader's authority. At the same time, his role as a scapegoat strengthens the cohesion of the group. The leader cannot let the child leave the group, as this would damage his authority.

Not giving money to the victim, then, entails a ritual angle which seems to exceed the practical aspect of this process. The presence of the child-victim in the group has different functions, which could be summarised thus:

(a) the hierarchical function: confirming the leader's power
(b) the function of social cohesion in the group: allowing some of the group members' aggression to converge on them
(c) the playful function: enabling fun
(d) the practical function: satisfying material needs (blankets, cardboard boxes, newspapers)
(e) the reassuring function: 'there is someone in the group who is weaker than me!'
(f) the ritual function: the status of child-victim is updated every day.

The second example, recounted by Paulo, concerns a child who had to steal and beg for other children. As in the previous example, this child was not the youngest of the group, but was but the weakest.[27] The victim's weakness is described in this way: 'He was the weakest because he did not know how to quarrel.[28] He had (physical) strength but was unable to use it. He was scared of us and did not know how to quarrel.' The Portuguese verb *brigar* refers to the act of quarrelling. In the way it is used here, however, it is not the act itself which is important but the form, the ritual of the quarrel. It is the words we choose and the ability to argue and talk back (the *papo*, or art of talking) which matter the most. In a confrontation, verbal abilities are more important than physical strength. A quarrel based on *papo* sounds like the bargaining between a vendor wanting to get a price and a customer trying to haggle. The outcome depends on what both parties are ready to concede (profit for one and marginal usefulness of the desired item for the other). But it also depends, just as much, on the verbal abilities of the speakers, as well as on their arguments. Bargaining - just like quarrelling - can entail 'losing face' (Goffman 1974) for one of the parties.[29]

Bargaining usually ends with the end of the negotiation, but the same does not apply to the quarrel discussed here. Indeed, children with verbal abilities impose themselves on children who lack these abilities. The situation in which bargaining happens is different from that of quarrelling. In a bargain, both parties can put a stop to the relationship. They both live in and belong to different milieus. In a quarrel,

[27] '*Nào era menor, mas era mais fraco. Entào a gente aproveitava.*'

[28] '*Brigar*'.

[29] For Erving Goffman (1974), 'face' corresponds to the identity an individual thinks they can legitimately claim.

children cannot avoid each other since they live in and depend on the same milieu. In other words, they cannot put an end to their connection.

We can find, as a result, the temporary submission of one party to the other. *Papo* is then of crucial importance. Denying this would be to say that the relationships between CSS can be explained only by physical obligation or by the harmony and complementarity that would exist between them. However, the answer can be found, in fact, between these two extremes.

The group is constantly watching the child-victim to make sure he does not escape. Just as in the previous example, his presence is necessary because the child has functions which are essential to the smooth running of the group itself. According to Paulo, the victim would not have been able to survive on the street without the group, and, moreover, a kind of bond[30] started to form with the group members because, he says, 'we were not continually mistreating him.'[31] To keep the victim from leaving the group, they started by forcing him to attack someone else. Then, the group would 'offer' their protection to the victim to defend him against the person he had attacked. The group was thus creating a situation that was strengthening the dependent condition of the child-victim.[32] As time went by, says Paolo, 'we realised that he (the victim) was a good boy'. So 'we took him with us[33] and found another weak child to take advantage of'.[34]

The previous victim then adopts the same exploitative behaviour. Paulo's group has always kept a victim among its members.[35] The group needs a victim because victims have the effect of stabilising the relationships between its members. A victim must be replaced by another one. As such we can speak of the rotation of child-victims. This means that the status of victim is a temporary one. Having such a child at their disposal can be interpreted as being an example of a collective survival strategy. For some time, the group keeps the child in their victim status. We can assume that it is the price some children have to pay in exchange for their introduction to life on the street.

When the group was using inhalants, the victim had to use more than the others to heighten the effects of the product.[36] It was then that some children would try to sexually abuse him.[37]

---

[30] '*Aproximaçào.*'

[31] "*Nos também nào maltratava ele toda ora.*"

[32] Paulo: '*Jogava logo uma proteçào pra ele ficar teleguidado pela gente.*'

[33] '*Botamos ele pra nossa parte.*'

[34] '*E arrumamos autro fraco pra gente se aproveitar.*'

[35] '*Sempre tinha um fraco.*'

[36] '*O papel du fraco é cheirar e ficar doidào.*'

[37] Benno Glauser (1990) also observed an example of victim sexual abuse in Asunción. The abusers were accusing the victim of enjoying homosexual relations. We do not have at our disposal any systematic study of the sexuality of CSS. Some Brazilian publications report a high homosexuality rate among these children. However, we think it is more accurate to talk about temporary or periodic bisexuality rather than confirmed homosexuality.

We see, then, a relation of interdependence between the victims and the group to which they belong, at least until the victims have accumulated enough experience to contest their status of victim.

A seventh function emerges from the second example, which we suggest calling the function of control or the function of experiment: the attacks required of the victim allow the group to test the reactions of their environment.

The different functions connected to the role of the victim are not equally important to the survival and well-being of the group. Moreover, not all victims are 'bearing' of all the functions at the same time. As such, we need to weigh their importance in relation to several factors:

(a) the organisation of the group and its leadership
(b) the age groups it includes
(c) the number of members it contains
(d) the presence of one or several victims
(e) the social and spatial context in which it acts

The group has mechanisms in place to emancipate the victim. At the core of this process is the challenge. Emancipation begins when victims realise that they also know how to quarrel.[38] They then challenge someone. Challenging someone is an important act because it corresponds with a strategy which either gives them personal respect or helps them to rediscover this respect. In the case of rediscovering respect, the challenge is heavily ritualised: its aim is for the individual to reaffirm their prestige or status on a regular basis. This strategy also helps in setting the limits which differentiate the individuals present. A challenge can be seen as a means to claim or to secure a certain identity and to set the boundaries of the personal sphere of the individuals involved in the confrontation. By setting limits, the challenge makes social relations in the group clearer. The established order in the group is confirmed when the challenger is unable to bear the consequences of the challenge. However, if the opposite happens, the order is altered as the challenge creates a new balance in the group. We can then see how the challenge is a factor in the group's order.

To leave their roles as victims, children have to be able to challenge someone.[39] The outcome of the challenge depends on:

(a) the skills learned by the victim
(b) the choice of the person to challenge
(c) the nature of the challenge

The challenge is usually against another child in the group. According to Paulo, the challenge itself is not only about using strength, but also about 'the form (of the challenge), the skill with which they steal, the art of talking'.[40]

---

[38] '*Brigar*'

[39] We will not consider here the case of the victims who emancipate themselves by receiving the 'clemency' of the group.

[40] '*Papo*'

We see that there is a complex mixture of, on the one hand, physical and violent elements, and on the other the skill with which the challenge is given and executed. As a matter of fact, the confrontation is a rite of passage: children leave behind their status of victims to gain the status of fully-fledged members of the group. The length of the emancipation process is different for every child and for every group. We can assume that in groups that are not strictly hierarchical the challenge is a constant process of social regulation. In that case, the challenge would be a functional substitute for hierarchical relations.

To conclude, challenges observe the following stages:

(a) the victims become aware of their possibilities
(b) they pick an opponent, the object of the challenge, and the ground the challenge will take place on
(c) they lay down the challenge
(d) the opponents want to subdue the victims
(e) there is a physical, practical (for example, theft), and symbolic confrontation
(f) the outcome of the challenge leads to a change in the victims' status, or on the contrary to their confirmation.

## 7.3 Solidarity, Complicity, Cooperation: The Social Bond or Ethics on the Street

The scientific literature on children in street situations speaks of the existence of solidarity and cooperative relationships between these children. They also report the violence that exists among them. However, we do not have at our disposal any extensive and systematic study of the nature of the social bonds which develop between these children. It is a complex problem, especially when it is connected with bonds of solidarity. In that case, this problem concerns, among other things, topics such as: moral judgement and the existence of the idea of justice amongst children in street situations (CSS) and thus their normative references and identity references, the different stages of the socialisation process, the cognitive structures on which the judgement of the child analysing a situation which raises problems of equity rest, the sense of responsibility, the nature of the semantic consensus which exists between children about equity, and the nature of the social control which presides over their relationships. Furthermore, the study of relationships of solidarity requires, beforehand, a clarification of the connections between morality and culture. Indeed, two positions go head to head. On one hand, Lawrence Kohlberg argues that 'morality is fundamentally different from culture for it holds an intent of universality' (Digneffe 1986, p. 24). On the other hand, the tradition of cultural relativism maintains that moral judgement is connected to the social and cultural context. While, according to Kohlberg, there 'seems to be universal forms of judgement and evaluation', this is not the case for the relativistic position.

Besides, we would also need to decide on the notions of heteronomy and autonomy in use, as well as on the different phases that characterise them respectively. Epistemological and methodological difficulties also arise when using theories developed in a very different context than the one we want to apply them to. Furthermore, when we are faced with relationships of solidarity, we find ourselves with moral problems to answer.

For all these reasons, it is not our intention to address the topic of solidarity between CSS. We wish to stress, however, that there is no reason to claim that CSS are lacking moral sense, and this despite the many obstacles on the road to their socialisation that hinder a continuous and harmonious development of their character. Their morals are above all contextual, and they have a strong sense of injustice when it comes to their own experiences. We will see this by studying how they judge their mothers and fathers. However, they are characterised by a tendency to judge others based on the consequences of their actions and not on their intentions. It then becomes difficult to distinguish between moral standards and social standards.

Moreover, for a standard to be moral, it needs to include two elements. The first element is the sense of obligation, the sense of having to perform an action because it is just and good. Thus, an action is performed, a move is made, because it is just *per se*, and this goes hand in hand with a vision of the world and of social relations. In the subculture of CSS, the exchange of services is of a pragmatic value, and used for survival. This value depends on the environment and does not have a normative foundation based on a definition of the general good.

The second element forming a moral standard is desirability (Durkheim). Individuals desire to apply a standard because they want to improve and surpass themselves. But social standards are defined by the sanctions that their transgression entails. However, social standards do not only depend on social control, for individuals interpret the standard in accordance with their lives, their sensibilities, their interests and needs. Yet it is according to this interpretation that a social standard can become a moral standard, with the opposite route being impossible. Depending on the context and on individual motives, similar types of behaviour can either have a moral dimension or, on the contrary, a lack thereof. It is then impossible to assess the significance of a moral component in the relationships between the children themselves, and between the children and adults in general. On the other hand, it is possible to find the presence of moral considerations in some of the children's remarks: for example, how they choose the victims of their attacks, or relationships with their parents.

When it comes to cooperative relationships, the practical element is primary. This practical element combines easily with a contextual judgement on the equity of the division of labour or benefits. So, in reality, there is no hermetic seal between cooperation on one side and solidarity on the other, provided, however, that we do not define solidarity in relation to a universal notion of justice.

Complicity is a relationship which can be based upon affinity and natural agreement. It can, just as well, come from the constraints a concrete situation, when the interests of some children are protected by the defence of the other children's interests. Cooperation and complicity are tightly connected. When we ask the seventeen-year-old Gordo, then, if he has friends, he answers: 'Friends? I am my own friend. What I do have is companions.'[41] This type of answer is fairly common among CSS. Another teenager speaks of *chegados* (newcomers) and *conhecidos* (acquaintances) when talking about the company he keeps. Their use of these phrases highlights the temporary aspect of bonds made on the street more than their fragility, even though these two aspects can often be seen together. Gordo also says about the other children, 'I entrust them with things, but I do not trust anyone.'[42] At most, he adds, 'If I were to trust people, it would be the little ones.'[43]

The distinction between *confio* (entrust) and *deposito confiança* (trust) is significant. *Confio* concerns the short term and situations that Gordo can fully control. This is confirmed by the fact that only the youngest children can get his trust. These children are dependent on older children because they lack street experience, and this lack of experience is therefore the foundation for Gordo's trust in the youngest. However, they rapidly learn the basics for survival and become gradually more independent, and thus more difficult to control. Trust decreases with the rise of the degree of independence in the youngest children. The notion of trust, as understood by Gordo, is paradoxical. Indeed, to him trust is based on dependence and controlling others. However, this is indeed a negation of trust, since its main characteristic is to be able to dispense with control as much as possible.

On the other hand, *deposito confiança* concerns long-term contexts. It is about extending credit to others. But for Gordo this is inconceivable, as living conditions on the street do not allow children to extend long-term credit. Ultimately, trust does not exist for Gordo. These two notions of trust illustrate the nature of social bonds between CSS. Children must live in symbiotic relationship with their environment, feeling it rather than observing it from the outside.

For Odair (sixteen years old), the most dangerous thing on the street is to have friends. For some time, this child was involved in drug trafficking in a Rio neighbourhood. It is likely that this experience has influenced his views on friendship. For Odair, sharing between children (of, for example, food, clothes, or money) is determined more by the fear of retaliation in case of refusal than it is by friendship.

On the other hand, CSS do not steal from any passer-by. They make choices which correspond to relevant strategies of opportunity, and under considerations which are not directly related to survival needs. These choices are interesting. Indeed, they allow us to notice that, on some occasions, children delimit what they can legitimately undertake. There is an implicit classification of the people using the street, a classification which could rest upon a specific cognitive structure.

Xavier (fifteen years old) says that he does not like stealing from anyone on the street: 'There are a lot of people that I do not even like stealing from.' He nevertheless does so sometimes, but reluctantly! Among the people Xavier does not like stealing from, we can find:

---

[41] '*Companheiros.*'

[42] '*Confio, mas nào deposito confiança em ninguém.*'

[43] '*Se eu for confiar, confio mais nos menorzinhos.*'

(a) pregnant women
(b) mentally ill people
(c) black people (he is black himself)
(d) priests (although he did steal a priest's car some time ago)
(e) nuns
(f) 'street children'. He does not like to steal from people who have a difficult life[44]

However, he has no qualms about stealing from the people he calls 'normal': white people and rich people. We have also found this among other children who define normality by skin colour and wealth. Thus, Xavier classifies people into three categories:

(a) People with a difficult life because they cannot defend themselves. This category is also subdivided into two subcategories of people. The first, people who are marginalised as a social class: 'street children' and 'black people'. The second, people who cannot defend themselves because of their physical condition: pregnant women and mentally ill people. Xavier implicitly includes himself in the first subcategory.
(b) People known as normal: white people and rich people.
(c) Those who, by their status, guide people with and take part in the spiritual realm: priests and nuns.

This classification is not based on an awareness of the mechanisms which lead to social inequalities. It is the result of a reproduction of the child's daily experiences.

Victimology teaches us that the behaviour, attitude, and habits of victims of attacks often play a significant part in the dynamics of the attack. The testimonies of these two children confirm this. The first child prefers to steal from men. He only attacks a woman if she is well-dressed and looks wealthy.[45] However, what triggers the theft from such a woman is rather an attitude of suspicion and fear directed towards children she sees on the street. If she hangs on to her handbag and picks up pace, the children are provoked, and react by stealing her handbag.[46] Her behaviour shows a judgement which is perceived by the children as provocation.

They feel labelled as thieves simply for being on the street. They feel attacked too by the woman's stigmatising attitude, indicating as it does the exclusion and rejection of these children. That is how theft acquires a vindictive connotation. From then on, it cannot be solely interpreted through the requirements of survival or through the enjoyment it brings to the child. Now theft must then interpreted through the self-image of the child as well.

Children also say that they feel no remorse or pity when they attack someone on the street. Paulo tells us, 'How could I feel pity when none of these people feel pity for us?' During an investigation by a Brazilian colleague, the testimony of a differ-

---

[44] '*Sofredor.*'

[45] '*Folgada.*'

[46] '*Só quando era folgada e passava junto da gente com medo e segurava a bolsa, aí a gente tomava mesmo.*'

ent child confirms this. He says, 'I think we have to steal when someone gives us a dirty look … because they are convinced that we are going to steal from them.[47] They avoid us.[48] When we sit next to a woman on the bus with no bad intentions and she gets up and leaves her seat, she is avoiding us.'

Xavier recounts an experience he had that day. He saw a young woman on the street: 'She looked at me in a funny way[49] and started to walk faster.' And this without any suspicious move from Xavier. To him, the ultimate provocation was that she deduced such a behaviour despite the shoeshine case he was wearing over his shoulder. This case, on the contrary, should have reassured the woman: he was on the street to work, not to steal. He then decided to have his revenge, and thought, 'I am going to walk faster so that she thinks I want to rob her. In this way, I mislead her on my intentions.' To avenge himself, Xavier simply wanted to scare her. He feels the mistrust of the adults as an unjustified judgement, to which he reacts in a very aggressive way. This reaction is closely connected to the problem of identity with 'street children', and to their references. It indicates the complexity of the motivations that lead children to attack adults.

If theft is the main element, it is not always committed without any normative reference. For fifteen-year-old Silvano, theft is justified if the victim is wealthy and the child who steals needs money.[50] Rather than attacking a defenceless woman, Silvano thinks it is preferable to hit a bank. This choice is not driven by moral considerations, but by the respect and admiration that being imprisoned for attempting to rob a bank would provide. Silvano adds, 'Being arrested for stealing a small watch or chain is not worth it.' For this child, the achievement is greater than the material profit of the theft. Incidentally, he does not even consider the possibility of a successful attack, since admiration comes from the incarceration. Indeed, stealing without being apprehended means staying anonymous, but, if caught, everyone is aware of the risks taken by the culprit. An intense need for social recognition is the reason for this attitude.

During a group interview, Paulo speaks up to reply to two other children who see no benefit in stealing, nor excuse for it. He starts by telling them that they cannot understand because they are not CSS. They cannot know the suffering and humiliation these children endure due to the contempt of adults. Even the little shoeshine boy has to go through these affronts. Paulo says that 'street children' are perceived as ferocious animals, marginal individuals, rapists and thieves, adding that he is humiliated by this contempt and mistrust. He says that 'for us, it is an adventure', and an adventure is a mixture of fun, risks and violence, with an unpredictable ending. Speaking to the other two children, Paulo repeats twice, 'Try being a shoeshine boy for just one day.'[51]

---

[47] '*Esse pivete vai querer me roubar.*'

[48] 'Sai *de perto da gente.*'

[49] '*Olhou prá minha cara assim.*'

[50] 'Se *eu tivesse muito apertado precisando de dinheiro.*'

[51] '*Experimenta só um dia só.*'

With his remarks, Paulo confirms that thefts can in part be attributed to the children's aggressiveness, and to what we could call a need for revenge, more than vengeance. The adults' contempt causes an imbalance in the identity of the child, an imbalance which leads to acts which are not practical or moral. Therefore theft, and simulated attacks, also have a playful connotation. Sixteen-year-old Luis does not disapprove of theft because, as he says, 'everyone follows their own heart'.[52] There is no standard that is valid for everyone because every situation is unique. However, stealing is bad[53] because you always end up being arrested. Luis explicitly says that, without this risk, he would not hesitate to steal,[54] but the risk is too great for the theft to be profitable. Luis' reasoning is based on practical rather than moral premises. The rejection of theft is not guided by the harm done to others but by his own experience: Luis was caught by the police during his first theft.

The playful aspect in the lives of CSS is important, but this aspect is not as intense for everyone. The playful element is divided between children, especially depending on age groups. We would like to focus on a few considerations regarding the presence of a playful element in theft and simulated attacks by using certain elements of the typology established by Roger Caillois (1958, pp. 31–91). For Caillois, 'a sequence of events that is known in advance, without the possibility of errors and surprises, clearly leading to a foregone conclusion, is incompatible with the nature of play' (op. cit., p. 39). He continues by claiming that 'play is based on the necessity to find, to invent instantly an answer which is free within the limit of the rules'. This margin which is granted to the player 'partly explains the player's enjoyment'.

Indeed, the rule invented by the child simulating an attack 'creates a fiction'.[55] The situation which results from it is in favour of the child. But not without conditions: they have to control the game played. In the simulation of an attack, the child's enjoyment comes from the revenge they take by instilling fear in their victim. However, children follow some rules, since they allow their victims to escape. Indeed, the game consists in gauging the simulation so as to avoid a reaction from the victim which would force the child to genuinely attack. In this case, the game would be over, and the child would lose.

The element of doubt which characterises this situation is also a necessary element of its playful dimension. Improvisation is primary at the start of the process of simulating an attack. The child waits for the victim's initial reactions to make the next move. They have to invent rules of conduct to keep the situation under control. Usually, the game becomes tighter as time passes. The child stops the game when the context is no longer suitable for the game to continue within, such as on the occasion of intervention by passers-by or the police. They will also give up when their need for revenge has been satisfied and there is no more enjoyment to be found in the game. It therefore seems possible to say that, in the case of such simulation,

---

[52] '*Cada um tem a sua cabeça.*'

[53] '*Nào é legal.*'

[54] '*E, ia ser o caso.*'

[55] Caillois, *op. cit.*, p. 39.

'*ludus*' and '*paidia*' tend to balance each other.[56] But, in the instance of theft, the playful element seems to be more centred on '*ludus*' than on '*paidia*'. In both cases, however, there is a constant combination of both elements.

Cooperation between children is the foundation of their collective survival strategies. It is practical and concerns different areas of action, and theft in particular. There are several forms of cooperation, but within each of them, we can find the pooling of individual resources in order to achieve a goal. Usually, this goal is collective, but in groups with a strong hierarchy, the goal is picked by the leader.

This does not allow us, however, to claim that the pursuit of the goal only serves the leader's interests. There are two reasons supporting this reservation. The first reason can be found in the numerous constraints of survival on the street. Even the strongest leader has formidable opponents, for instance the police and other leaders on the street. As such they have to take into consideration the other children's interests. If they do not do so, they put themselves in great danger.[57] The second reason concerns the division of groups of children according to their respective schedules. As a result of this division, there is an increased independence of the members from the group. Affected children can then turn to other sources which meet their needs and are closer to their interests.

The level of cooperation between children varies depending not only on the nature of the goals, the difficulty of reaching them, and the urgency of reaching them, but also on the participants' interests, and therefore their motivation, as well as on the group's social integration. All these factors also determine the type of cooperation: forced or voluntary. It depends as well on the means used to maintain the group's social integration. Voluntary cooperation means that the structure of the group members' individual motivations converge towards the objectives pursued by the group (whether they are ad hoc groups or permanent groups, highly hierarchical groups or non-hierarchical networks). But this alone is not sufficient, as this structure also has to include the means chosen by the group to reach their predetermined goals. If these conditions are not met, we can speak of forced cooperation. In reality, we will find a mixture of these two types of cooperation. The world of CSS is not homogeneous enough on a psychosocial level for us to be able to determine the type of cooperation which is predominant. We can only assume that voluntary cooperation is the most common type of cooperation. While the versatility of survival strate-

[56] Caillois distinguishes four principles within the game, among which are '*paidia*' and '*ludus*' (p. 48). '*Paidia*' concerns, among other things, a principle of amusement and free improvisation; he 'embraces the spontaneous demonstrations of the play instinct' (p. 76). This last characteristic only partially applies to theft simulation. '*Ludus*' concerns the 'taste for gratuitous difficulty' (p. 75) and to 'a growing need to follow gratuitous conventions' (p. 48). '*Ludus*' is also calculation and combination. This principle creates an obvious problem: in order to have conventions, you need a partner. But in simulation and theft, the 'partner' is not playing! On the other hand, these two situations are only partially playful. All this shows why they are only partially related to Caillois' model.

[57] To our knowledge, there was at least one event of a leader being executed by other children for having abused his power, through mistreatment and the repeated confiscation of inhalants for his own use. The execution of a second child, for similar reasons, also seems to have happened before the beginning of our study.

gies is an important condition to survive on the street, this versatility is ill-fitted for forced cooperation. However, justifying any claim on this matter requires an extensive study of the children's motivational structures.

Several testimonies, including Emilio's, reveal that some children obtain inhalants even if they cannot afford to pay for them. In general, this does not mean that the drugs are free of charge, as the child who receives them has to pay off their debt later. However, there are situations in which children cannot afford to pay for the drugs, but yet they can still obtain them for a certain amount of time. Several observations must be made about this:

(a) compensation does not always need to be monetary or in kind
(b) the beneficiary can be forced to do favours for those who gave them the product
(c) a child who receives something they cannot give back loses part of their autonomy. The increase in the power of their 'creditor' constitutes a significant disadvantage
(d) free access to drugs is a phenomenon which seems to be part of the logic of a hierarchical relationship rather than one of solidarity
(e) the dependency of the debtor is a survival strategy for the child, or children, to whom they are indebted
(f) the benefit for the debtor is to be a member of the network

Only a study of the motivations to deliver free drugs would allow us to reach the conclusion that there are elements of solidarity and cooperation involved. For now, we will focus on the utilitarian hypothesis.

Theft is an activity which illustrates well the collective survival strategy which relies on the collaboration of all the children involved. We can find four constants in the strategy of Colen's group:

(a) Theft is carried out in specific *pontos*. A *ponto* is a place (among them plazas, squares, crossroads, car parks, supermarkets, stations, parks, public transport, wasteland, beaches, pavements, or canopies) with spatial and social (environmental) characteristics which are favourable for survival activities, such as odd jobs, theft, drug use, begging, or rest. It is a public space in which children organise both their profitable and recreational activities.
(b) A *ponto* never coincides with the place where children sleep at night. A child who steals at the night-time *ponto* makes a big mistake, for they jeopardise the safety of the other children. With this mistake, the guilty child '*fica sujo no pedaço*'.[58] This means that, through their action, the child made a *ponto* unsuitable for the children to use. A *ponto* is constructed, it is conquered, it is the result of much effort, and losing it creates uncertainty and new risks for the group. As such, everyone needs to follow a certain discipline. This individual discipline is in itself an expression of the collaboration which exists between CSS. It is a rule that must be followed even when an extremely favourable situation arises.

[58] Literally, 'remains dirty in the turf'.

(c) Children change *ponto* on a regular basis. There is therefore a rotation between *pontos*: children change *pontos* every day and only come back to one place once it has become safe again. A group must then be able to make use of a specific area to optimise the conditions of its safety. Since the space is not expandable as needed, the choice of each *ponto* must be made with great care.
(d) Preferably, children only steal during specific times of the day. They generally steal shortly before lunch and dinner, and only steal between meals if a suitable situation arises. Stolen items are easily passed on to hawkers and other receivers of stolen goods. The search for food is not a problem. Children split into groups of two or three in order to steal.

They prefer to act when their victim is relatively isolated from other passers-by so as not to be stopped by them. For example, a potential victim is identified while in a covered market, but is not attacked at that time. The child waits for the victim to leave the market and only acts when the victim crosses a square near the market.

This way, the child has two advantages. First, there are fewer people in the square and the risk of being stopped is reduced. Second, the child can easily disappear through one of the many streets leading to the square. Every morning after waking up, children from the group go looking for the most promising *ponto*. This prepares the ground by scouting the area. Theft is not an improvised activity but one that requires the skills and collaboration of each child. A child with such skills is an 'expert'.[59] Those who are not 'experts' have to beg, and are disdained by the members of the group of child thieves.

Colen recounts an episode which illustrates certain practices used, among other things, to secure the cooperation of the group members. After collectively using inhalants, the leader challenges all the group members. He commands them to walk barefoot on a pile of nails to prove their bravery. Children who refuse to obey will be expelled from the group. The children voluntarily accept the challenge. This challenge has the characteristics of a ritual, despite being partly induced by the effects of the drugs. In any case, it is possible to discover two functions of a ritual in this episode: of confirming the leader's authority, and of strengthening the cohesion of the group.

The distribution of profit from stolen goods affects the role of the leader as much as the quality of the social bond between the group members. This distribution can take the form of:

(a) everyone giving their profit to the leader
(b) the leader dividing the money into equal shares, regardless of the share provided by each child. Even the child-victim receives a share[60]

[59] '*Esperto*' (deft).

[60] A similar case concerning Salvador, Bahia was brought to my attention by Antônio Nery Filho, a professor at this city's federal university. Children wash the windscreens of cars that stop at a traffic light. Everyone's share is proportionate to the amount of work done. However, the money coming from gratuities is not the result of the children's work and is, therefore, divided between the children into equal shares. In this example, two criteria preside over the division of money. The

(c) the leader proposing for everyone how to use the money: clothes first, then food
(d) if a member of the group is without money, the leader giving the child their share in kind (clothes or food)
(e) the leader takes a share equal to every other child's

Even though we have not seen any unquestioned leadership among the children of Praça Carioca, the testimonies of the oldest children (Paulo, Odair, Colen, Emilio, Gordo, Marco), like what was said by Paulo, allow us to distinguish at least five functions of a leader:

(a) choosing places for meetings and activities
(b) deciding whether to declare a site as *sujo* (a place which has become dangerous for the group) or not
(c) maintaining order in the group
(d) preserving the *ponto*
(e) keeping contacts in the police

If the group cohesion is primarily the leader's responsibility, the social bond between children does not rely on mutual trust. For instance, when the children go to the beach to swim, they entrust their money to the child-victim (who is also the least skilled child in the group). The child-victim can only go in the water once the other children are done swimming. The group does not entrust their money to the most trusted child, but to the child who is unable to take advantage of the situation and run away with the 'hoard'. The choice is made based on the lack of skills of the child to whom the money is given, not on the trust they have in this child. The behaviour of the child-victim is not dictated by a sense of solidarity towards the other children, but by a fear of repercussions and a lack of personal resources.

The absence of mutual trust is incompatible with bonds relying on solidarity, but it is compatible with cooperative relationships. The conditions required to trust someone are material. It is possible to trust someone only if that person does not leave a specific spot and stays visible and reachable: trust and physical presence are inseparable. In this case, the problem of trust exists in relation to a concrete situation: who can you confidently entrust with money? The answer is clear: only the person who does not need to spend it! Here there is no reference to the individual qualities which make a person trustworthy. Colen thinks that individuals behave according to their needs. But these needs are themselves determined by the circumstances. When there are no material resources on hand, individuals seize the opportunities they have. In Colen's terms, trust is a matter which depends on the circumstances and on entirely material factors. The relationships between these children are influenced by the level of survival skills that each child has gained, as well as by their personal charisma. We have witnessed this aspect, particularly when analysing the problem of the victim.

---

first one is proportionate to the children's individual effort and highlights their skill. The second one, which is an egalitarian criterion, is applied because the sum brought in is not the result of work.

In general, for equal skills, we have equal status. For children with important survival skills, one of the rules is to maintain control over the learning process that they offer to children less skilled than they are. Their safety and well-being on the street are at stake. Seventeen-year-old Paulo, an expert in *capoeira*, says: 'I am not going to teach it to others, because suddenly they become better than me. Then, they want to hit me and subdue me.' On the street, contrary to what one might think, rare goods are primarily not material goods (money, food, clothes), but rather intangible goods such as safety and physical integrity. We can add to this the prestige given to a child by the skills he or she learned on the street. Paulo thus wants to protect his goods when he refuses to teach *capoeira* to anyone.

Solidarity and trust are virtues, but the practice of these virtues is subject to the need to protect such rare goods. This protective dynamic is present at every level of competence, not only the highest levels (such as Paulo's). At the lowest levels, the distance in terms of skills between the dominant child and the apprentice child is smaller. In these cases, it is more difficult to durably protect the acquired skills.

On the street, there can be different consequences to other children learning new skills:

(a) a rise of the competition for survival in a given territory
(b) a rise in cases of voluntary cooperation between children
(c) the creation of new networks (dyads, triads or other). In this scenario, the 'newly skilled children' subjugate newcomers and the cycle can start again.

The acquisition of skills is therefore more absorbed by a permanent restructuring of the social bonds between the children than by new forms of solidarity.

Paulo indirectly links trust and respect. He says, 'Where there is respect (from people), there is also morality.'[61] Here, morality is the standards which control social relations in a given social context. Children respect morality when they conform to the practices of those they meet for the first time: 'If we arrive in a new place, we must respect the people already there'. In return, they acquire respect themselves. But this position is ambiguous, for it seems to concern primarily children with limited street experience. For those with skills, this obligation to respect is not considered: 'We were respected, because we put pressure on others.'[62] Respect is made up of a mixture of fear and admiration towards those who know how to impose themselves with their physical resources and symbolic skills. The phrase '*nào dar mole*', which is used here, means to not give rise to an attack, to avoid giving the opponent an excuse to attack.

The fluctuations which characterise life on the street force children to redefine their relationships with the entirety of their environment daily. Furthermore, the great emotional load that CSS carry with them makes them react violently to the smallest annoyances. The result is an extremely unstable social bond.

---

[61] '*Aonde, que aonde existe respeito, tem a moral.*'

[62] '*Dava respeito porque nos nào dava mole pra eles.*'

## References


Amado, J. (2013). *Captains of the sands*. Penguin Classics.

Caillois, R. (1958). *Les jeux et les hommes*. Paris: Gallimard.

Carlini, S. (1986). *As Familias e as Funçàes das Crianças de Rua: Algumas Pistas para sua Compreençào*, São Paulo (unpublished manuscript).

Cohen, A. (1955). *Delinquent Boys. The culture of the gang*. New York: The Free Press.

Di Méo, G. (1991). *L'Homme, la Société, l'Espace.* coll. Géographie. In: *Travaux de l'Institut Géographique de Reims*, n°79–80, 1990. 20 ans de TIGR, 20 ans de géographie, sous la direction de M. Bazin, J. Domingo et A. Marre. pp. 118–119.

Digneffe, F. (1986). Morale de justice ou morale de responsabilité: le débat entre L. Kohlberg et C. Gilligan à propos du développement du jugement moral. *Déviance et Société, 10*(1), 21–38.

Dubet, F. (1987). *La galère: jeunes en survie*. Paris: Fayard.

Fischer-Ferreira, M. (1979). *Meninos da rua*. São Paulo: IBREX.

Glauser, B. (1990). Street children: deconstructing a construct. In A. James & A. Prout (Eds.), *Constructing and reconstructing childhood. Contemporary issues on the sociological study of childhood* (pp. 143–157). London: The Falmer Press.

Goffman, E. (1974). *Les rites d'interaction*. Paris: Editions de Minuit.

Houchon, G. (1990). Pratiques et réseau: éloge de l'ambiguïté. *Déviance et société, 14*(2), 213–222.

Mucchielli, R. (1965). *Comment ils deviennent délinquants. Genèse et développement de la socialisation et de la dissocialité*. Paris: Editions sociales françaises.

Riaño-Alcalá, Y. (1990). Las Galladas: Street youth and cultural identity in the Barrios of Bogota. York University (unpublished manuscript).

Short, J. F., & Strodtbeck, F. L. (1965). *Group process and gang delinquency*. Chicago/London: University of Chicago Press.

Thrasher, F. M. (1927). *The gang*. Chicago: University of Chicago Press.

Whyte, W. F. (1943). *Street corner society*. Chicago: University of Chicago Press.

Yablonsky, L. (1979). The delinquent gang as a near-group. In E. J. Clark & D. H. Kelly (Eds.), *Deviant behavior. Readings in the sociology of deviance*. New York: St Martin's Press.

# Chapter 8
# Girls in Street Situations and Prostitution

**Riccardo Lucchini**

## 8.1 Girls in Street Situations[1] Are Not Prostitutes[2]

Among children in street situations (hereafter CSS) there are also girls. Yet these girls only rarely appear in the scholarly literature. There is a similar phenomenon here to that concerning the field of juvenile delinquency. Indeed, there have been very few attempts to adapt the "male theories of delinquency to girls" (Campbell 1981, p. 65). This despite some estimates that, in the USA, 10% of gangs are composed exclusively of girls (op. cit., p. 89). While the systematic study of CSS has begun, it focuses almost exclusively focus on boys. The situation is the same with the institutions dedicated to CSS. For most of these institutions, the question of GSS does not seem to constitute a central concern (de Almeida 1986, p. 59). In Brazil, for instance, assistance projects make boys their priority, even if girls have also access to them. Often programmes for girls focus on young prostitutes or prostitutes' daughters. This contributes to the conflation which is often made between GSS and prostitution. We will come back to this point.

While it is true that, compared to boys, girls are in a minority on the street, they are far from absent. Most estimates around the world report between a range of 9% to 25% of girls making up the street population. In Kanpur, India, the percentage is 17.3% (Pandey 1991, p. 107), while it is 13.7% in the Indian state of Madhya Pradesh (Phillips 1994, p. 33). In the Philippines, one estimate suggests that girls make up 19% of the population of CSS (Silva 1991, p. 107). A recent study put the percentage of girls among CSS at 9% in Nairobi, Kenya, and 17% in Juarez, Mexico (Aptekar 1993a, b, p. 2). Research on four Ethiopian towns found that 24% of CSS were girls (UNICEF 1993, p. 16). Stefan Roggenbuck (1993, p. 133) states that 35% of CSS in Sào Paulo are girls, a proportion he notes is relatively high. Across Brazil,

[1] Hereafter GSS.

[2] This chapter is updated from Lucchini, R. (1994). *The street girl. Prostitution, family and drug*. University of Fribourg (Working Paper 243).



R. Lucchini, D. Stoecklin, *Children in Street Situations*, Children's Well-Being: Indicators and Research 21, https://doi.org/10.1007/978-3-030-19040-8_8

the percentages vary from place to place: in Rio de Janeiro it is 13%, in Recife 14%, Salvador 11%, and in Fortaleza and Goiânia 10% (de Souza 1992, p. 99). In Asuncion, Paraguay, girls represent 12% of the population of CSS (Espinola et al. 1990, p. 22), in Lima, Peru, it is 14%, while in Cochabamba, Bolivia, the percentage is 12% (Myers, p. 359). Another recent study in Lima gave a proportion of 17%.

These figures indicate the over-representation of boys among CSS. Unfortunately, they do not allow for a rigorous comparison between situations in different parts of the world. Indeed, some of these figures refer only to children who do not return home in the evening, while others refer to all children who spend some time on the street. In the latter case, which includes the three categories of children said to be in 'risk situations' – "children of the street", "children on the street" and "abandoned children" – the percentage of girls rises somewhat. On the other hand, these studies raise attention to the fact that most GSS are distantly supervised by an adult from their family or an older brother. As such, speaking of Latin America, Mark Lusk (1994, p. 7) writes: "street girls are more likely than boys to be found working in conjunction with a street family – that is to say a conjugal group that resides in the street or parks on a full or part time basis [...] Parents make every effort to retain the girl in the home environment". It is here that from a young age they perform all the domestic duties of adult women. This approach is also valid for young women in the India. Their presence in the street "is mainly because of the availability and nature of jobs in the urban area. In the case of girls they are involved in household chores such as collecting, water, cooking and looking after siblings" (Phillips 1994, p. 33). However, as Amrita Chatterjee (1992, p. 14) writes, "studies show that employment for girls outside the home often ceases around the time of puberty to conform with socio-religious practice: parents are extremely reluctant to expose their daughters to male attention".

The small number of girls on the street in comparison to boys does not alone explain the absence of scholarly work afforded to GSS. This absence likewise contrasts with the abundance and proliferation of mass market publications on the girls who are on the streets of cities in the global south. This leads to a conflation between GSS, prostitution, and other forms of exploitation. As Lewis Aptekar (1988, p. 44) writes it, girls are not considered part of the same category as boys: "they are given a different niche, one that is more often associated with prostitution". This association must be linked to the social perception of female sexuality. As Nanette J. Davis (1977, p. 265) writes, "originally defined as offensive and immoral, female sexuality, especially within a monogamous relationship, is accepted as normal and appropriate". This point of view is supported by Loes Brünott (1986, p. 293), who argues that men have imposed upon women "their definitions of marriage, eroticism and sexuality".

But we know that the large majority of GSS do not take part in prostitution. We also know that among very young girls who sell sex and who come from the most disadvantaged social stratas, only a tiny minority belong at the same time to the category of CSS. This distinction is already present in a 1985 unpublished report on prostitution in Latin America. Quoting a Colombian journalist, the author writes that "when a young girl leaves home, she has the choice only between joining a group of children or falling into prostitution" (Barruel de Lagenest, 1985). Aptekar also writes that the "most common claim for finding fewer girls in the streets has been that they are taken off the streets to become prostitutes. This situation has been described, particularly by the media or international organizations, as inevitable and total, but in fact the actual number of prostitutes is far less than this hypothesis would predict" (Aptekar op. cit., p. 2).

Besides, how is it possible to classify often very young children – between ten and twelve years old – as professional prostitutes? We find here the expansion of the classification which cannot be justified scientifically or ethically. These children are victims of sexual abuse, even if they receive a few pennies or a little food and drink for their services. This therefore nothing to do with prostitution. Moreover, the younger girls, aged eight to ten years, are often sexually exploited in the company of their mother – who will also be very young – who themselves practice prostitution. These cases also, for the most part, do not belong to the of CSS. In one of the rare surveys made of street girls who "are prostituting", it is written that they do not realize "their situation and above all the conditions of exploitation they are submitted to" (de Almeida op. cit., p. 63). The problem of the sexual exploitation of GSS exists and must be taken seriously. But this is not comparable to prostitution. While it is true that girls living on the street sometimes turn to prostitution, it is not correct to identify them as professional prostitutes. We will see why.

The act designated as prostitution does not have a precise definition, and no single definition is satisfactory. It cannot be defined as simply an exchange of money for sexual services. In addition to monetary exchange, most definitions involve the absence of affective relations between the partners and the immediate payment of the monetary counterpart of the sexual act (Thio 1978, p. 169). Some other authors also define prostitution in terms of the commercial exchange of sex and emotional indifference between the partners: "Prostitution is sexual intercourse on a promiscuous and mercenary basis, with emotional indifference" (Clinard and Meier 1979, p. 394). By this definition, if one of the three elements is lacking, the act cannot be defined as prostitution. One finds again these three dimensions of prostitution in the definition given by Robert King Merton and Robert Nisbet (1977, p. 245). For these authors, the instability of the relationship is fundamental in order to distinguish prostitution from sexual acts which, even when they have a monetary dimension (the marriage of convenience, for instance), takes place in an institutional setting: "The prostitute's affront is not that she trades but that she trades promiscuously and with emotional indifference".

The absence of emotional tie or of pleasure in the sexual act which appears in numerous definitions of prostitution has been criticised for its subjective character (Fossé-Poliak 1984, p. 260). Indeed, if one takes the subjective dimension into account, "one is immediately confronted with the diversity of points of view" (Ibid.). Finally, the professional character that accompanies sexual activity appears in several definitions of prostitution. This takes in not only the temporal dimension and thus its routine character, but also the competencies and the learning of these competencies by the woman designated as a prostitute. This routine character appears in Wilhelm Bernsdorf's (1955, p. 593) definition of the prostitute, understood as a woman who is "giving herself sexually in exchange for money, be it publicly or secretly, to a high number of men without making differentiation or choice". Professionalism and venality become the dimensions most often accepted when talking about prostitution.

However, the professional element of the definition is not universally accepted. For Kathleen Barry (1986, pp. 302–303), prostitution is always accompanied by "a fundamental violation (consisting in) transforming the body and the sexuality of women into objects in order to exchange them on the market". Barry shares the position of the UNESCO group of experts who in 1986 refused to name prostitution as a profession. Here prostitution is considered as "an exchange where the woman's body is assimilated to a commodity and where the woman is lowered to the status of an object" (op. cit., p. 299). As we see, the definition of prostitution as a status and as an activity originates a debate which is far from resolved, and which is impossible to resolve here, because the very criteria used for these definitions work through different argumentative registers. For some, prostitution is objectively a violation of the fundamental rights of the human person, while for others, it is subjectively a right that has to be respected. The debate inevitably takes on a normative character.

However, what must appear in any sociological analysis are the characteristics of the phenomenon itself before any moral consideration. The four dimensions (professionalism, venality, promiscuity, emotional indifference), diversely present in the above mentioned definitions, all appear to us as being useful. Prostitution is thus defined as a transaction of a venal character and of a professional nature, which involves promiscuity and the absence of an affective relationship between the partners. The principal difficulty resides in the fact that, at the level of practices, these dimensions of prostitution do not have an absolute character, but a gradual one. In other words, the intensity, the importance of each of these dimensions can vary considerably from one case to the next. Yet this affects the quality of the sexual act itself. As with most deviant behaviours, we find a continuum (see Fig. 8.1 hereunder).

Concrete behaviours are located between the two extremes of the continuum. The position of behaviours on the continuum depends on cultural, identitary, and contextual factors, which have to be identified from case to case. The classification of behaviours on this continuum is also complicated by the fact that the dimensions defining prostitution may vary independently. It is not easy to determine with certainty at what point on the continuum a sexual act becomes prostitution or stops being prostitution. Despite these difficulties the idea of a continuum is useful,

| | | |
|---|---|---|
| Deviance:<br>maximal presence of the four components (professionalism, venality, promiscuity, emotional indifference) | (1)<--------------------------->(2) | Conformity:<br>total absence of the four components (professionalism, venality, promiscuity, emotional indifference) |

**Fig. 8.1** Continuum of conform and deviant sexual intercourse

because it allows to show why it is imprudent to identify GSS with prostitution. Moreover, when CSS speak of the girls who are with them on the street, they do not speak in terms of prostitution. Prostitutes do not share their daily lives as is the case with GSS. The prostitutes belong to an out-group, while GSS are members of an in-group. Here sexuality does not have a commercial character. Even if the sexual act is characterised by a certain promiscuity that is not always without violence, it is not assimilable to prostitution. This does not exclude the fact that certain girls get into prostitution while remaining members of a group of CSS. However, this activity is restricted within certain limits. In the opposite case, the girl leaves the group or the network of CSS, and joins the category of prostitute women.

The assimilation of GSS into the terms of prostitution is therefore one of the factors that renders them less visible. Indeed, they are classified in a category which is not that of CSS. One gets the impression that the 'street girl' does not exist, or should not exist. This is a phenomenon which is both cultural and cognitive. Indeed, the street world is above all a masculine space. The presence of girls on the street upsets the values and representations of adults. Unease sets in, and the explanation of this presence goes through a pathologization of the girl and of her family.

The marginal girl and the delinquent girl are soon associated with sexuality and with the fantasies and prohibitions which accompany it. This troubles the judgement and consideration that men and women have for the girls who are on the street. With the boy, sexuality appears as natural: it needs no particular explanation, and does not disturb the order of things. Female sexuality, on the contrary, is perceived as a potential danger. It has to be exorcised more than prevented. It is acceptable only within a clearly delimited institutional structure. As the street is perceived as a place of licentiousness and anomie, the female sexuality that is linked to it is deemed definitely deviant.[3]

While GSS are associated with sexuality and pathology, boys are associated with delinquency. As Anne Campbell (1981, p. 13) writes, the explanation of female delinquency itself "is sought in individual pathology, and a young female criminal is more likely to be labelled as maladjusted or afflicted with behavioural or emotional problems than as simply delinquent". When a boy steals or is trafficking in order to survive on the street, this is considered to be something natural. On the contrary, when a girl trades sex, "one admits the existence of instincts which transform the woman into a prostitute" (Pastoral do Menor 1988, p. 11). This attitude towards girls is not limited to the countries of Latin America: it is found everywhere. While "boys tend to be arrested for offenses involving stealing and various sorts of mischiefs, girls are typically charged with sex offenses which are euphemistically described as 'delinquent tendencies', 'incorrigibility', or 'running away'" (Adler and Adler 1979, p. 523). This is confirmed by the analysis of Ruth Shone Cavan and Theodore N. Ferdinand (1975, p. 2018), who characterize the delinquency of girls by high rates of "runaway, truancy and incorrigibility". Then these same authors

[3] On the contrary, prostitution is not considered so troubling, as it is an institutionalized practice. Even if it takes place in the street, it is, while not considered legitimate, nevertheless an accepted deviance.

specify that "in mid-adolescence, girls were most frequently charged with sex offenses and disorderly conduct". This is also confirmed by Campbell (1987, p. 451) in her studies girls who are members of street gangs. Overall, in works published before 1970, two features characterize the girl frequenting the street: psychological problems and a deviant sexual behaviour.

The deviant behaviour of the girl is thus more strongly stigmatized than the boy's. Moreover, as Freda Adler and Herbert Marcus Adler observe, among sociologists and criminologists the study of female deviance has not given rise to an interest comparable to that by male deviance (Adler and Adler, op. cit., p. 524). This stigmatization is thus also influenced by the attitude of the scholars. Indeed, "because girls were different from boys, it was assumed a generation ago that delinquent girls, like nondeliquent girls, were simpler to understand" (Ibid.). This stigmatization is partly caused by the behavioural expectations the community has of girls. The demand made of girls is that they be obedient at home and at school, they spend the night at home, and they do not have sexual relations (Cavan and Ferdinand, op. cit., p. 220). In the specific case of GSS, the stigmatization is stronger still than of the deviant girl compared to the deviant boy. Indeed, it is on her that the self-righteous focus their indignation, and to her the state services react, subjecting her to their degrading rigour.

It is therefore incorrect to assimilate GSS to prostitutes. This conflation is in opposition to facts, and it is the consequence of a stigmatization that affects women when they leave home for public spaces. It is true that the conditions in Brazil in which we find the 'lower prostitution', that is to say the one practiced on the street, facilitates the identification of GSS with prostitutes. A study of Rio de Janeiro shows that prostitutes there rarely depend on a pimp (Dulce Gaspar 1985, pp. 73–75). When there is one, his power is not comparable to that of his European equivalent. The woman is thus relatively independent, and she regulates her activities according to her personal needs. This is also true of the 'intermediary prostitution' taking place in rooms rented for this purpose (*prostituiçào de zona*).[4] In other cities like Salvador, however, only prostitution on the street allows the prostitute this independence (Espinheira 1984, p. 52).[5] It is also the case that when prostitution is associated with drug trafficking, the woman's independence is further reduced.

That said, none of this can allow us to underestimate the severity of the sexual violence to which the girl is exposed. We will see this. While reliable estimates do not exist, and are probably impossible to produce, testimonies suggest that a majority of girls leave their parental home for reasons concerning domestic sexual violence. Stepfathers, fathers, half-brothers and neighbours are generally responsible for this violence. Recent research concerning the Philippines, Thailand, Colombia, and Kenya reveals the precocious character of sexual intercourse among CSS. Here

[4]The *zonas* are important establishments, with up to sixty rooms and as many prostitutes. The rotation of clients is important, as an average of twenty clients per prostitute was reported (see Dulce Gaspar, op. cit., p. 11).

[5]This author specifies, however, that even this form of prostitution sooner or later ties up the woman with organizations limiting her independence.

"sex represented a mixture of pleasure or recreation, a source of income or a possibility of shelter, sometime even of power (in the case of group rape) [...] Sex is a bargaining chip to obtain food, shelter, or any favour". The study also reports on "cases of collective rapes of the female members of gangs [...] rape as punishment or initiation into the gang". In certain cases, like in Bogotà, studies speak of a "survival prostitution on the street" (Barker 1994, p. 41). However, all this does not yet allow us to assimilate the GSS into the category of professional prostitutes.

## 8.2 The Single Parent Family

Not one of the girls we have been interviewing comes from a complete family. Most of them do not know their father. Either they have never met him, or he left home when they were only a few months old. Furthermore, while all the girls knew their mother, only one of them lived with her exclusively until adolescence, before she was placed in an institution. The other girls have been variously placed with their grandparents, uncles and aunts, or with a foster family. Finally, in one case the girl was placed in an institution while still very young. Two girls have lost their mothers, respectively when aged three and six. All the girls have therefore experienced different forms of placement in care and have alternated between different homes.[6]

All the girls mention bad treatment, but the focus is placed on the absence of affection and of respect for their personhood. Their offence, and generally their episodes of running away, appear to be more of a means of protest against a lack of identitary recognition than a search for adventure or a means of survival. The affective and identitary dimension of the process, which leads the girl to leave the familial home or her place of care, seems to be more important than in the case of boys. In a study of English children who have left their family home for significant periods of time or who have been placed in the care of the state, some researchers have found an interesting difference between girls and boys. The proportion of girls is more significant among the younger children. According to the authors, this could indicate "a greater ability of females to move out of the risk situation which in turn may be a consequence of agencies seeing females as more vulnerable and giving them priority" (Stockley et al. 1992, p. 9). The socio-economic and cultural differences between countries like England and Argentina, as well as a lack of documentation, do not allow us to know whether something similar exists in certain countries of Latin America. It remains a fact that the girls in our study have all experienced the absence of the father, of abandonment and placement in care at a

[6]The familial situation characterizing our sample cannot be simply extrapolated to the population of GSS as a whole, even if the very deficient information we have on GSS may make us think that the incomplete family is a feature shared by most of them. We cannot extrapolate this information in a pure and simple manner, especially for one reason: the girls studied were all placed in an institution for girls, having experienced significant 'behavioural' problems. Here the institution made a selection which ended in a concentration of cases qualified as 'risk cases'.

young age. With one exception – the short time presence of the mother and the stepfather – they come from single mother families. It is therefore necessary to take into consideration this type of family, and the status of the poor woman who raises her children alone. It is certain that some important differences exist according to the place the single mother family lives and its socio-cultural conditions. Indeed, some elements like economic constraints, access to a parental network ('availability of kin') and the cultural context ('cultural predispositions') are determinants of the forms taken by the different types of familial organisation (Morgan 1993, p. 246).

Socio-economic development and cultural change, as well as the structure of the familial group and the status of the woman in this group, all influence the woman's behaviour. It is therefore useful to ask how these parameters intervene in the relationships a woman establishes with her children. In turn, socio-cultural change is also linked to the question of female deviance. Indeed, the mother's status in the domestic group as well as her behaviour are both linked to the question of the child's departure for the street (Miranda Ferreira 1986, Woortmann 1987, Aptekar 1988, 1992, 1993a, b, Kilbride 1991).

As Nanette J. Davis (op. cit., p. 248) writes, "lower fertility, privatization of the nuclear family, segregated labor market, consumerism, and social distribution based on equality of competition, not equality of results, have profoundly altered family and gender structures, and probably worsened women's condition, especially among already disadvantaged groups". This evolution has been especially manifest since the 1950s, but does not touch all the social groups and all the countries in the same manner. As Mercer L. Sullivan (1993, p. 66) observes, "explanations of the relationship between family form and poverty have long been controversial in social science". The convergence between the phenomena of poverty and single mother families among the cultural minorities of the United States has sustained a long controversy, says Sullivan, which is far from resolved on "the role that culture plays in the processes that produce both female-headed households and poverty"(Ibid).

We do know that 60% of the children in African American neighbourhoods come from single mother families (Body-Gendrot 1993, p. 195), and that, according to another source, 85% of black children born in the beginning of the 1990s will for some period of time live in a family headed by a woman (McLanahan and Garfinkel 1988, p. 110). In contrast, research for the year 1987 showed that the total number of American children living with only their mother was 21%. This represents a considerable increase: in 1960 the proportion was only 7% (McLanahan et al. 1991). We see, then, that black children are heavily overrepresented. In Brazil, at different times and in different cities, we find similar percentages of single mother families. A 1985 study of Recife found that a woman was the family's head in 29.8% of cases, in Belem, 1973, this percentage was 28.2%, while in Salvador, 1970, it was 26.8%.[7] A similar situation can be found in East Africa, where in the beginning of the 1980s it was estimated that single mother families accounted for 35% of all families (Aptekar 1993a, b, p. 10).

[7] On Recife, see Quintas (1986); for Salvador: Woortmann (1987); for Belem: de Andrade Gonçalves (1979).

While to some authors "the dislocation of the black family appears as the major problem in the ghettos" (Body-Gendrot, op. cit., p. 196), we also see that "the inner-city black female-headed household has been praised as an innovative adaptation to disadvantaged economic conditions" (Boone 1989, p. 145). The innovative character of the modes of adaptation to extreme situations of shortage, as experienced by single mother families in ghettos, is also underlined by the analysis Sullivan offers of three neighbourhood units in New York City. Speaking of a black neighbourhood, Sullivan writes that "they have developed complex ways of supporting children in kin-based networks" (op. cit., p. 74). The situation here involves young fathers not living with the mother of their children. Niara Sudarkasa (1993, p. 84) makes a similar observation on the help given to single mother families by men belonging to the kinship network, noting that researchers have neglected to highlight the help given by sons, brothers, or uncles to the woman who is head of the household.

However, the mutual aid network also depends on the resources of the community the single mother family lives in. It is estimated that 30% of single mother black families in the United States live in neighbourhoods suffering extreme poverty, where the only resource is public assistance (McLanahan and Garfinkel, op. cit., p. 117). In this case, the available resources for material mutual aid are quite weak. Data for the United States showed that in 1983 half of single mother families were poor, compared to only 12% of nuclear families. On this topic, some authors speak of a "feminization of poverty" (McLanahan et al., op.cit. p. 54). This process is also found in the countries of the European Union, where single mother families represent 10% of households with children, and where the rate of poverty is higher than the national average when the head of household is a woman (Michel 1993, p. 12).

This poverty is, generally speaking, longer-term and is more significant than that experienced by nuclear families. This poses the problem of inherited poverty. According to a study made by the Rand Corporation, "a black teenage girl who has difficulties at school and who lives in a poor family abandoned by the father has a one in four probability of becoming a single mother. For a white teenage girl, raised by her two parents in an environment without financial and school problems, this probability is one in one thousand" (Halimi 1989, p. 37). In turn, the children of these black teenagers are then the most vulnerable to long-term poverty (Huston 1991, p. 9). Regarding marriages, we can note that they begin to decline at the turn of the 1970s. The proportion of married individuals, we note, "declined among black Americans from 64% to 49% between 1970 and 1983, while rising from 62% to 65% among the Hispanic population" (Clignet 1988, p. 267).

As Aletha Huston (op. cit.) notes, it is important to distinguish between persistent poverty and transitory poverty. Indeed, these two types of poverty differently affect familial organization and thus the child's situation in the familial group. Yet poverty alone does not explain the child's departure from home, nor does the mother's behaviour towards the child, and not all poor children from the slums quit their homes. Still, we must recognise how poverty influences the familial organization, and the respective positions of men and women in the familial group (Lucchini 1993b).

In addition, slums – notably in Latin America – are not totally homogeneous in socio-economic terms. There are sometimes important differences regarding material conditions (income, wealth) among the inhabitants of the same slum (UNCHS 1981; Santos 1982; Cannat 1988; Rochefort 1988; Leser de Mello 1989; Kasarda and Parnell 1993; Riaño and Wesche 1994). These differences influence the possibilities of building networks of mutual aid between single women. However, the weakness, even absence of state social aid of the in the slums of Latin America stimulates the creation of such networks. As Rosa M. Cañadell John F. Ugen write (1993, p. 49) regarding Chile, a number of factors stimulating the self-organization of poor women can be distinguished. Among these factors, two are particularly important. The first concerns the familial role of the woman who becomes the family head after the man's departure. This change gives a new legitimacy to extra-familial activities which allow the woman to provide for the needs of her family. We may note that this legitimacy is often already established, as the women going into work can be a condition of even a nuclear family's survival if the family is poor. The second factor is constituted by the lack of political organisations and unions, alongside the weakness or absence of state social policy, that pushes women to fill this gap. In this case, the political aspect is an important component of women's action. All of this also influences the image these women have of themselves and the relationships they have with their children, and with the man when he is at home. When this taking on of new functions is accompanied by an improvement in the image of self and by community awareness, there is an improvement in the quality of family life.

Regarding violence exerted on children, nothing allows us to attribute the cause of it to the single mother family, or to the woman. Some studies have shown that it is within the frame of the isolated nuclear family that violence against children is at its highest (Levinson 1989, p. 54), while others have come to the conclusion that the family type exerts no influence on violence towards children (Ibid. p. 55). This is not surprising if one takes into account the high number of factors that produce domestic violence towards children. On the contrary, mutual aid networks, by linking single mother families together, reduce this form of violence. Social control as well as material resources and the cooperation entailed by the networking of two or more domestic units explains this result. As Philip Kilbride writes regarding the United States, "enhancing people's social support networks is also an effective measure for the prevention of child abuse" (Kilbride, op. cit., p. 131). Other studies have shown that social isolation of the woman, including if she is married, is linked to a rise in the mistreatment of children. The woman's feeling of solitude reinforces this tendency further still (Polansky et al. 1985, p. 39). The constitution of mutual aid networks in the slums is most often the work of women. If this is accompanied by an improvement of the woman's status, one would assume that violence towards children would consequently diminish. Indeed, as Kilbride (op. cit., p. 131) writes, the heightening of the woman's social status is accompanied, even in the different cultures, by an apparent decrease of familial violence committed on children. The situation is evidently more complex, since the woman who is head of the household does not always live alone. This is the case in families where the woman has children from several men who live with her only for relatively short periods of time.

Besides, not all single mother families look alike. Indeed, there are important differences between a family composed of a young woman who has never been married and her children, and a family with a widow or an older woman who has been married at its head. Any discussion of the single mother family has to consider parameters like the age and the marital history of the woman (Sudarska, op. cit., p. 83). As Cristina Szanton Blanc (1992, p. 37) notes "the female headship phenomenon is socially diverse both within and across countries. The determinants of headship and its significance also vary". This entails different consequences for the children and their mother from one country to another, from one region to the next. However, we see widely that a child who has been raised by their mother alone is more frequently the victim of mistreatment than a child who lives in another familial context (Levinson, op. cit., p. 55).

Among black Americans, the single mother family has always been perceived as a legitimate form of familial organization (Ibid. p. 85). As a consequence, the children born within such families have never been considered to be illegitimate. This legitimacy can be considered as a factor which potentially reduces the possibility of the mother exerting violence on the child. Where such constitutive principles of matrifocality are preserved, the same phenomenon can be found among the black populations of countries like Colombia and Brazil.[8] But in the case of a black population which has gone through an important process of deculturation (in terms of the valorization of the nuclear family and of the authority of men over women), and whose economic situation is precarious, the image of the single mother family changes and the situation of the woman and of her children deteriorates severely.

The woman often places a child in the care of a female neighbour, a parent, or in an institution in order to be able to provide at least the minimum to support her other children. When such cases multiply, anthropologists speak of a "circulation of children" (Fonseca 1985, 1988; Scheper-Hughes 1985, p. 312), and even a "voluntary" circulation of children. In fact, the placement is not only a survival strategy, but also a means of allowing the woman to set up a link with another woman. The children are "sometimes given as a gift in order to cement the relationship between the birth mother and the foster home" (Scheper-Hughes, op. cit., p. 50). This does not mean that the child who has been placed in care will have a stable home, and, indeed, the often changing economic conditions of the foster family itself lead in turn to this family sending the child elsewhere or back home.

We note also that this placement of children in care is not exclusive to single mother families, but also concerns other types of family. The circulation of children also functions not only through informal adoptions, but also through the practice of abandonment. When living conditions are very precarious and infant mortality very

[8] On Columbia see Aptekar (1988); for Brazil, see Woortmann (1987) and McCarty (1981).

high, the mother will sometimes not give her newborn a name. She seems to protect herself against developing too strong an attachment to the child, who is still at significant risk of dying in the near future. Several children were not only unbaptized, "but did not have any name until they began to walk, or until a serious illness (and eventuality of death) would provoke a hasty baptism". In these cases, "unnamed babies are simply called *ne-ne* (baby) or given a Brazilian generic name, Ze (Joe) or Maria. Adult affection for *ne-ne* is diffuse and not focused on any particular characteristics of the infant as a little persona" (Ibid. pp. 311–312).

The behaviour of poor women in general, and in particular of women who are the family head of the single mother family, cannot be explained by the culture of poverty alone. The culture of poverty is conceived as constituting a homogeneous whole, enclosed and clearly delimited with respect to other systems of values and references. Even if Oscar Lewis – the creator of the concept – relativizes somewhat the closed character of the subculture of poverty, the whole constituting it seems to remain very homogeneous.[9] In truth, the diversity of human cultures "should not be conceived in a static way" (Lévi-Strauss 1973, p. 381). In other words, any culture is forming and developing through contact with other cultures. The diversity of human cultures "is less the function of the isolation of groups than of the relationships linking them together" (Ibid., p. 382). This indicates that one cannot delimit a culture or an ethnic group "by innate and unchanging cultural and mental characteristics, by specific and permanent features" (Porshnev 1978, p. 319). Porshnev joins Lévi-Strauss when he writes that "[the] point is not that a certain people possess a certain stable cultural element while its neighbour do not have it or have it in a modified degree. No, it is the difference itself that constitutes the fact of culture" (Ibid. p. 142). According to Porshnev, it is the frontier between different cultural entities which constitutes the essence of a culture. It is therefore the opposition of differences that constitutes cultural dynamics. A certain ambivalence in the heart of any culture is enabled by the contact and confrontation between different cultures. Indeed, for Porshnev, a culture is constituted precisely by the totality of frontiers or contact lines which demarcate it from other cultures: "an exceedingly complex totality of accumulated interethnic borders of lines of contact" (Ibid. p. 143).

The norms and the practices specific to the culture of poverty, then, define themselves in contrast to other cultural wholes: such as the middle classes. This has to be considered when tackling the question of the construction of meaning by different social actors, and as such also when analysing the question of abandonment, the circulation of children, and violence against children. In other words, these concepts do not always mean the same thing when we move between cultures, social environments, and time periods.

[9] Oscar Lewis (1963, p. 618) actually observes that the poors know certain values specific to middle classes, proclaim certain among them, but cannot live according to these values.

## 8.3 Sociability, Identity and Drugs

We have seen that the girls of our study come from single mother families. In the most disadvantaged stratas, in Argentina as elsewhere in Latin America, the instability of the conjugal union is important. The phenomenon of single women with several children, living unmarried with men who leave them after short periods of time, is a common one (David 1987, p. 333).

### *8.3.1 Sociability*

To explain their departure from home, all of the girls in our study mention they have been victims of violence or prohibitions. However, none of them go directly to the street. Only Mara leaves her mother. The others leave various housing situations, like foster families or institutions. These departures are therefore from very different contexts, but the common thread is that these girls, as with most CSS, feel a deep need to justify their departure from home. It is presented as a solution to personal problems. When the girls speak of their past existence on the street, their accounts often take the form of an excuse. Yet these excuses are "accounts expressed in socially approved vocabularies in which one admits the act in question is bad, wrong or inappropriate but denies full responsibility" (Visano 1990, p. 145). This, however, does not mean that the child refuses membership of the street world: quite the opposite (Ibid.).

These girls often do not go directly in the street, but first seek refuge at a girl friend's home. They are soon placed in institutions, and it is only later that they arrive on the street. For some of them, prostitution is an intermediary phase located before their arrival in the street. Certainly during this phase, the girl is not a 'street girl', since she does not share the daily life of CSS. For the girls who will go onto street, this is a transitional phase. Some others alternate between phases of professional prostitution and phases of casual prostitution. We do not know how the passage from prostitution to the street takes place. What we do know is that CSS do not speak of their female friends in terms of prostitution, and no girl in our study who has practiced prostitution before staying on the street sees the two situations as being the same. What we observe here is that prostitution and street life are two distinct periods of their lifetime.[10] This is also confirmed by the account of a street educator who clearly distinguishes between the street and the milieu of prostitution. According to this educator, the street requires that boys be even tougher than would be expected of men. In the case of women, there are two situations. In the first, the girl embraces femininity and at puberty she passes in the other milieu, that of prostitution. If, on the contrary, she wants to stay in the social sphere of CSS, then

[10] Authors like Stefan Roggenbuck (1993, pp. 104–105) and Dolly Conto de Knoll (1991, p. 141) also refuse the identification of GSS with prostitutes.

she also has to adopt the tough manners of the street.[11] There is no compromise between the two social spheres: the girl cannot simultaneously be a professional prostitute and a 'street girl'. She is the one or the other, because the social rules and the rhythm of daily life are too different from one case to the other.

Two factors seem to influence the character of the girl's prostitution, be it transitional or permanent. The first is the age at which the girl practices prostitution, and the second is the existence, or absence, of a pimp or a network that exploits the girl. Two situations then arise. The first one is characterized by the very young age of the girls who practice prostitution – twelve to thirteen years old – and by the absence of her insertion into an exploitative network. The second, in contrast, is that of an older girl who is exploited by a pimp or integrated into a network. In this case the conditions are met prostitution becoming a lasting and non-transitional condition.

Girls, as with boys, do not become GSS overnight. They follow a route, a movement towards the street.[12] This movement comprises four stages: (1) the girl leaves the domestic home and goes to the home of a female friend home; (2) she is placed in an institution; (3) she practices prostitution; (4) she stays on the street for some time. One observes that when a girl finds her place in a group of CSS, she generally abandons prostitution as a primary activity. However, the movement ending in the street is not a straight one. Indeed, returns to the preceding stage are frequent, and most girls do not leave the domestic home alone, generally being accompanied by a friend.

This process is illustrated in an exemplary manner by the case of Mara. She comes from a small town in the province of Mendoza, and she has never known her father. She is the youngest of her mother's children and, at the time of her running away, all of her brothers and sisters were married or had otherwise left the house. Her mother works as a servant. This absence of adults gives Mara much liberty. She is twelve when she leaves home for the first time. This departure is the consequence of her a punishment delivered by her mother, which Mara considers unjustified and violent. It is unjust because her mother punishes her for a minor act disobedience: she went out to dance, despite her mother prohibiting this. Mara specifies: "my mother saw me and struck me. I remember she struck me with a cable and she almost killed me, she cut my hair, she left no hair on my head. So I left".

This maternal behaviour is perceived as very repressive as Mara's friends' mothers allow their daughters to go out to dance. The maternal punishment is described as being exaggerated, inappropriate, and therefore unjust. Yet Mara makes no judgement of her mother, despite the severity of the punishment. She only says that her mother is an old-fashioned woman, unable to understand the ways of the teenagers. As it is recounted, this episode is not dramatic and it may occur in the most diverse social groups. In fact, the episode that trigger's Mara's departure is not the most important thing. It is, rather, a symptom, which reveals the existence of an

[11] We will come back to this point when analysing the identitary function of theft committed by girls.

[12] As we have shown elsewhere (Lucchini 1993a), this movement is double: spatio-temporal and identitary.

uneasiness and an imbalance in the relational and familial life of the child. Factors of an affective, material, psychological, and social nature influence the child's threshold of tolerance when facing events happening in their immediate surroundings, and likewise influences their perception of these events. The attraction exerted by the extra-familial sphere on the child is also influenced by these factors.

Mara finds refuge at a female friend's home. As she does not want to return home, she is placed in an institution, from which she later escapes. She does not run away alone, but in the company of other girls. On the institution, Mara speaks against the shared presence of girls placed there for diverse offences: from robbery to murder, prostitution to running away. She says: "it is as if I was in another world". This mixing of diverse cases, that would rightly require diverse interventions, cannot be correctly managed if the institution does not have the appropriate material and human resources at its disposal. Running away from the institution is thus the result of the institution's inadequacy to and absence of response towards the children's needs.[13]

Running away is also an adventure undertaken with several others. As well as being a response to the lacks of the institution, it is therefore also a playful enterprise. With her companions, Mara rents a room in an old lady's flat and practices prostitution for a while. She is twelve years old. She enjoys this life: "I saw my mother working all day long to earn some pesos [...] What she was earning in one day, I could earn within half an hour". She practices prostitution in this way for a year, without ever living like a 'street girl'.

After one year, Mara leaves Mendoza together with a female friend in order to go to Buenos Aires. The reason for this departure is be the death of one of her friends, who was shot by the police. In the capital, the two girls establish themselves in one of the big stations of Buenos Aires, Retiro, highly frequented by CSS. At night they sleep in coaches. Like other girls of our study, Mara practices occasional prostitution. Regular prostitution is associated with the danger of being kidnapped, and of being identified by the police. In fact, being identified as a prostitute is contrary to the anonymity required for survival in the street. As such Mara practiced prostitution only to compensate for lack in other survival strategies, generally becoming necessary twice a week. When she practices prostitution, she never does so on the street by approaching potential clients. She leaves the street and goes to the home of the man asking her so. She entered this activity by responding to a man's demand: he wanted her to go to his friend's house. Mara makes a clear separation between this activity and the street world she is frequenting. No disapproval of the other children towards prostitution is indicated in her accounts, only the danger of being arrested by the police.

Regarding forms of sociability among girls, we distinguish four types of groups: the network, in which a significant number of children participate (between fifteen and thirty); the small group formed only by girls; the mixed group of boys and girls;

[13] One finds interesting analysis of the dynamic of running away, as well as on the mechanism that on the contrary would see the child stay in the institution (see Newman 1989).

and eventually the couple, formed by one boy and one girl. The girl participates in all of these groups, since they are complementary in their functions. The couple formed by some older boys and girls is occasionally the exception to this rule. In this case, the couple has meet their survival needs by themselves. This last situation is primarily found when the couple has a child.

This participation in different groups allows the girl to satisfy a greater number of material and social needs. As we will see, affective needs remain more difficult to satisfy if no adult is present. The network is a form of flexible organization of relationships between individuals, and so according to their needs and contacts the children participate in other types of groups. Besides, the members of the network are not all CSS. Some of them do not come to the street every day, and some others go back home at night. Moreover, the children not going back home do not sleep at the same spot, and the children never move together, fearing being the target of police repression.

Despite the memberships of multiple sub-groups, the network remains an important reference for the children who are part of it. The network as a reference point is characterized by three dimensions.

The first dimension is spatial, as the network is named for where the children meeting place: here it is the group of the *Obelisco* (Obelisk). The children identify themselves with this place and by its name. From an identitary point of view, this place and this name allow the children to share a common reference. The second dimension allowing the children to identify themselves with the network is a social one. Despite the memberships to others sub-groups, a child specifies: "After all, we were a gang". There is therefore no contradiction between these multiple memberships and membership of the network. This is explained by the complementarity and subsidiarity of these groupings. Furthermore, identification with the network predominates over identification with sub-groups. This explains why the network is perceived as whole.[14] The third dimension is hierarchical. A young man respected by all the children is recognized as the leader of the *Obelisco* network. He is well-known even beyond the area of the *Obelisco*, and his reputation protects the children of the network when they are visiting some other areas of the city. This leader enables a strong identification of the children with the network. He personifies the network. He also fulfils an affective function for the children who, like Mara, do not have a reference adult. The spatial and hierarchical dimensions take precedence over the social dimension, and give the network its consistency. Its identitary function is more important than its instrumental function. On the other hand, the instrumental function takes precedence in the sub-groups in which the children participate, being associated with survival strategies such as stealing, seeking food, night refuge, and drugs.

[14] The network, as it exists in the case of the children we have observed in Rio de Janeiro, cannot be reduced to Lewis Yablonsky's notion of the 'near-group'. In the Brazilian case, the network cannot be characterized by any of the three identifications - spatial, social, hierarchical – we find in the Argentinian case.

This kind of network cannot be identified with to the gangs studied by Thrasher, White or Miller, nor to modern gangs in the United States. In comparison to the latter, the network does not involve systematic violence or dealing hard drugs, it is not armed, it is less structured, it does not defend an ethnic group or an exclusive territory, its function is not to fight against an adversary by negating its right to exist, and there is no mixing of children, adolescents and young adults in the same organization. Besides, the strongly organized and hierarchical gang generally excludes membership of other relatively autonomous sub-groups. Loyalty to the gang cannot be divided. Moreover, the gang is not an organization that resolves survival problems.

The network, on the other hand, divides into small groups grounded in feelings of sympathy, but also on the needs of survival on the street. Some members of the network also go back home at night: for instance, most of the girls belonging to Mara's network return home when the day is over. Some others withdraw from the group in the company of a boy who they will spend the night with. The members of the network also change with notable frequency. If at night the network divides into multiple sub-groups, this is also true at certain moments during the day. Mara is member of a group composed of three girls, but she is the only one staying on the street day and night. The others return home at night. Occasionally some other girls coming to buy marijuana join this group, and sometimes these girls stay on the street the whole day, instead of going to school. They share some joints, and the rewards of the occasional theft. To these girls, the group has an essentially playful function, and the function of diversifying their routine. Their relation to the street is not the same than the one characterizing CSS.

The children never steal in their chosen place of residence. They also oppose any children not belonging to their network who come to their area intending to commit an offence. Such acts bring the places the children occupy to the attention of the police, and the children will then be obliged to leave the spot. This represents an significant loss for the children, who then have to compete with other groups in order to replace the lost territory. The children say that a theft perpetrated in proximity of where they stay "burns our parade" ("*quemar nuestra parada*").[15]

Concerning the activity of stealing from passers-by on the street, the children adopt a standardized strategy. This strategy demonstrates an acute sense of observation, as well as a very good knowledge of the reactions of victims. Generally, this kind of stealing requires the cooperation of two children. The example of the theft of a necklace allows to illustrate the adopted strategy. One of the children walks along the street, preceding the person chosen as the potential victim, while the other one walks at their side. The second child commits the theft by tearing off the necklace, and runs away immediately. The function of the first child is to confuse the victim and disrupt their reaction. To do this, the child adopts two strategies. Either they get in the path of the victim in order to delay their pursuit, or they ask

[15] In Brazil, the children use a similar expression to indicate the consequences of a theft committed in their place of residence: "*sujar el pedaço*", which can be literally translated by "to mess up the piece (plot)". This means that for a period this place becomes unfit for survival activities.

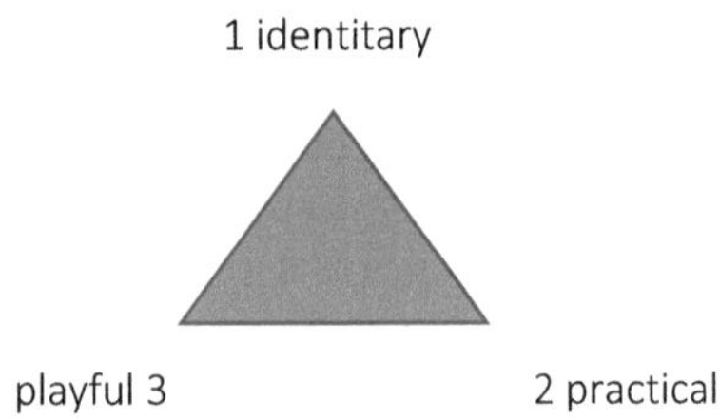


**Fig. 8.2** The triple function of theft

the victim what has happened and pretend to be willing to help recover the necklace. It is then that they can depart, following a path that allows them to leave the scene of the crime without difficulty. Rainy days and the night are favourable to theft, when there are few people on the street and the police are absent. Moreover, power cuts and the rain protect the children from the reactions of their victims.

For the girl, theft is not simply a survival strategy. It is also a means to acquire respect from the boys. Her courage and her skilfulness allow her to become their equal. The boys do not look at her as a girl anymore: her status changes. By taking the same risk as boys, she ceases to be only an object of their desire: as someone perceived as being willing to take risks, she earns their respect. The active participation in theft gives the girl an authority which confers respect on her. In this case, the theft has a triple function like shown in Fig. 8.2.

Here, the girl adopts masculine attitudes and behaviours in order to "be on a par with men".[16] It is also not rare for girls to dress like boys, with oversized clothing conceal their feminine body. They cut their hair very short, for the likeness to be complete. It becomes difficult to differentiate the girl from the boy.

The theft committed by the girls is therefore not only a material contribution to the group: it equally, perhaps even more so, has an important symbolic dimension. If we take the example of the girl's occasional prostitution, the difference between this and theft appears immediately. This activity brings material advantages for the group – money, food, and clothes – but it does not have the same consequences with regards to the identity and status of the girl. In this case she does not become the boy's equal. In the boy's opinion, the girl is only using her feminine attributes, which therefore gives her no special merit. Risk-taking and the competencies evident in committing thefts do not appear in with prostitution, and the girl does not become perceived as the boy's equal.

## 8.3.2 *Identity*

Like the boys, the girls underline the importance of what they have learned in the street. In this regard, it is possible to differentiate three attitudes. The first is that of the girls mentioning the physical tests they have undergone in the street: resisting

[16] This is according to an educator from *Childhope*, during an interview with CSS.

the cold, hunger, and aggression among them. These are the difficulties linked to material survival in the street. Here, the street is lived in a defensive mode, and the child's resources are used in a permanent struggle against shortage and aggression. The street is experienced as a dangerous and testing world. The second attitude concerns the pleasures of what is found in the street: alcohol, marijuana, and sex. This pleasure is essentially physical, and the playful dimension is important. The third attitude is one of transforming the street into a substitute for the family. This is a minority position, and concerns first of all girls who know how to gain the respect of the other children.

On the street, the girl is at once a GSS and a woman. She is perceived by adults as a 'street girl' and as a prostitute simultaneously.[17] Here we find a double stigmatization which does not affect boys. Yet these boys themselves do not perceive their female friends as prostitutes, even if the girls occasionally practice prostitution. To the boys, the prostitute is a woman practicing the profession of prostitute. When GSS fall into exploitation networks controlled by pimps, they no longer belong to the world of CSS, even if they continue to frequent the same space as the other children. The clothing, behaviour, and habits of prostitutes differ from those of 'street girls', and prostitutes themselves refuse to be identified as 'street girls' (Roggenbuck, op. cit., p. 105). To the CSS, the prostitute belongs to a different social category.

Regarding the street girl's attitude towards sexuality, it is possible to distinguish between three different cases. There is first the girl for whom sexuality is reduced to constant harassment from the boys. In this case, the problem of the relationship with male companions is an insoluble puzzle. Indeed, the girl comes to sees this relation only in terms of submission to the boy's desires for domination. This attitude is reflected in Elsa's account, when she says, "I prefer to have them leave me than to be marked, as they say". For Elsa, the woman has to decide the type of relationship she wants to have with a man, but she does not see how the woman could emancipate from this constraint. When speaking about the mark sexual relations leave on the girl, Elsa mentions the stigmatization the boys make her endure. She refuses such a modification of her identity, and besides, Elsa sees the behaviour of the girl who does not share her fears and scruples. This increases her uneasiness, as a 'victim-girl'. The attitude of the 'victim-girl' towards the boys is thus focused on sexuality. Boy/girl relationships come down to a struggle. The other aspects of the relationship between the two sexes are secondary.

At the other extreme, we have the case of girls for whom having sexual relations does not correspond to a loss of autonomy, and even less to submission. Two cases are found here. The first is that of girls who benefit from the respect of their companions. They can also benefit from the protection of boys who occupy a position of leadership on the street. This is the case for Mara. The second case is that of girls who has sex without choosing to do so, but considers this part of life on the street. In this way it can be considered by the girl to be a survival strategy. The girl

[17] Aptekar (1988, p. 165) makes the same observation of Columbia.

understands sexual relations as freely consented to, and not as imposed on her by the boy, and she thus perceives herself as a partner and not as a victim. In contrast to the 'victim-girl', she does not see relationships with boys only in terms of sexuality, subordination, or escape. These girls correspond to the type Stefan Roggenbuck calls the *barraza* (as we will see below).

Finally, there is the case of the girl forming a couple with a boy. This is termed by Roggenbuck the *esposa*. The couple does not live separately from the other children of the network, but they are a sub-group of it. Generally, these couples are respected by the other children. For the girl, it is a situation of relative peace, since she is for a time protected from the advances of other boys. But the stability and duration of these couples is low. Indeed, the children find difficulty in maintaining lasting emotional relationships. Moreover, the conditions of street life considerably reduce the chances of a couple persisting for a long period of time. As one girl says, "couples last longer or shorter: four months… one month… one week". As Patrick Larvie (1992, p. 34) writes, it is not always appropriate to speak of a "survival sexuality" for CSS.

It is therefore insufficient to consider this sexuality solely in socio-economic terms, and thus as being entirely different from the sexuality of non-marginalized people. As Larvie notes, "the sexuality of street boys and girls is, for external observers, generally linked to questions of health and of poverty (prostitution, venereal diseases, AIDS, sexual abuse and pregnancy)" (Ibid.). However, it is true that the sexuality of CSS is experience through constraints like a lack of privacy, violence, instability of relationships, and exploitation.

These three cases can be linked with the typology established by Roggenbuck (op. cit., p. 104) for the GSS of Bogota. Roggenbuck distinguishes between the *soltera*, the *barraza*, and the *esposa*. The *soltera* is a very young girl who has a little experience of the street, yet who is respected by the boys of the group she is part of. She has no sexual relations with the boys. The *barraza* has sexual relations with several boys, without forming a couple. The *esposa* is the girlfriend of one of the boys, with whom for a time she forms a stable couple.

To understand the attitude and behaviour of these girls, one has to take into account the sexual violence which they have often been enduring before coming to the street. Furthermore, in the case of the most deprived families, the lack of privacy characterizing familial life means the child is confronted with the sexual life of adults from a very young age. We do not know how this precocious experience influences the attitudes of children towards sexuality. But the image the girl has of sexuality cannot be separated from the image she has of her mother and of her father, or of the adults replacing them, such as stepmothers or stepfathers. These images become an important component of her own identity, as a girl and as a woman. The same identitary scheme applies to boys. One may suppose that in the case of the 'victim-girl', attitudes towards boys are determined by a maternal image linked with prostitution.

This is striking with Elsa. Her grandparents take her into their care after her mother and stepfather leave. Her grandmother tells her that her mother is a prostitute, though Elsa defends herself by saying that her grandmother never tells the truth: she refuses to believe what she is told. Elsa also recalls that one of her aunts called told her she was an outrage, a capricious, selfish, deceitful, and unreliable girl. All of this affects the image Elsa has of herself. As such, she fears relationships that could lend credence to the things her family told her. The relationships Elsa has with boys are influenced by the image she has of herself. She therefore defends herself from the identitary consequences of a sexuality which could confirm what her family said. Yet those GSS who like Elsa fear sexuality suffer more than others from the pressures to which they are subjected. The 'street boy', in turn, has few inhibitions regarding sexuality. On the contrary, "he constantly seeks physical contact with women without concern for age, height, or beauty" (Dominguez 1990, p. 14).

GSS who have endured sexual violence at home are numerous. The perpetrator of these acts is usually one of the mother's companions. Yet the mother's reaction to this behaviour is as important as the act itself, and this reaction is directly linked to the departure of the girl for the street, as well as to her self-image. It influences the girl's behaviour and her attitude towards sexuality, as well as towards her male friends on the street. Elsa's case illustrates this. When the mother does not react to her stepfather's abusive behaviour, she develops a deep feeling of injustice. But most abuses occur during puberty (around eleven to fifteen years), when the child's ego and identity at an important point of construction. As such, the construction of a coherent self-image is disturbed, and the relation to the other becomes characterized by instability.

### 8.3.3 *Drugs: The Characteristics of Consumption and Its Effects*

The purchase of marijuana and of medicines is financed by the resale of stolen goods. When the children sell the entirety of their takings to the same person, this is called *reducir* (to reduce). This practice allows them to get some money quickly and simply, reducing the number of intermediaries as well as the time to acquire the money necessary for the purchase of drugs. The consumption of drugs (marijuana and medicines) and of alcohol is a general feature among the girls of our study. Yet no one mentions any obligation to consume the drugs, nor the existence of any ritual linked to this consumption. The most consumed products are, in descending order, marijuana, medicines (Artane, eyedrops which the child takes through nostrils, and names Pentolato),[18] and alcohol. More seldomly CSS consume cocaine. Other hard drugs are absent, but they seem to be replaced by mixtures of alcohol and medicines. On the other hand, there is no mention of the consumption of inhalants: glue, stain-

[18] Artane is a anticholinergic commonly by CSS in Brazil and in other countries of Latin America. In its medical administration, the anticholinergic is primarily prescribed for "early adverse effects during antipsychotic treatment". The abusive consumption of anticholinergics may induce "toxic psychotic states with hallucinations. The psycho-stimulant effect may be felt as pleasant" (Rafaelsen et al. 1979, p. 73). This explains the circulation of Artane among CSS.

remover, lacquer, varnish, propulsive gas, or organic solvents like toluene, ether, or chloroform. This is surprising, as inhalant consumption, particularly using shoemaker's glue or stain-removers, is the most common drug use among CSS in Latin America. Three reasons may explain the absence of these substances.

First, marijuana is readily available. It is abundant and cheap. Some college girls, who are not part of the *Obelisco* network of children, come here to buy their joints, and often stay with the group for the day. One girl on the street says, "a joint (*porro*) costs the same as a kilo of apples. Anybody can buy a joint". When marijuana is at their disposal, CSS prefer it to inhalants. When marijuana becomes rare, expensive, and when its market more professionalised, there is a shift towards using inhalants.

The second reason is probably found in the consumption of Artane. This medicine produces long-lasting hallucinations of great intensity. As a hallucinogen it is therefore more efficient than marijuana and inhalants. A turn of events in Brazil indicates that a link between the consumption of Artane and the absence of inhalant use among the girls of our study is plausible. The consumption of Artane among CSS in Sao Paulo has fallen considerably after the product became subject to medical prescription, and after its price rose considerably risen due to the establishment of a parallel market. The younger children who had no means of paying the new prices have then substituted inhalants for Artane (Carlini Comtrim and Silva-Filho 1988, p. 203). This phenomenon of the replacement of one product by another is not an isolated one: it appears every time a product becomes rarer or more expensive. So, in a slum of Brasilia, inhalants replaced marijuana when the price of the latter rose significantly, caused by the professionalization of the cannabis market (Lucchini 1993a, b, p. 182). As Richard H. Blum et al. (1976, p. 15) write, the "multiplication of use is encouraged by the substitutability of one drug for another".

The third reason is attributable to the fact that the use of inhalants is primarily a male practice. The girls consider the inhalants as a product not suited for them, and prefer consuming medicines. One finds this tendency across cultural and national border. In Europe, like in Latin America, consuming inhalants is linked with the feeling of a loss of femininity. The boys themselves will stigmatize girls who use inhalants, and the girls fear this stigmatization.

What is immediately apparent in the girls' consumption practices is the importance and the frequency of the mixtures of alcohol and medicines. These mixtures exist despite the easy access to marijuana. Occasionally, however, marijuana becomes difficult to come by. In Mara's group, the children replace it with alcohol, particularly with wine. As Mara says, "when there was no marijuana any more, we had to drink wine and wine and again wine". This insistence on the quantity of wine necessary to replace marijuana indicates the existence of an addiction towards cannabis, and to psychotropic drugs in general. This addiction is also evident in the need for drugs the girls of our study mention in their accounts. All say that giving up drugs has been a difficult test when they have left the street to move into a foster home. The existence of such an addiction is also testified by the consumption of mixtures of alcohol and medicines, the effects of which on moods and the senses is considered important. More seldomly, marijuana itself is consumed together with wine or liquor.

On the other hand, we do not find any examples of the mixture of marijuana and medicines. The consumption of large quantities of medicines without any mixture also happens, but at less significant levels than the consumption of other products. The girls will do this only in very exceptional circumstances. When Mara wants obtain have some special effect, to have a trip, she mixes a medicine (Artane) and wine. This gives her the impression of flying, and all movements being made in slow motion. An irrepressible desire to laugh accompanies this experience. The consumption of Artane also leads to aggression and to a decrease in inhibitions: "I felt able to do anything, even to kill someone", says one of the girls. She continues: "I reacted badly if someone made a comment".

The effects are thus not always the same. This variety is also found in the case of marijuana. Smoking a joint generally produces relaxation and laughter, as well as some mild hallucinations, but it may sometimes also lead to aggressive behaviours, which the user explicitly attributes to the joint. This is the case with a girl who attacked a boy with a piece of broken bottle in reaction to him delivering a dubious compliment accompanied by an disrespectful gesture. "With the joint, I had a great deal more courage", she says.

It is not surprising that the effects children attribute to the same products may vary. The principal effect of a substance remains the one described by pharmacology, but its description varies according to the experience of the child and the social context of consumption. This effect depends, of course, on the quantity consumed, and on the concentration of active ingredients contained in the substance. It also depends on personal disposition and mood at the moment of consumption, as well as on the previous experiences of the user. The expectations they have towards the consumed product also influence its effects. The mixtures of substances used by the children and the dosages this implies are another factor in the diversity of effects. It would therefore be necessary to control all these parameters to be able to precisely evaluate the effects of the different substances use by CSS. In the child's life environment such control is impossible.

This explains why, varying by circumstance, marijuana may enable relaxation or may lead to aggressive behaviour, or why a certain mixture of medicines and alcohol can variously produce aggression or apathy. Any attribution of certain effects to a given substance has to take into account a margin of uncertainty. This, however, still leaves the possibility to attribute a principal and recurrent effect to the different substances used by the CSS (Medina-Mora et al. 1982; de la Garza Gutiérrez et al. 1985; O'Connor 1986; Angel et al. 1987; Medina-Mora 1987; Carlini-Comtrim and Silva-Filho 1988; Carlini-Cotrim and Carlini 1988; Ministeiro da Saude/Ministeiro de Justiça 1989; UNFDAC 1990; Ortiz 1991; Ives 1991; Bucher et al. 1991; Bucher 1992, pp. 65–88; Lucchini 1993a, b, pp. 116–118). This principal effect will then be one of the major components intervening in maintenance of a consumption habit. As Blum et al. (op. cit., p. 15) write, "many compounds have somewhat similar effects; one can sedate or relax oneself with over-the-counter sleep aids, with barbiturates, with tranquilizers, with cannabis, or with alcohol. Conversely, one compound can have several effects, depending on, for example, expectations, dosage, biological rhythms, or the drug effect suggestions offered by others. One may seek substitute effects not ordinarily envisioned by drug classification schemes".

### 8.3.4 The Relationship to Drugs

The use of drugs by GSS, as well as their attitudes towards these substances, is influenced by their life before coming to the street. It is striking to see the relation that exists between the past of the GSS who practiced prostitution and her consumption habits. In these cases, the girl arrives on the street with already existing consumption habits. These girls are already addicted to certain products like medicines (here Artane) and alcohol, and the mixture of both. Drugs are linked prostitution as they allow the girl to overcome the any inhibitions she has. As she says, drugs gives her the courage necessary to practice this activity.

The link between drugs and a past practicing prostitution is therefore a particular case. It is not representative of drug use by CSS in general, whether boys or girls.[19] On the other hand, the consumption of marijuana and the occasional mixture of this substance with alcohol concerns all CSS. It seems, then, drug use among GSS with a past in prostitution, and/or an experience of rape (by the stepfather or other member of the family), accompanied by the absence of maternal reaction, presents a different situation than that of the other children.

The case of girls being addicted to drugs before coming to the street is not only different from that of other CSS, but also from the European heroin addict or the individual addicted to multiple drugs. As we have noted, this drug consumption is linked to a short period of professional prostitution. When the girl arrives on the street, she is faced with a world differing from that of prostitution. She no longer has only one activity – the selling of sexual services – but, on the contrary, a multitude of activities, and she makes new experiences. Drug use takes on another dimension: it is no longer the means of allowing the girl to face the daily life of prostitution and its brutality.

The meaning of drug has changed: from a monofunctional role it has become plurifunctional. At the same time, the journey on the street is accompanied by new references. At least in its early stages, the adventure and excitement of life on the street confers to daily life a different dimension than those the girl experienced when practising prostitution. The change of environment comes with to a modification of drug use. For instance, the consumption of cocaine is more frequent with the professional prostitute. On the street, these girls prefer products with hallucinatory effects, while in the context prostitution drug use is oriented towards

[19] The existing literature on drug use among CSS is poor. Regarding GSS it is non-existent (at the time of writing, in the 1990s).

a reduction of inhibitions. The consumption of cocaine can also be explained by easy access.

We have isolated four functions of drug use among GSS. These are the playful, hedonistic, and identitary functions, as well as the function of reducing inhibitions (Fig. 8.3).

The individual character of the function of particular drugs indicates that drugs use meets a personal need and sometimes also a personal motivation. On the other hand, the collective function is governed by a group dynamic. The association between the individual or collective nature of the function and dependent use is legitimate when drugs is used to meet the user's identitary or emotional needs. It is therefore not prudent to associate toxic addiction with the individual character of the functions the drug fulfils. On the other hand, the needs and the motivations leading to consumption of psychotropic substances are a determining factor in the genesis of an addiction.

Different functions are associated with different substances. Marijuana, with its laughter and hallucinations, is associated with the playful function. The hallucinatory effects of Artane may lead us to think that this medicine, when consumed by itself, is also associated to this function. But this association depends on the consumed quantity, as well as, from an identitary and emotional point of view, on what influences this consumption. The collective nature of the playful function is explained by the sharing of the product among the children. Moreover, use takes place within the group and its effects are shared by all the children.

Marijuana and wine, when consumed separately, are also associated with the hedonistic function. It is the pleasure given by the act of consumption which is primary, and the effect of the substance itself is relatively secondary. The hedonistic function is individual in nature, and the hedonistic and playful functions are

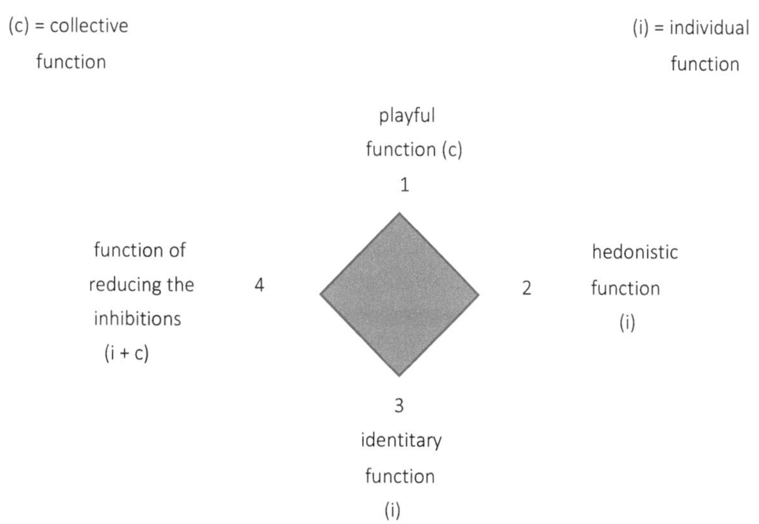


**Fig. 8.3** The functions of drug use among children in street situations

generally connected to each other. Mixtures are as associated with the remaining two functions. The mixtures of Artane and wine, marijuana and wine, and marijuana and Artane are associated with the identitary function, and to the function of a reduction of inhibitions. The uses associated with the two first functions, playful and hedonistic, correspond to a soft use of drugs. On the other hand, the mixtures are above all associated with a hard mode of using drugs. There is no hard or soft drug as such, there are, rather, soft or hard uses of psychotropic substances. Mixtures, independent of the substances used, generally correspond to a hard mode of consumption. Moreover, when drug use is used to fill a lack, it is the hard mode that is predominant. On the other hand, if drug use serves primarily the playful and hedonistic functions, then the soft mode predominates. Children pass from one mode of consumption to the other fairly regularly, and the exact reasons for this alteration are largely unknown.

Concerning drug use among the GSS of our study, it is difficult to distinguish between the different functions in order to determine which is the most important. As the functions of drug use are interconnected, it is normal that we encounter such difficulties. This also means that the products may be linked to several functions. But the question of the relative importance of the different functions is central, because it concerns the user's addiction. When consumption concerns above all the identitary function and the function of reducing inhibition, then the user's degree of addiction is more important. The playful and hedonistic functions are linked to the soft mode of drug use and to a relatively weak addiction.

With regards to the multifunctionality of drug use, this cannot be simply associated with an absence of addiction. We will see this by comparing the case of GSS and that of the 'junkie', as well as that of CSS in Rio de Janeiro.

### *8.3.5 The Identitary Question: The Street Girl and the 'Junkie'*

The identitary function relates to drugs when they come to compensate for deficiencies of a self unable to produce meaning. Drugs compensate for the emptiness this deficiency implies. In these cases, self-image is also negative or even non-existent. This creates a feeling of unreality and of an inability to manage basic existence, as well as a feeling of exclusion from the social environment, especially from family. The absence of communication with this environment is the most important symptom of a deficient system of identity (Lucchini 1985, pp. 106–137; Lucchini 1986, pp. 12–43). The identitary function of the drug is present when the user does not know how to organize their experience of the world. A feeling of isolation dominates the individual's emotional and social life. The identitary function of drug use, then, serves as "an attempt at organizing the image of self" by the user (Olievenstein 1983, pp. 130–131).

As such, the weaker the identitary system, the more important the identitary function of drug use. The degree of dependency on drugs also increases. The structural weakness of the identitary system is also the consequence of a prolonged absence of counter-roles – father, mother, or other responsible adults – during the child's socialization. The concept of counter-role concerns the people serve who as models when a child is learning what specific roles involve. While these counter-roles fulfil the function of models and have an influence in the construction of identity, they are also associated with learning about social prohibitions. During socialization, the counter-role is an object of identification for the child. It becomes an essential element for the knowledge acquired in this socialization to be enacted. The absence of stable counter-roles during childhood is accompanied by problems adapting to the social environment. Drug use the serves as an attempt to compensate for these difficulties of adaptation.[20]

In the extreme cases, the experience is chaotic and senseless. The individual then looks for something else, a new relationship to the objects that constitute their environment. The Italian writer Alberto Moravia, in the novel *La Noia* (*Boredom*), produces an outstanding analysis of the disturbed relationship the protagonist of his novel maintains with the world. Boredom or the absence of reality appears in Moravia's protagonist from "a sense of the absurdity of a reality which is insufficient, or anyhow unable, to convince me of its own effective existence" (Moravia 1999, p. 5). Moravia continues, "boredom is not only the inability to escape from myself but is also the consciousness that theoretically I might be able to disengage myself from it, thanks to a miracle of some sort" (Ibid., p. 6). Moravia's protagonist has the obscure sense that there is no relationship between himself and the things of the world, and that boredom is ultimately incommunicability. This absence of communicability, of relation to the things gives him the impression that he has no relationship even with himself. Moravia's analysis is quite appropriate to the case of the addict drug user, who takes drug in order to compensate for an absence of reality which is at the same time an absence of identity or of a coherent identitary system (Mead's I/Self/Me, or Freud's Id/Ego/Superego).

The behaviour of people who are addicted to drugs is the result of complex relations between the environment, their personality, and the drug. When the identitary function is predominant, the degree of addiction is also the strongest. While we know little about how an addict is 'made' and how they 'function', it seems possible to formulate the hypothesis, according to which the compulsive consumption of drug is a conduct adopted in order to give normative consistency to one's identity. Drugs would then be utilized not as an means of mediating between a deficient identity and its social environment, but rather in order to give consistency to both. Moreover, the addict's consumptions of drug is the result of a complex system composed of cultural, social, economical, legal, psychical, psychiatric,

[20] It is interesting to observe how in a different socio-cultural context – that of Switzerland – many addicts do not seem to have any recollection of their childhood, or a quite vague and confused memory. The absence of counter-roles offers a partial explanation of this. With other addicts, the recollection of childhood is seen as a separate world, narrow and isolated, characterized above all by a submission to the familial environment. It is an omnipresent and oppressing mother, as well as a weak or absent father, which characterize this environment. In both cases, self-image is deficient and negative.

biological and pharmacological elements (Lucchini 1986, pp. 31–33). In the cases where drug use is linked primarily to the identitary function, the degree of addiction is high. On the other hand, the playful and hedonistic functions do not *a priori* produce addiction. Indeed, their presence can counter-balance the effects of the identitary function.

The case of GSS thus differs from that of the 'junkie' who is addicted to multiple drugs. At least two particularities distinguish this user from GSS. First, all their resources – material, social, and affective – are spent looking for drugs. They cannot dedicate themselves to anything else. They represent the highest degree of addiction, and their drug use is monofunctional. The 'junkie' seeks, at a basic level, to avoid a lack, but also hopes to find again the pleasure of the first hit. The monofunctional character of their consumption is visible in the mechanical and repetitive character of their drug-taking. The absence of syringes and thus of shooting up among GSS is another important element that differentiates them from the 'junkie', and as such they do not encounter the risks associated with the injection of heroin. With the 'junkie' there is a very strong imagery of the syringe and of the needle penetrating into the vein. All this is a constitutive part of the addiction toward heroin.

As we have noted, the search for and consumption of drugs are only one of the activities of GSS. Drugs do not monopolize all her resources, in terms of time and material means. But beyond this it is above all the girl's participation in the social life of the street's that differentiates her from the socially isolated 'junkie'. This participation enables a diversification of activities and sources of sensory stimulation. This is the case even if street life also produces repetition and boredom.

### 8.3.6 Girls in Street Situations and the Use of Inhalants on the Street

The concept of inhalants covers different substances and products, with much variation in chemical components and their proportions. This naturally complicates the study of the long-term effects of the consumption of volatile substances. We can distinguish four principal classes of substances. First is the glue adhesives. These products contain volatile substances, among which the most known is Toluene. Shoemaker's glue (*cola de sapateiro*), used by CSS, belongs to this first group. Aerosols constitute the second group of substances. These contain propellants, usually CFCs (halocarbons), which produce effects when inhaled. The third group comprises the butane and propane, found in the cigarette lighters. The first of these two products is the more common. Though these products are easily accessible, they nevertheless do not belong to the range of substances consumed by CSS. The last class of substances is constituted by what one calls "other solvents" (Ives 1991, pp. 9–12). These solvents are in liquid form, and among them the stain-removers are the most widespread products. Easy to obtain, they are known under the name *Thinner*. The consumption of volatile substances produces excitement, euphoria,

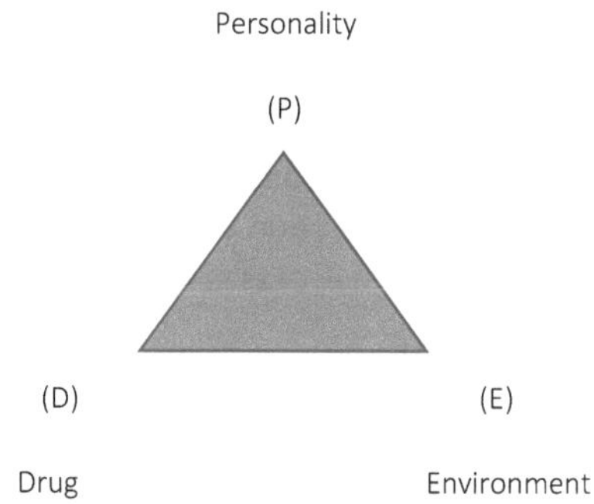


**Fig. 8.4** The triadic relations between personality, drug and environment

and sometimes, when they are used in high quantities, hallucinations. The inhalants taken most by CSS are *Thinner* – it is also easy to control the quantity of liquid with which the material that used for inhalation is moistened – and glue. When the child is under the influence of glue, he faces significant difficulties in speaking and articulating words. He also loses his capacities of concentration. The children say that the effects produced by the glue last as long as those produced by *Thinner* (Gutierrez et al. 1992, p. 67).

We have seen that the case of GSS using drugs is not comparable to the case of the heroin addict. Their case differs also from that of CSS using inhalants. These girls occupy an intermediary position between the heroin addict and the child who uses inhalants. Regarding the case of children consuming inhalants, we refer back to the analysis we have made in another work (Lucchini 1985, pp. 163–198). Any reflection on drug use and addiction necessarily looks the personality of the consumer (P), their social environment (E), and the product consumed (D). These three elements are interdependent and give a systematic character to drug use. P, E and D thus form a triad (as shown in Fig. 8.4).

The interactions between the three elements of the triad explains not only the existence of a relationship of addiction toward the drug, but also the absence of such a relation. Regarding the consumption of inhalants among CSS, the environment seems to be the more important element of the triad (Ibid., p. 171 and *passim*). This consumption is linked to the subculture, and its norms, beliefs, habits, and rites that characterize the child's daily life.[21]

Yet this does not mean that drug consumption is evenly distributed among these children. Some differences exist regarding mixtures and consumed quantities. Consumption of inhalants, and particularly of shoemaker's glue, ensues more from the logic of social control than from a pathology of personality. As we shall see, it is a form of consumption where the principal characteristic is – as with GSS in Buenos Aires – multifunctionality. Besides, one cannot deny that CSS, like manu other adolescents, adopt risky behaviours. Simply, drug use, and more specifically that of inhalants, is integrated into a lifestyle. This corresponds to a temporary

[21] Several authors (Carlini-Cotrim and Carlini 1988; Bucher et al. 1991; Medina-Mora 1987) stress the importance of the subculture in relation to consumption of inhalants.

survival strategy. All this is closely linked to the problem of the presence of states of addiction in CSS consuming inhalants. On this question, the use of mixtures of different products and the frequency of this is significant. Indeed, the more frequently mixtures are consumed, the more likely we are to find a state of addiction. This is the case when a child uses the mixture in an individual and habitual way, and when consumption has ceased to be part of a collective practice in the group to which the child belongs.

We can assert that the more the practice of consuming mixtures is a collective one, that is, the more it is instrumentalized and ritualized, the weaker will be the degree of addiction accompanying it. This is the case when the consumption of mixtures is not an aim in itself, but a means to a specific end, such as when facing a situation that contains certain dangers or challenges.[22] In such cases it is the social context, more than deficiencies in the identitary system, which explains consumption.

The consumption of inhalants by CSS cannot be considered a destructive behaviour. Their case is not comparable to that of the addict who "is able to know his own reality only through addiction, risk and dependency", and who "looks for an all-powerful protective substance on which they depend to keep their anxiety at tolerable levels" (Charles-Nicolas 1989, p. 91). Among the children we have studied in Rio de Janeiro, consumption of inhalants is above all a collective practice. While it is true that solitary consumption also exists, we have not observed it as a unique mode of consumption. This is important, for such consumption "could constitute an important sign of the subject's psychic vulnerability and of the risks they are exposed to" (Angel et al., op. cit., p. 19).

As Gloria Aurora Champion de Castro (1998, p. 121) writes, "pharmacodependency on inhalants is a phenomenon which is above all a social one". The consumption of inhalants among marginalized populations is a phenomenon in which the psychological component is less important than the social and economic factors (Garza Gutiérrez et al., op. cit., p. 11). A Mexican study shows that the children working in the streets of Monterrey who consume inhalants generally come from families in which one of the parents has left, in which the number of children is high, who have a very low income, and where there is precedent with regards to alcoholism and pharmacodependency (Ibid., p. 4).

However, these studies do not allow to draw conclusions concerning the presence or the absence of addiction. Indeed, nor do they tell us about the motivations of consumption, nor the specific relationship the user establishes with the product they use. Champion de Castro (op. cit., p. 121) suggests a triple distinction between pharmacodependency as a symptom, a syndrome, and a disability. The first form concerns the use of a product that diminishes the effects of a conflictual situation, and does not imply lasting consumption. The second is concerned with "a persistent use that can be in relation to existential and contextual constraints, with a multiple and diverse aetiology" (Ibid.). The last form of dependency is "a process of

[22] The most frequent mixtures are between alcohol and medicines such as Artane, Diazepam, Optalidon, and cough syrups.

progressive deterioration accompanied by a lasting, compulsive and growing consumption, as well as by a heavy pathology of personality" (Ibid.).

None of these forms of dependency seem to us to characterize, as such, the situation of CSS. In most of these cases, we see transitory and cyclical forms of dependency which combine symptom and syndrome. There is thus no pure form of dependency, and the consequences of the consumption of inhalants are tempered by its multifunctional character. This activity is hardly compatible with a drug consumption that monopolises all of the child's energy and resources. The ecology and rhythms of survival on the street are factors that, in terms of dependency, limit the effects of consumption, and other factors strengthen this protective effect. We have already mentioned the often collective character of consumption. The purchase is also a collective affair. The use of inhalants stands as a challenge towards the adults that the children perceive to be stigmatising them. This challenge and this provocation together form of claim of a collective identity for the children as CSS (Lucchini 1993a, b, pp. 168–169 and 188–189).

A Brazilian study informs us of the reasons the children offer when asked why they consume inhalants (Bucher et al. 1991, pp. 18–21). We find that the reasons put forward may be classified into two categories. The first concerns justifications that we call instrumental: the child uses inhalants to help them better perform a task at hand. This category, the most important (comprising 42% of the answers), covers activities like stealing (24%), running and playing (12%), or quibbling (6%). The second category concerns reasons we designate as compensatory. In this case, the child consumes inhalants in order to *curtir*, which means "to pass the difficult moments the best one can" or "to escape boredom". This category represents 12% of the responses. There is a further category of children who say they are not willing to do anything after having consumed inhalants (28%). We observe, then, that the playful and instrumental function is more important than the function of compensation. Furthermore, the more important this function, the less addicted is the user. This also explains why many children are able to suddenly give up their inhalant use when required.

We have said that consumption of inhalants by CSS is multifunctional. Figure 8.5 (hereunder) depicts this multifunctionality.

These functions may be split into two categories. The first comprises functions that are of a collective nature, the second concerns individual functions. In the first case, the effects of consumption are collectively experienced and contribute to the functioning of the network or the group. Among the functions of this first category, we find:

(a) the playful function
(b) the provocation, claiming, and contestation function
(c) the ritual function
(d) the identitary function

This last function is closely associated with the provocation, claiming, and contestation function. When the children claim a collective identity as 'street children', they contest the stigmatization attached to it. The collective and public

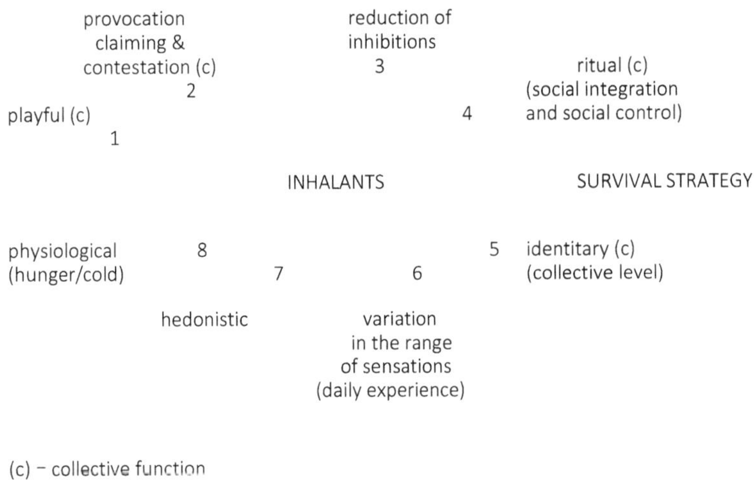


**Fig. 8.5** The multifunctionality of inhalant consumption by children in street situations

consumption of inhalants is closely linked to this fact (Lucchini 1993a, b, pp. 140–147).

The second category comprises the individual functions. They are as follows:

(a) reduction of inhibitions
(b) variation in the range of sensations
(c) hedonistic
(d) physiological

Here consumption of inhalants responds to the child's individual needs. When the child has consumed inhalants, they undertake things they would not have done without having taken drugs. The variation in the range of sensations concerns the modification of visual and aural perceptions. In these ways the child reacts against a daily routine which can serve to produce boredom. The physiological function concerns the struggle against cold and hunger.

The plurality of functions of inhalant consumption combines with the multiplicity of survival strategies on the street. This constitutes a considerable barrier to the development of a dependency of an addictive type. When multifunctionality diminishes, the relationship the user has with the drug modifies. A reduction of the number of functions accompanied by the maintenance of a constant consumption contains within it a growing risk of addiction.

The reduction of the multifunctionality of inhalant consumption is accompanied by a rupture in the existing balance between collective functions and individual functions. We may also foresee two situations. In the first, the collective functions of inhalant consumption are strengthened to the detriment of individual functions. In this case, consumption entails a low dependency and the child is able to cease consumption overnight. In the second situation, the case is the opposite: the individual functions prevail over collective ones. In the most extreme case, only the function of compensation subsists. Here, consumption responds to needs generated by significant difficulties of a relational and identitary order. The situation most favourable to the development of an addiction of a classical type – when "nothing but the product counts" – appears when a monofunctionality of consumption coincides with an impoverishment of the child's survival strategies. What can be observed is that many children experience some cycles of hard consumption and some cycles of soft consumption. These cycles are not irreversible and repeat over time.

While proceeding to a comparison between CSS who use inhalants and the drug consumption of GSS, one has to take into account these consumption cycles through which the child passes. One also must consider the existence of an alternation between a hard mode of consumption and a soft mode for GSS. This means that the number of functions attached to drug consumption is an important criterion, but not a sufficient one when comparing these two cases of drug use. In order to adequately compare them, we would have to consider a number of dimensions, such as, how the consumption is acted on, the number of the functions involved in consumption, the individual and/or collective character of these functions, and the hard and/or soft mode of consumption. This list is not exhaustive, but in the present state of research the indicators needed to specify the dimensions of consumption in the two populations are not yet available.

Why suggest that GSS occupy an intermediary position between heroin addicts and CSS who consume inhalants? What does the notion of 'intermediary position' mean?

The notion of position concerns the type of relations GSS maintain with drugs. This relation is defined by the constraints drugs exert on the user's daily life, and so such a relation can exclude any activity not linked to drugs: finding, purchasing, and consuming them. In the case of the heroin addict, their drug consumption monopolizes all of the personal resources. This is not the case for CSS using inhalants, for whom consumption is only one activity among others. This consumption coexists with numerous other activities specific to the life on the street.[23]

GSS with a past in prostitution do not consume inhalants, but rather medicines, marijuana and alcohol. They also more frequently move towards consuming mixtures. The nature of the consumed products, as well as the use mixtures, indicate the presence of a different relation to drugs.

The identitary and affective function of drug use is important. It therefore produce a stronger dependency with GSS than with CSS who use inhalants. However, this dependency is attenuated by the insertion of the girl into the world of the street and her survival activities. While it is not of the same order of the heroin

---

[23] The omnipresence of inhalants on the street renders them more accessible than heroin is for the 'junkie'. Besides, as inhalants are not illegal drugs, they are not associated to the scene that exists for hard drugs. The accessibility of inhalants, as well as the absence of a specific milieu allowing its purchase and its consumption, does not oblige the children to leave their daily environment, the street.

addict's dependency, it nevertheless remains significant and its consequences cannot be underestimated.

Drug consumption therefore does not the same significance across the three categories of users we have considered. For the children who use inhalants, consumption is characterized by the predominance of social factors. In the case of GSS, this influence diminishes while personal factors take on more importance. With the heroin addict, drug use is focused on the product and conditioned by personal problems. The dependent relationship to different substances thus evolves according to these parameters.

## References


Adler, F., & Adler, H. M. (1979). Female delinquency: Minor girls and major crimes. In J. Edward Clark & D. H. Kelly (Eds.), *Deviant behavior. Readings in the sociology of deviance*. New York: St Martin's Press.

Angel, P., Botbol, M., & Facy, F. (1987). *Adolescence et solvants*. Paris: Echo-Centurion.

Aptekar, L. (1988). *Street children of Cali*. Durham: Duke University Press.

Aptekar, L. (1992). *Some conceptual and methodological issues in research on street children*. San José (Unpublished manuscript).

Aptekar, L. (1993a). *A cross-cultural approach to the study of street children*. San José (Unpublished manuscript).

Aptekar, L. (1993b). *Some conceptual and methodological issues in research on street children*. (Unpublished manuscript).

Barker, G. (1994). Recherche sur la connaissance du SIDA, les attitudes et les pratiques des jeunes de la rue. In BICE (Ed.), *SIDA. Les enfants aussi*. Geneva: BICE.

Barruel de Lagenest, J.-P. (1985). *La traite des femmes et la prostitution en Amérique latine*. (Unpublished manuscript).

Barry, K. (1986). La prostitution est un crime. *Déviance et Société, 10*(3), 299–303.

Bernsdorf, W. (1955). Soziologie der Prostitution. In H. Giese (Ed.), *Die Sexualität der Menschen, Handbuch der medizinischen Sexualforschung*. Stuttgart: Enke.

Blanc, C. S. (1992). *Urban children in distress: An introduction to the issues*. Florence: UNICEF.

Blum, R. H., Blum, E., & Garfield, E. (1976). *Drug education: Results and recommendations*. Lexington: Lexington Books.

Body-Gendrot, S. (1993). *Ville et violence. L'irruption de nouveaux acteurs*. Paris: Presses universitaires de France.

Boone, M. S. (1989). *Capital crime. Black infant mortality in America*. London: Sage.

Brünott, L. (1986). La prostitution comme travail. *Déviance et Société, 10*(3), 293–297.

Bucher, R. (1992). *Drogas e drogadiçao no Brasil* (pp. 65–88). Porto Alegre: Artés Medicas.

Bucher, R., da Costa, A. C. L., & de Oliveira, J. A. (1991). Consumo de inhalantes e condiçoes de vida de menores de periferia de Brasilia. *Revista ABP-APAL, 13*(1), 18–26.

Campbell, A. (1981). *Girls delinquents*. Oxford: Basil Blackwell.

Campbell, A. (1987). Self definition by rejection: The case of gang girls. *Social Problems, 34*(5), 451–466.

Cañadell, R. M., & Ugen, J. F. (1993). Chilean women's organizations. Their potential for change. In *Latin American Perspectives* (79, Vol. 20, No 4).

Cannat, N. (1988). *Sous les bidons de la ville*. Paris: L'Harmattan.

Carlini-Comtrim, B., & Silva-Filho, A. R. (1988). O abuso de Artane por meninos de rua de São Paulo. *Jornal Brasileiro de Psiquiatria, 37*(4), 201–203.

Carlini-Cotrim, & Carlini, E. A. (1988). The use of solvents and other drugs among homeless and destitute children living in the city streets of Sao Paulo, Brazil. *Social Pharmacology, 2*(1), 51–62.

Cavan, R. S., & Ferdinand, T. N. (1975). *Juvenile delinquency*. Philadelphia: Harper and Row.

Champion de Castro, G. A. (1998). *Introducción a los estudios sociales y comunitarios sobre los inhaladores. Disolventes, inhalantes*. Mexico: Consejo nacional contra las adicciones.

Charles-Nicolas, A. (1989). Les principaux outils conceptuels de la psychopathologie des toxicomane. *Aspects médicaux, psychologiques et sociaux des toxicomanies*. Geneva.

Chatterjee, A. (1992). *India: The forgotten children of the cities*. Florence: UNICEF.

Clignet, R. (1988). Discontinuité de la vie familiale. *Cahiers Internationaux de Sociologie, LXXXV*, 257–275.

Clinard, M. B., & Meier, R. F. (1979). *Sociology of deviant behavior*. New York: Holt, Rinehart & Winston.

Conto de Knoll, D. (1991). *Die Strassenkinder von Bogotà*. Frankfurt/Main: Verlag für Interkulturelle Kommunikation.

David, P. R. (1987). Children in despair: The Latin American experience. *Journal of Comparative Family Studies, XVIII*(2), 327.

Davis, N. J. (1977). Feminism, deviance, and social change. In E. Sagarin (Ed.), *Deviance and social change (pages)*. London: Sage.

de Almeida, M. T. F. (1986). Alternativas para a menina de rua. In *Revista de administraçào municipal*, XXXIII, No 178, IBAM.

de Andrade Gonçalves, Z. (1979). *Meninos de rua e a marginalidade en Belém*. Belem: Salesianos do Pará.

de la Garza Gutiérrez, F., de la Vega, B., & Zúñiga, V. (1985). Control Social y Uso de Drogas en Menores que Trabajan en la Via Publica. *Salud Mental, 8*(3), 3–7.

de Souza Minayo, M. C. (1992). *O Limite da Exclusão Social. Meninos e Meninas de Rua no Brasil*. Sào Paulo: Hucitec/Rio de Janeiro: Abrasco.

Dulce Gaspar, M. D. (1985). *Garotas de Programa. Prostituiçào en Copacabana e Identidade Social*. Rio de Janeiro: J. Zahar.

Espinheira, G. (1984). *Divergência et Prostituiçào*. Salvador: Tempo Brasileiro.

Espinola, B., Glauser, B., Ortiz, R., & Ortiz de Carrizosa, S. (1990). *En la calle: Menores trabajadores de la calle en Asuncion, Paraguay*. Asuncion: Imprenta El Grafico.

Fonseca, C. (1985). La circulation des enfants dans un bidonville brésilien. *Annales, 40*(5), 991–1018.

Fonseca, C. (1988). Menores carentes. In B. Trillat (Ed.), *Abandon et adoption*. Paris: Autrement.

Fossé-Poliak, C. (1984). La notion de prostitution. Une définition préalable. *Déviance et Société, 8*(3), 251–266.

Gutierrez, R., Vega, L., & Pérez, C. (1992). Caracteristicas psicosociales de los menores en la calle. *Anales Instituto Mexicano de Psiquiatria*, 63–70.

Halimi, S. (1989). Misère à l'américaine dans l'autre Californie. *Le Monde Diplomatique, Le triomphe des inégalités* (No 5, p. 37). Paris.

Huston, A. C. (1991). Children in poverty: Developmental and policy issues. In A. C. Huston (Ed.), *Children in poverty*. Cambridge: Cambridge University Press.

Ives, R. (1991). *Soluble problems: Tackling solvent sniffing by young people*. London: National Children's Bureau.

Kasarda, J. D., & Parnell, A. M. (1993). *Third world cities, problems, policies and prospects*. London: Sage.

Kilbride, P. L. (1991). Female violence against related children: Child abuse as a modern form of deviance in Kenya. In M. F. D. Raybeck & J. S. Savashinsky (Eds.), *Deviance. Anthropological perspectives*. New York: Bergin & Garvey.

Larvie, P. (1992). *A Construçao Cultural dos Meninos de Rua no Rio de Janeiro: Implicaçoes para a Prevençao de HIV/AIDS*. Rio de Janeiro: AIDSCOM/University of Chicago.

Leser de Mello, S. (1989). Un barrio y sus familias. *Médio ambiente y urbanización, 8*(29), 54–64.

Levinson, D. (1989). *Family violence in cross-cultural perspective*. London: Sage.
Lévi-Strauss, C. (1973). *Anthropologie structurale deux*. Paris: Plon.
Lewis, O. *Les enfants de Sanchez*. Paris: Gallimard.
Lucchini, R. (1985). *Drogues et société. Essai sur la toxicodépendance*. Fribourg: Editions universitaires de Fribourg.
Lucchini, R. (1986). *Une substance psychotrope n'est pas encore une drogue. Réflexions sur le devenir toxicodépendant*. Fribourg: ISES (Working paper No. 90.
Lucchini, R. (1993a). *Enfant de la rue. Identité, sociabilité, drogue*. Genève/Paris: Droz.
Lucchini, R. (1993b). Paroles de femmes marginalisées au Brésil. In N. Michel (Ed.), *L'enseignement social chrétien* (pp. 141–170). Fribourg: Presses Universitaires de Fribourg.
Lucchini, R. (1994). *The street girl. Prostitution, family and drug*. University of Fribourg (Working Paper 243).
Lusk, M. (1994). *Latin American street children: A regional perspective*. Santa Fe (Unpublished manuscript).
McCarty, P. (1981). *Social Structure in Latin America: A Case of Child Abandonment*. (Unpublished manuscript).
McLanahan, S., & Garfinkel, I. (1988). *Single mothers, the underclass and social policy*. Baltimore: Urban University Press.
McLanahan, S., Astone, N. M., & Marks, N. F. (1991). The role of mother-only families in reproducing poverty. In A. C. Huston (Ed.), *Children in poverty*. Cambridge: Cambridge University Press.
Medina-Mora, M. E. (1987). Aspectos epidemiológicos del uso de substâncias inhalantes en la República Mexicana. *Salud Mental, 10*(4), 11–19.
Medina-Mora, M. E., Ortiz, A., Caudillo, C., & López, S. (1982). Inhalación Deliberada de Disolventes en un Grupo de Menores Mexicanos. *Salud Mental, 5*(1), 77–81.
Pastoral do Menor (1988). Menor-Mulher. Quem é esta menina, adolescente, São Paulo.
Merton, R. K., & Nisbet, R. A. (1977). *Contemporary social problems*. New York: Harcourt, Brace, Jovanovich.
Michel, A.-M. (1993). En Europe l'escalade de la pauvreté. *Le Monde Diplomatique, Manière de voir* (No 20, p. 12). Paris.
Ministeiro da Saude/Ministeiro de Justiça. (1989). *Consumo de Drogas psicotrópicas no Brasil, em 1987*. Brasilia: Centro de Documentação do Ministério da Saúde.
Miranda Ferreira, M. D. G. (1986). Mulheres espancadas. E seus filhos? In M. H. F. Steiner (Ed.), *Quando a criança nào tem vez*. São Paulo: Pioneira.
Moravia, A. (1999). *Boredom*. New York: New York Review Books.
Morgan, P. S. (1993). Third world urbanization, migration, and family adaptation. In J. D. Kasarda & A. M. Parnell (Eds.), *Third world cities. Problems, policies and prospects*. London: Sage.
Myers, W. E.. (année). Les enfants des rues: comparaison entre quatre études menées en Amérique du Sud. In *Revue Internationale du Travail, 128*(3), pages.
Newman, C. (1989). *Young runaways: Findings from Britain's first safe house*. London: . Children's Society.
O'Connor, D. (1986). *Glue sniffing and volatile substance abuse: Case studies of children and young adults*. Aldershot: Gower Press.
Olievenstein, C. (1983). *Le destin du toxicomane*. Paris: Fayard.
Ortiz, A. (1991). *Family characteristics of inhalants users versus non-inhalants users*. Mexico City: Instituto Mexicano de Psiquiatria.
Pandey, R. (1991). *Street children of India*. Allahabad: Chugh Publications.
Phillips, W. S. K. (1994). *Street children in India*. Jaipur/New Dehli: Rawat.
Polansky, N. A., Gaudin, J. M., & Ammons, P. W. (1985). Loneliness and isolation in child neglect. *Social Casework: The Journal of Contemporary Social Work, 66*(1), 38–47.
Porshnev, B. F. (1978). Opposition as a component of ethnic self-consciousness. In R. E. Holloman & S. A. Arutiunov (Eds.), *Perspectives on ethnicity*. The Hague: Mouton.
Quintas, F. (1986). *Sexo e marginalidade*. Petropolis: Vozes.

R.E. Dominguez, op. cit., unpublished manuscript, Mendoza 1990, p. 14.

Rafaelsen, O. J., Mendlewicz, J., & Hollister, L. (1979). *Abrégé de psychopharmacologie*. Brussels: Éditions de l'Université de Bruxelles.

Riaño, Y., & Wesche, R. (1994). Changing informal settlements in Latin American cities. In A. R. M. Ritter, M. A. Cameron, & D. H. Pollock (Eds.), *Latin America and the Caribbean to the year 2000*. New York: Praeger.

Rochefort, M. (1988). Problèmes généraux de la production du logement des pauvres. *Revue Tiers-Monde, XXIX*(16), 1043–1081.

Roggenbuck, S. (1993). *Strassenkinder in Lateinamerika*. Frankfurt am Main: Peter Lang.

Santos, M. (1982). *Ensaios sobre a urbanisaçào latino-americana*. São Paulo: Editora HUCITEC.

Scheper-Hughes, N. (1985). Culture, scarcity, and maternal thinking: Maternal detachment and infant survival in a Brazilian shantytown. *Ethos, 13*(4), 291–317.

Silva, T. (1991). Highlights of situation studies on street children in the Philippines. In R. Pandey (Ed.), *Street children of India*. Allahabad: Chugh Publications.

Stockley, D., Canter, D., & Bishopp, D. (1992). *Young people on the move*. Guildford, University of Surrey: Rowntree Foundation.

Sudarkasa, N. (1993). Female-headed African American households. In *Harriette Pipes McAdoo, Family ethnicity: Strength in diversity* London: Sage.

Sullivan, M. L. (1993). Absent fathers in the Inner City. In W. J. Wilson (Ed.), *The ghetto underclass*. London: Sage.

Thio, A. (1978). *Deviant behavior*. Boston: Houghton Mifflin.

UNCHS. (1981). *United Nations Centre for Human Settlements. The residential circumstances of the urban poor in developing countries*. New York: Praeger.

UNFDAC. (1990). *Abuso de Drogas entre meninos meninas de rua do Brasil*. São Paulo: Editora Ave Maria.

UNICEF. (1993). *Street children in four selected towns of Ethiopia*. Addis Ababa: UNICEF.

Visano, L. (1990). The socialization of street children: The development and transformation of identities. *Sociological Studies of Child Development* (Vol. 3).

Woortmann, K. (1987). *A familia das mulheres*. Rio de Janeiro: Tempo Brasileiro em co-edição com o Conselho de Desenvolvimento Científico e Tecnológico.

# Chapter 9
# The Agency of Children in Street Situations

Daniel Stoecklin

## 9.1 From Agency within Structure...

Empirical evidence shows that many children in street situations (CSS) consider themselves to have a greater level of choice in the streets than in other places, such as their homes, schools, or institutions. This is a surprising observation as it contradicts the common view that the street is a hostile and often dangerous space, not appropriate for children. In light of this contradiction, it is tempting to say that CSS lack maturity, as they do not acknowledge the immediate dangers of street life or their long-term interests. But what they do not acknowledge, in fact, is the origin and legitimacy of the discourse about 'normal childhood'. From the context of their own situations this discourse turns into a judgment, reflecting the widespread reaction to deviance. These antagonistic judgements reinforce the social dynamics prevailing in the streets.

Sociologists therefore have to consider the accounts of CSS, and public reaction to them, as revealing aspects of the social dynamics they seek to understand. Some children's marginalized. Moreover, the preference for the street, compared to other spaces, tells something fundamental about their situation: we cannot merely relate them to personal skills and accept the common evaluations in terms of immaturity. This is because those accounts that contradict common expectations, like the sense of freedom children feel in the street, are bound to an alternative ethos which may have become invisible as they become 'freedom' a child claims to have in the street may also result from the very social process that has turned 'competence' into the dominant narrative of the 'entrepreneurial self' that characterizes modernity. Dominant narratives can therefore constrain as much as they can empower the discourses of CSS.

Updated from Stoecklin 2018b, with permission by The International Journal of Children's Rights.



R. Lucchini, D. Stoecklin, *Children in Street Situations*, Children's Well-Being: Indicators and Research 21, https://doi.org/10.1007/978-3-030-19040-8_9

The duality of the symbolic world through which social dynamics evolve will be addressed in this chapter through the concepts of agency and structure. The two concepts are so closely related that I will suggest that they are in fact referring to the same thing – the symbolic order – viewed from two different angles. But let us first start with the dominant view that conceives of agency and structure as separate, before coming to the reasons for merging them. This will be done with some empirical examples to support this change of focus.

Very broadly speaking, the dominant view holds that agency refers to the capacity of actors to influence the ways in which society functions, and structure refers to the social barriers that constrain this capacity to influence. The dominant account separates agency and structure, and reifies them as two 'substances' that are in conflict. Meanwhile, in childhood studies, the agency-structure opposition has evolved towards a paradigm of interdependence, synthesized in the vision of agency *within* structure (Leonard 2016). A detailed presentation of these developments is beyond the scope of this book. However, it should be noted that most of the authors conflate structure with institutions, hence opposing actors (or agents) to structures (or institutions). This dichotomy stems from other binaries, especially that of individual and society, which should be critically perceived as nothing more than mind-body dualism put in sociological terms: individuals (and their agency) would be the minds moving around within a body (society, institutions) that has its own logic and functions. It therefore seems that the dualism of agency and structure is still very much influenced by organicism. Consequently, it is necessary to draw on theories that mark a real departure from dualistic views. Structuration theory (Giddens 1984) is such a theory, marking a groundbreaking contribution to social theories insofar as it does not conflate structure and institutions. Figure 9.1 reflects this tripartite process of structuration.

Giddens exits dualistic conceptions by introducing the notion of 'duality of the structure', where structure is located between actors and institutions. Giddens' structuration theory moves "beyond the structure-agency dichotomy through suggesting that the two concepts are interrelated. Hence, rather than asking whether structures influence people or people influence structures, Giddens articulates how structures are both constraining and enabling" (Leonard 2016, p. 118). Structure

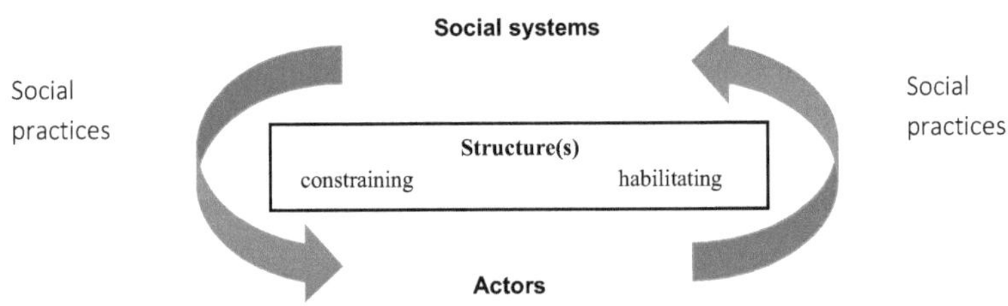


**Fig. 9.1** The process of structuration. (Giddens 1984)
Adapted from Nizet (2007, p. 16), (translation from French into English), with the arrows representing social practices

hence has a 'duality': it is simultaneously a medium and an outcome of social practices. Giddens identifies structure as an abstract entity that is recursively constraining and enabling of practices, and as such people's agency is not only an outcome of structural features, but also a means for influencing social systems.

The centrality of 'structure', separated from 'system', is of essential importance here. Structures link actors and social systems through social practices. Social systems are 'Reproduced relations between actors or collectivities, organised as regular social practices' (Giddens 1984, p. 25), and hence 'social systems' and 'actors' are bound together by 'structures' which "can be identified as sets or matrices of rule-resource properties [...] recursively implicated in the reproduction of social systems" (Giddens 1979, p. 64). Meanwhile, Giddens does not clearly locate agency, but I believe that the duality of structure opens the possibility to see agency as 'structure in the making'. This is only implicit in Giddens' approach, but can be seen in the recursiveness he emphasizes:

> By the duality of structure, I mean the essential recursiveness of social life, as constituted in social practices: structure is both medium and outcome of the reproduction of practices. Structure enters simultaneously into the constitution of the agent and social practices, and 'exists' in the generating moments of this constitution. (Giddens 1979, p. 5)

This dual nature of structure can be seen in its instantiations: discourses on action (which frame action) and actions on discourse (which frame discourse). These instantiations can be found in language, and the centrality of language is underlined in Giddens' theory:

> Giddens (1984) has focused on the idea that structures are both external to social actors and also receptive to their actions. Giddens refers to processes of structuration, whereby individuals interact with these structures through their routine engagement with others. Interactions help to change structures as well as reinforce them. Thus, the conversations we have with each other are constrained by our language and our expectations of others. At the same time, in and through these conversations we reinforce these rules and also refine and expand our understandings of those within the frame of the dialogue. While we tend to work and live within fixed points of predictability, we cannot completely predict the outcomes of our actions and interactions with others. (Wyness 2018, p. 74)

It is relevant to note that the symbol theory developed by Norbert Elias (1991) is close to the Giddensian conceptualization of a symbolic structure that is at the same time a means and an outcome of social interactions:

> Ancestral experiences can be deposited in the concepts of a language, and can thus be handed on through a line of generations of considerable length [...] Deposits of earlier experiences can be reinforced, blocked and, for all we know, perhaps even extinguished by those of later generations (Elias 1991, p. 16).

The Eliasian perspective insists more on the dimension of time: symbols are both means for present and future interactions and outcomes of past interactions. Moreover, Elias insists on the link between thought and language:

> It can be an abbreviated version of the audible use of language, but whether longhand or shorthand, audible or inaudible, language and thought are inseparable. Without learning a

> language, i.e. without learning to communicate with other human beings by means of sound-symbols, a person could not perform the kind of thinking which enables human beings to come to grips with the kind of problems that arise from everybody's co-existence with others, human or non-human (Elias 1991, p. 78).

It is hence possible to consider that, through the words that are used by actors, their language is a 'solidified' reflection of their thoughts, and acts as a structure that constrains but also enables further thoughts, including the thoughts of later generations. The dual nature of the symbolic structure of language conforms with practical reality: the fact that actors can mobilise symbols without exactly knowing the origin of the symbols they use proves that experience is not only made of *a posteriori* syntheses but also of *a priori* categories, the latter being the outcome of the experience of former actors. (I will come back, at the end of this chapter, to *a posteriori* and *a priori* thinking when dealing with forms and content). Experience is thus also structured by the agency of former actors. Consequently, with this long-term chain of experiences accumulated and passed over from one generation to another, it becomes very problematic to differentiate agency and structure: they result from each other. A diachronic perspective therefore reintroduces the dynamics that are hidden by the synchronic perspective. The latter opposes structure and agency on the grounds that structure is a constraining force, but why would agency not, as well, be constraining? Why would the agency of specific individuals not constrain those of others?

The idea of constraints located only on the side of structure is therefore misleading, but this remains the dominant account:

> Structures can be viewed as barriers or constraints which can become more visible and tangential in contexts where people's motives and actions are thwarted. For the most, part structures are understood as guides, regulations and rules that are located within a much broader context that enable as well as constrain the actions of individuals (Wyness 2018, p. 73).

Structure is therefore commonly used as another word for institutions: "dominant approaches within sociology such as Marxism and feminism have tended to focus on the roles of economic, political and social structures" (ibid.). There is a confusion here between structure and institution, a confusion that Giddens avoids by proposing a conceptualization of structuration as a three-level process (see Fig. 9.1). Giddens places structure in between actors and institutions (social systems) as it is the only way to recognize the dual nature of structure, as both the means and outcomes of social practices. His approach underlines the symbolic nature of structure. In Bourdieu's works, by contrast, structure is more closely associated to institutions, as fields (the French *champs*) are delimited by their influence: the boundaries of a field are said to be delimited in terms of "where the influence of specific actors ceases to exist" (Bourdieu 1984, p. 25). This corresponds to a territorial representation of the social world more than a symbolic one. In Giddens' theory structure is a symbolic mediating element between actors and institutions, whereas in conflict theories (including Bourdieu) structure is equated with one of the two oppositional poles, and hence associated with dominant classes.

I choose to focus here on the implications of Giddens' structuration theory for the understanding of the agency of CSS, which of course also has implications for the sociology of childhood. There have been some attempts to reconcile structure and agency within the sociology of childhood. These originate in an ethical and political dimension of childhood studies, namely the rejection of the notion that children are incapable of exerting agency (Garnier 2015). In turn, theoretical developments have intervened in the political debate:

> In some respects, the bringing together of structure and agency opens up the potential to reconceptualise children and childhood within this debate. Could children have agency if this agency was always understood in terms of ongoing constraints on children's actions? Could we generate sufficient space within the heavily structured lives of children such that we start to view children as creative and competent and capable of changing the structures of our actions? The stumbling block to recognising children's agency is that children rarely figured within analyses of social structures (Wyness 2018, p. 74).

In my view, structuration theory contributes to seeing children as structuring actors as well. But providing a more empirical foundation of the agency-structure relation remains work in progress, and much remains to be done within childhood studies. Some connections between major sociologists, even if they have not worked specifically on children and childhood, can be quite important for this endeavour. Nigel Thomas and I have strived to emphasise the mutual contributions of the capability approach and recognition theory (Thomas and Stoecklin 2018). Another promising path, in my view, lies in comparing the latest works of Norbert Elias with Anthony Giddens' structuration theory, underlining possible connections between symbol theory (Elias 1991) and structuration theory (Giddens 1984) in terms of structure seen as a symbolic "'virtual order' of transformative relations":

> To say that structure is a 'virtual order' of transformative relations means that social systems, as reproduced social practices, do not have 'structures' but rather exhibit 'structural properties' and that structure exists, as time-space presence, only in its instantiations in such practices and as memory traces orienting the conduct of knowledgeable human agents. (Giddens 1984, p. 17)

Language, as analysed by Elias in his symbol theory, can be viewed as exhibiting structural properties that are instantiated when people speak, read or write, and which do not exist *per se*. I will show in the next sections of this chapter that the language commonly used by actors and the thoughts reflected through it can be subsumed into very general 'thinking horizons', through which perceived reality is rearranged. This is the development I am making with the proposition that structure is the form taken by agency, in the same way that discourse is the form taken by language. The conclusion has tremendous scope: structure and agency are the same thing – the symbolic order – viewed in its duality.

## 9.2 … to the Structure of Agency

I will now highlight the agency of CSS alongside the development of a theoretical framework focusing on forms of agency. The idea that agency itself has an internal structure (Stoecklin and Fattore 2018) is pursued here. My turn here to *the structure of agency* has been motivated by structuration theory (Giddens 1984).

I first relied on the two elements that are distinctive in the structuration theory, and on which other theories put less emphasis, namely choice and reflexive monitoring:

> Agency concerns events of which an individual is the perpetrator, in the sense that the individual could, at any phase in a given sequence of conduct, have acted differently. Whatever happened would not have happened if that individual had not intervened. Action is a continuous process, a flow, in which the reflexive monitoring which the individual maintains is fundamental to the control of the body that actors ordinarily sustain throughout their day-to-day lives (Giddens 1984, p. 9).

If we consider that structure constrains and enables practices, then it is logical to see individual choices and reflexive monitoring as also reflecting these constraints and enactments. Power is therefore not only located in structures, it is also instantiated in each individual action:

> Agency refers not to the intentions people have in doing things but to their capability of doing those things in the first place (which is why agency implies power: cf. the Oxford English Dictionary definition of an agent, as 'one who exerts power or produces an effect'). (Ibid.)

This is compatible with a relational approach to agency (Oswell 2013, Leonard 2016, Esser et al. 2016; Raithelhuber 2016), as individual projections necessarily encounter each other in a symbolic structure that is a "'virtual order' of transformative relations". When the complex links between choice and reflexive monitoring are highlighted, we come closer to a vision whereby agency itself has a structure.

In this chapter, I will strengthen this turn to *the structure of agency* by relying on symbol theory (Elias 1991). The dual nature of language resides in its capacity to put in 'solid' form (discourses, writings…) the fluidity of thought, while, simultaneously, participating in the structuration of thoughts. How then could one situate language within an oppositional view of structure and agency? In my view, it is not possible. Rather, the theory of symbol reinforces the view that structure and agency are not opposed, but the same thing, a symbolic realm that must be viewed in its duality. The dual nature of language, constraining thoughts and enabling them, is the concrete instantiation and reflection of the duality of the symbolic world we live in. (For Elias the symbolic world is the fifth dimension, adding to the dimension of time and the three dimensions of space.) Consequently, if language is neither simply on the side of agency nor on the side of structure, then this central reality of our lives named 'language' or 'symbolic structure' has structural and agentic functions. It is the functions of language that are structural and agentic, and therefore one should not situate structure and agency as two substances, but rather as two features of only one thing: language. This brings us to see that the structure-agency debate is an outcome of a substantialist view of society, deriving from the old substantialist separation of body and mind. Sociology remains trapped in Cartesian dualism as long as it opposes agency and structure, and as long as it confuses the latter with institutions.

This turn to *the structure of agency* is of paradigmatic importance. It is also fundamental to understand the choices and strategies of CSS. The starting point was the observation that CSS have to create opportunities in order to compensate for the lack of resources they are equipped with in the street. It is therefore important to come back to some empirical examples before further developing the theory.

## 9.3 Agency as Creation of Opportunities

As presented in chap. 6 (on survival strategies), Riccardo Lucchini has shown, drawing on Cusson (1981), that an opportunity is constructed when the actor is able, thanks to his or her resources, to "take advantage of given circumstances to achieve his [or her] ends" (Cusson 1981, p. 64). The creation of opportunities is hence dependent on the triangle of relations between the resources of an actor (affective, cognitive, cultural, social, physical), the intentions of the actor, and the occasions found in the environment.

The following example shows how an opportunity can develop or not. On the square of Shanghai North railway station (which is now the 'Old North Station'), Lan, a five-year-old boy, grabs onto passers-by with the hope that they will give him a few coins. However, since his hands are especially dirty, passers-by mostly respond with insults; sometimes they also kick him or hit him with their umbrella. Huang, another boy around the age of eight, begs as well. But, unlike Lan, he ostentatiously shows his dirty hands and pretends he wants to touch passers-by, but without ever actually touching them. Faced with the risk of having their clothes dirtied, passers-by promptly give him a coin in order to get rid of him before he touches them. This 'pressured begging' is thus effective for because the child has integrated into his strategy the fact that passers-by are repulsed by the idea of being touched by the 'child with the dirty hands'. This shows that the child is aware of the disgust that the people of Shanghai feel towards his dirtiness. He can then use this knowledge wisely: what is, *a priori*, an obstacle – their revulsion – can be turned into a resource.

Children can thus, to a certain extent, transform their environment, through the transformation of an occasion (here, well-dressed passers-by) into an opportunity. Children also beg from poorer people, a fact they recognise from the way they dress, but they are less likely to receive a coin and, if they do, it will most likely be one of lesser value. These passers-by are relatively indifferent about the prospect of being touched, as their clothes are already not the cleanest anyway. We noticed that Lan, the youngest of the two beggars, behaves the same way no matter how passers-by are dressed: he grabs onto people whether they are dressed well or poorly. This is something Huang does not do: he never touches well-dressed people (and only sometimes touches poorly dressed people), because he understands what their priority is. He is able to empathise with passers-by and understand that, for them, not being dirty is more important than giving a coin away.

Through this simple example, we can see that the actor's resources (affective, cognitive, cultural, social, physical) are essential in order for the actor to be able to connect occasions to act with his or her intentions or goals. Taking advantage of an occurrence requires cognitive resources in order to recognise that it is an occasion to act. The strategies we can observe among these children are then indicators of the degree of development of their symbolic competences. In this instance, the occasion that is the arrival in Lan's field of vision of a passer-by, no matter who, well dressed or not, is an event that Lan seizes for what he perceives it to be: an occasion to act, to beg. Lan seizes this opportunity in an undifferentiated way: every passer-by is worth imploring, and he grabs onto them with the hope of obtaining their commiseration. This very young beggar maintains a kind of magical thinking: he believes that the more he insists, the higher his chances of receiving money. Reality proves him wrong: he receives blows, but very rarely coins.

The transformation of an occasion to act into an opportunity, and therefore into a more elaborate begging strategy, requires a more active investment from the child and thus symbolic competences. Huang knows that the arrival of a well-dressed passer-by does in itself not constitute a sufficient chance to provoke his or her pity. He must adopt a more complex strategy, and he uses his dirty hands as a resource for this purpose. From destitute little hands, supposed to provoke pity, they become weapons, enabling him to threaten the sartorial dignity of well-dressed people. The child thus acquires a certain power that turns the occasion into an opportunity. Children who know how to use their dirty hands as a resource can take advantage of the circumstances in order to achieve their goals: they are then in a position to negotiate a kind of agreement not to touch the passers-by's clothes on the condition that the passers-by give them something in return. This is a gestural transaction that children can establish to their advantage, particularly through a blackmail strategy which consists in getting the passers-by to understand that if they give something, their clothes will not be dirty.

This example shows that things happening in an actor's environment can be identified as opportunities when the child relates them to his or her own goals. This is possible thanks to their personal resources, notably their cognitive resources. But with the description of the two different strategies adopted by Lan and Huang, we can highlight something more: the active construction of opportunities stemming from social interactions is possible only when the actor's personal skills have reached a sufficient level of understanding of the goals of others. Some empathy is needed. But how is this empathetic understanding achieved? This question will be dealt with in the next section.

## 9.4 Understanding Is Interpreting

As Herbert Blumer has argued, understanding is always interpretation:

> The term 'symbolic interaction' refers, of course, to the peculiar and distinctive character of interaction as it takes place between human beings. The peculiarity consists in the fact that human beings interpret or 'define' each other's actions instead of merely reacting to each other's actions. Their 'response' is not made directly to the actions of one another but instead is based on the meaning which they attach to such actions. Thus, human interaction is mediated by the use of symbols, by interpretation, or by ascertaining the meaning of one another's actions. This mediation is equivalent to inserting a process of interpretation between stimulus and response in the case of human behaviour (Blumer 1979, p. 19).

The construction of opportunities is therefore possible only when the actor uses symbols to interpret the actions of others. These symbols intervene, so to speak, between the occasion to act (the stimulus in Blumer's terms) and the actual behavior (for Blumer, response) that embodies a strategy to reach one's goals. The symbols mediating the perception of a situation (stimulus) and the reaction to it (response) are socially constructed. This approach sheds more light on the symbolic mediation. But does it really go beyond Max Weber's definition of social action? In his definition of "that action of an individual which is influenced by the actions and behavior of other persons and by which its direction is determined" (Weber 1978a, p. 7), Weber does not speak of the symbolic space mediating reciprocal actions. When referring to "an action in which the meaning intended by the agent or agents involves a relation to *another* person's behaviour and in which that relation determines the way in which the action proceeds" (Ibid.), Weber does not specify what this relation is made of.

We must wait for other formulations by Weber to come closer to this. According to Weber, "action is 'social' insofar as its subjective meaning takes account of the behavior of others and is thereby oriented in its course" (Weber 1978b, p. 4). How the *meaning* is constructed and how this meaning involves a *relation* to other persons is specified by Weber in the following terms:

> The 'meaning' to which we refer may be either (a) the meaning actually intended either by an individual agent on a particular historical occasion or by a number of agents on an approximate average in a given set of cases, or (b) the meaning attributed to the agent or agents, as types, in a pure type constructed in the abstract. In neither case is the 'meaning' to be thought of as somehow objectively 'correct' or 'true' by some metaphysical criterion (Weber 1978a, p. 7).

But the problem with Weber's approach is that the 'pure type constructed in the abstract' is an ideal-type that serves as a heuristic tool for the sociologist, and is not necessarily an experiential symbol used by actors to attach meaning to behaviors. His classification of types of conduct are made along four ideal-types: rationally-purposeful action, value-rational action, affective action, and traditional action. These ideal-types are intended to analyse human conduct:

> An ideal type is formed by the one-sided accentuation of one or more points of view and by the synthesis of a great many diffuse, discrete, more or less present and occasionally absent concrete individual phenomena, which are arranged according to those onesidedly emphasized viewpoints into a unified analytical construct (Shils and Finch 1997, p. 90).

Yet this sociological understanding is not congruent with actors' own reflexivity about their actions. After all, actors do not reflect on their own action in these abstract terms. They use symbols that are socially constructed but not to such an abstract level. In other words, the analytical concepts of the sociologist are not the pragmatic categories of the actors. This reminds us of the criticism of Bourdieu's intellectualism, placing as it does the objective reality reconstructed by the sociologist over the subjective and practical reality of actors (Latour and Woolgar 1979, Boltanski 2009). A possibility for avoiding this trap can be found in the notion of 'sensitizing concepts', defined as "directions to look at" (Blumer 1969), and that I will also call 'thinking horizons' as this, in my view, is heuristically relevant.

## 9.5 Thinking Horizons and the System of Action

If, as suggested above, the symbols actors use are mediating their perception of a situation and their reaction to it, then these symbols must pragmatically link stimulus and response within a set of symbols that illuminate experience by common sensitizing concepts, or directions to look at (Blumer 1969). Such sensitizing concepts are experiential, whereas Weber's four ideal-types of social action are analytical. The number of sensitizing concepts that are common enough to be able to act as symbols through which action can be understood is quite low. I contend that there are five such concepts, namely activities, relations, values, images of self, and motivations (hereafter also referred to with the acronym ARVIM). These five sensitizing concepts are able to function as 'thinking horizons', enabling actors to make sense of one another's conduct: they may understand an action in terms of activities, relations, values, images of self, and motivations. These sensitizing concepts correspond to common questions humans commonly ask each other: what do you do? who do you know? what do you think?, who are you?, what do you want? These questions are the most commonly asked questions (in this form or another) in innumerable contexts. They correspond to the most pragmatic 'thinking horizons' that people have in mind when interacting.

Consequently, whereas the four ideal-types of social action identified by Weber (rationally-purposeful, value-rational, affective, traditional) are analytical categories used by sociologists, the five sensitizing concepts (activities, relations, values, images of self, motivations) are 'thinking horizons' used by actors. These "thinking horizons" are depicted in Fig. 9.2 (below).

The 'thinking horizons' (ARVIM) are bound to the eidetic reduction (phenomenology) of reality made by social actors, an operation that is necessary to classify things and attribute meaning to them. The five dimensions (ARVIM) in the actor's system can therefore be viewed as 'reductions of the reductions'. They can be called 'second degree reductions'.[1]

The eidetic reduction of reality (language) and praxis (experience) are recursively bound together: the fictional reduction of reality (eidetic reduction) directs the praxis (system of action) which in turn directs the fictional reduction of reality (language). Giddens goes beyond the kind of syntactical sociology of the linguistic turn (inspired mainly by Saussure and Chomsky), considering "the mutual co-ordination of language and praxis" (Giddens 1984, p. 80). Elias (1991) puts this in terms of linkages between language and thought, as seen above. ARVIM are efficient eidetic reductions of reality because they are pragmatic categories: they enable us to reduce the margins of error in the interpretation of our social interactions,

---

[1] In French '*réductions au carré*'.

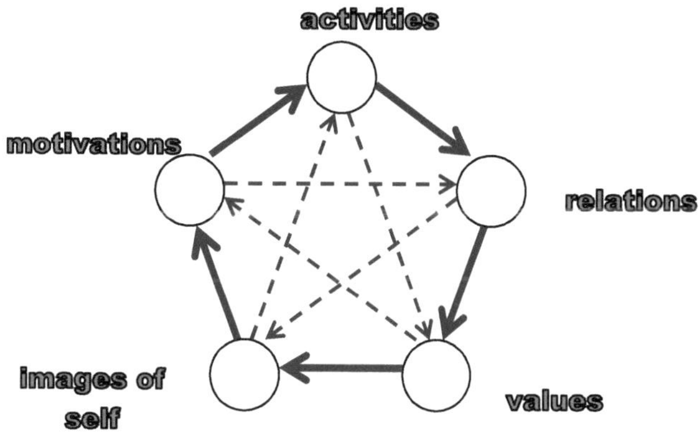


**Fig. 9.2** The 'actor's system'. (Stoecklin 2013)

as they function as triggers for legitimate questions (what do you do? who do you know? what do you think?, who are you?, what do you want?). They instantiate pragmatic trial-error procedures in the actor's inquiry (Dewey 1991). These meaningful horizons to which items of experience are attached by social actors are not necessarily discursively elaborated in these terms: actors may not use the words 'activities', 'relations', 'values', 'images of self' or 'motivations' (ARVIM) during their interactions. Nevertheless, these 'thinking horizons' are eligible to include sensations, vague impressions, things that are difficult to put in words. ARVIM are sensitizing concepts linked to sensations, through the lenses of which the actor reads and interprets reality.

Actions (*praxis*) are not reduced to activities, but encompass the whole system. ARVIM are "sensitizing concepts" (Blumer 1969, p. 148) functioning as "directions to look at", propositions with a content that is not given beforehand (Le Breton 2004, p. 41). The social construction of reality (Berger and Luckmann 1966) implies that these five dimensions of experience are not considered in the positivistic Durkheimian approach of *sui generis* social facts, but on the contrary as sedimented interpretive categories functioning as "thinking horizons" (Stoecklin, 2018a) or social lenses through which actors read and interpret their environments and attach meanings to experienced reality through their subjective inquiries (Dewey 1991).

The model is called the 'actor's system' because it is assumed that one's system of action is the constantly evolving outcome of the links between these components of personal experience. As such, ARVIM can be seen as ideal-types (Weber 1978b) for the researcher in order to arrange "concrete individual phenomena" (Shils and Finch 1997, p. 90) along "those one-sidedly emphasised viewpoints into a unified analytical construct" (Ibid.). But they are not only ideal-types, they are also commonly used 'thinking horizons', and this duality of ARVIM is what makes them into sensitizing concepts. ARVIM are hence schemes presiding over practical and discursive consciousness, conducive to stabilised interactions (modes of action) in specific social systems. Modes of action are "typical ways of acting according to dominant 'thinking horizons' that link together concrete items of perceived reality"

(Stoecklin 2018b, p. 561). With five commonly found 'thinking horizons' (ARVIM), there are consequently five modes of action, or visible forms of the practical arrangement of daily life: entrepreneurial, relational, moral, identitary, and motivational (Ibid.).

The entrepreneurial mode of action focuses on activities that produce objects exterior to oneself (*poiesis*) and strategies believed to be the most efficient to achieve one's goals (corresponding to Weber's "rationally-purposeful action »). The relational mode of action puts emphasis on relational configurations (it is close to Weber's « traditional social action » when it favours habits and routines that reproduce the social status and positions of actors). The moral mode of action is based on the belief in the inherent worth of specific values (Weber's « value-rational action »). The identitary mode of action bases on the intersubjective definition of self (it partly corresponds to Weber's « affective social action » as drives also inform subjective identity). The motivational mode of action is the most complex one. It has no correspondence in Weber's typology of social action, it is closer to inquiry (Dewey 1991).

Motivation has a contemplative aspect, and this is why I first called this mode a "contemplative mode of action" (Stoecklin, 2018b). More precisely, motivations are built through rearranged elements of consciousness derived from experience. Therefore consciousness is evolving with perceived things and is at the same time rearranging these things. This bi-directional construction is what John Dewey calls 'inquiry', which he defines as "the controlled or directed transformation of an indeterminate situation into one that is so determinate in its constituent distinctions and relations as to convert the elements of the original situation into a unified whole" (Dewey 1991, p. 108). Any person is an inquirer, not just the scientific researcher. Inquiry, be it loose or systematic, is a mode of action I call 'motivational', as it conveys motives that are stemming from observation. One looks around, as well as 'within' oneself, and finds 'things out there' becoming motives because they are related to shapes that grow within oneself. Motivations include a large spectrum of cognitive procedures, from images emerging from the unconscious (dreams) to logical operations of induction and deduction (scientific process). These diversely elaborated manifestations are all bound to the ontological capacity of humans to adjust to the environment through reflexive thinking.

With the identification of five modes of action – similar to Max Weber's "ideal-types of social action" (1978b), with the difference that Weber's typology is more abstract than 'modes of action' that are more experiential – it is possible to come closer to the experiential categories, or symbols, used by actors when they are thoughtfully orienting their conduct in concrete interactions. They are using 'thinking horizons' to attribute meaning to each other's conducts, and in doing so they are reinforcing the impact of routinized 'modes of action' that are constraining and enabling their practices. Modes of action are therefore not only ideal-types constructed by the researcher, they also derive from the pragmatic eidetic reductions through which actors make sense of their environment. 'Modes of action' are hence operational in studying the meaning-making processes that preside over social structuration.

Something has been added here to Blumer's focus on meaning-making. The actor's system is a good candidate to serve as an operational and heuristic device for the analysis of 'structure' as it reflects the "virtual order of transformative relations" (Giddens 1984, p. 17). I presuppose that the five commonly used 'thinking horizons' (ARVIM), captured through "sensitizing concepts" (Blumer 1969) are bound together and form a matrix. The actor's system represents a matrix of "rule-resource properties" (Giddens) in the form of discursive categories (ARVIM) which simultaneously reflect and orient practical consciousness, as they are both generative (plain arrows in Fig. 9.2) and delimiting of (dotted arrows in Fig. 9.2) one another. These rules (generation and delimitation) are stemming from the properties of the 'sensitizing concepts' (ARVIM) themselves as, similar to language in general, meanings are constructed through the associations of words that themselves are generating and delimiting all possible 'thinking horizons'. Words and their associations are always, to some extent, open to be defined by the locutors. Consequently, the 'thinking horizons' that have become the most pragmatical (ARVIM) function as *a priori* categories that serve as practical 'forms' in which a diversity of experiences can be subsumed.

The 'actor's system' is a matrix reflecting the links between the dimensions of experience. This matrix is conducive to a theory of action focusing on the systemic transformations of experience through experience itself (Stoecklin 2018b). This matrix is coherent with structuration theory (Giddens 1984), but it remains to be checked empirically to what extent the structural properties of the 'actor's system' are timeless and spaceless, in other words where and when we find accounts of experience in terms of activities, relations, values, images of self, and motivations (or synonyms of these notions). So far, comparative research confirms the relevance of the actor's system for understanding the experiences of CSS in different countries (Aptekar and Stoecklin 2014), and further research is underway to reconstruct typical ways of experiencing the street and the institutional order.[2]

The emergence of the 'actor's system' (Stoecklin 2013) originates in the 'Child-Street System' (see Chap. 3 in the present book) as a new matrix for a theory of action (Stoecklin 2013, 2018a, b). The aim of the 'Child-Street System' was to reconstruct types of street experiences, to have a better understanding of which aspects of their street experience are important to each child. The children's acts and discourses described the elements that formed their experience. These indicators could be in regard of a single subject, a single dimension of the experience, or different ones. This allowed us to link the dimensions of the experiences lived by CSS together, and to show the 'system of relations between the child and the street', hence the name 'Child-Street System', a model which stems from research first conducted in Rio de Janeiro (Lucchini 1993) and which then evolved in the field in Mexico and Uruguay (Lucchini 1996). I used this model for my doctoral thesis in China (Stoecklin 2000). Later on, this model was used for practical applications by NGOs which intervened with CSS.

But the complexity of its nine interdependent dimensions posed practical problems in intervention programs, which I tried to solve by simplifying the tool

[2] Stoecklin, *The participatory capability of children in street situations in Brazil and China.* A four-year project (starting in 2019) supported by the Swiss National Science Foundation (Grant No 10001A_179098).

(Aptekar and Stoecklin 2014). The new model, with five dimensions, has a more general scope, as it can be used in any context because it is less 'street-driven' than the 'Child-Street System'. The 'actor's system' (Stoecklin 2009, 2013, 2018b)[3] has now a decade of developments. I originally called it 'actor's system' as I constructed the model through actors' accounts of their experience. I think that 'system of action' provides a synthetic view of how action is constituted by systemic links among 'thinking horizons' that actors use to inform (give a form to) their practices. Major developments of this theory have been made thanks to its connection with structuration theory (Giddens 1984). Another development is in the connection with Mead's theory of the Self (Mead 1934), which allows for a highlighting of the "transformability" of the actor's system, and suggests a theory of situated agency (Stoecklin 2018b).

## 9.6 Transformability of Situated Agency

According to George Herbert Mead, individual identity is formed by the self-consciousness that stems from relationships with other individuals. By perceiving themselves from the point of view of others, individuals create a 'Me'. They perceive the object they are to others and thus become an object to themselves, an object they refer to by saying 'Me'. The 'Me' incarnates itself in institutions: "the institutions of society are organized forms of group or social activity-forms so organized that the individual members of society can act adequately and socially by taking the attitudes of others toward these activities" (Mead 1963, p. 222). However, this adoption of the attitudes of others is a constant source of tension. The internalisation of this 'object' that is the 'Me' conflicts, in a greater or lesser way, with the 'I', which is "the response of the individual to the attitude of the community as this appears in his own experience" (Mead 1963, p. 167). From this results a 'Self' that mediates this tension: the 'Self' is the compromise between the 'Me' (role expectations) and the 'I' (personal reaction to role expectations).

We can thus draw a parallel between Mead's 'Self', as a social formation (which he calls 'society'), and Giddens' 'structure', located between the actors and the social systems: "For George Herbert Mead, 'society' simply corresponds to a formation that stems from the relations between the 'individuals' and 'institutions'- it is their mediation, just like the 'Self' mediates the relations between the 'I' and the 'Me'" (Côté 2015).

If we clarify now that this 'structure' can be lived by individuals in the experiential terms of the actor's system (ARVIM), then we can deduce that individuals express their 'Self' through 'thinking horizons' which thus represent as many possible forms taken by the dialogue between individuals and institutions. This enables us to clarify the 'type of organisation' that social activities follow, and which has been mentioned earlier when we quoted Mead: the 'forms of social activities' are

[3] The English version appeared in the publication of 2013. I mainly refer here to this publication.

organised around modes of action (entrepreneurial, relational, moral, identitary, motivational) in which the individuals recognise each other, and according to which they create their own 'Self'. Depending on the contexts and on the dominant modes of action, individuals thus develop, to varying degrees, an entrepreneurial self, a relational self, a moral self, an identitary self, and a motivational self. From this, we can also deduce that the activities, relations, values, images of oneself, and motivations are the dominant forms taken by institutionalised 'social activities'. These forms are dominant because they are pragmatic.

The agency of CSS is therefore linked to the things they are able to indicate to themselves, as they stand in greater or lesser tension with the 'objects' constructed through the institutional order. Nevertheless, their agency is not somewhere outside this order. It is constrained by it, and this is why I equate agency with structure: it is the form structure takes thanks to these 'objects'. The structure is not something that exists outside (or before) particular actors: it is the form taken by social practices with the participation of these actors. Social practices would not be exactly the same if these specific actors were not there. In one word, the structure is enacted: it does not exist other than through individual enactments. Of course, single actors are not able to transform the whole system (although some are more powerful than others), and sedimented social practices have massive impact on the formation of the 'Self'. But this does not allow us to situate structure outside of or in opposition to the agency of actors: structure is accumulated agency as well as new agency in the making.

This vision allows us to avoid the substantialist conception of social structures and individual selves. It identifies 'emergent products', or 'objects', as the result of the forms taken by dominant 'thinking horizons', forming a structure of pertinences. This can be visualised through the dimensions of street experience that are relevant to CSS, namely the elements of the child-street system (Lucchini) and, more generally, the dimensions of the actor's system (Stoecklin 2013). We can now come back to the issue of agency as a construction of opportunities: this construction is always framed by the structure of pertinences. The development made above underlines a very central point: the child's agency is not just framed by structural constraints (giving more or fewer occasions to act), it is also linked to the child's ability to identify, name, and deal with occasions that are identified through the dominant dimensions of the structure of pertinences and the modes of action associated with them. As the act of giving meaning to 'things that happen' is socially constituted, there is no agency that is not an instantiation of structure. Hence agency and structure are the same thing, expressed in its dynamic manifestation (agency) and it its systemic form (structure). In Meadian terms we could speak of the 'acting self' and of the 'structured self', and hence see that it is always a structured self that is acting, and, reversely, that acting is always structuring the self.

Consequently, an occasion to act exists only according to one's interests, which are socially constructed through dominant 'thinking horizons'. The fundamental importance of language is therefore highlighted, as it also affects the qualitative aspects of the actor's resources: the more nuanced the language we have, the more elaborate agency can be. This has tremendous impact on one's motivations. Underscored here is the importance of the impact of language on motivations, through the dialogue between one's resources and one's goals, and this has been empirically verified in the previous chapters of this book (see notably the survival strategies analysed by Riccardo Lucchini in Chap. 5).

Another form of language is gestural language, as we have seen with the example of Lan and Huang, with their dirty hands used more or less strategically. It is, compared to the '*papo*', a very basic language. Nevertheless, all cases show that agency tends to espouse the forms of the context, through 'structures of pertinences' expressed in dominant modes of action. The form and content of agency are context-dependent. It is the street context, specific in each country, in each city, that is peculiar, and hence the content of agency espouses the structural forms of each context. (This point questions Bourdieu's notion of 'habitus', as this is supposedly 'transposable' from one context to another.) The less differentiated ideal representations of children in China (seen in Chap. 2) explain why the forms of agency are also less differentiated:

Cultural and interactional elements are closely linked to the structure of the street-space. Recognising this is fundamental in order to understand the variation, from one context to another, in the flexibility available to 'street children'. Children living on Chinese streets experience less diverse situations than children in other contexts. This greater homogeneity refers to macroscopic factors specific to China. In China, CSS are not in a position to become as independent as children in different contexts, especially in Latin American contexts.

We can thus generally see that children's agency strongly depends on the social representations of childhood in a given context, and that we must therefore focus on the relationship between the two. That is how we can speak of 'situated agency'.

"I use the term 'situated' to mean that agency always takes place in given contexts. Hence, agency takes place in the family, at school, in the street, etc. 'Situated agency' therefore means agency in context" (Stoecklin 2018b, p. 560). Children who are able to build opportunities have more chances to survive on the streets. This is why context (the street) is always built: children also create the situations, they are not just passive objects of circumstances. They create 'objects' like 'the group', 'the street', 'opportunities', 'survival strategies', and so on. These objects become part of one's identity, and consequently street situations can also be viewed, from the actor's point of view, as an integration into the symbolic order. This is how we can understand the 'paradox' of integration in a marginal group as being still a movement towards recognition from and participation in wider society:

> Structure does not mediate the relationship between individual and society (dualism), it integrates one into the other (duality). Hence, the theory of situated agency locates agency as both inside and outside individuals. It operates within them and without them. Agency is the structured and structuring entity (…). It is both habilitating and constraining. The duality of structure in Giddens' theory has inspired my vision of the duality of agency. I have come to the conclusion that agency and structure are the same thing. The core point in the theory of situated agency is that agency is located in the structure itself. This change of perspective is of paradigmatic importance. Agency is a set of symbolic resources bound together by the rules of generation and of delimitation, fundamental to their habilitating and constraining duality (Stoecklin 2018b, p. 581).

Therefore situated agency is always linked to wider social configurations. This is the next point I am turning to now.

## 9.7 Situated Agency and Social Configurations

The sociology of configuration developed by Norbert Elias evokes "a more realistic picture of people who, through their basic dispositions and inclinations, are directed towards and linked with each other in the most diverse ways. These people make up webs of interdependence or figurations of many kinds, characterized by power balances of many sorts" (Elias 1978, p. 14). Configurations can be illustrated by the metaphor of the game – Elias uses card games and football as examples:

> "The concept of figuration draws attention to people's interdependencies. What actually binds people together into figurations? Questions like this cannot be answered if we start by considering all individual people on their own, as if each were a *Homo clausus*" (Ibid., p. 131), because the game is "the outcome of the actions of a group of interdependent individuals" (Ibid., p. 129). This dynamic sociological perspective does not conceive of societies as "no more than congeries of individual atoms" (Ibid.), and allows us to envision how the "behaviour of many separate people intermeshes to form interwoven structures [which] can be neither understood nor explained by reducing them to the behaviour of their separate participants" (Ibid., pp. 131–32).

Within a single context we can encounter rather different types of relations with the street-space, depending on the child. We must then understand 'the street situation' through this diversity. In the Chinese case, the relations that on one hand beggar children and on the other wandering children have with the street-space are different because every type of child experiences a different combination of the cultural factors (social representations and prejudices) and structural factors (migration policy, demographic policy) that influence their daily interactions. This influences what the children do in order to circumvent these factors of stigmatisation, and to what extent they manage to put into place strategies that allow them to have a certain detachment and to attain skills and autonomy on the street.

Children who beg are the least autonomous type of children, and the most exposed to the victimising factors of the hierarchy of social relationships on the street. Wandering children are the most independent, but also the most targeted by the police. Children cannot engage in any gainful activity independently, as they are constantly reminded of the alternatives of being at the service of a protector or being subjected to police arrests. As for runaway children in Shanghai, they barely have the opportunity to stay on the street, as surveillance and repression take place very early in their attempt to attain freedom, which is seen as devious. As social actors, the children are then more or less unable to develop the sufficient autonomy they need to escape victimisation.

In a comparative approach, the variation of the 'Child-Street System' is to be linked with the particular configuration of interdependences specific to each context. These configurations influence certain dimensions of the 'Child-Street System' as much as they evolve through the inclusion of specific actors (for example assistance programmes) and the strategies that these actors help to make possible for these children. Accepting the existence of this dynamic invites us to consider in a critical way the determinist approach and the pessimistic vision that present these children exclusively as victims without resources. CSS play an active part in the transformation of their environment, but we must, however, note that, depending on the contexts, they contribute to varying degrees to this 'construction', which presupposes that the actors have a certain autonomy.

Considering the child as an actor is then not simply claiming that the child is autonomous, but, on the contrary, looking to see which forms his or her agency takes. It is this variability of agency that we must highlight in order to have a better understanding of the modes of social integration. This has nothing to do with certain rhetorics about the so-called freedom of 'street children' that try to turn them into idealised heroes. The Chinese case specifically illustrates a situation in which the children's agency is relatively limited. We must connect this form of agency with the specific social configuration it fits within. In China, the interdependence between the actors present in the street-space is different from that in most other contexts, as there is no intervention program that is independent from the state. During the last 20 years, Chinese policy has become more favourable towards the needs of CSS, going from a repressive approach to a more social approach (Cheng 2008, 2009a, 2009b; Cheng and Lam 2010; Gao et al. 2018). However, the agency of institutionalised children still needs to be observed, especially through the way the General Comment on Children in Street Situations (UNCRC 2017) has been received. This General Comment was adopted in June 2017 by the Committee on the Rights of the Child, and it gives guidelines on the respect of the rights of CSS to every state that is part of the Convention on the Rights of the Child. Nevertheless, in the 1990s, social configurations of the street-space in China were 'relatively' simple, as they were made up, above all, of three types of actors: the police (associated with closed institutions), bosses (city employers), and children (accompanied by a supervising adult or not). These collective actors are part of a particular structure of the street-space, which comes from a configuration connecting these actors together through interdependences based on three types of relations:

(a) a relation of exploitation-protection between bosses and children: the beggar children are all accompanied by supervising adults, themselves subject to city bosses (*laoda*) who take advantage of them in exchange for shelter and an agreement with the police.
(b) a relation of bribery between bosses and police officers: bosses who use children bribe police officers in exchange for their impunity. It is impossible to judge the extent of this practice based only on a few empirical observations, but these observations confirm its existence.
(c) a relation of repression between police officers and children: children who are not under the protection of a boss are more likely to be arrested by the police, sent to an institution, or sent back to the rural area they came from. This is

especially the case for wandering teenagers who try to do without the 'protection' of a boss because they refuse to be exploited.

What connects these individuals in configurations is the hierarchy of social relationships on the street and the supervision of children that results. It is the relation of exploitation-protection that, for accompanied beggar children, connects together the dimensions of their experience. Here, it is clearly the entrepreneurial mode of operation which is predominant, in terms of the efficiency of begging. This mode of operation gives a rather specific form to the child's agency when this entrepreneurship is practiced in an illegal manner. But most beggar children are obliged to survive in illegality: field observations show that they are mostly *Heihaizi*[4] girls, namely girls born outside of the one-child policy (dating from 1979 and abrogated in 2015). The agency of beggar children in the 1990s in China thus took the form of extreme vulnerability, compared to actors who could abuse their power through the structural contradictions between planning policies and policies for liberalisation. We can clearly observe the connection between the microsocial level and macrosocial factors: the extremely limited room for manoeuvre of children in the street-space is structured by significant political and economical factors. The strategies observable in CSS are therefore indicative of social configurations. Agency is the dynamic expression of the structure.

Wandering teenagers try to free themselves from the 'bosses' through the creation of gangs (here the dominant modes of action are relational and identitary), but their efforts are promptly extinguished by police interventions. The older and less submissive children, those who start to develop an identitary connection with the street (through group sociability or work), are thus precisely the ones targeted for repression. The processes of identity re-equilibration are thus easier to observe among teenagers for whom social response and police repression are direct, that is to say, not mediated by a supervising adult. The secondary deviance that these young people develop is a way for them to compensate for the damage to the Self caused by stigmatisation and repression: social reaction forces positive self-evaluations that will, in turn, extend the continuous participation in the activity defined as 'deviant'. Defiant attitudes towards passers-by are then clearly observable. The challenge can take the form of mockery, as illustrated by the following example:

CSS share with migrants the stigma of the 'outsider' (Becker 1963), in other words of those who, for city dwellers, come from the outside (*waidilaide*). Beggar children address migrants with more familiarity, calling them 'uncle' (*shushu*; a father's younger brother). I was myself called *shushu* (uncle) by CSS, and when my wife accompanied me on the field, they called her *ayi* (aunt). But while the younger beggar children would address us by these nicknames during our direct interactions, the wandering teenagers would use these expressions in an indirect and ostentatious way: as soon as they saw me appear on the square of the railway station in Shanghai they would shout "*shushu*", obviously hoping that passers-by would hear them. By doing this, they were using the occasion that was my presence in order to create an

[4] « Black children » (undeclared).

opportunity that would generate identitary advantages for them: highlighting to the Shanghainese people that they are worthy of their esteem since a 'person from an outside country' (*waiguoren*) shows them sympathy. At that time, Chinese people still had great curiosity for anything that came from abroad. By fictitiously integrating me among them, these teenagers therefore made their 'in-group' (beggars, migrants, foreigners) bigger, seeking to give a more positive definition of themselves to the Shanghainese people. They were thus contesting the stigmatisation against them by mocking it. They did not address me primarily, but, through me, they addressed the passers-by. I represented an opportunity that they had seized in order to send a message.

They do so in order to modify the boundaries of inclusion (in-group) and exclusion (out-group). This unusual inclusion of the foreigner can be partly explained by a semantic similarity: in the Chinese word *waiguoren* (foreigner, a person coming from an outside country), we can find the *wai* (outside), from the word *waidilaide* (coming from the outside). However, semantics cannot explain everything. When children accost us by using a familiar nickname they show a certain confidence, as they have been seeing us for a long time and have started to trust us, and, at the same time, they introduce a hint of mockery towards the Shanghainese people and, possibly, towards the migrants who reject them also.

This example thus shows that, as suggested by the 'system of opportunity' (Cusson 1981), an occasion must first be recognised, and this recognition is always connected to the structure of pertinences that prevails in a given context. The occasion embodied by a 'foreigner' is more pertinent in China because of the configuration of the street-space (triadic relations from which the wandering teenagers try to escape), but also more deeply, because of the language itself: the similarity, in Chinese, between *waiguoren* (foreigner) and *waidilaide* (migrant) allows for me (the valued foreigner) and them (a depreciated group) to be brought into proximity. Thus the teenagers create a kind of cognitive dissonance through which they transform constraints into resources. They use what tormented them to create an opportunity, namely an increased value of identity that serves above all their self-esteem, a redefinition of identity going hand-in-hand with their deviant career.

'Secondary deviance' becomes the most satisfying solution to the problems created by the process of stigmatisation (Lemert 1967, p. 55). In order to compensate for the damage to the Self caused by stigmatisation, the deviant starts by finding positive or valuable aspects in his or her situation. The negative social response forces individuals to evaluate themselves positively and, thus, extend the continuous participation in the deviant activity (Becker 1963).

This example also shows us that structure is, indeed, both constraining and enabling. Secondary deviance can be evaluated as a weak agency, because it does not turn the social order around; it is a mistake: it acts more indirectly, and in the long run, on the symbolic order. The concept of agency often fails because we invest it with too much haste for change. Even in a configuration that demands restricted forms of agency, children have a flexibility that helps the social system to evolve. It is the structure itself that generates these forms of agency: the relationship between the child and the migrant allows for a strategy of identitary proximation which is lacking in their relations with the Shanghainese people. The identitary demarcations forced by the Shanghainese people promotes this identitary proximation towards the migrants. Indeed, beggar children are rapidly aware of this identitary demarcation and, instead of suffering it, they use it. The child beggar's strategy of greeting migrants by calling them 'uncle' (*shushu*) corresponds to an attempt to create an 'in-group' which is directly connected to the stigma that rural people in the city face indiscriminately, the label of 'outsider' (*waidilaide*). For the beggar children and their supervising adults, this conflation in the stigmatisation of rural people and migrants thus becomes a resource to eradicate the statutory distance that separates them from other migrants, as minimal as it might be, and this allows them to prompt these migrants to help them, since they are 'related' (vicariously, through the term *shushu*).

This Chinese example thus highlights the consubstantial connection between structure and agency. It enables us to shed light on other fields, through this connection between agency and structure. In this way we can develop a better understanding of the links between an institutional environment and the agency of the CSS, in different contexts. Indeed, in a more complex configuration (contexts richer in diversified interrelations) – in other words where other actors (especially NGOs) step in to enforce child protection regulations – interactions enable a more complex social structuration, and thus more flexibility for CSS: "It has been shown that the course of the game is relatively autonomous from every single player, given that all the players are approximately equal in strength" (Elias 1978, p. 129). In other words, the introduction of new institutional actors noticeably complicates the interrelations and, in general, when the political legitimacy of assistance programs independent from the state is acquired, this richer structuration of interdependences is to the advantage of the children: they can diversify their strategies and their networks, which gives them certain protections, direct and indirect. However, adding complexity to the configurations also has drawbacks. One of its adverse effects is the 'institutional tourism' of CSS (Aptekar and Stoecklin 2014), which contributes to keeping them on the street and does not change anything of the institutional order that is the cause of their obligation to survive on the street. The middle ground remains difficult to attain, and that is why empirical research is absolutely necessary in order to have a better understanding of the social structure and, thus, to adapt policies.

## 9.8 Agency as an Alteration to the Structure of Pertinences

The creation of opportunities has been observed through the example of Lan and Huang, who use their dirty hands for 'pressured begging'. This agency is relatively limited and does not, fundamentally, modify the structure of pertinences valid in this context, as passers-by keep seeing them as a nuisance. In order for a modification of the structure of pertinences to be possible, there needs to be more than simply the accommodation of the child from the point of view of others, as in the case of Huang, who understands what the interest of passers-by is and so pretends to threaten them to touch them in order to receive charity.

As previously observed, CSS are objectified through a stereotypical image of 'street children', which sees them as victims and/or delinquents depending on the ideal representation of childhood in a given context. These social representations convey restrictive normative expectations, but CSS can also use them strategically. It is at this moment that children can, to a certain extent, modify the structure of pertinences to their advantage. Yet, this capacity is more often observed as a group agency, through the coordination of actions which enable persisting advantage.

Normative expectations refer to things that are expected, and therefore to things that are relevant to the actors who formulate these expectations. The whole of these expectations thus forms a 'structure of pertinences'. According to Giddens (1984), what is characteristic of a structure of pertinences is that it is both constraining and enabling. It is therefore *through* this structure of pertinences that children give meaning to their situation on the street and develop their agency. This interpenetration between social practices and representations (mentioned in Chap. 2) can thus also be found at the level of the structure of pertinences, that we can visualise with the 'actor's system' as a negotiated symbolic order. What is therefore negotiated are the modes of action, in other words ways of doing things which are guided by specific preoccupations (which I call 'thinking horizons'). In a way, the actors fight to make their 'thinking horizons' prevail. To carry out this fight, actors have at their disposal economic, social, and cultural forms of capital (Bourdieu 1984) that differentiate them.

In Bourdieu's theory, the different forms of capital (economic, social, cultural, symbolic) play one over the other. Lacking economic capital, and with less of the differentiated social capital that is usually prevalent in middle and higher classes (in terms of differentiated networks), CSS have to make smart use of the cultural habits of people from these classes, in order to obtain some advantages from them. They have to be able to place themselves in the shoes of the other. They have to make a very subtle analysis of the situation, and hence they mobilize primarily their cognitive competences.

It is thus with more or less skill, and recognition of their forms of capital, that actors negotiate the symbolic order. There needs to be a certain congruence between the order of individual preferences and the symbolic order that is predominant to have a chance to influence it from 'the inside'. That is why agency is not opposed to structure, but tends to match it, without mimicking it perfectly. Agency is the dynamic expression of structure negotiating itself. We therefore cannot artificially separate agency from structure, because it is consubstantial. There is no agency independent from structure. We can thus return to the subject of the creation of opportunities (with which we started this chapter) to show that this agency goes hand in hand with structure. Indeed, if agency takes the form of the structure of pertinences, it is because the necessary capacities to practice one's agency are all related to the environment.

Agency is made of the combination of the following capacities: (a) the capacity to act purposively (goal-oriented action); (b) the capacity to relate objectives and objects (in both directions); (c) the capacity to attribute meaning to the environment (hence identifying occasions to act).

All these capacities are related to the environment, and more precisely to the structure of pertinences that are valid in a specific context: goal-oriented action (Weber 1978b) itself relies on the capacity to relate objectives and objects, in both directions, and hence to attribute meaning (value-oriented action) to the environment. Occasions to act are identified by actors who do already attribute meaning to people and things in their environment (through specific values, i.e. a structure of pertinences). An occasion is therefore never something that happens really outside the actor's appraisal: the event is an event for someone, and this person is embedded in their environment, and so they therefore refer to the structure or pertinences that are deemed valid in this environment. Consequently, the agency of CSS is linked to the structure of pertinences that is negotiated in their context.

This underscores a very important point, as mentioned regarding Lucchini's use of the 'opportunity system' of Maurice Cusson (1981), in Chap. 5 of this book. While "[a]n occasion occurs within an actor's environment without their personal intervention" (Lucchini, Chap. 5), this component of the system of opportunity nevertheless needs to be "perceived and elaborated upon – for example, categorised as favourable or unfavourable – in accordance with the actor's skills (resources), interests and social affiliation" (Ibid.).

Indeed, the actor does not intervene in order for something to happen, but he or she intervenes mentally (and not yet physically) *a posteriori* by identifying this thing as an event. Yet this mental intervention by which the thing is identified as an occasion to act is a phenomenological reduction (eidetic): the noumenon (the thing in itself, what is currently happening) is reduced to a phenomenological category, indexed to a language category, through a structure of pertinences which has been socially developed (actor's system). The actor identifies the thing as an occasion to act *because* this thing is filtered by these frequently used thinking horizons. In other words, the identification of an occasion to act is socially constructed. This occasion to act is then a kind of constructed stimulus. Subsequently, an action orientated by a goal is a projection that stems from the social construction of reality. The actor's intentionality is not asocial. It is orientated by the thinking horizons building stimuli which, without these specific thinking horizons, would not be perceived. What the actor sees in the environment is, therefore, already the result of a socialisation of the thinking horizons. We saw this with the example of the Chinese children who strategically use the word *shushu* (uncle) to induce a reaction: the closeness with the migrants for the beggar children is in line with an entrepreneurial mode of operation (increasing the chances of profit), while the closeness with the researcher (myself), artificially created by the teenagers, is in line with the identitary mode of operation (gaining esteem). This shows that the identification of an 'occasion to act' is filtered by the structure of pertinences which prevails in a given context.

That is how we can understand the agency of the CSS as creations of opportunities (Cusson 1981), which we can now specify take the shape of the 'structure of pertinences' that marks a particular context. What is pertinent on the street is socially debated, and it is among these conflicting points of view that CSS orientate themselves: the more the argument creates contrasting points of view, the more the child is able to develop an 'inventive' agency. On the contrary, the more the argument is reduced by unequivocal dominant discourses, the more the child finds it difficult to seize occasions to act, as they are less differentiated. The actor's agency therefore takes on the shape of diverse structural forms. We can represent this variability through a continuum. On one end of this continuum we can find a monomorphic agency; this is the case when only one thinking horizon (ARVIM) monopolises the function of social stimulus. On the other end, we find polymorphic agency.

## 9.9 Forms and Contents of Agency

These reciprocal adaptations between forms and contents of reflexivity lead us to go back to Kant, for whom the reality of the world amounts to the experience we make of it (the 'phenomenon'), the essence (the 'thing in itself', or 'noumenon') remaining inaccessible:

> The world as experienced is called by Kant *phenomenon*. The thing in itself is the *noumenon*. Our knowledge of the world, including all our scientific knowledge, is concerned with things as experienced. However much one might wish it, science does not apply to *noumema*, but only to *phenomena*. (Martindale 1960, p. 217).

Kant adds that we know phenomena, namely things as they appear to us, in two forms or orders: the order of the 'contents', which are contingent, in other words based on experienced facts (empirical cognition and *a posteriori*), and the order of the 'forms' (transcendental cognition and *a priori*), which are deduced from the observations made through experience (op.cit.). Yet while Kant thinks that there are *a priori* categories which are universal and atemporal, Elias considers that there are *a priori* categories but that they are contingent to groups, and that they are transmitted through learned symbols. I choose to favour this second option by postulating that knowledge is a recursive dynamic: what is experimented is reconstructed *a posteriori* (empirical cognition) and re-injected in the order of the *a priori* forms (the words or analytic concepts we use). *A priori* forms are themselves the result of repeated empirical findings, which have given a certain stability to these language categories. The contents of experiences are thus indexed to words or language categories which then act as 'containers' (*a priori* forms) that have withstood successive empirical tests to which they were subjected. The definition of a word is then always the definition of what covers or 'includes' the word based on an experience that confirms the pertinence of the word or the concept used to designate the factual object.

In the long run and through use words then hold *a priori* knowledge, not requiring automatic empirical verification. We 'trust' words, we 'take them for granted'. That is why we do not need to call to mind the characteristics of the street every time we mention an action on the street in order to make the action understandable. We have enough empirical experiences that have already been subsumed under the words 'actions' and 'streets' to know what we are referring to *a priori*. The 'actions' of children on the 'street' are then seen as deviant only if they are outside of the common use of this space in a given context. Because *a priori* knowledge functions by analogy, there is always an evaluation of the norm or of the deviance of an 'action' happening on the 'street' that is made in relation to one's own experiences of the street-space. These evaluations then highlight the normative discrepancies between 'street' actors and their observers. The culture of these observers, in terms of class cultural capital as much as in terms of belonging to a socio-cultural group for whom the street is not their main living or survival environment, thus always affects the description of the 'actions' of children on the 'street'. Yet this evaluation is, at least in part, incorporated by the children themselves in their own reflections about their 'actions' on the 'street'.

Consequently, the child's subjective construction of the object 'street', as a space in which it is possible to act according to certain modes and not others, is already influenced by the social response to behaviours prior to the child's own experience of the street. To put it plainly: children do not enter the street as if it were virgin grounds. This space is already charged with meanings, which the child did participate at first, then partly take on before also partly rejecting it, depending on their personal path. Subsequently, the choices they make, the re-assembling they do subjectively – in short, what we call their agency – these are all highly influenced by the meanings attached to the street-space in a given society. The most pertinent choices are always in line with these representations, because only these appropriate choices can make it possible to avoid the stigmatisation that affects deviant choices. Dominant representations thus form a structure, which we can call the 'structure of pertinences', which gives form to empirical contents: this structure (or form) classifies behaviours, and designates them in a normative way, as conforming or deviant. This therefore implies that the agency always tends to take the form of the structure of pertinences, and that, unlike the dominant outlook that separates agency and structure, it is not opposed to structure. It is, in fact, the dynamic expression of the structure. Likewise, role is the dynamic expression of status: the role relates to the ways of fulfilling the obligations associated with the rights conferred by a status. In the same way that a role is a practical instantiation of a status, agency is a practical instantiation of structure. It is one and the same thing, seen in different ways: in its phenomenological manifestation, and from a noumenal perspective. We can now understand that agency is the observable phenomenon while structure is the noumenon inaccessible to our senses. Agency reveals structure.

This perspective counteracts the dominant view which separates structure and agency (and which stems from the mind/body split that has prevailed in the West since the advent of Cartesianism). This separatist vision is thus at the origin of the conception of agency in terms of opposition, comparable to the presumed superiority of mind over body. The mind is valued (also since the advent of an individualism of Christian origin), the body is despised. Since the spirit has been declared immortal, imprisoned in a mortal body, these representations of independence and freedom as having to break free from a constraining structure (like an aging or sick body) has resulted in multiple dichotomies derived from them: subject/object, individual/society, agency/structure, and so on. That is why it seems that the epistemological break in social sciences is not yet complete: they are still too steeped in Cartesianism and individualism.

However, this emancipatory or oppositional vision involves categories of judgement (just and unjust) that stem from a mystical vision (celestial and terrestrial) which has not been sufficiently challenged. That is to say, the oppositional vision of agency and structure is a dualism of religious origin, which, paradoxically, is not detected by its proponents despite the fact that most sociologists are atheists. This paradox must therefore question the current epistemology of social sciences. But let us set this aside for now in order to focus on the observation bias produced by this implicitly religious vision of the separation of body and mind: namely concerning how the resulting structure/agency opposition leads the sociologist's focus solely towards the 'deviant' behaviours of the actors who challenge authority. It is quickly claimed that, by these behaviours, these actors show their opposition to structure. The blindness and analytical confusion thus provoked by the agency/structure opposition then strengthens the observation bias: the behaviours that stray from the expected role are the only ones we consider as a reflection of an agency. In other words, we mistake agency with 'role distance', which is then observed as a manifestation of the 'room for manoeuvre' which persists despite itself in the structure.

The focus on agency as being opposed to structure then leads to a vision of the social system as a labyrinth out of which it is best for the actor leave unscathed or, better yet, grown up. There is, then, often only one step to take for the 'engaged' sociologists, that of designating the institutional walls that we should take down. This oppositional position is somehow romantic. I personally succumbed to it more than once before I could, through a critical reflexivity, free myself from it. I believe that the sociologist's ethics should not be primarily guided by his or her own self-image as an engaged citizen, which he or she can absolutely be, but by the consequences of his or her axiological positioning in the face of the realities experienced by the observed actors. The sociologist must then be even more careful before condemning a 'structure' or a 'system', as what he or she perceives is not necessarily free from a specific education, which is not the education of the actors who live and stay there. Without this care, sociologists could find themselves coming back and living in a context in which they may want to shine through the mythical figure of the sociologist liberator.

It is then extremely important not to mistake agency with role distance, and not to consider that it is a form of resistance to the role expectations (structure of pertinences) which is, simply by being dissenting or oppositional, morally superior to these role expectations. Role expectations also have their moral justifications and it is not pertinent to claim, once and for all, that they are merely a reflection of the domination of one class over others, or of a group of individuals over others, the latter group being alienated or in search of potential liberation. However, it is clear that where a habitus is imposed insidiously, and even more when it spreads through a violence explicitly claimed as legitimate by an individual or a group that considers themselves entitled to decide in the name of all (dictatorships, authoritarian regimes, and so on), it is necessary to consider that the oppositional forms of agency are indeed observable in role distances, in the unsaid, in the avoided, and so on.

This imputation of a 'revolutionary' attitude is even more ascribed to children, especially those living in spaces dominated by injustice, because it is strengthened by Rousseauism. The ideal image of the 'authentic' child has indeed, since Rousseau, generated behavioural expectations (a Western structure of pertinences of sorts) far removed from those that are considered as legitimate in social spaces where Christian individualism did not have a similar development. The case of China, for example, is emblematic in this regard: there are no CSS who have the ideal image of the authentic child as a reference. This ideal image has not been spread enough in China for us to be able to find, among the population, an adherence to the image of 'the street child as a victim of the system', an image that has been successfully proposed by NGOs in different cultural contexts. This is not simply because of a political context that diminishes the ability to criticise the system. It is more fundamentally fixed in a different ideal image, much more widely spread in China, namely the image of the obedient child, representing the ideals of filial piety (*xiao*). The children living or surviving on the streets of China therefore do not have the benefit of the benevolent gaze we can find in the West towards the figure of the child-victim, the desperate hero of a hopeless fight. They find only pitying or hostile reactions, according to a moral code in which individualism remains, despite the effects of globalisation, subjected to a more collective ethics in which the importance of reputation, concerning family above all else, engages every member of the group, and punishes even more harshly the disparities which could threaten this collective identity.

In Latin America and Africa, even though Christian individualism has come further there, we can also find dynamics ruled by community logics rather than individualistic ones. What a disappointment then for Western participants, who have been fed Rousseauist individualism, to realise that CSS that they are trying to help do not necessarily, and maybe only strategically, claim to be innocent victims, and even less to be revolutionary children trying to overthrow the unfair social order! Most of the time, they are children who partly assume the contradictory discourses about them and who adapt to a greater or lesser extent, and this ability to adapt to the paradoxical definitions of their situations is precisely the agency we may miss: because of the Cartesian approach, which makes the opposition or dichotomy of body/mind the model of the structure/agency opposition, the accommodating behaviours of CSS are therefore seen as a capitulation to the unfair order. Their entry into a violent career, based upon the subjugation of others, is not seen as an emancipation (they are not the good Jesus…), but as a reproduction of the unfair social order. This is how we can then speak of 'paradoxical overadaptation': "The concept of 'paradoxical overadaptation' leads to the disappointing realisation that the best adapted for survival on the street are the least adapted to conventional social dynamism, in other words, the codes of life in society" (Samusocial International 2014, p. 7). However, this accommodation, including under the form of a progression in the deviant career, is indeed an instance of agency. It tends to take the structural form of society, namely the form that takes the structure of pertinences in a given context. This sends us back to the old debate about form and content.

Form and content are analytical categories. Empirically, there is no form without content, and every content has a form. The disjunction between form and content is a rationalist operation, that is made for the sake of analysis. Synthesis can be achieved only when form and content are merging. This is another way to address the old philosophical and scientific debate of the links and tensions between rationalism and empiricism, and that informed the emergence of sociology in the Neo-Kantian nineteenth Century. There is no room here to enter into these historical developments. What is more relevant is to underline a constant feature of sociological theory: that all of the theoretical models that sociologists use and develop are forms deriving from empirical observation. However, once they have been modelised in figures, reduced to their function as analytical grids, these models appear as 'empty' of experience. The definition of habitus (Bourdieu 1984) looks like a form without a content. This is also true for the definition of structure in Giddens' theory. The actor's system model is also a form waiting to be filled with contents.

As models stem from empirical observations, they are the analytical forms that empirical contents have taken in the view of the theorist. The sociologist and the layperson actually perform similar operations: they reconstruct *a posteriori* (synthetic knowledge) what has been experienced and reinforce or reassemble *a priori* forms (common sense language and sociological concepts). Meanwhile, in the actor's system, by contrast with habitus (Bourdieu 1984) and structure (Giddens 1984), the concepts that serve as *a priori* forms are 'thinking horizons' that are also shared and used by actors in their daily lives. This makes a difference, which is pragmatic. The concepts of the actor's system (ARVIM) are pragmatic because they help make the link between experience and theory, content and form. They realise the synthesis of content and form. Any actor can at once name a personal experience that can be indexed to activities, relations, values, image of self, and motivations (responding to questions like: what do you do? who do you know? what do you think?, who are you?, what do you want?). This is not the case with concepts like 'rules' and 'resources' (Giddens 1984) or 'dispositions' (Bourdieu 1984) that first would need to be defined and explained to respondents before they would be able to index some item of their experienced world to such concepts, concepts that are already too 'analytical' (or not 'synthetic' enough).

This pragmatic approach enlightens the following parallel: agency and structure are in the same relation as content and form. Agency is the content of structure, and structure is the form of agency. There is empirically no separation between agency and structure, they are the same thing but viewed as content or as form. It is the analytical approach, typical of scientific rationalism, that makes them seem different, and sociological theories can even speak of structure (form) without necessarily relying on contents (taking empirical examples). This is because the logical deductions that can be made theoretically among the other concepts (forms) that are seen as components of structure (rules and resources for Giddens, dispositions for Bourdieu) have enough of a rational character. In the end, the 'analytical game' can end in a purely speculative 'playing with words'. In order to avoid these endless speculations, the concepts (forms) have to have the sort of empirical grounding that makes language significant. This is the case of the concepts used in the actor's system: they are sufficiently grounded in actors' experiences to be able to function as 'content-form', favoring synthetical knowledge. They are experiential concepts and because of this they are able to function as 'thinking horizons' that actors use in their inquiries (Dewey 1991) to orient their conducts. Their pragmatic character comes from the practicality of the testing of the environment that actors constantly perform in their inquiries, and hence Dewey's conception of accommodation ('learning by doing'), as a pragmatical process, can be further specified and confirmed with this model.

## 9.10 Agency as Construction of 'Objects'

The tremendous consequence of the empirical indissociability of form and content is that agency and structure are also indissociable. They are not two opposing substances. Hence the view of agency *versus* structure, and even agency *within* structure, disjoining content and form, is actually a purely analytical product that is not congruent with reality. In reality, no form can exist without a content, and vice versa. Agency is the content of structure and structure is the form of agency: they are in fact the same thing. What should this thing be called? I see no other concept than the 'symbolic order of action', or simply 'action', to speak of something that is simultaneously the form and the content of human practices. This is why the 'actor's system' can be renamed the 'system of action': the specification of the features of this model, which is itself an analytical process leading to synthetical knowledge, have now allowed us to reach the point where the model can be renamed. This change exemplifies how further theoretical developments are recursively integrated in concepts, which therefore evolve.

'Thinking horizons' are resources for giving meaning to practices, and these resources are bound together by specific rules: any meaning given to a practice, by indexing it to a 'thinking horizon', generates and delimits the contents and reorganisations of the other thinking horizons (ARVIM). Consequently, the systemic relations (generation and delimitation) among the dimensions (ARVIM) organise (structure) the assemblages (agency) made by actors. Agency has the structure of the intersubjective organisation of signification, and hence structure equates to how actors negotiate their own assemblages. This intersubjective organisation of significance, as the symbolic space where personal assemblages are negotiated, refuses to situate agency as individual possession. This view is shared by other authors who also consider that assemblages are not made through purely subjective and individual fantasies but are socially structured: "agency neither starts nor finishes with any individual agent" (Oswell 2013, p. 269). Yet it remains to be explained how negotiation among different assemblages occurs.

In conflict theories, the attribution of a higher negotiation power to dominant classes or groups rests on problematic and mostly implicit premises. Bourdieu's theory is preeminent in this regard. It assumes that the actors best placed within a 'field', in terms of different forms of capital (economic, social, cultural, cognitive) have the ability to impose their own assemblages, and to make it become common sense (the *doxa*). The different forms of capital are also assumed to be cumulative, recursively reinforcing each other. With this double assumption, Bourdieu contends that the naturalisation of the common sense (*doxa*) occurs by means of 'symbolic violence', which supposes that dominated classes or groups are alienated as they misrecognise the process by which *doxa* is naturalized. But Bourdieu himself doesn't explain how this happens! This is what Paul Costey (2004, p. 21) points out when he says that Bourdieu's formulations dissimulate «the entity that allows the passage from something that is passively incorporated into something that is actively exteriorised».[5]

Specifying the 'rules-resources properties' of structure (Giddens) may help in understanding how action is negotiated through the symbolic order. It is possible to come closer to the negotiation itself if we acknowledge that the symbolic order is always negotiated in contexts, but that the rules (generation and delimitation) that are organizing individual assemblages among their 'thinking horizons' (ARVIM) transcend these contexts. The 'rules' of individual reflexivity are not context-specific. This position is coherent with genetic epistemology (Piaget 1932), whereby the organisation of intelligence is not equated with particular contexts, but rather supersedes them (and therefore allows for the transferability of schemes). The intelligence of a species follows universal rules (the contrary could only be true if Darwin's theory of evolution was invalidated.) What is context-specific is the content of experience that enters into the legitimation of the intersubjective symbolic order that structures this context.

We can see this precisely with the case of CSS: street life is structured by the experience that enters into the legitimation of the intersubjective symbolic order that structures this specific context. The assemblages made by 'upper' or 'dominant' classes who do not live in the streets are not relevant in this context. Street life may be 'policed' by them (mainly in terms of the privatisation of public spaces, and 'safeguarding the public order'), but their values and practices are not seen as legitimate by children (and adults) who live in the streets. The group dynamics of CSS (presented in Chap. 5 by Riccardo Lucchini) are therefore also mediated by their opposition to values that the 'outside' world tries to impose on them, including the most well-intentioned practices of NGO staff intervening for the child's 'best interests', referring to art. 3 of the Convention on the Rights of the Child. This will be further addressed in Chap. 10.

This is how we can better understand why CSS may resist even the kindest intentions to rescue them from street life, especially in the stage of the street career Lucchini calls the 'honeymoon with the street' (see Chap. 4 of this book). In this phase of the street career the child feels at their most empowered, because the negotiated assemblages of the group of children he or she belongs to are close enough to his or her own subjective assemblages and distinct enough from the 'outside' world. This is especially observable through us/them distinctions and the corresponding constitution of 'in-groups' and 'out-groups'. This then raises a sense of membership, and with it the corresponding acquisition of a specific, valorised, collective identity. As has been shown, the stages of the street career depend on a

[5] Translation by the author.

series of changes, mainly a subjective reappraisal of objective factors that do not necessarily have to change to allow a subjective change. The child makes a different evaluation of the situation, and passes then to another phase of the street career. The importance of subjective appraisal is underlined here, but this is only a methodological way to highlight the link between micro and macro factors: children in street situations use substances (drugs) to mediate the tension between their inside world and the outside world.

The multifunctionality of drug use among CSS as depicted in Chap. 8 of this book by Riccardo Lucchini, valid for girls and boys, can be reinterpreted under the light of agency/structure. Lucchini identifies four functions in the use of drugs: playful, hedonistic, identitary, disinhibitory. The playful and hedonistic functions correspond to a soft use of drugs, and the identitary and disinhibitory functions signal a hard use. The latter may be linked to a greater tension between the child and its environment, in terms of conflicting normative expectations and abusive behaviours stemming from power asymmetries. A softer hedonistic and playful use of drugs is likely to happen in situations where this tension is lower. The kinds of agency CSS may develop through hard or soft drug use are therefore quite different: escapism in the case of the hard use of drugs and fun in the case of soft use qualify different degrees of tension in interactions. A softer use of drugs accompanies more relaxed interactions. Heavy addiction is more prevalent in contexts where interactions are tense. A very interesting link can be made with agency once we consider, as suggested, that agency is the form of structure: where this form stems from more relaxed interactions, the actors can make softer use of products such as drugs. These 'artificial paradises' have the function of either accompanying, in ludic and hedonic terms, the subjective reassemblage of reality in the case of soft use, or, in the case of hard use of substituting for a reality marked by too much tension an artificially built otherness. It is possible therefore to link drug use to social configurations, and not merely (as is usually made) to individual characteristics. The social dimension of addiction has notably been underlined by Riccardo Lucchini in his earlier works (Lucchini 1985).

We can see here that configurations marked by heavy tensions among social actors are less compatible with the soft use of drugs (of any kind, including alcohol) because the space for subjective and intersubjective reassemblages of reality is shrinking. Conversely, where the soft use of drugs is predominant it is because it is compatible with social configurations marked by less conflict. Heavy drug use is linked to more violent contexts. In extreme cases of violence, it is however nevertheless possible to survive even in the absence of drug use, such as when they are not available, as is shown by the survivors of concentration camps. There are however a few, provided they were not subjected to extreme physical violence, who were able to survive without becoming mentally ill. Those who survive without too much damage to readapt to 'normal' daily life were primarily those who, during captivity, managed, in whatever ways possible, to maintain, in the imagination, images of a 'normal' world outside the camp.

The case of the French composer Olivier Messiaen is emblematic. He survived the atrocious conditions he had to endure while in captivity in a concentration camp in Silesia thanks to his perseverance in composing music, especially the *Quatuor pour la fin du temps* during the winter of 1941. This example is a good demonstration of the phantasmatic ability at the heart of a subjectivity that assembles or reassembles outside reality in an inside world, enabling the individual to resist this 'objective' reality. Without actually transforming the present reality, the composer's agency is spread over a much longer term and postponed in time. He is today among the most renowned of French composers. There is therefore a temporality of agency, it does not redefine the contours of the structure at once. It is, therefore, also a matter of agency, not simply of resilience: it is not a matter of a return to a prior state, like a metal regaining its original shape despite the pressure applied to it,[6] but, indeed, a transformation of the system of action, through an intense activation of memories and projections, in other words is by the effect of a specific will. It is the motivational mode of action that is then strongly solicited.

It is possible that the depth of the motivation depends on an already relatively optimal equilibrium between the 'other horizons' of thinking which, in an individual, structure the action. This would be an avenue to explore. Still, in any case, the career of a prisoner locked up under extremely difficult conditions, as was the case for Messiaen, enables us to formulate the following hypothesis: an actor's ability to transform the social configuration, even in a postponed way, proves the symbolic nature of agency, being assumed that the symbolic is the *sine qua non* condition for the educational transmission of human language. The postulate on which this hypothesis is based could only be invalidated if we succeeded in proving that human language is not made of learned sound sequences, which overwhelmingly predominate innate sound sequences. We can then reasonably consider that the hypothesis formulated here requires empirical verification, since it is falsifiable. (The falsifiability of the hypothesis exists because the postulate can, potentially, be invalidated.) This empirical verification consists in finding concrete examples proving that an actor's ability to transform the social configuration is symbolic, more than physical, since the possibility of this transformation taking place in a postponed manner can only be connected to the symbolic nature of agency, which 'moves' abstract objects and not simply concrete objects.

The example of Olivier Messiaen, as well as those of the CSS who in different ways make use of drugs in order to cope with reality, confirm the existence of a 'third realm' in between actors and environment. This symbolic space, called 'structure' by Giddens, 'habitus' by Bourdieu, and 'system of action' by myself, is nothing actually new. What is new is how we name and define it. It has been identified as 'poetry' by Friedrich Albert Lange (1828–1875), a philosopher and social reformer considered a founder of the neo-Kantian movement. Surprising as it may seem at first sight, 'poetry' is a good word to qualify this 'third', symbolic, realm. Following Lange, Martindale asks

> what reality a thing has other than that of the representation of a subject. There is no fundamental reason why dissolving the world into the facts of consciousness should be preferable

[6]This is the physical origin of the application of the notion of resilience in social sciences (see Cyrulnik and Jorlan 2012).

to reducing consciousness to physical things. There must be a third reality transcending the physical and the psychical. (Martindale 1960, p. 221)

According to Martindale, Lange situates this third reality in poetry:

Kant would not understand, what Plato before him would not understand, that the 'intelligible world' is a world of poesy, and that precisely upon this fact rests its worth and nobleness. For poesy, in the high and comprehensive sense in which it must be taken, cannot be regarded as a capricious playing of talent and fancy with empty imagination for amusement, but it is a necessary offspring of the soul, arising from the deepest life-roots of the race, and a complete counterbalance to the pessimism which springs from an exclusive acquaintance with reality. (Lange 1950, pp. 231–232).

This is quite coherent with the centrality of language (Elias 1991), structure (Giddens 1984), habitus (Bourdieu 1984), or any other model (like the 'system of action' presented here): a symbolic realm mediates social interactions, and therefore the relation of actors to institutions stemming from those interactions. This symbolic realm has a 'structure' that is reflected in social configurations. The structural features of social configurations (tensions more or less marked) allow different kinds of agency, because agency takes the form of structure (or, conversely, structure informs agency). Agency and structure are two ways of decoding the same phenomenon, namely human action.

The construction of 'objects', real or imaginary, is therefore a social process, and the 'objects' constructed by CSS are indicative of the social configurations they live in. There is no agency free of structure and no structure empty of agency. The lives of CSS inform us about larger social configurations, and this is how the expression 'children in street situations' takes on its full meaning: they live in situations constituted by very large social configurations, by a multiplicity of actors, and not in a world that can be reduced to an 'underworld' for which they should be held responsible. Meanwhile, the specificities of different public spaces oriented by specific public policies are also shaped by the users of these public places. Consequently, agency being contextual, the agency of CSS expresses the structural form of a specific public place in terms of the dominant modes of action that are legitimate in this specific place. There are, in the same cities, places that are marked by a predominance of one of the modes of action over the other: entrepreneurial, relational, moral, identitary, motivational. It seems possible to make social maps that are an alternative to those based on more classical socio-economic indicators. Alternative maps could base on the prevalence of different modes of action in different places. This localised and contextualised approach, far from the blind adoption of an unproblematic transposability of the Bourdieusian 'habitus', would be conducive to specifications of what we may call 'situated agency'.

This is where we clearly see that narratives, embodying dominant accounts, do not only constrain but also enable specific 'presentations of self', and consequently CSS play with this duality of the symbolic order: depending on the persons they get in touch with, they may claim they are victims, or they may claim they are heroes, using the camouflage strategy depicted by Riccardo Lucchini (in Chap. 5). Their agency is playing with these structural features of the symbolic order. This is why agency should be seen as the dynamic outcome of structure, or the symbolic order: namely, the capacity to build new 'objects' through this symbolic order.

There is a link of co-determination between macrosocial factors and the development of children's competences. In other words, their agency is directly connected to the structural forms that stimulate them. The feeling of competence itself, and the esteem it provokes and which influences the motivation to stay or to leave the street, depends mostly on the social validation of the 'objects' that the exercised competence relates to, or through which this competence develops itself. The analysis of the 'street career' carried out by Riccardo Lucchini (Chap. 6) shows, indeed, that it depends on the way the child rebuilds 'objects', with some notable objects including 'the street', the 'group', 'family', and the 'shelter'. This subjective reconstruction is influenced by the factors highlighted in Fig. 6.1 (Chap. 6) of the present book: ways of going to the street, references and identifications, symbolic and instrumental competences, level of integration/participation in the social life on the street, movement between different fields (street, family, institutions), necessities and motivations of the child, ways of leaving the street, and institutional and adult perception.

There is, therefore, no unequivocal interpretation of socially pertinent 'objects'. This interpretation is rather specific to each actor, depending on his or her own experience. This experiential variability of socially constructed 'objects' is, indeed, what makes it impossible to consider institutions as unequivocal entities. They are equivocal and protean: everyone projects on them and take from them variable elements. Consequently, we cannot achieve a unique definition of the 'social system' as a structured group of institutions, because the structure takes specific forms stemming from the agency of social actors: it is their successive assemblages (Oswell 2013) that give renewed forms to the social system. We are now aware of the malleability of the social, that it cannot be reduced to an 'object' with clear contours and, even less, to a fixed reality. The social always takes form through individuals. It is not, as claimed by Durkheim, a social fact which engenders itself (*sui generis*). But at the same time radical constructivism is not an appropriate perspective either, because individuals always build meaning through prior constructions, which they might modify but from which they, themselves, come from as actors: their subjective reconstructions depend on the social positions they occupy and in which they have been placed socially. They are not the absolute masters of the 'objects' they rebuild.

Therefore, the image that children take on themselves, as more or less competent individuals on the street, is an image which that is socially constructed, in a specific context. They pick 'objects' that seem pertinent to them through an already socialised interpretation of reality. We could not, then, separate agency and structure, as if they were two different entities or 'substances', as the subjective and identitary aspects connected to children's agency, and that the researcher gathers through his or her interviews, are the expression of a structure of pertinences. The observed actor selects as pertinent things, 'objects', the contours of which are derived from a social definition of reality through a 'language' (Elias 1991). The things perceived by the actor as pertinent are therefore objects which are already socially constructed.

These objects are connected to each other through the mental operations that organise and arrange them and that 'language' establishes, and any new object integrates itself into the structure thus constituted. 'Language' thus creates a 'structure of pertinences'. Grammar is, itself, a reflection of this structure: mnesic traces, memorial images...

That is what leads me today to suggest that agency takes the shape of the structure of pertinences in a given context, and thus that agency and structure are not separate but, on the contrary, two aspects of the same reality. Agency is the dynamic part of structure, just as speech is the dynamic part of grammar. Agency produces, through the roles played by actors, the performativity of social grammar: the structure of pertinences. Agency is structure as it is performed. It never exhausts all of the possibilities of the structure of pertinences (things can be put together in thousands of different ways), but it is somehow the structure as it is performed. And since it is not anything else but a performed part of structure, we can thus say that it is structure as it is experienced in a specific time and place. That is why I establish an equivalence between agency and structure: agency is the instantiated form that structure takes.

The identification of agency with structure has been possible with the 'actor's system' (Stoecklin 2013), suggesting that agency has itself a structure. This adaptation of the theory of structuration (Giddens 1979, 1984) is conducive to the understanding of complex links between resources and behavior. In another field of study, this potentially explains why researchers find no linear correlation between children's possessions and children's well-being (Ben-Arieh 2008, 2014; Rees et al. 2016). Yet well-being is also associated with forms of agency (Stoecklin, *in preparation*). This child's capacity to influence its environment is rather fuzzy, ambivalent, and full of meanders. This is because context is the outcome of a recursive social dynamics. Hence agency takes specific forms or modes of expression.

More research on the forms of agency are thus required. This might contribute to our understanding of why CSS may have a sense of well-being despite their objective vulnerability (Stoecklin 2015). It might also allow us to understand the confused feelings linked to their ambiguous status and place in society, leading to the "paradoxical overadaptation" to street life (Samusocial 2014). The rejection of dualism – coherent with both structuration theory (Giddens 1979, 1984) and the experiential approach (Dewey 1991) that is also contained in the 'actor's system' (Stoecklin 2013) – implies that there cannot be any relation between an objective element and a human behavior without the mediation of meaning-making processes. It is therefore this *symbolic interactionism* that is the object of study. These developments revert 'symbolic interactionism' from a paradigm into an object: it is the sociological object *par excellence*, in a way forgotten by sociologists who confuse their objects with specific populations (stating that they are "working on street children", for instance). Going back to symbolic interactionism treated as the 'object' of sociological studies, and not just as a perspective, illuminates the intuition that "children in street situations" is "a concept in search of an object", deserving renewed sociological research and theorization.

## References


Aptekar, L., & Stoecklin, D. (2014). *Street children and homeless youth: A cross-cultural perspective*. Dordrecht/Heidelberg/New York/London: Springer.

Becker, H. S. (1963). *Outsiders: Studies in the sociology of deviance*. New-York: The Free Press.

Ben-Arieh, A. (2008). The child indicators movement: Past, present, and future. *Child Indicators Research, 1*(1), 3–16.

Ben-Arieh, A. (2014). Social policy and the changing concept of child well-being: The role of international studies and children as active participants. *Zeitschrift für Pädagogik, 60*. Jg., Heft 4. Weinheim/Basel: Beltz Juventa, S. 569–581.

Berger, P. L., & Luckmann, T. (1966). *The social construction of reality: A treatise in the sociology of knowledge*. New-York: Anchor Books.

Blumer, H. (1969). *Symbolic interactionism: Perspective and method*. Englewood Cliffs: Prentice Hall.

Blumer, H. (1979). Symbolic interaction. In H. Robboy, S. L. Greenblatt, & C. Clark (Eds.), *Social interaction. Introductory readings in sociology*. New York: St Martin's Press.

Boltanski, L. (2009). *De la critique. Précis de sociologie de l'émancipation*. Paris: Gallimard, NRF essais.

Bourdieu, P. (1984). *Questions de sociologie*. Paris: Editions de Minuit.

Cheng, F. (2008). *Negotiating exclusion: An ethnographic study of the street children in Shanghai, China*. Hong-Kong: University of Hong-Kong (Unpublished doctoral dissertation).

Cheng, F. (2009a). The efficiency of Chinese welfare policy for street children: A perspective of the street children. *Journal of Social Sciences, 4*, 11.

Cheng, F. (2009b). Failure of the traditional childcare model and the causes of street children: An ethnographic study of the street children in the Shanghai Railway Station neighborhood. *Society, 5*(8).

Cheng, F., & Lam, D. (2010). How is street life? An examination of the subjective wellbeing of street children in China. *International Social Work, 53*(3), 353–365.

Costey, P. (2004). Pierre Bourdieu, penseur de la pratique. Tracés. *Revue de sciences humaines, 7*, 11–25. Online since 21 January 2009, connection on 08 August 2018. http://journals.openedition.org/traces/2773. doi: https://doi.org/10.4000/traces.2773.

Côté, J.-F. (2015). *George Herbert Mead's concept of society. A critical reconstruction*. Boulder: Paradigm Publishers.

Cusson, M. (1981). *Délinquants, pourquoi?* Paris: Colin.

Cyrulnik, B., & Jorlan, G. (2012). *Résilience. Connaissances de base*. Paris: Odile Jacob.

Dewey, J. (1991). Logic: The theory of inquiry. In J. A. Boydston (Ed.), *John Dewey: The later works, 1925–1953* (Vol. 12). Carbondale: SIU Press. (Originally published in 1938 by N.Y. D.C.: Heath & Co).

Elias, N. (1978). *What is sociology?* New York: Columbia University Press.

Elias, N. (1991). *The symbol theory*. London: Sage.

Esser, F., Baader, M. S., Betz, T., & Hungerland, B. (2016). *Reconceptualizing agency and childhood: New perspectives in childhood studies*. New-York: Routledge.

Gao, Y., Atkinson-Sheppard, S., Yu, Y., & Xiong, G. (2018). A review of the National Policies on street children in China. *Children and Youth Services Review, 93*, 79–87. https://doi.org/10.1016/j.childyouth.2018.07.009.

Garnier, P. (2015). L'"agency" des enfants. Projet scientifique et politique des "childhood studies". *Education et sociétés, 36*(2), 159–173. https://doi.org/10.3917/es.036.0159.

Giddens, A. (1979). *Central problems in social theory. Action, structure and contradiction in social analysis*. London: Macmillan Press.

Giddens, A. (1984). *The constitution of society: Outline of the theory of structuration*. Berkeley: University of California Press.

Lange, F. A. (1950). *The history of materialism*. New-York: Humanities Press.

Latour, B., & Woolgar, S. (1979). *Laboratory life: The social construction of scientific facts*. Beverly Hills: Sage.

Le Breton, D. (2004). *L'interactionnisme symbolique*. Paris: Quadrige/PUF.

Lemert, E. (1967). *Human deviance. Social problems and social control*. Englewood Cliffs: Prentice Hall.

Leonard, M. (2016). *The sociology of children, childhood and generation*. Los Angeles/London/ New Delhi/Singapore/Washington DC: Sage.

Lucchini, R. (1985). *Drogues et société. Essai sur la toxicodépendance*. Fribourg: Editions Universitaires Fribourg.

Lucchini, R. (1993). *Enfant de la rue. Identité, sociabilité, drogue*. Genève/Paris: Droz.

Lucchini, R. (1996). *Sociologie de la survie. L'enfant dans la rue*. Paris: Presses Universitaires de France.

Martindale, D. (1960). *The nature and types of sociological theory*. London: Routledge & Kegan Paul.

Mead, G. H. (1934). *Mind, self, and society*. Chicago: University of Chicago Press: Charles W. Morris.

Mead, G. H. (1963). *L'esprit, le soi et la société*. Paris: PUF (Translation from the 1934 original version in English)

Nizet, J. (2007). *La sociologie de Anthony Giddens*. Paris: La Découverte.

Oswell, D. (2013). *The agency of children. From family to global human rights*. Cambridge: Cambridge University Press.

Piaget, J. (1932). *The moral judgement of the child*. New York: Harcourt, Brace Jovanovich.

Raithelhuber, E. (2016). Extending agency. The merit of relational approaches for childhood studies. In F. Esser, M. S. Baader, T. Betz, & B. Hungerland (Eds.), *Reconceptualizing agency and childhood : New perspectives in childhood studies*. New-York: Routledge.

Rees, G., Andresen, S., & Bradshaw, J. (2016). *Children's views on their lives and well-being in 16 countries: A report on the Children's Worlds survey of children aged eight years old, 2013–15*. York: Children's Worlds Project (ISCWeB, www.isciweb.org).

Samusocial International. (2014). *La Suradaptation paradoxale. Une notion clé dans l'abord clinique et psychopathologique des enfants et jeunes de la rue. Cahier thématique*. Paris: Agence française de développement.

Shils, E. A., & Finch, H. A. (1997). *The methodology of the social sciences (1903–17)*. New-York: Free Press.

Stoecklin, D. (2000). *Enfants des rues en Chine*. Paris: Karthala.

Stoecklin, D. (2009). L'enfant acteur et l'approche participative. In J. Zermatten & D. Stoecklin (Eds.), *Le droit des enfants de participer. Norme juridique et réalité pratique : contribution à un nouveau contrat social* (pp. 47–71). Sion: IUKB/IDE.

Stoecklin, D. (2013). Theories of action in the field of child participation. In search of explicit frameworks. *Childhood, 20*(4), 443–457.

Stoecklin, D. (2015). Vulnérabilité et capabilité de l'enfant. Dans: *Promotion et défense des droits de l'enfant: Enjeux théoriques, pratiques et philosophiques*. Université de Genève: Global Studies Institute, pp. 33–43.

Stoecklin, D. (2018a). Freely expressed views: Methodological challenges for the right of the child to be heard. *Child Indicators Research*. Article first published online: February 5, 2018. https://doi.org/10.1007/s12187-018-9527-6.

Stoecklin, D. (2018b). Institutionalisation of Children's rights: Transformability and situated agency. *The International Journal of Children's Rights, 26*(3), 548–587.

Stoecklin, D., & Fattore, T. (2018). Children's multidimensional agency: insights into the structuration of choice. *Childhood: A Journal of Global Child Research. 25*(1), 47–62. Article first published online: November 29, 2017; Issue published: February 1, 2018. https://doi.org/10.1177/0907568217743557.

Thomas, N., & Stoecklin, D. (2018) Recognition and capability: A new way to understand how children can achieve their rights? In: C. Baraldi & T. Cockburn (Eds.), *Theorising childhood.*

*citizenship, rights, and participation*. Palgrave McMillan, Studies in Childhood and Youth, pp. 73–94. isbn: 978–3–319-72672-4. https://doi.org/10.1007/978-3-319-72673-1.

UNCRC. (2017). General Comment No. 21 (2017) on Children in Street Situations. CRC/C/GC/21. https://www.crcasia.org/wp-content/uploads/2016/04/G1717034.pdf. Accessed 27 Oct 2018

Weber, M. (1978a). The foundations of social theory, 1. The nature of social action. In W. G. Runciman (Ed.), *Max Weber: Selections in translation. I*. Cambridge: Cambridge University Press.

Weber, M. (1978b). In G. Roth & C. Wittich (Eds.), *Economy and society: An outline of interpretive sociology*. Berkeley: University of California Press.

Wyness, M. (2018). *Childhood culture and society in a global context*. London: Sage.

# Chapter 10
# A Rights-Based Approach with Children in Street Situations

**Daniel Stoecklin**

## 10.1 From Ideals to Practices

What does a rights-based approach look like with children in street situations (CSS)? The directions already suggested (Aptekar and Stoecklin 2014) can be revisited since the adoption, in June 2017, of the General Comment (No 21) on Children in Street Situations, by the Committee on the Rights of the Child (UNCRC 2017). In this chapter, I will use the theory of situated agency (outlined in Chap. 9) to propose an interpretation of the limitations in the translations of ideals into practices. This will involve some insights into the capability approach applied to children's rights (Stoecklin and Bonvin 2014b). This approach helps in identifying the factors that convert (or do not convert) formal freedoms (the provisions contained in the Convention on the Rights of the Child) into real freedoms (rights as they are concretely exerted). The recursivity of normative standards and social practices will be highlighted. The recursive nature of social dynamics has already been suggested in Chap. 2, when we talked about the interpenetration of the social representations of 'street children' and social practices, and in Chap. 9 with the idea that children are not only constrained but also enabled by dominant narratives. Finally, the logic of public policies will be analysed, showing how there is often a confusion between the final beneficiaries and the target population.

But first of all, something must be said about the difficulties in separating science and intervention, as in this chapter especially it will appear that we cannot speak of marginalized populations, such as CSS, without incidentally switching from analytical to ethical considerations. The important body of knowledge about children's participation in public decision making (White 2000; Kirby and Bryson 2002; Tisdall 2008; Percy-Smith and Thomas 2010; Cockburn 2013; Warming

---

Updated from Stoecklin & Bonvin 2014a, b, with permission by Springer and from Stoecklin 2017, with permission by The International Journal of Children's Rights.

 
R. Lucchini, D. Stoecklin, *Children in Street Situations*, Children's Well-Being: Indicators and Research 21, https://doi.org/10.1007/978-3-030-19040-8_10

2013; Johnson 2017) and in development (West 2004) is still at pains to explain what exactly perpetuates the discrepancy between the ideals of children's rights and the actual experiences of CSS. The practical impact of knowledge produced by the sociology of children and childhood can be enhanced only if the actual limits of both academic work and intervention strategies, and their interdependence, are recognized. This is a topic this chapter is also concerned with.

Among international instruments to protect CSS, provide them with adequate services and let them participate in the solutions to street life or homelessness, the United Nations Convention on the Rights of the Child (UNCRC 1989) is of course of ongoing importance. But although the UNCRC has been ratified quasi-universally (the USA is the only country that has not yet ratified the UNCRC), there is a long way to go between its provisions and their implementation. This is because the transformation of the formal freedoms represented by the provisions of the UNCRC into real freedoms is mediated by factors of conversion.

Within the framework of the capability approach, it has been suggested that children's rights can be considered as individual entitlements (Stoecklin and Bonvin 2014a, b; Bonvin and Stoecklin 2016). Figure 10.1 helps visualize the transformation of these entitlements into a capability set and finally into achieved functionings.

Figure 10.1 depicts the process of transformation of formal freedoms into real freedoms. The factors converting children's rights (considered as entitlements, and therefore situated in the left box in diagram 1) into effective rightful functionings are therefore central to understanding how formal freedoms transform into real freedoms, or, in other words, how ideals are translated into practices: "The capability approach holds that children's capacities evolve along both individual and social factors that promote or obstruct the conversion of their formal rights into real freedom" (Stoecklin and Bonvin 2014b, p. 133).

This perspective helps us understand children's choices, and hence agency, as the outcome of a recursive process binding together a large set of factors that are largely only partially perceived by the actors. In other words, there is no strict correspon-

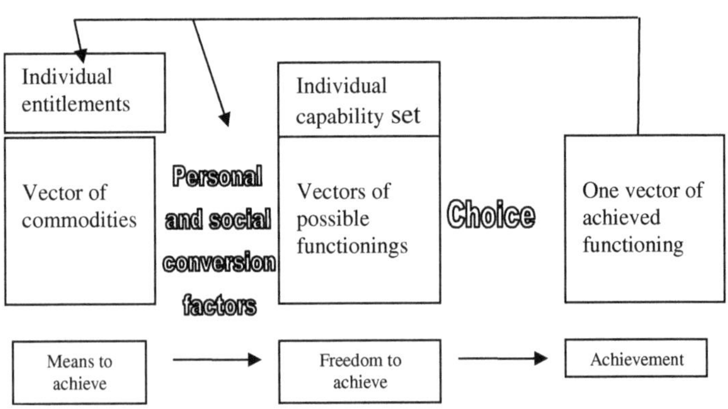


**Fig. 10.1** From entitlements and commodities to achieved functionings (Stoecklin and Bonvin 2014b, p. 134)

dence between the objective measure of the factors converting entitlements (here children's rights) into a set of possible functionings and the appraisal of these potentialities by the actors (the children). This is probably even more the case with CSS, who do not have access to the same information as children who are more integrated in spheres, primarily families and school, where these factors are more likely to be discussed, and hence become present in children's minds.

This point reminds us of the processual nature of agency (seen in Chap. 9). Interesting parallels can be traced here, underlining the recursivity in this transformation of ideals into practices. In the capability approach, context is merely equated with institutions. We find the same kind of confusion between context and institutions as in the dominant approach merging structure with institutions. Consequently, 'context' can be approached in terms of 'structure'. Yet, as we have seen through structuration theory (Giddens 1984), structure is primarily a 'symbolic order' before it turns into a more 'solidified' or 'sedimented' institutional order. In Chap. 9, I suggested that structure and agency are bound together by discursive forms: 'thinking horizons'. Agency and structure are therefore recursively bound together. This brings about the idea that 'context' itself is the outcome of a recursive system of interpretations, dominated (possibly in turn) by different modes of action: entrepreneurial, relational, moral, identitary, and motivational. When applying this recursivity to the capability approach we can see that the choices made by CSS for specific functionings (entrepreneurial, relational, moral, identitary and motivational) have a retroactive effect on their entitlements.

In fact, 'context' is more winding than linear. This linearity might be a problem if it was not completed (as in Fig. 10.1) by retroactive effects. This suggests that context is a recursive system of action. A link with the structure of pertinences (seen in Chap. 9) can be made. As shown in Chap. 9, agency is linked to structural features, notably the "structure of pertinences" stemming from a shared language. This shared language also reifies and legitimates the social positions in which, of which, and from which actors speak. Their discourses are not only positional: they also reflect their positional projections, that is, how they perceive their positions and which positions they would like to have. These positional projections made through discourses are also, of course, observed with CSS. They embody their use and reconstruction of 'objects' – like 'the street', the 'family', the 'group', that are relevant for them. This structure of pertinences, methodologically captured through the child-street system (see Chap. 3), also deals with 'objects' like the different forms of capital – economic, social, cultural and symbolic (Bourdieu 1992) – things that do not exist per se, but which are always 'relevant' categories for social distinction, in the eyes of the actors. It is hence problematic to consider the forms of capital as determining forces, as if they exist objectively, outside of actors' appraisals. Yet the different forms of capital that are valorised in a given society are also accumulated because of this valorisation. Their accumulation is therefore what in the end reinforces their importance in the social positioning of actors. They will progressively build their ability to choose among different options available to them through the very accumulation of capital itself. If we take, for example, social capital, we can see why the ability to exert agency may be more restricted for CSS: as they have less differentiated social networks (compared to the middle and upper classes), the range of opportunities they can choose from is more scarce.

The different forms of capital hence become resources (what the capability approach calls entitlements) that are recursively integrated in the actors' interpretation of reality. This explains why CSS, lacking the cultural capital of the passers-by they are confronted with, try to 'create' opportunities: as we have seen in Chap. 9 with Lan and Huang using their dirty hands to put pressure on passers-by. Do they use rights to create opportunities? No: they essentially create opportunities in ways that are not based on the Convention on the Rights of the Child. That is too far from their perception. The UNCRC does not (yet) become an occasion they can turn into opportunities. They lack any introduction to and schooling on the UNCRC. 'Entitlements' in the form of rights are therefore not, or hardly ever, converted into a capability set for these children. CSS are not, however, the only child population who is not trained in children's rights, although some intervention programs include this training in a progressive way. Even children in rather rich countries, like Switzerland, largely ignore the rights they are declared subjects of.

In other research on the framework of the capability approach applied to children's rights we gained some insights that highlight the complexity of the translation of formal rights into real rights. Children's participatory capability in organized leisure activities in Switzerland has been analysed, with "children's participatory capability" defined as "the capacity of the child to effectively participate in the definition and fulfilment of choices that affect his/her own life" (Stoecklin and Bonvin 2014a, p. 66). In the Swiss context of organized leisure, three forms of participatory capability have been identified: adaptive participatory capability, innovative participatory capability, and cooperative participatory capability. Adaptive participatory capability describes a situation in which the motivation of the child to attend a leisure center is enhanced by the pleasure of meeting people and the relaxation provided by activities within the framework of organized leisure, the resources of which offer a series of activities and the freedom to not participate actively. Innovative participatory capability is encountered when children are highly motivated either to carry out their own projects or to transform certain resources (individual or institutional), and the institution offers adequate and personalized support to their requests. Cooperative participatory capability refers to a situation of greater interdependence between the child and the institution: the resources of the actor and those of the institution are mutually recognized by the children and the staff, and there is a reinforced cooperation. This form of participatory capability optimizes the possibilities of creating a self-determined space, based on the co-construction of project frameworks, an elective logic, the acquirement of necessary resources, and the autonomy of users. These three forms of participatory capability can meet the needs of different children at different times in their lives (Stoecklin et al. 2017).

Observation and analysis of children's participatory capability reveals that the process of transformation of formal freedoms into real freedoms is fuzzy. The forms of participatory capability depend on differential combinations of economic, political, organisational, and personal factors (Stoecklin and Bonvin 2014b, p. 138), pervading different levels (micro, meso, and macro) of the social dynamics. These complex multifactorial and multilevel interactions mediate the transformation of ideals into practices. Implementation of guidelines never happens as the drafters of the guidelines imagine it would. They may have a clear-cut vision of what should be done, but how and to which extent it really will be done is out of their reach. Their goal-oriented plans are defeated by unforeseen and loosely understood dynamics, which are usually addressed, in rather vague formulations, in terms of 'risks' or 'threats' in a SWOT analysis (Strength, Weaknesses, Opportunities, Threats). This is why empirical observations are so important. They may enrich the follow-up processes with new indicators more congruent with real social dynamics, rather than with indicators that are merely an operational translation of a SWOT analysis, indicators made from the only point of view of the implementers of new guidelines through a top-down perspective.

Hence, when it comes to the General Comment (No 21) on Children in Street Situations, (hereafter GC on CSS) some cautious considerations about its implementation process should be raised. The perspective of "translations" (Hanson & Nieuwenhuys 2013) is an important contribution to understanding the multiplicity and multidirectionality of the things that are actually "translated" from ideals into practices and vice-versa. Figure 10.2 represents these multiple directions in the case of the GC on CSS.

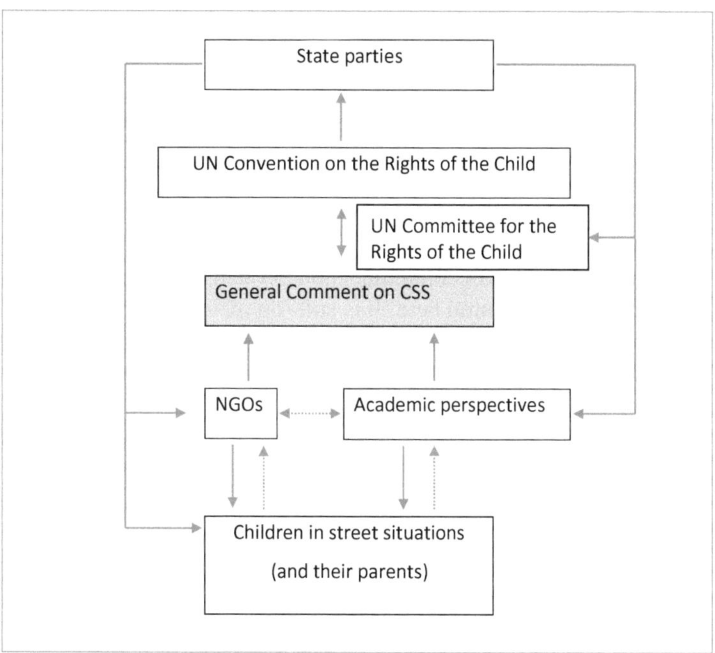


Plain arrows : formal channels of communication, participation and representation.
Dotted arrows : informal channels of communication, participation and representation.

**Fig. 10.2** Translations in the GC on CSS (Stoecklin 2017, p. 822)

By distinguishing between formal and informal channels of communication (represented respectively by plain and dotted arrows in diagram 2), it has been suggested that the perspectives of CSS, and those of the scholars who try to understand them, have largely "been lost in translation" (Stoecklin 2017).

The GC on CSS is an attempt to give guidelines towards the enjoyment of children's rights with a focus on the specificities of CSS. The translation of formal freedoms (the rights of the child) into real freedoms (real enjoyment of these rights) is therefore framed, but not yet realized, by the GC on CSS. It is only once the GC on CSS is implemented that CSS will be able to better enjoy their rights. This is the fundamental rationale behind the elaboration of this general comment, similar in this endeavour to all other general comments, that are in the end nothing more than a means for the optimal implementation of the Convention on the rights of the Child for specific groups of children. This position of 'intermediate stage' between the UNCRC and the children can be seen, in broader sociological terms, as the intermediate stage occupied by the structure placed in between institutions and actors. It is therefore necessary to analyse how this structure functions.

Analysis of this 'structure' (the GC on CSS as a symbolic structure) informs us about its dominant components. As structure is, in Giddensian terms, made of resources and rules, one must seek to uncover the main resources and rules that are present in the GC on CSS. Analysis of the main 'modes of action' or 'thinking horizons' conveyed through this 'structure' (the GC on CSS as a symbolic structure) informs us about the dominant habitus pervading child rights governance. I suggest that the dominant 'modes of action' or 'thinking horizons' conveyed through the GC on CSS are mainly conveyed by the 'activities' and 'relations' that are deemed desirable for CSS, hence mainly an entrepreneurial mode of action, and to some degree a relational mode of action.

We can also see in Fig. 10.2 which stakeholders are the main sources of this entrepreneurial mode of action contained in the GC on CSS: the actors benefitting from more formal channels of communication through which to express themselves. CSS themselves are not central here. It is still 'on their behalf' that the GC on CSS favours some dominant modes of action (entrepreneurial) that in fact primarily reflect how the 'implementers' of the CRC see themselves. They see themselves as 'entrepreneurs', and consequently tend to consider CSS through this 'thinking horizon', stereotyping them through a new perspective that makes them 'subjects of rights', and hence 'actors', the new naturalized category through which street life should be read and understood. The problem is that the attribution to someone else of the capacity to be a 'subject of rights' or an 'actor', while this person is not herself using these categories to define herself and act accordingly, is only a new imposition of status without any corresponding reflexivity regarding the person that is 'elected' to this status conferred by others, along their own agendas.

This is why sociologists should be extremely cautious when NGOs speak of CSS as being 'social actors': NGO staff may not mean the same thing as sociologists do. While the concept of 'social actor' can be used as a heuristic device to analyse how individuals act socially, once it is used in a normative way – as is mostly the case with NGOs making the positive connotation of 'actor' into a slogan, synthesizing the entrepreneurial mode of action that is socially valued –there is a switch from an analytical endeavour to a normative one. This switch remains rather unnoticed, as people think they are speaking of the same thing. But the sociologist who talks about 'social actors' in the sense of individuals acting according to their perceptions of the reactions of others to their own behaviours, and to their perceptions of the intentions of others (see Chap. 9), are not talking of the same thing that NGO staff who, primarily in public relations messages, use the expression 'social actor' in the sense of an entrepreneur who is socially oriented, someone who actively displays solidarity. Consequently, major confusions stem from the equivocal meanings conveyed by the expression 'social actor' in different arenas.

The concept of social actor is often simply used in a relatively superficial sense, giving the image of a child who would be an 'actor of society', 'actor of his or her own life project', or even 'actor of his or her own choices'. These meanings reduce the concept of social actor assigned to the child to what would be an appropriate place to give them, in the sense of an 'essential actor' of something, a project, a community, society, etc., in short, of something that defines and encompasses them, or to which they belong. This use of the notion of social actor thus identifies the child as an actor of something exterior to them. Yet, one cannot simply be an 'actor' of something that is exterior to oneself; a 'social actor' is an individual engaged in the construction of meaning that engages and rearranges his or her own interiority, in relation to what surrounds them.

The paralleling, and especially the confusion, of the notions of subject of rights and social actor therefore stems from a still insufficient theorisation of the social actor as well as of the subject of rights. It is through the connection of these two concepts that we can notice some aporias.

Indeed, the notion of subject of rights implies that there is a 'subject' (the child) who holds an 'object', namely rights. If we apply this 'possessive' vision to the social actor, we must then ask what the object held by this social actor would be. This object cannot be the 'social', society, the community, or even a project or a choice: even a choice, in appearance personal, is the product of social transactions. Consequently, the social actor (be it a child or an adult for that matter) cannot demand, from anyone, these things as possessions: they can only participate or resign themselves. We can observe here that the figure of the 'holder' of inalienable rights ignores negotiation, as if it were already resolved. Yet it is not because one is declared 'holder' of inalienable rights that the realisation of these rights is automatic. On the contrary, a succession of transactions, of varying duration, is necessary for the formal rights to translate into real rights. We could even say that difficulties are only beginning when a right is written: we still need to claim responsibility for it, enforce it, make it last, and so on. Nothing is ever set in stone. And the 'fuel' of these transactions is human reflexivity.

We can then observe that the only 'object' that social actors really 'possess', and on which they can act directly, is their own reflexivity: in other words, their capacity to see themselves as an 'object', by adopting the different perspectives from which others perceive them, in exactly the same way as they perceive others. We find here the construction of the Self, as problematised by George Herbert Mead: the individual "enters his own experience as a self or individual, not directly or immediately, not by becoming a subject to himself, but only in so far as he first becomes an object to himself just as other individuals are objects to him or in his experience; and he becomes an object to himself only by taking the attitudes of other individuals toward himself within a social environment or context of experience and behavior in which both he and they are involved" (Mead 1934, p. 116).

Consequently, claiming that individuals are 'holders' of rights is only going half of the way: they are 'creditors' of rights and must be able to make states, who are 'debtors' of these rights, respect them. The state owes them their rights, yet often only partially settles this debt. What is the underlying reason for this injustice? Is it simply a matter of a lack of will and/or economic resources, as is often said? Or is there a deeper reason? Here is where the aforementioned insufficient theorisation of action, and thus of the social actor, comes into play.

With the theory of situated agency we can make out things that used to be invisible, namely here the fact that the subject-object relation is mediated by 'objectives' built through the symbolic order (language), a 'structure' of meaning situated between the social actors. Symbolic interactionism, which is the perspective focused on the interactions guided by symbolisation, gains depth here in that it is possible to identify 'thinking horizons' (ARVIM) that structure the modes of action. Subsequently, social actors are able to transform the symbolic structure that mediates their interactions. They do so through practices that are 'personalised' implementations of the rights that matter to them. These rights are not necessarily the same as the ones that have been institutionalised in international treaties. These are 'living rights' (Hanson and Nieuwenhuys 2013). The theory of situated agency helps us gain a better understanding of these living rights as expressions of specific modes of action. We can find some claims of living rights as procedures of the exercise of different modes of action.

In contrast, we can identify the dominant mode (or modes) of action in international treaties. The dominant mode of action in the Convention on the Rights of the Child seems implicitly to be the entrepreneurial mode of action: it is the ethos of the responsible individual, as mentioned in the introduction (Chap. 1), that presides over the 'regime of truth' (Foucault 2012) of children's rights whereby children are represented as needing access to entitlements necessary for them to become responsible adults.

The theory of situated agency leads me to suggest that if children can participate, as social actors, in changes to the symbolic structure, of which the CRC is a part, then they must be able to do so through all the modes of action at their disposal (the five modes of the actor's system; see Chap. 9). Yet the institutional mechanisms derived from the entrepreneurial mode of action remains marked by this mode of action, to a point where the realisation of the rights of the child is thought mainly through actions oriented by efficiency, called purposeful rational action by Max Weber (1978). The list of the indicators of implementation of the rights of the child is a part of this mode of action, which is meant to measure the impact of the adopted standards in the very short term. Yet the impact of human rights on human behaviours is measured in the extremely long run. There is an incompatibility between the short-term measure and the measured phenomenon, that, indeed, requires that the rights that individuals are declared subjects of be included in the code of conduct of these individuals: this subjectification passes through values, images of self, motivations, and finally activities, before fully deploying its effects at the level of relations. The actor's system enables us to take a glimpse at this systematic progression of the 'objects' called 'child rights' in the consciousness and actions of the actors.

Adults and children, as actors taking part in the implementation of the Convention on the Rights of the Child (CRC), first act on their own reflexivity. Their reflexivity needs to evolve before it can, through their practices that evolve accordingly, have an effect on their interactions. In other words, the elements on which they can act are not chiefly external structures, but, first and foremost, their own representation of themselves, their own reflexivity, their own internal system of action. That is why this chapter has an inclusive title (A rights-based approach with CSS), and this inclusion is not simply in regard to the tokenistic participation of children in processes managed by adults – seen as 'decoration' by Roger Hart (1992) – but a reflexive participation. Yet this participation has not been thematised by the scales of participation, which all remain focused on the distribution of the power of the 'decision-makers' (child or adult) as if it were a zero-sum game, where the power of decision gained by the children would be lost by the adults. However, reflexive participation is a non-zero-sum game: what is gained by some is also gained by the others, for they benefit from the 'broadening of perspectives' that reflexivity offers. This relation also works in the way of a narrowing of perspectives, and what is lost by some is therefore also lost by the others. That is particularly the case when an ideology comes to forcibly constrain social actors and limit their point of view by aligning it with the only authorised point of view. The Portuguese writer Fernando Pessoa admirably describes this relation between subjects and the objects they reflect upon, in this truthful verse: 'For I am the size of what I see' (Pessoa 2006).

That is why an inclusive approach to the rights of the child, *with* CSS, supposes that we make space for other modes of action besides the one that is currently predominant in the CRC, namely the entrepreneurial mode of action. There cannot be any genuine inclusion of these speakers without an evolution of this text.

The implementation of the Convention on the Rights of the Child demands, indeed, conceptual and operational developments likely to facilitate the transition from the slogan 'child as subject of rights' to the realisation of the potentials of the social actor. The perspective of the child 'social actor' is still relatively undocumented today, and as a result there is still much work to be done on the interdisciplinary analysis of children's capacities to reach their potentials. This perspective brings out many questions about a complex reality. To address and transform this complex reality in a participative way requires, however, simple tools. These tools must be accessible to and malleable for social actors, otherwise we remain ensconced in social engineering. They must be based in the potential of transformation inherent to the actors themselves. Being active does not simply mean having activities (the instrumental level of the action), but, in a much broader sense, building the meaning allocated to these activities, through the other dimensions of experience (relations, values, images of self, and motivations), that, together, form a *praxis*. Why exactly does the entrepreneurial mode of action pervade children's rights? This is the question I address in the next section.

## 10.2 Which Human Rights Agenda?

There is no single human rights agenda, but a diversity of conceptions of human rights. Children's rights are also meshed into this multiplicity. The endeavour and intended impact of the GC on CSS can be scrutinized once we link it to the schools of thoughts in children's rights (Hanson 2012) and the preeminent directions of human rights. This analysis will allow us to better understand why the GC on CSS is primarily oriented by an entrepreneurial habitus.

We can start by recalling the following three postulates:

1. Natural rights are historic rights.
2. They came into existence at the beginning of the modern era, together with an individualistic perception of society.
3. They are one of the principal indicators of progress (Bobbio 1996, p. VIII).

Through the years having passed since these three postulates were first identified by Bobbio (1996) as early as 1951, they can now be considered as confirmed. Widely acknowledged historical accounts of humankind stress the historicity of the individualistic conception of human rights, and hence their centrality in modern states based on the rule of law and corresponding to the rational-legal authority of which Max Weber (2013) speaks. The history of human rights is embedded in an individualism that arose in Europe with the Renaissance.

Human rights are rooted in the vision of the 'abstract' individual. Individualism is therefore a humanism (de Singly 2005). By proclaiming that God is dead, we place humans at the centre of the world and bestow the sacred on individuals:

> "since each of us incarnates something of humanity, each individual consciousness contains something divine and thus finds itself marked with a character which renders it sacred and inviolable to others. Therein lies all individualism: and that is what makes it a necessary doctrine" (Bellah 1973, p. 52).

Humanism is then simply the transfer of the sacredness of God onto humans. The replacement of God by the abstract individual is the logical consequence of the cult of reason that appeared in the eighteenth century, during the Age of Enlightenment: "The cult, of which he is at once both object and agent, does not address itself to the particular being which he is and which bears his name, but to the human person (*la personne humaine*) wherever it is to be found, and in whatever form it is embodied" (Bellah 1973, p. 48). It is then not childish egocentricity but, indeed, a new moral attitude:

> "individualism thus extended is the glorification not of the self but of the individual in general. It springs not from egoism but from sympathy for all that is human, a broader pity for all sufferings, for human miseries, a more ardent need to combat them and mitigate them, a greater thirst for social justice" (Bellah 1973, pp. 48-49).

Human rights are thus born out of this historical construction which is, with the modern era, rooted in an awareness of being the architects of our own happiness, of finding the authenticity within ourselves (Rousseau), and of listening to our own inner voice. Yet this attitude is not purely selfish. There is, in individualism, an awareness of belonging and of the necessity of collective solidarity, for if I am what

I do, I am also what I do to others and what others do to me. Entrepreneurial habitus is rooted in this awareness of being a social individual, and human rights are the embodiment of this attitude, the institutionalisation of this vision. They are an instrument aiming to 'supervise' as much as to deploy individual behaviour.

Durkheim was among the first sociologists to problematise the appearance of individualism, but he distinguished between selfish individualism, which is an ego centric attitude, and abstract individualism, which can be seen as a religion. In modern societies, it is the 'abstract' individual that represents the new superior moral authority:

> « not anymore [the authority] of gods or kings, but of a commonly shared Reason. The public interest must prevail, even within individualist societies, which is not always the case. There can be overindulgence coming from the 'particular' individual, as man gives in to his endless needs instead of obeying to reason. The ideal individual must hence be held together by society, which offers institutions in order to contain him and prevent such egoistic drifts » (Martucelli and de Singly 2009, p. 12).[1]

This institutionalisation of individualism constitutes a framework, and Durkheim identifies the school as being at the centre of this framework. In other words, as pupils, we have all been socialised via individualism, that is, we have all been brought up to perceive ourselves as individuals, first of all through the assessment of our individual competences: through the grading system at school. More broadly speaking, "central institutions of modern society – basic civil, political and social rights, but also paid employment and the training and mobility necessary for it – are geared to the individual and not to the group" (Beck and Beck-Gernsheim 2001 pp. XXI–XXII). We can thus see human rights as an increasingly important extension of the institutionalisation of individualism, and particularly of the liberal vision of the individuals who are said to have 'free will'. It is even possible to detect in it a new form of religiosity: "the religion of the individual was socially instituted, as were all known religions. It is society which fixes for us this ideal as the sole common goal which can rally our wills" (Bellah 1973, p. 54). According to Durkheim, individualism has "become the basis of our moral catechism" (Ibid., p. 45). Durkheim was the first to declare that individualism is a religion: he wrote that it is "a religion in which man is at once the worshiper and the god" (Ibid., p. 46). Since Durkheim, it has become common to consider collective representations as social constructions, and consequently it is also a question of illuminating human rights as a fictional symbolic order that humans give themselves in order to regulate their relations. Human rights are thus rooted in the fiction of humanism.

This fiction of humanism is a religion, religion as "a system of human norms and values that is founded on a belief in a superhuman order" (Harari 2014, p. 234). Moreover, the humanist 'religion', placing human beings in the centre of attention and hence making human rights a core issue, should be further refined into subbranches. Yuval Noah Harari, the author of a very successful account of the history of humankind, makes distinctions between three such branches, namely liberal humanism, socialist humanism and evolutionary humanism (Harari 2014, p. 260).

[1]Translation by the authors (original text in French).

Liberal humanism is centred on the assumption that individuals have free will, and consequently they are considered as the centres of decisions about themselves (Harari 2014). The goal of human rights in the liberal conception of humankind is therefore to maximise individual freedom. Taking due note that the freedom of one individual stops at the borders of the freedom of another individual, liberal humanism sees human rights primarily in terms of negative freedoms: human rights are obligations to not infringe on one another's freedoms, and the state's foremost obligation is to not interfere in private affairs. Responsible selves are hence those who accept a minimal role of the state in safeguarding the conditions for free will to fully express itself, notably in terms of free trade. The liberal branch of humanism is expressed in the first generation of human rights (Verhellen 1999), namely the civil and political rights – freedom of expression and of opinion, freedom of the press, freedom of association – that stem from the Declaration of the Rights of Man and Citizen (DRMC 1789) during the French Revolution.[2]

With the second generation of human rights (Verhellen 1999), starting with the Constitution of Russia in 1918, economic, social, and cultural rights are put at the forefront: rights to minimal standards of living, the right to work, the right to health, the right to education, and so on. These rights are positive freedoms: the state is meant to actively promote the conditions for the effectuation of these rights. The state embodies the collective will and is therefore held responsible and obliged to do act in order to guarantee access to these rights, which are seen as the necessary conditions for collective progress. This socialist humanism contests the individualistic view of liberal humanism:

> Socialists believe that 'humanity' is collective rather than individualistic. They hold as sacred not the inner voice of each individual, but the species *Homo sapiens* as a whole. Whereas liberal humanism seeks as much freedom as possible for individual humans, socialist humanism seeks equality between all humans. According to socialists, inequality is the worst blasphemy against the sanctity of humanity, because it privileges peripheral qualities of humans over their universal essence. For example, when the rich are privileged over the poor, it means that we value money more than the universal essence of all humans, which is the same for rich and poor alike (Harari 2014, p. 258).

Consequently, socialist humanism addresses the causal factors and raises questions around the unequal distribution of wealth (Rizzini and Lusk 1995). In their efforts directed towards social justice and equality, some rights-based programs go as far as advocating for the redistribution of economic resources to the optimal well-being of all (Schumacher 2011). According to Harari, both liberal and socialist humanism display "a revamped version of the monotheist conviction that all souls are equal before God" (Harari 2014, p. 258). Evolutionary humanism, on the contrary, has "broken loose" (Ibid.) from these monotheist foundations. Among the representatives of evolutionary humanism, the most known but also the most problematic "sect of humanism" (Ibid.), we find the Nazis:

> "In contrast to other humanists, the Nazis believed that humankind is not something universal and eternal, but rather a mutable species that can evolve or degenerate. [...] This is why

[2] *Déclaration des droits de l'homme et du citoyen.*

the Nazis said that the Aryan race, the most advanced form of humanity, had to be protected and fostered, while degenerate kinds of *Homo sapiens* like Jews, Roma, homosexuals and the mentally ill had to be quarantined and even exterminated" (Harari 2014, p. 258).

Humanism therefore should not be seen as an angelic view of humanity: even the Nazis shared with liberal and socialist humanists the idea of the unique and sacred nature of humans, which led to one of the greatest nightmares of all time.

The common feature and the differences between the three branches of humanism discussed above are reflected in the Table 10.1 below.

Important differences appear in the ways the three branches of humanism translate the uniqueness and sacredness of human beings into realizations that get as close as possible to this decreed human 'nature'. There is some kind of cosmic realization that underlies all humanist religions, and hence also a risk of engaging humanity in a grand disaster. It is not clear, however, whether evolutionary humanism corresponds to 'solidarity rights' (Verhellen 1999, Quennerstedt 2013), the third generation of human rights: the right to freedom, to a safe environment, to the expression of one's own culture, to autonomy, and so on. Yet a link can be made between these rights that are embedded in a vision of global interdependence and the evolutionary vision of the common fate of humankind. This suggests that it is important to prevent the rise of a specific ideology that would reduce the fate of humankind to the protection of a specific characteristic that is supposedly indisputable, like the Nazi's ideology concerning the 'Aryan race'.

Today transhumanism, with its mythical figure of the 'enhanced man', is perhaps just another version of the endeavour to improve the human species, with hints of eugenics – since enhancing the human can also be understood as diminishing its defects. It is in fact also sharing in the liberal fiction of the 'free will', by placing 'autonomy' as the new frontier towards which humanity (or more precisely the rich) is striving: becoming autonomous, to the point of reaching immortality, is a dream that is nowadays pursued with the belief that bio-technologies can make it become true (Harari 2016). While Nazism was an evolutionary fiction with hints of socialist humanism (the official name of the party was the 'national-socialist' party), transhumanism is a mixture of the liberal and evolutionary branches of humanism: it

**Table 10.1** Humanist Religions – Religions that Worship Humanity (Harari 2014, p. 260)

| Liberal humanism | Socialist humanism | Evolutionary humanism |
|---|---|---|
| *Homo sapiens* has a unique and sacred nature that is fundamentally different from the nature of all other beings and phenomena. The supreme good is the good of humanity. | | |
| 'Humanity' is individualistic and resides within each individual *Homo sapiens*. | 'Humanity' is collective and resides within the species *Homo sapiens* as a whole. | 'Humanity' is a mutable species. Humans might degenerate into subhumans or evolve into superhumans. |
| The supreme commandment is to protect the inner core and freedom of each individual *Homo sapiens*. | The supreme commandment is to protect equality within the species *Homo sapiens*. | The supreme commandment is to protect humankind from degenerating into subhumans, and to encourage its evolution into superhumans. |

does not care a great deal about equality, and even assumes that only the richest individuals will actually be able to reach total autonomy.

What does all of this have to do with CSS? It in fact plays a quite central role, because the three branches of humanism tell three different narratives about marginalized populations such as CSS, and these narratives have huge consequences for them.

With humanism we glorify the unique and sacred nature of individuals. From 'peripheral' creature of God, the individual who has become centre of the world can take the shape of any human. In that respect, the 'street child' is emblematic of a vision of the world that is combines in three modes:

The delinquent child: for liberal humanism, where the 'free will' of the individual grounds its political philosophy, the 'street child' can only be deviant. The narratives about CSS will readily resort to explanations of a culturalist type, explaining the child's deviance by his or her social admission in dangerous classes. Here, theories of differential association (Shaw and McKay 1969; Snodgrass 1985; Sutherland 1992) form the foundations of explanations expressed in terms of learnt deviance. Regarding children, their deviance is thus likely to be explained in terms of immaturity and delinquent socialisation. In the end, the temptation is great to conclude that these children simply made 'wrong choices' and, consequently, that they are responsible for their own situation.

The victim-child: this is the ideal-typical image conveyed by socialist humanism. In view of their wretched situation, the marginality of 'street children' can be raised to a figure of authority, as they represent the archetype of the marginalised abstract individual, a tragic incarnation of the authentic individual dealing with the dramatic conditions that humanity itself is responsible for. If they are nonetheless proclaimed as actors, it is here only the effect of a romantic vision that is easily associated with the socialist humanism that cultivates the heroic figure of the revolutionary. Here, theories of domination and alienation are central.

The failing child: according to evolutionary humanism, the 'street child' represents a decline in human condition, and one could not value a being who represents a degenerate category. The child's failure is explained through biological theories, and the potential consequences of this genetic interpretation of social reality are evidently horrifying. No current political regime would dare resort to declared eugenics programs, but 'hygienist' approaches are relatively close to this point of view, and in these programs interventions are based on the idea of re-socialisation for those whose socialisation has been inadequate.

In the two branches that derive from monotheist religions, the CSS is seen as either a delinquent or a victim. For the evolutionary branch, the CSS is an outcast: he belongs to a subculture that is described as intrinsically felonious. That is why, in countries with a tradition of monotheistic religions, there is an oscillation between types of intervention based on the repression of the deviant child and those based on the rehabilitation of the victim child. This is especially the case in Latin America, which is why we can find the delinquent child/victim child dichotomy in the works of many authors who have worked there (see Lucchini 1993). Epstein (1996, 2000), for instance, compares how the state and non-governmental organizations in Brazil and the USA respond to homelessness in youth and children. He takes as a starting point the conflict between homelessness and the state's aim of social and political inclusiveness. He critically assesses whether or not the state can reform its existing programs to include the special needs of CSS: there has been more flexibility in the non-governmental sector, even in some cases accepting how street life has changed the children and how these changes have contributed to them gaining new skills, a flexibility that has not been taken over by the government. While pointing out that NGOs in the developed world have worked with and taken on existing technocratic points of view, Epstein (1996), considers the state in Brazil to be unable to provide CSS with what the state's mandates should be, and this is why most of the programs for CSS have come from the non-governmental sector, including churches. The analysis of Epstein (Ibid.) regarding the case in Brazil is still valid today, as it illustrates how grassroots organizations are often taken over by more powerful state institutions. A resurgence of 'cleaning the streets' operations have in fact been observed in recent years (Rizzini 2003; Rizzini et al. 2012). This attitude has something to do with the liberal doxa accusing the poor of being responsible for their situation: that they simply made wrong choices. This is, of course, highly contested by socialist-oriented programmes (mostly NGOs) who oppose to what they see as a state-organized repression of the Christian-like icons of the victim child. Such oppositions can only emerge in countries that had a strong monotheist religious culture, even if it has faded away in most areas of public life.

The approach of re-socialisation for the failing child is more present in countries without a monotheistic religious tradition, and consequently, countries in which the child is not seen through the models of a divine order that gave humans the freedom to choose (God chased Adam and Eve from the Garden of Eden because by eating the apple they made the wrong choice), nor through the mythical figure of the victim (Adam and Eve once punished). If 'street children' are failing, it is because they disobeyed other human beings (their parents, authorities) or because they have been insufficiently socialised by them. Such an approach of re-socialisation is dominant in China, for example (Stoecklin 2000; Cheng 2006, 2008, 2009a, b; Lam and Cheng 2008; 2010). We have mentioned (in Chap. 2) that the ideal representation of the Chinese child – obedient, disciplined, productive – influences the social reactions to the presence of children on the street, and thus limits their room for manoeuvre. However, empirical research still need to be done in order to gain a better understanding of what I call the 're-socialisation of the failing child'.

In China, the phenomenon of CSS has not drawn much attention from the academic world. It was until the year 2000 that a substantial pioneering in-depth analysis of CSS was made in this country (Stoecklin 2000) (see sect. 2.2.), followed by other works on the dynamics of exclusion (Cheng 2008), Chinese policy towards CSS (Lam and Cheng 2008), the subjective wellbeing of CSS (Cheng and Lam 2010), and welfare policy (Cheng 2009a, b). The latter show that China has adopted a 'protective' policy model, with the aim of sending CSS back to their families, including by forceful measures. Cheng criticized the current Chinese welfare policy for not meeting the needs of CSS, and called for more respect of their personal choices and consideration for their life conditions (Cheng 2009a). On the basis of an ethnographic study of 49 CSS in the neighborhood of Shanghai Railway Station, Cheng (2009b) highlighted major factors leading to street situations, such as family dysfunction, rural-to-urban migration, and children's search for autonomy. He related these factors to social transformation at the macro level, especially the gap between the normative childcare model determined by the traditional views on the family and the real life conditions of children which have forced many to run away to find alternative life opportunities. The crisis of Confucian notions of parental authority (Naftali 2014) is reflected in colliding socialization processes, leaving practitioners with many uncertainties about their role and responsibilities.

The hesitations, doubts, and reversals in China are therefore also to be connected with a moral order that oscillates between Confucianism and communism. 'State Confucianism' remains, for political reasons, a highly centralised discourse. Changing guidelines thus has a huge impact on local practices. But the difference between the West and China has foundations that go beyond the contingent political systems. The positions expressed in the West, through the icons of the delinquent child versus the victim child (as victim of the system), are also to be sought in monotheistic religious traditions, not only in multi-party systems. On the contrary, the single-party system alone does not explain the centrality of the figure of the failing child. Confucianism has an extremely important role in this. We should therefore not limit the study of children's rights to the measures taken by the states present at the Convention on the Rights of the Child, as these politico-administrative measures are made on specific cultural and religious grounds that highly influence the allocation of responsibilities and thus the commitment of actors to the topics on the agenda. Besides, the theme of 'children in street situations' is less on the agenda today than it was one or two decades ago. This highlights the importance of cultural and religious habitus: in China, just as much as in the West, there is a return to religion. This could also be a cause explaining the general trend in the world of intervention to use the figure of the victim child (Poretti et al. 2014). The matter of responsibility is thus reinforced, but we are still far from agreeing on who is to blame.

With 'street children', we are then confronted with a question for humanity and with an injunction to take responsibility for the situations experienced by these children. This, necessarily, translates into negotiations on shared responsibility. Once it is time to assume a social contract in which God is absent, human rights are the expression of the social negotiation that distributes responsibilities between the actors and the institutions that represent them. Children's rights arrived on the scene of this permanent negotiation relatively late, it taking two hundred years to go from the rights of man and of the citizen, first created for adult males, to a specific convention for children. However, this convention is interpreted in different ways precisely because the different actors distribute and claim responsibilities in different ways. This negotiation moves on several axes – childhood image, competence, rights of children, difference dilemma – and it is then possible to identify the gatherings of actors around these criteria as strengthening dominant views (Table 10.2).

Hanson identifies four school of thoughts in the children's rights movement, highlighting that this movement is not uniform but on the contrary composed of competing normative and ideological perspectives (Hanson 2012, p. 63). He shows that:

**Table 10.2** Schools of thought in children's rights (Hanson 2012, p. 63)

| | Paternalism | Welfare | Emancipation | Liberation |
|---|---|---|---|---|
| Childhood image | Becoming | Becoming and being | Being and becoming | Being |
| Competence | Incompetent | Incompetent, unless | Competent, unless | Competent |
| Rights of children | Protection rights | Protection rights | Participation rights | Participation rights |
| | | Provision rights | Provision rights | |
| | | Participation rights | Protection rights | |
| Difference dilemma | Special rights | Special rights | Equal rights | Equal rights |
| | | Equal rights | Special rights | |

(a) The paternalistic view on children considers them only with regards to what they will become as adults. Along this traditional viewpoint, children are seen as 'becomings', not yet as 'beings'.
(b) The welfare approach, closer to protection rights than to participation rights, still dominates today's child welfare sector, at both national and international levels (Hanson 2012, p. 76).
(c) The emancipation or empowerment approach, directed more towards participation rights, considers the child as being competent as long as the contrary is not evidenced (the burden of proof lies with the adult).
(d) The liberationists consider children as independent actual citizens ('beings') who make competent and rational decisions, and therefore claim for equal rights to those of adults (Hanson 2012, p. 74).

When we now compare these four schools of thought in children's rights and the three branches of the 'humanist religion', we see that those who are the most liberal are the liberationists. Liberationists consider that children should have equal rights with adults, whereas the three other schools of thought consider (differently) children's special rights. The emancipation or empowerment approach also strongly builds on the idea of individual competences, as they place the burden of proof regarding children's incompetence on the adults. The welfare approach is closer to socialist humanism, in the sense that burden of proof on children's competence is placed on children: for welfarists, children have to prove that they are competent in the same way as socialists will consider a social class as a 'class for itself' (*classe pour soi*) only once it has reflected on its own interests and consequently overcomes the alienation of the 'class in itself' (*classe en soi*). Finally, the paternalistic view is evolutionary: it considers children primarily as becomings, who are incompetent as long as they are children, and hence in need of protection granted by special rights that must prepare them to become responsible and competent adults. This does not mean necessarily mean that children's participation is undermined; it is rather strictly organized and directed by adults who are entitled with the obligation to train children in the direction of enhanced qualities of humankind. The *Hitler-Jugend* were the most tragic example of this paternalistic evolutionism. Today, a paternalistic vision of children's rights is only to be seen in socio-political contexts that are still close to or reoriented by authoritarian regimes.

The general movement is towards more participation rights. The more children's rights are oriented towards participation rights – that is, civil and political rights – granted without restriction of age, the more it aligns with a liberal humanism based on the postulate of the individual's free will. However, this does not go without major problems and tensions, because the underlying assumption of humans' free will is flawed.

The postulate of free will is largely disputed. Socialists contest the notion of free will since Marx insisted on the process of alienation making people unaware of the social components of the construction of their subjectivities. Consciousness, according to Marx, stems from the conditions of existence (infrastructure) that determine the ways people think and the institutions they build (superstructure).

The notion of alienation then refers to the production of objects seen as exterior to oneself and through which things become "estranged" from us (the German word *Entfremdung* gives a better idea of the remoteness that is implied by the term alienation), a status of exteriority which is then perceived as a more or less taxing 'external' influence. Marx used the notion of alienation to talk about the state (Israel 1972), which then appeared to individuals as exterior to them despite being nothing but a 'we'. It is fundamental to use this notion of alienation in the sense of exteriorisation, and not in the more common sense of madness: the latter is derived from the loss of possession over oneself,[3] and is most commonly used in Marxist-inspired sociology, as it highlights the domination of the powerful in relation to which the disadvantaged classes alienate themselves – no longer possess themselves – as they recognise the bourgeois habitus as normal.

More generally, the exteriorisation of a thing, through the language that fixes it by giving it a name and a meaning that then seems intrinsic to it, puts this thing in a position of exteriority, facing us, even in confrontation. Subsequently, the materiality of the physical world can also be a product of symbolisation. Alienation is then not only a negative movement of loss of self, it is also a movement constative of the world that 'surrounds' us. This construction of the world is fundamental and it is especially important to see that this construction is a reflexive process that gives things a sense through which they acquire their meaning. If this is valid for any thing that can be 'exteriorised', then it is also valid for this thing that we call a right. In other words, all human rights, and especially children's rights, are objects that induce subjective senses through which they acquire their meaning.

Socialist humanism, based on the Marxist paradigm, thus contests that individuals exercise free will. However, according to Marx, free will remains attainable only through class consciousness, namely the consciousness of belonging to a social class and, consequently, the knowledge of the social determinants that affect this social class. To free oneself of these determinations (primarily thought in terms of domination) is, according to Marx, to pass from a class in itself to a class for itself; from a class that has an objective existence but without its members being aware of it, to a class that has a subjective existence, that thinks of itself as a class and that, consequently, defends its class interests. Incidentally, CSS would probably be con-

[3] The verb used here is the possessive 'to alienate oneself' (*sich entfremden*).

sidered by Marx as *Lumpenproletariat*, a pejorative term that he used to designate the proletarians unable to think of themselves as a social class.

For this perspective, even if children may act in strategic ways they are not necessarily able to significantly alter their situations (Moran-Ellis 2013), because the circumstances under which children may change small scale settings are not of their own choosing (Leonard 2016). In fact, neuroscience seems to tell us that we are all 'alienated', as research in this field has uncovered unconscious determinants of our supposedly 'free' decisions (Libet 1985; Wegner 2002; Chun et al. 2008). While geneticists consider biological determinism as an impediment to free will, sociologists have since long identified social determinants, such as belonging to a certain class, ethnicity, familial configuration, and so on, that mediate the relationship between the subject who chooses and the chosen object.

Further specifications of these mediations can be made, as suggested in Chap. 9, by looking at them as embedded in the thinking horizons depicted by the 'actor's system'. ARVIM symbolise dominant modes of action that mediate the influence of institutions over individuals (structured action) and of individuals over institutions (structuring action). Consequently, individual decisions cannot be 'free' as they always stem from the duality of the symbolic world, which also orients individual preferences along the socially shaped importance given to the different thinking horizons (ARVIM). The 'free choice' of activities, relations, values, images of self, and motivations is therefore merely an illusion. The narrative of the 'free will' is the fiction that liberal humanists hold to, despite scientific evidence that 'free choice' is possible neither sociologically nor biologically. This fiction has become an ideology, or even a religion (Harari 2014).

Science should in fact deconstruct the humanist religion. The distinction between the three sub-branches of humanism (liberal, socialist, evolutionary) and the comparison with the four school of thought in children's rights is a step in this direction, which allows us to critically read children's rights governance (including the CRC, its additional protocols, and notably the general comments) under the light of conflict theory, highlighting the conflictual normative positions that underpin the elaboration, dissemination, and evaluation of these internationally recognised guidelines. They are social constructions based on ideological assumptions that are meshed together in consensual texts. During this process, radical claims are abandoned in favour of more consensual positions, and hence the most emancipatory struggles are in the end not translated into an institutionalized set of norms. This reflects the 'paradox of institutionalisation', whereby we can observe the "extent to which emancipatory struggles can be sustained through processes of institutionalisation" (Stammers 2013, pp. 282–283).

The paradox of institutionalisation (Stammers 2013) disqualifies the claims and discourses that are felt to be too distant from the dominant discourse, even if they might have been foundational of social movements or academic works that sustain alternative views and findings. Indeed everyone can tell a story, but in the end it is the ability to make one's story legitimate that counts. This ability is of course not only linked to personal skills, it also involves social positions invested with more or less prestige. The 'distinction' (Bourdieu 1979) of the actors positioned with high economic, cultural, and social forms of capital therefore serves to reproduce their dominant modes of action. As the dominant mode of action in a globalised neo-liberal economy is an entrepreneurial mode of action, the legitimacy of the claims expressed by different stakeholders tends to be evaluated in entrepreneurial ways.

It is the entrepreneurial mode of action that actually differentiates the claims that are converging towards the legal-rational consensual guidelines for children's rights: relevant claims are those that are expressing proactive attitudes, supposedly reflecting the 'free will' and the 'good will' of claimants. The claims that are deemed irrelevant are not necessarily rejected on the basis of a lack of speaking ability in the claimants, but rather on the basis of their insufficient compliance with the entrepreneurial mode of action.

An example of this necessary bind between NGOs and the entrepreneurial mode of action that dominates corporations (and hence important potential contributors) is given by the slogan "Invest in a street child".[4] It naturalizes the entrepreneurial mode of action, implying that donations for 'street children' programmes are investments in future citizens. The image of the donor shifts from philanthropist to businessman. Compassion gives way to rational choice. This example illustrates that the agenda of intervention rests on a more profound "regime of truth" (Foucault 2012): the economic ideology of growth pervading human development (the becoming child), and with it the need to protect the resources (including human resources) that are conducive to optimizing the output of responsible adults. This explains why the entrepreneurial mode of action and a paternalist approach to children's rights can go hand in hand, and this is why big companies, when they develop 'corporate social responsibility' towards children, are more attracted by protection rights and less by provision and participation rights.

Some voices are therefore simply inaudible just because they do not match the dominant accounts and the underlying regime of truth. Consequently, the translations of the voices of CSS into the few voices that synthesize the claims of the 327 children that have been consulted for the GC on CSS (UNCRC 2017) is an instantiation of the regime of truth that revolves around protection and growth. More generally, in NGO publications similar deformations of children's voices can be witnessed, primarily through the selection of the 'most touching account'):

> "The deformation comes from the very actors, mainly NGOs, that try to 'save' these children. It is inscribed in their own views about these children, produced in strategies, meta-plans, coordination meetings, and eventually in a specific vocabulary used by street workers, before it is reproduced in more or less strategic ways by the children themselves. Hence, the voices of children that have the highest probability of reaching the point of institutionalisation (through formal channels like those involved in the GC on CSS) are those who express their reality in the appropriate terms, actually the terms that have been learnt from educators and other responsible staff within NGOs. Everything that is not audible to the people who are in direct contact with these children will hardly find its way up the channels informing and formating the GC. It appears then, that a GC formulated in terms of rights, even if it is a very good perspective indeed, and probably the best one, is far from being truly informed

[4] English translation of the French original « *Investissez dans un enfant des rues* », on a poster produced by Terre des hommes in 2014.

> by children's voices. The rights-based language necessitates that one has a moral consciousness of the abstract individual, seen as an equal. This is possible under conditions that are not survival conditions. The legal-rational domination (Weber 2013) is typically a form of domination arising in developed and centralised nation-states. It is not the dominant mode of thinking in street environments which are closer to traditional and charismatic forms of domination. Hence, the barrier experienced by children is not just a cultural barrier, it is a structural barrier: the social system they experience is marked by traditional and charismatic forms of domination, and we want them to express themselves in legal-rational terms" (Stoecklin 2018, pp. 558–559).

The 'paradox of institutionalisation' is therefore sustained by the very actors who have been 'cheated' in the first instance by the regime of truth that keeps them in the position of 'becoming': the children. While sociability in the street environment is mainly based on a charismatic-traditional domination, this experience of the street space and the significations that stem from it cannot find legitimacy within arenas and institutions that are working with a legal-rational domination. Conversely,

> "the recommendations, as institutionalised in the present GC on CSS, can hardly take account of the complexity and heterogeneity of street situations which, to a large extent, get 'lost in translation'. Hence, the discrepancy between the labels used in the General Comment – CSS and SCC – and the underlying protectionist view. The 'paradox of institutionalisation' is a matter of conflictual influence: any struggle, sooner or later, faces the necessity to compromise, to some extent, with other views involved in the process. The question therefore is not whether or not struggles are mitigated in the processes of institutionalisation, but rather how much, or to which extent, they have to compromise" (Stoecklin 2017, pp. 854–855).

The discourse on children's rights is not free from domination. It in fact consolidates the legal-rational form of domination, which favours protection rights, as these are much easier to reach a consensus on than the provision and participation rights. Protection rights are also closer to the vision of the individual self. We therefore have a sort of paradoxical image of marginalized children who are at the same time captured through the lenses of paternalist and liberationist approaches: a becoming child with strong individual competences, not yet able to know his or her own interests while already acting as gang leader. This paradoxical status locates the CSS at the crossroads of traditional-charismatic authority and legal-rational authority (Weber 2013). If this child wants to be heard in the political arena, he must espouse the latter and abandon the former. Yet this cognitive dissonance is what impedes full participation of the child in the implementation of his or her own rights: they cannot just jump from one symbolic world to the other. Most feel trapped in between:

> "The exit from the street is in this view a complex passage from one kind of authority to another, and not simply a change of place. In this sense, children who are 'out-of-place' (Ennew and Connolly 1996) are actually out of the authority that rules or intends to rule the majority. This is why reintegrating them into 'mainstream society' is a disciplining endeavour (Foucault 2012)" (Stoecklin 2018, p. 577).

What then is the 'regime of truth' (Foucault 2012) that underpins the GC on CSS? As consensus building rests on the 'paradox of institutionalisation' (Stammers 2013) whereby extreme positions are cut out, we have a kind of mixing of the three forms of humanism (liberal, socialist, and evolutionary), of the four schools of thought on children's rights (paternalism, welfare, emancipation, and liberation), and of the three generations of human rights (civil and political rights; economic, social and cultural rights; solidarity rights). Everyone is able to tell a story, but in the end what counts is the ability to make one's story legitimate. An overarching principle presides over this legitimation: the entrepreneurial mode of action. Entrepreneurship is the hidden 'regime of truth' that underpins children's rights. Variations within this concern questions like "who has to take the lead?" or "who is more entrepreneurial here?", while the fundamental basis is a mode of action placing performance as the yardstick of human rights. They are to be translated into indicators of growth, exactly like growth in the economy has become the dominant ideology. Human rights are therefore informed, shaped, and transformed by the neo-liberal doxa (Bourdieu 1994) which turns 'growth' into a natural law. This new ideology says that everything grows, and consequently we have to favour growth in every domain.

The tensions between the schools of thought in children's rights therefore tend to be pragmatically reduced because of this common overarching vision of growth as the natural order. The debates between the defenders of the first generation of human rights and those who favour the second generation are becoming less acute, as with the end of the Cold War the new overarching ideology is rising. The dichotomy is no longer 'liberty over equality' versus 'equality over liberty', or 'free will' versus 'collective will', but economic growth versus nature: human rights are more and more thought in relation to the question of their contribution or opposition to 'economic growth' and the 'preservation of nature'. Making 'economic growth' a natural law therefore cuts human rights out of the picture. This neo-liberal ideology is not compatible with human rights. The GC on CSS is thus a text in which we can see a tremendous effort to push neo-liberal ideas aside, but as it is still the dominant ideology the drafters of the GC on CSS could not avoid some hints of neo-liberal thought. They had to build consensus by including the most indisputable claim of neo-liberalism: the idea that all stakeholders have to be actively involved, in an entrepreneur-like attitude, in the amelioration of the lives of CSS. The sociological paradigm of the social actor has therefore been captured by the ideological vision of children as entrepreneurs. The social actor orienting one's line of conduct according to 'thinking horizons' (ARVIM) has been 'lost in translations' that reduce action (praxis) to activities (poiesis). This reduction stems from the entrepreneurial mode of action that has become prevalent in modernity, extending from the new elite (the capitalist bourgeoisie) down to the marginalised (CSS): everything is measured against performance indicators. It's a tricky game, as some start with heavy handicaps.

With the paradoxical wedding of a nature associated with growth (the neo-liberal dogma) and human rights associated with a collective will embodied by the state (the socialist dogma), we find ourselves in a configuration where any actor can hold a legitimate position as long as he or she has the power to 'make a difference'. This power is measured primarily in economic terms: the typical language of entrepreneurship. The 'returns' and how they are measured have become the criteria to legitimize actions. The motto 'go in the direction where you can expect substantial returns', dominant since the sixteenth century (the 'Great Discoveries'), has been generalized, and it is now re-emerging, after a rather socialist-driven conception of human rights (the second generation of human rights), in the liberal agenda of children's rights, coupled with a vision of human rights as the main basis for human evolution.

In the Western world, at least, no one really argues for a paternalistic approach to children's rights, and the welfare approach is put into question. The debate is oriented by the emancipation and liberation lines of thought. These are leading strands that create tensions among liberal humanists around the unresolved question of 'free will'. Article 12 of the CRC is probably where these tensions are on most prominent display, as the obligation of authorities to take into account the opinion of the child is concerned with how views are expressed (freely), the range of matters on which these views are expressed (all matters affecting the child), the consideration that is given to these views (due weight given in accordance with the age and maturity of the child), and, first of all, who forms the views (the child who capable of forming 'own views').

As the provisions of the UNCRC are linked together, the principle of evolving capacities (art. 5 UNCRC) is often taken as an argument to orient the implementation of children's rights through the emancipatory approach (the child is considered competent, unless others prove the contrary) or the welfarist approach (the child is seen as incompetent, unless he proves the contrary). Neither of these orientations contest the individualistic view of liberal humanism, whereby the seat of thought is located in the individual self. This centring on one's own feelings has, since Rousseau (Harari 2016, p. 261), become the 'taken-for-granted' horizon (regime of truth) that links rather different processes, like child development and economic growth, in one single paradigm. Economic growth becomes the *ultima ratio* because it is supposed to contribute to child, and hence human, development. The entrepreneurial mode of action informs human rights – the subject of rights being an individual person – because it is the overarching horizon of human responsibility: to become oneself by one's own efforts. How and to what extent this endeavour is indebted to the collective dimension of human cooperation (firstly through language and shared meanings) is put aside, as if each individual was be a text without context. This is why using the expression 'children in street situations' is so important: it puts context around personal stories. It brings back the scene on which the child plays.

The scene on which children play is sustained by public policies. The next and final section of this chapter suggests that the translation of children's rights agendas into policies is dependent not just on the existence of guidelines such as the GC on CSS, but foremost on the typical images of 'street children' that pervade social representations.

## 10.3 From Agendas to Policies

There is not a single children's rights agenda, but several, as we have seen with the three humanist religions (Harari 2014) and with the four schools of thoughts in children's rights (Hanson 2012). Analysis of these branches should be further refined. But whatever the sub-branches, the different routes of the children's rights agendas are translated into public policies.

What we have seen about the typical images of 'street children' (deviant, victim, and failing), in relation to the three forms of humanism (liberal, socialist, evolutionary), now leads us to revisit the classifications of intervention programs.

Sarah Thomas de Benitez (2011) classifies programs for CSS in three categories: (1) the correctional, reactive or repression-oriented model, whereby CSS are seen as deviants; (2) the rehabilitative or protection-oriented model, seeing CSS as victims; (3) the human rights-based approach, which considers CSS as citizens whose rights have been violated.

The second and third categories are in fact relatively close, and their convergence reinforces socialist humanism. But, as we have seen before, the approach based on children's rights is not unequivocal: there are several humanisms (Harari 2014) and several schools of thoughts in children's rights (Hanson 2012). In the GC on CSS, we find that socialist humanism is dominant, but that there is also a strong influence from liberal humanism. We can see this in a more precise way if we consider the components of any public policy. Every 'social problem' is constructed through representations of reality, of which the political expression includes balances of power (Müller 2010). Public policy is also constructed as:

> "a series of intentionally coherent decisions or activities resulting from structured and repeated interactions between different public and, sometimes, private actors, whose resources, institutional links and interests vary, with a view to resolving in a targeted manner a problem that is politically defined as collective in nature". This group of decisions and activities gives rise to formalised actions of a more or less restrictive nature that are often aimed at modifying the behaviour of social groups presumed to be at the root of, or able to solve, the collective problem to be resolved (target groups) in the interest of the social groups who suffer the negative effects of the problem in question (final beneficiaries)" (Knoepfel et al. 2007, p. 24).

This definition of public policies connects three entities depicted in Fig. 10.3:

1. The political and administrative authorities are "in charge of the elaboration and implementation of institutional policies, for which operating logic is deposited in federal and cantonal public law […] These public actors are endowed with a (legal) monopoly over the production of administrative decrees". (Knoepfel et al. 2007, p. 102). Through their actions, they influence the rights and obligations of target groups and final beneficiaries.

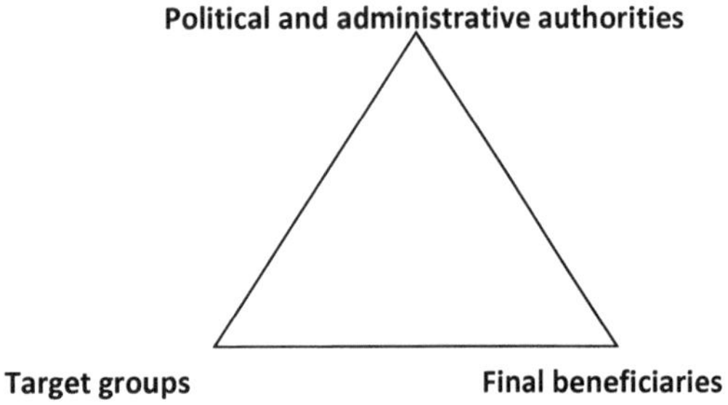


**Fig. 10.3** The collective actors of public policy (Knoepfel et al. 2007)

2. Target groups are those identified as the cause of the problem that requires State intervention: "Institutional politics is hence directed towards modifying target groups' behaviours to resolve a collective problem. Such dynamics tend to profit to the group of final beneficiaries" (Knoepfel et al. 2007, p. 103). If one identifies young people as the target group (as 'the problem', for example: young people's violence), one develops interventions supposed to change their behaviours, whereas if one identifies them as final beneficiaries (as 'affected by the problem of violence') then there will be an intervention identifying violence as written in social relations, hence in a perspective not individualising but social. One will identify target groups (causing the problem), including among the "politico-administrative actors in charge of the elaboration and implementation of their respective substantial policies" (Ibid.). In other words, failures in the setting up of participatory policies (according to the recommendations based on the CRC) are also a part of the problem of violence ('violent expression' of a speech not listened to elsewhere).
3. Final beneficiaries suffer from the negative effects of a problem "whereas the institutional policy seeks to resolve a problem and improve the situation with its implementation" (Ibid.). If one identifies young people as the final beneficiaries of a pro-active policy of youth, then they should benefit from the change in behaviour of the target groups especially since these target groups and the changes to make would be identified with them. Their participation is, therefore, essential to a youth policy that would be proactive, pertinent, effective and efficient. Thus, by integrating young people's participation to the resolution of the collective problems that preoccupy them, one can produce substantial policies (aimed at target groups), policies that would, themselves, benefit from «[…] the positive effects brought about (in theory) by the state intervention, for which the objective was to modify third party groups' behaviours, as they were deemed to be troublesome" (Ibid., p. 104).

We note that this is a 'technocratic' definition, with a unique decision-making centre (the State), which corresponds to the typical ideal of socialist power; whereas in a neo-liberal world, power is decentralised. Today, this decentralisation is such that we do not really know who is in charge anymore. But 'public policies' are the State's prerogative indeed. It would then be a matter of replacing the importance of public policies within the political (Arendt 1951). 'The political' mentioned by Arendt is a kind of space where anything is possible, in opposition to what we commonly call 'politics', which is only a utilitarian instantiation of it. Arendt talks about 'political freedom' (Poizat 2013, p. 43) as a 'space' in which individuals can move. Hence, individuals build "horizons of possibilities" through their own reflexivity. I suggest here that this "space" where everything is possible can be visualized through the "thinking horizons" (see Chap. 9) and their systemic connections. We now realise that among the possibilities, we only favour a few of them: the entrepreneurial mode of action is favoured by neo-liberal policies, to the detriment of the relational, moral, identitary and motivational modes of action (they are also present, but on a minor mode).

That is how we continue to view children in street situations as relatively passive 'final beneficiaries', and that we only concede them an actor capacity if they show entrepreneurship: if the child becomes, as some say, 'actor of his/her own life'. It is also this reduction of the "thinking horizons" to the entrepreneurial mode of action that can explain why the three types of intervention (repression, protection, rights-based) identified by S. Thomas de Benitez (op. cit.) can be more or less combined. With the entrepreneurial mode of action, the approach based on child rights is tinted with a protection of the entrepreneur in the making … What varies, inside this dominant paradigm, is the definition of the target population: the one that causes the problem, the one that constitutes an obstacle to the realisation of the ideal (the child entrepreneur).

A fine-tuned classification of rights-based institutions should therefore be made by looking at the definition of the target groups in each of the studied programs, because the target groups (defined as the groups that cause the problem) are different in each approach. For the repressive approach, those causing the problem are CSS themselves; for the protective approach, the target groups are all those who cause the departure to the street such the dysfunctional family, abusive adults, gangs, drug dealers, exploiters and so on; and for the rights-based approach, the target group is the state that has ratified the UNCRC and which therefore bears the responsibility to see to it that all rights are made accessible to all children.

We notice that the constituent parts of a public policy are oriented by particular frames (liberal, socialist, evolutionary humanism). The implementation of the GC on CSS remains to be observed. It can benefit from this type of causal analysis, situating actors around the dominant positions that are founded on the mythical figures of the delinquent child, the child victim, and the failing child. The rights that will be favoured in the concrete implementation of the GC on CSS indeed strongly depend on the image we have of the 'final beneficiaries', and consequently of the 'target populations'. In the end, these mythical figures (the deviant child, the victim child, the failing child) will preside over the interpretations of the GC on CSS that different states will make when they translate it into their own public policies. State parties will do this by putting the 'final beneficiaries' in the shoes of one these three mythical figures. It is possible that the two primary and opposite political paradigms of the twentieth century – the liberal conception of individual responsibility (that freedom is more important than equality) and the socialist conception of collective responsibility (that equality is more important than freedom) – will give way to the evolutionary conception of responsibility and solidarity rights (where development is more important than both freedom and equality). This is however not necessarily good news, unless development is reassessed and redefined with all stakeholders.

## References

Aptekar, L., & Stoecklin, D. (2014). *Street children and homeless youth: A cross-cultural perspective*. Dordrecht/Heidelberg/New York/London: Springer.

Arendt, A. (1951). *The origins of totalitarianism*. Schocken books.

Beck, U., & Beck-Gernsheim, E. (2001). *Individualization: Institutionalized individualism and its social and political consequences*. London: Sage.

Bellah, R. N. (1973). Durkheim, individualism and the intellectuals. In R. N. Bellah (Ed.), *Emile Durkheim on morality and society*. Chicago: The University of Chicago Press.

Bobbio, N. (1996). *The age of rights*. Cambridge: Polity Press.

Bonvin, J.-M., & Stoecklin, D. (2016). Children's rights as evolving capabilities: Towards a contextualized and Processual conception of social justice. In G. Graf, G. Schweiger, & M. Cabezas (Eds.), *Ethical perspectives 23* (Vol. 1, pp. 19–39).

Bourdieu, P. (1979). *La distinction. Critique sociale du jugement*. Paris: Editions de Minuit.

Bourdieu, P. (1992). *The logic of practice*. Stanford University Press.

Bourdieu, P. (1994). *Raisons pratiques*. Paris: Seuil.

Cheng, F. (2006). The street Children's street life and the victimizations against them: An ethnographic study. *Youth Studies, 9*, 1–9. (in Chinese).

Cheng, F. (2008). *Negotiating exclusion: An ethnographic study of the street children in Shanghai, China*. Hong-Kong: University of Hong-Kong. (unpublished doctoral dissertation).

Cheng, F. (2009a). The efficiency of Chinese welfare policy for street children: A perspective of the street children. *Journal of Social Sciences, 4*, 11.

Cheng, F. (2009b). Failure of the traditional childcare model and the causes of street children: An ethnographic study of the street children in the Shanghai Railway Station neighborhood. *Society, 5*, 8.

Cheng, F., & Lam, D. (2010). How is street life? An examination of the subjective wellbeing of street children in China. *International Social Work, 53*(3), 353–365.

Chun, S. S., Brass, M., Heinze, H.-J., & Haynes, J.-D. (2008). Unconscious determinants of free decisions in the human brain. *Nature Neuroscience, 11*(5), 543–545.

Cockburn, T. (2013). *Rethinking children's citizenship. Studies in childhood and youth*. Basingstoke: Palgrave Macmillan.

De Benitez, S. (2011). State of the World's street children: Research (Street children. Series 2). In *Consortium for street children*. London.

de Singly, F. (2005). In Editions de l'Aube (Ed.), *L'individualisme est un humanisme*. La Tour d'Aigues.

DRMC (1789). *Déclaration des droits de l'homme et du citoyen*. Accessed 29 Oct 2018 https://fr.wikipedia.org/wiki/Déclaration_des_droits_de_l%27homme_et_du_citoyen_de_1789

Ennew, J., & Connolly, M. (1996). Introduction: Children out of place. *Childhood, A Global Journal of Child Research, 3*(2), 131–145.

Epstein, I. (1996). Educating street children: Some cross-cultural comparisons. *Comparative Education, 32*(3), 289–302.

Epstein, I. (2000). Dependence served: Rhetorical assumptions governing the education of homeless children and youth in the US. In R. Mickelson (Ed.), *Children on the streets of the Americas* (pp. 99–107). New York: Routledge.

Foucault, M. (2012). *Du gouvernement des vivants – Cours au Collège de France. 1979–1980* (Edition établie par M. Senellart, sous la direction de F. Ewald et A. Fontana). Paris: EHESS - Gallimard-Seuil.

Giddens, A. (1984). *The constitution of society: Outline of the theory of structuration* (p. 1984). Berkeley: University of California Press.

Hanson, K. (2012). Schools of thought in Children's rights. In M. Liebel (Ed.), *Children's rights from below. Cross-cultural perspectives* (Studies in childhood and youth) (pp. 63–79). Basingstoke: Palgrave MacMillan.

Hanson, K., & Nieuwenhuys, O. (2013). *Reconceptualizing Children's rights in international development. Living rights, social justice, translations*. Cambridge: Cambridge University Press.

Harari, Y. N. (2014). *Sapiens. A brief history of humankind*. London: Vintage.

Harari, Y. N. (2016). *Homo Deus. A brief history of tomorrow*. London: Vintage.

Hart, R. (1992). *Children's participation from tokenism to citizenship*. Florence: Innocenti Research Center.

Israel, J. (1972). *Der Begriff Entfremdung. Makrosoziologische Untersuchung von Marx bis zur Soziologie der Gegenwart*. Hamburg: Rowohlt.
Johnson, V. (2017). Moving beyond voice in children and young people's participation. *Action Research, Sage, 15*(1), 104–124.. Article first published online: April 4, 2017; Issue published: March 1, 2017. https://doi.org/10.1177/1476750317698025.
Kirby, P., & Bryson, S. (2002). *Measuring the magic? Evaluating and researching young People's participation in public decision making*. London: Carnegie Young People Initiative.
Knoepfel, P., Larrue, C., & Hill, M. (2007). *Public Policy Analyses*. Bristol: The Policy Press.
Lam, D., & Cheng, F. (2008). Chinese policy reaction to the problem of street children: An analysis from the perspective of street children. *Children and Youth Services Review, 30*(5), 575–584.
Leonard, M. (2016). *The sociology of children, childhood and generation*. Los Angeles/London/New Dehli/Singapore/Washington, DC: Sage.
Libet, B. (1985). Unconscious cerebral initiative and the role of conscious will in voluntary action. *Behavioral and Brain Sciences, 8*, 529–566.
Lucchini, R. (1993). *Enfant de la rue. Identité, sociabilité, drogue*. Genève/Paris: Droz.
Martucelli, D., & de Singly, F. (2009). *Vers une sociologie de l'individu. Les sociologies de l'individu* (pp. 10–33). Paris: Armand Colin.
Mead, G. H. (1934). *Mind, self and society*. Chicago: University of Chicago Press.
Moran-Ellis, J. (2013). Children as social actors, agency, and social competence: Sociological reflections for early childhood. *Neue Praxis, 43*(4), 303–338. ISSN 0342-9857.
Müller, M. (2010). Doing discourse analysis in critical geopolitics. *L'espace politique, 12*(3), 1–21. (online), Accessed 29 Oct 2018 https://www.alexandria.unisg.ch/59906/1/Müller_2010_Doing%20discourse%20analysis%20in%20critical%20geopolitics_Espace%20Politique.pdf.
Naftali, O. (2014). *Children, rights and modernity in China. Raising self-governing citizens* (Studies in childhood and youth). Basingstoke: Palgrave Macmillan.
Percy-Smith, B., & Thomas, N. (2010). *A handbook of children and young people's participation. Perspectives from theory and practice*. London/New-York: Routledge.
Pessoa, F. (2006). *A little larger than the entire universe*. Penguin Classics.
Poizat, J.-C. (2013). *Hannah Arendt, une introduction*. Paris: La Découverte.
Poretti, M., Hanson, K., Darbellay, F., & Berchtold, A. (2014). The rise and fall of icons of 'stolen childhood' since the adoption of the UN convention on the rights of the child. *Childhood, 21*(1), 22–38.
Quennerstedt, A. (2013). Children's rights research moving into the future–challenges on the way forward. *The International Journal of Children's Rights, 21*, 233–247.
Rizzini, I. (2003). *Vidas Nas Ruas*. Rio de Janeiro: Editora PUC-Rio.
Rizzini, I., & Lusk, M. W. (1995). Children in the streets: Latin America's lost generation. *Children and Youth Services Review, 17*(3), 391–400.
Rizzini, I., Princeswal, M., Caldeira, P., & Bush, M. (2012). *A efetivação de políticas públicas no Brasil. O caso das políticas para crianças e adolescentes em situação de rua*. Rio de Janeiro: CIESPI-PUC-Rio.
Schumacher, S. (2011). *Children in street situations in South Africa* (Master of advanced studies in Children's rights). Sion: IUKB.
Shaw, C. R., & McKay, H. D. (1969). *Juvenile delinquency and urban areas*. Chicago: The University of Chicago Press.
Snodgrass, J. (1985). A biographical sketch and review of the work of Edwin H. Sutherland. *History of Sociology, 6*(1), 55–67.
Stammers, N. (2013). Children's rights and social movements: Reflections from a cognate field. In K. Hanson & O. Nieuwenhuys (Eds.), *Reconceptualizing Children's rights in international development. Living rights, social justice, translations* (pp. 275–292). Cambridge: Cambridge University Press.
Stoecklin, D. (2000). *Enfants des rues en Chine*. Paris: Karthala.

Stoecklin, D. (2017). The general comment on children in street situations: Insights into the institutionalisation of Children's rights. *The International Journal of Children's Rights, 25*(4), 817–869.
Stoecklin, D. (2018). Institutionalisation of children's rights: Transformability and situated agency. *The International Journal of Children's Rights, 26*(3), 548–587.
Stoecklin, D., & Bonvin, J.-M. (2014a). The capability approach and Children's rights. In C. S. Hart, M. Biggeri, & B. Babic (Eds.), *Agency and participation in childhood and youth, International applications of the capability approach in schools and beyond* (pp. 63–82). London/New Dehli/New York/Sydney: Bloomsbury.
Stoecklin, D., & Bonvin, J.-M. (2014b). Cross-fertilizing Children's rights and the capability approach. The example of the right to be heard in organized leisure. In D. Stoecklin & J.-M. Bonvin (Eds.), *Children's rights and the capability approach. Challenges and prospects* (Children's well-being: Indicators and research 8) (pp. 131–152). Dordrecht/Heidelberg/New York/London: Springer.
Stoecklin, D., Bonvin, J. -M., & Sedooka, A. (2017). Sociologie de l'enfant acteur. Capabilité participative dans les loisirs organisés. Rapport au Fonds national suisse (FNS), projet de recherché 100017_153589. (Research Report).
Sutherland, E. H. (1992). Criminology. In E. H. Sutherland, D. R. Cressey, & D. F. Luckenbill (Eds.), *Principles of criminology* (11th ed.). Lanham, Boulder/New York/Oxford: Rowman & Littelfield Publishers.
Tisdall, K. M. (2008). Is the honeymoon over? Children and young peoples' participation in public decision-making. *The International Journal of Children's Rights, 16*(3), 419–429.
UNCRC (1989). *Convention on the rights of the child (UN, 1989)*. Accessed 27 Oct 2018 https://www.ohchr.org/en/professionalinterest/pages/crc.aspx
UNCRC (2017). *General Comment No. 21 (2017) on children in street situations*. CRC/C/GC/21. Accessed 27 October 2018 https://www.crcasia.org/wp-content/uploads/2016/04/G1717034.pdf
Verhellen, E. (1999). Facilitating children's rights in education: Expectations and demands on teachers and parents. *PROSPECTS (BRUSSELS)*., 223–231.
Warming, H. (2013). *Participation, citizenship and trust in children's lives* (Studies in childhood and youth). Basingstoke: Palgrave Macmillan.
Weber, M. (1978). Economy and society. In G. Roth & C. Wittich (Eds.). Berkeley: University of California Press.
Weber, M. (2013). *La domination*. Paris: La Découverte.
Wegner, D. (2002). *The illusion of conscious will*. Cambridge, MA: MIT Press.
West, A. (2004). Children and participation: Meaning, motives and purpose. In D. Crimmens & A. West (Eds.), *Having their say: Young people and participation: European experiences*. Russell House: Lyme Regis.
White, S. (2000). Depoliticising development: The uses and abuses of participation. In D. Eade (Ed.), *Development, NGOs, and civil society*. Oxford: Oxfam.

# Chapter 11
# Conclusion

**Daniel Stoecklin and Riccardo Lucchini**

## 11.1 Children in Street Situations: A Concept Uncovering Many Objects

In the introduction, we presented the reasons that made us see the expression 'children in street situations' (CSS) as a heuristic device that functions to illuminate a particular 'object'. With this concept, we started the search for an object. What is this object? Throughout the different chapters of this publication, we have collected different 'objects'. The heuristic function of our expression has then worked, as it enabled us to collect social objects illuminated by this expression. But is there a specific 'object' that would subsume all of the others, which would then only be particular aspects of it? The answer to this question can only be found once we have summarised the object, or objects, that each chapter has shed light on. We will then be able to see if they are aspects of a single object that encompasses them.

The first 'object' we identified, in the introductory chapter (Chap. 1), is the child itself. We are of course speaking of the individual as an 'object' of representations; representations which are more or less respectful of the individual's reflexivity. The most stigmatising representations are on the side of the 'substantialist' designations that associate the child with implicit projections about the space they are in – the street, seen as dangerous, unpredictable, dirty, and so on – that, consequently, seem almost intrinsic to the child. We have highlighted the objectification of children who are labeled as depreciated objects, listing the different names that have been applied to them. As a result, the social treatment of the 'street child' can only be violent: the child is apprehended as an 'object' that disturbs, and that it is necessary to move by forcibly introducing him or her into a process of standardisation. In contrast, our approach aims to understand the reflexivity of the CSS, as this contributes to shedding light on the broader context that conditions the child's path. We thus highlight the child's capacity as a reflexive actor, rooted in self-analysis. In this way, we consider the discourse of the child as the expression of a Self (Mead 1963), negotiating the image he or she wants to give of him- or herself, in accordance with the per-



R. Lucchini, D. Stoecklin, *Children in Street Situations*, Children's Well-Being: Indicators and Research 21, https://doi.org/10.1007/978-3-030-19040-8_11

ceived tension between behavioural expectations (Me) and his or her own aspirations (I). This discourse on the 'Self' reflects the actor's capacity to become an object for him- or herself. This objectification, unlike the previous ones, is not stigmatising, as it is self-made and thus does not fail by substantialism: the child does not perceive him- or herself as having the characteristics of the street, but as an individual with a specific relationship with the street-space. It is this relationship that is the object of our analysis and that is why we immediately stressed that "we consider that the object is neither the subject nor society, but the social process that is linking them together" (Chap. 1).

The substantialist vision of the 'street child' as an object is therefore denounced (in Chap. 2) as both stigmatizing and ontologically problematic: as objects are constructed by human subjects, human beings cannot have a substantial ontology, they can only be relationally defined. Any definition of a population demonstrates only the perspective of the definer. It cannot capture the ontology of the defined. Reducing someone to a static object, allegedly circumscribing its ontology, not only violates the right of this person to self-determination, but also precludes the possibility of relational identity. Labelling someone else not only confiscates the freedom of those labelled, it also imprisons the labellers, as it annihilates one's capacity to reflect on the self in relational ways. Every time in human history such substantialist reductions took precedence over relational identities, it resulted in massacres. This is why it is so important to abandon the label 'street children'. The expression 'children in street situations', by contrast, puts emphasis on situations, and hence on the relational dynamics of such constructions. Labelling 'street children' is an objectification that turns persons into objects, namely objects of intervention. Human beings are then 'abstracted' – that is, extracted from their context, which is a relational reality. They become a concept, a category, which is 'capable of existing in the absence of the object' (Jacquard 1997, p. 25), because the object has been emptied of from its own reflexive capacity. In other words, no particular child's voice is even needed to speak of 'street children': we already know who they are!...

The same reduction of personality to a social category has been made for numerous social categories, with dramatic consequences. 'Street children' are no exception in this regard. This stigmatizing label is socially constructed and certainly not just the result of natural inequalities (as the fate of being born in a family deprived of different capitals). This particular social construction induces the violence that these children are subjected to. The violence directed towards 'street children' comes from their objectification itself. This is why it is so important to reverse this perspective, and speak of CSS: it obliges us to address the situations, and hence the social constructions that led to their developments, and therefore to identify the 'objects' on which intervention is necessary as social processes and symbolic orders. This perspective displaces the targets: it is not people that have to be curbed, but processes.

Among the processes at play, the child's meaning-making, as an evolving capacity, is central. This has been shown particularly in Chap. 3. The 'child-street system' (Lucchini 1993) has been elaborated through the children's own reconstructions of reality. In turn, it can serve as a tool to understand how children connect things together and hence build objects. Each dimension (time, space, relations, activities, sociability, identity, motivations, gender) is an 'object' for the subject (the child) who actively elaborates the meaning of street life through the subjective links made among these 'objects'. In this chapter, we have shown that there is a link between the 'objects' upon which the child's subjectivity reflects and the 'objectives' he or she pursues. We have suggested that children's behaviours are not oriented by an instrumental economy (means-goal), as rational choice theory would contend.

The street is not just a means to attain goals. The child's motivation is much more complex: individual choices are socially constructed (Stoecklin and Fattore 2018), notably through social processes like identification, interpersonal relations, and negotiations of values. The 'child-street system' therefore triggered our reflections about the links between 'objects' and 'objectives' that have been developed later (notably in this book in Chap. 10). Besides, we have also shown that the child's subjective reconstructions (the 'objects' he or she thinks of) are also to a great extent influenced by the group. The group thus elaborates common objectives that reconstruct new 'objects' for every member. The importance of collective agency is underlined here by the consideration that any network is made up of "ties between actors (individual or collective) that form a mobile resource base for the accomplishment of specific objectives with particular conditions" (Houchon 1990, p. 213). Consequently, socialization and sociability (the sixth dimension of the 'child-street system') should be considered as not restricted to the street-space. Hints of the influence of larger contexts are suggested in Chap. 3, and these are then developed further throughout the book.

Among the 'objects' that children reconstruct we also find the relationships they have with persons of reference, like the bond with maternal and paternal figures with which the child may identify or take distance from (as has been shown in Chap. 4). The possible conflicts arising from multiple maternal and/or paternal figures are yet not sufficient to explain the child's movement to the street: it takes some catalysing event for the child to decide to stay in the street, for a more or less long time, and this event therefore becomes the 'object' around which all the images of the mother, of the father, and of siblings will eventually revolve. The departure for the street hence involves the construction of such specific 'objects', that are described as 'events'. Meanwhile, events and their respective importance are reconstructed through other factors. The child's appraisal of danger plays a vital role. Other factors, such as the geographical distance between home and the place where the child has found some sort of social integration in a peer group, also modulate the importance of past events and their influence on survival strategies. Space and time (two dimensions of the 'child-street system') are actively reinterpreted, and past events may become less important than new issues more directly linked to immediate survival and self-protection. The most pressing needs therefore tend to become the new 'objects' of preoccupation, and favour immediatism.

A 'less-harm' principle tends to preside over the child's choices, but to follow this principle the child must develop awareness of the symbolic rules, and not just the physical dimensions, of street life. Survival strategies (dealt with in Chap. 5) have led us to the heart of symbolic constructionism. We have shown that children need to use their reflexive skills not only to adapt to the conditions of street life but also to create opportunities. These opportunities are much more linked to verbal competences than to physical ones. It is the plasticity of discourses that allows CSS to construct opportunities that stem from the combination of (a) the resources of the actor (affective, cognitive, cultural, social, physical), (b) the occasions to act they encounter, and (c) their intentions or goals (Cusson 1981). This active elaboration of opportunities is an imaginary construction of 'foreseen objects'. Once an opportunity is realised it may become an 'object' the child can now count on, and upon which the child reflects to elaborate renewed objectives. The objects that acquire stability turn into routines or things that are considered normal and expectable. The elaboration of routines requires a minimal stabilisation of some modes of action. The strategies of CSS therefore lean on the modes of action that are most relevant and appropriate in the street environment.

Several strategies have been listed: the camouflage strategy (changes of identity, manipulation of nicknames and of age), strategies combining physical and symbolic resources (the case of Paulo in Chap. 5), and strategies for the self-protection and self-affirmation. Most of these strategies are non-confrontational, the child using the language of a vulnerable person and playing the role of a victim. These strategies are linked to the relational, moral and identitary modes of action. Less elaborate strategies, like stealing, are closer to instrumental-rational action (Weber 1978), or the entrepreneurial mode of action. It is interesting to see that children begin with less elaborate modes of action, and symptomatically newcomers are usually tested on their ability to steal, as a kind of 'exam' to be admitted in the group. Some develop more complex strategies, and hence routines, as they get experienced with street life. This confirms that there is a cumulative dynamics of the elaboration of objects, from the most concrete to the most abstract (this is further developed in Chap. 9).

The processual nature of street life is further highlighted with the notion of the 'street career' (developed in Chap. 6). The street career is made of different phases in which the street situation has a different signification in the child's eyes. This changing signification is mapped onto the eight dimensions that are constitutive of these changes, namely: (1) the child's ways of going to the street, (2) the child's references and identifications, (3) the child's symbolic and instrumental competences, (4) the child's level of integration/participation in the social life on the street, (5) the child's movements between different fields (street, family, institution), (6) the child's necessities and motivations, (7) the child's ways of leaving the street, (8) the child's perception of institutions and of adults. These variables 'producing' the different stages of the career of the CSS are all 'objects' reflexively elaborated by the child. As Fig. 6.1 (Chap. 6) suggests, these factors are interdependent. Consequently, the subjective change of any of these factors has consequences for the overall system. While the objective reality is not necessarily changing, the child's perception of it can evolve tremendously, and what has been experienced as exciting may soon lose its appeal, or the converse. The career of CSS therefore has a strong subjective trigger.

This is important to consider, as intervention for and with CSS can succeed only if the child's subjective appraisal of the situation is understood. A group of CSS is composed of individuals who are situated at different phases of their street career. Any intervention which would simply take the group out of the street and propose similar activities to all members therefore has no possibility of having a lasting impact on all of the children. One has to decipher the different phases of the street career, and an appropriate way to do this is to speak with each individual child about each of the eight elements of the street career in order to see how each child specifically reconstructs these 'objects'. The career of CSS can thus be viewed as being linked to differentiated symbolic objects that these children are able to actively construct: their representations of the eight elements in the diagram above are fundamental in the choices they make and the directions they take. This leads us to conclude that the modalities of leaving the street are also linked to these abilities to construct and to modify symbolic objects. The plasticity, or on the contrary the rigidity, of these symbolic objects is linked to dominant social representations, and therefore the child's trajectory will also depend on the level of negotiation that is allowed in the public sphere (as has been highlighted when addressing social representations in Chap. 2).

The more or less dynamic nature of the children's reflexivity is also reflected by the speed at which they evolve in the different stages of their street career. The stages of the career of CSS can, indeed, be seen as different orientations in relation to the objects they construct. These phases thus reflect modifications of the constructed objects. Here too we also glimpse a recursive relationship between objectives and objects: they are both in turn changing and changed, enabling and constraining. Structuration theory (Giddens 1984) thus enables us to show the importance of sociability (Chap. 7) in the construction of objects and objectives. The sociability of peer groups encounters spatial, social, and material constraints. But there are also many emotional aspects that mark the relations between CSS.

There is a vicious cycle between the instability of peer groups (notably in the example of China, with the extremely short duration of social relationships) and the instability of street life itself on account of changing circumstances (retroacting on the instability of peer group). This produces huge difficulties in constructing objects of identification. We can here recall the relation between the construction of abstract objects (culture) and safety (the domestication of dogs, for instance, is a way to achieve more emotional stability, and hence more safety) that is also observable with homeless youth in developed countries (Aptekar and Stoecklin 2014). CSS lack stable territories, by contrast with gangs that control territories (mainly in the slums), and hence their 'subculture' is also less stable. Their relationship with the street is more functional and instrumental than identitary. There are thus no strong marks of identification among CSS, whereas these marks (especially tattoos) are widespread within gangs occupying territories. The fragmentation of the street space is reflected in the less elaborate or less complex sets of objects (culture) that are constructed.

The 'objects' that are constructed by CSS remain rather basic, and linked to survival. This confirms that it is only when freed from survival preoccupations that humankind can develop a complex culture, where abstract objects like philosophies gain importance over practical instruments and tools. Many reports of a lack of safety at night-time reflect the constant fear of violence (also linked to police repression), which is an impediment to more abstract constructions. Sociability is therefore not grounded in abstract ideals: roles are diffuse and activities are shifting, allowing for the development primarily of near-groups and dyads; nothing like the 'big society' resting on a social contract sustained by legally binding conventions. The objects are less elaborate because of the preoccupation with material security over the satisfaction of identitary needs. Alternation, in turn, is more favorable to the construction of objects (by comparison of different spaces and their respective sociabilities), and this may also explain the movements of CSS. They escape boredom by alternating between spaces and hence developing more complex 'objects', but this nevertheless depends on constraints that are exerted on them. This is why we can say that alternating is also a survival strategy.

The issue of the body as an object is reflected through interviews conducted with girls in street situations (GSS) (Chap. 8): survival strategies explain how girls construct their bodies as potential sexual 'objects'. These transformations are not linked to the emotional indifference and the commercial character of prostitution, but to sexual abuse. It is therefore quite stigmatizing for them to be treated as 'prostitutes'. But here again the label has tremendous effects on identity, and reinforces the potential stigmatization of all women using the public spaces in their own ways, not framed by the normative standards of machismo. GSS therefore have more difficulties in constructing opportunities than boys do, because their objectives are less recognized. A more flexible way of constructing alternative objects is found in the consumption of drugs (Chap. 8). The fantasies and fictions that drugs induce make them quite attractive, especially when no other means to change reality is at hand. The polymorphic and polyvalent structural aspects of the group finds is reflected in the very high plasticity of diffuse impressions, and sometimes hallucinations, reached through drug use.

The functions of drugs associated with soft use (playful, hedonistic) and hard use (identitary, disinhibitory) illustrates the fact that the use of these products mediates social relationships. This has been taken further to inform the agency-structure debate (in Chap. 9). It has been suggested that the agency of CSS includes resistance to the values of 'out-groups', the latter including even well-intentioned social workers who intervene to safeguard their 'best interests' (art. 3 UNCRC). This is how we can better understand why CSS may resist even the kindest intentions to rescue them from street life, especially in the stage of the street career Lucchini calls the 'honeymoon with the street'. In this phase of the street career, the child feels most empowered because the negotiated assemblages of the group of children he or she belongs are close enough to his or her own subjective assemblages and distinct enough from the 'outside' world. This is especially observable in the us/them distinctions, and the corresponding constitution of 'in-groups' and 'out-groups'. Hence the sense of membership, and the corresponding acquisition of a specific valorised collective identity, is raised. As has been shown, the stages of the street career depend on a series of changes, mainly a subjective reappraisal of objective factors that do not necessarily have to change to allow a subjective change. The child makes a different evaluation of the situation, and passes then to another phase of the street career. The importance of subjective appraisal is underlined here, but this is only a methodological way to highlight the link between micro and macro factors: CSS use substances (drugs) to mediate the tension between their inside world and the outside world.

The multifunctionality of drug use among CSS, valid for girls and boys (Chap. 8 of this book), can be reinterpreted under the light of agency/structure. A very interesting link can be made with agency once we consider, as suggested, that agency is the form of structure: when this form stems from more relaxed interactions the actors can make softer use of products such as drugs. In any case, these products are enhancers, more than substitutes, for imagination. We have evoked the power of imagination with the case of the French composer Olivier Messiaen, who was able to survive a concentration camp by sustaining his ‘inner world’ by composing music, hence putting the ‘outside reality’ at a distance. The comparison with the strategies of CSS who similarly put the ‘outside world’ at a distance, with drugs as mediators, confirms the importance of this ‘third realm’ in between actors and environment. The ‘system of action’ helps us come closer to this symbolic space that has been viewed as ‘structure’ by Giddens (1984) and ‘habitus’ by Bourdieu (1984).

Imaginary objects are socially constructed, and they are hence indicative of specific social configurations. The imaginary objects constructed by CSS are reflections of larger social configurations. ‘Street situations’ are outcomes of intersubjective constructions of a multiplicity of actors, and not just the ones found living or surviving in the streets. These constructions are conflictual, as the legitimacy of the constructions of ‘outsiders’ is questioned by the ‘insiders’. The in- and out-groups constructed by CSS are a clear illustration. This is why ‘situated agency’ takes on the structural form of interactions (modes of action) that are considered legitimate in a specific place. The correspondence between agency and structure is therefore quite local. Tensions arise when either the agency of CSS or the structure of an outside organization (NGOs, the state, the police, the business sector) tries to impose itself over the other. Tensions are resolved when one gives up. And those who give up are CSS, because the ‘outsiders’ are too strong. Resisting them is almost like a death sentence: you cannot survive for a long time in the streets. That is unless this space becomes invested with rights, which is an ideal pursued notably by the General Comment on Children in Street Situations (hereafter GC on CSS, UNCRC 2017). How this might happen will therefore be of great interest not only for researchers but foremost for people surviving in the streets. With the notion of ‘situated agency’ we thus favor contextualised analysis of ‘modes of action’, and therefore a sociology of multiple transformations that is multidirectional and less deterministic than the Bourdieusian notion of ‘habitus’, and also more concrete than the Giddensian notion of ‘structure’.

The theory of situated agency (Chap. 9) holds that social systems are outcomes of interpretations. This helps us understand that behaviours are framed by the meaning given to reality by means of the limited and limitative symbolic world instantiated by language. The most pragmatical categories commonly used (‘thinking horizons') are structured and structuring, hence building up a "'virtual order' of transformative relations" (Giddens 1984, p. 17) which can be visualised with the 'actor's system' (Chap. 9). Drawing on the use of the actor's system in research on children's organised leisure,[1] research on children's agency in Australia (Stoecklin and Fattore 2018), and research on children's well-being in Switzerland (Stoecklin 2018a), this emerging grounded theory (Strauss and Corbin 1990) sees the institutionalization of children's rights in connection with specific "modes of action" (Stoecklin 2018b). The latter are "typical ways of acting according to dominant 'thinking horizons' that link together concrete items of perceived reality" (Stoecklin 2018b, p. 561).

Children learn distinctive modes of action that are relevant in their social environment. They 'assemble' reality according to the 'thinking horizons' that are most pragmatic in the different environments they experience. Their capacity to be included as competent members depends on such pragmatic choices. These choices embody the objectives of the actors, and they can be transformed into gratifications only if they are compatible with the 'thinking horizons' prevailing in a specific context: the objects that can be reached (whether material or symbolic) are linked to the objectives ('thinking horizons'). In a word: you find what you seek. And what you seek is structured by dominant accounts sedimented into 'thinking horizons'. Agency hence has a structure. Agency is not opposed to structure, seen as a barrier to self-realization: it espouses the form of the structure, along cooperative 'thinking horizons'. This view of 'structure within agency' emphasizes cooperation, including negotiations (which also rest on cooperation), whereas 'agency within structure' reduces individuals to opponents, trying to escape domination (which is always located 'outside' them). The theory of situated agency assumes that individuals cannot just be oppressed or oppressing; it considers that they are both (of course to various degrees, according to spheres and social positions). It gives way to a more nuanced vision of social dynamics. And street life is also made of such nuances.

In Chap. 10, it has been suggested that evolutionary humanism might take on more importance in the twenty-first century than both liberal humanism and socialist humanism, and that consequently 'freedom' and 'equality' might be reassessed in new ways. Children's rights are therefore of crucial importance, as this reassessment should be made with the largest number of possible stakeholders, including children. Their 'participation rights' are central, and their implementation today will have tremendous impact on future children's ability to actively take part in this debate and not just remain the object of it. Yet today, even in countries that are promoters of child participation, reality is far from compliant with the ideals. In Brazil, for instance, the gap between the legal framework of children's rights and their concrete implementation is significant (Rizzini and Strickland 2014; Cheng 2009a, b), and this highlights the institutional limits to children's agency (Stoecklin 2014; Stoecklin and Bonvin 2014a, b). In Brazil, CSS are largely not supposed, expected, or encouraged to participate in any decisions about their lives (Rizzini

[1] SNSF Grant 100017_153589.

1996, 2010). In some kinds of institutions, like the Children's Rights Council in the municipality of Rio de Janeiro, young people find more encouragement to participate, but this older youths, while poor and marginalized, do not necessarily have an experience of life on the streets, and there is little evidence concerning the effects of new laws and amendments of existing legislation in Brazil on the real freedom of children (Rizzini et al. 2012; Rizzini and Bush 2013; Rizzini and Strickland 2014).

The three forms of humanism (liberal, socialist, and evolutionary) have become politico-philosophical traditions that are conducive to specific institutional arrangements. They are sedimented hierarchies of civil, political and social rights (Quennerstedt 2013). These hierarchies are the visible tip of the iceberg, hiding the immersed part that is the political projects or 'regimes of truth' (Foucault 2012) that support the existing institutional arrangements. But these political projects are still all connected to humanism. The goal remains the same –a better life for humans – but following different routes. The General Comments, and hence the Committee on the Rights of the Child, try to balance these liberal and socialist views. This is particularly apparent in the GC on CSS (UNCRC 2017): the very long list of "the State should…" formulations makes one think of a kind of socialist-type five-year plan, while, on the other hand, the stakeholders are presented as having 'free will' and therefore as potential allies in the overall strategy. The belief that corporations would freely adhere to the GC on CSS sounds rather naive, but the tone, as it must be, is positive and optimistic. What makes it possible to come up with such a mishmash of liberal and socialist visions in a single UN document? How does this consensus among conflicting views emerge? What makes it possible to have the enemies dining at the same table? And how do they emerge from this strange dinner?

It seems that the only way for them to reach consensus is that they must share an overarching 'regime of truth' (Foucault 2012), namely the ideology of growth. It can be argued that growth is the central value shared by all governments, and that these oppositional political arrangements called 'liberal' and 'socialist' are only two practical ways to reach, by different routes, the same goal (Harari 2014). Whether during the Cold War or after, with this 'single thought' (*pensée unique*) no government ever explicitly and practically pursued a 'degrowth' policy, even though this option was advocated internally and internationally by changing numbers of stakeholders. So what makes the ideology of growth an overarching regime of truth? Is it just the result of evolution that has no reason (Harari 2014)? The logical, but meaningless, outcome of specialisation, which is the logic of evolution? Can we assume that liberal economy is compliant with the law of evolution? Credit is based on trust in the future, and the latter was made possible through the scientific revolution and the idea of progress (Harari 2014, pp. 344–347). With the idea of progress brought about by the scientific revolution thus came the prospect that, thanks to scientific discoveries, there will always be a 'growing pie'. This liberal narrative of capital investment for later profits could only take ground on the optimism conveyed by scientific discoveries and associated technological progress. Yet isn't this just a rather 'liberal' narrative of evolution, a fiction that is actually a sympathetic ally for the ideology of the 'invisible hand'?

It looks like the neo-liberal "pensée unique"[2] deliberately forgets to think about the qualitative sociological dimensions of growth. In his work on the social division of labour (1893), Emile Durkheim noted that the specialisation of roles in the division of labour (which he called 'organic solidarity') was not happening with an aim of sustaining economic growth thanks to competition (like the English liberal Spencer argued), but it rather had the function of social integration: the shrinking of collective consciousness associated with the vanishing traditional world ('mechanical solidarity') had to be replaced, and the division of labour was the functional dynamic that allowed both differentiation between individuals and cooperation among them. The growing autonomy of the individual consciousness, gradually escaping the total grip of the collective consciousness, was accompanied by an anomie that leaves individuals alone with choices and responsibilities that they do not always know how to assume. This individualization process, as painful as it might sometimes be, is nevertheless also a chance for self-realization. Consequently, modern selves have developed an ambivalence towards marginalised positions. CSS are therefore seen simultaneously as a menace to social integration and as a romantic figure of freedom. This ambivalence is itself an outcome of a liberal narrative of evolution, whereby progress is to be achieved by a 'free will' that expresses itself in ways that are socially conformist, being appraised in the terms of success, performance, entrepreneurship, and independence that have become the main indicators of a 'normal' growth. Growing in the streets is therefore seen as quite far from the standards of 'normal growth', as it does not allow for financial success. Street life may only secure short-term financial independence, and even this is not guaranteed. Street life is a deadlock, and children should therefore be removed from it and placed on promising paths eventually conducive to the highway of economic growth.

The hidden assumption that the 'correct ways' to human progress are on the side of economic growth is so strong that it even seems unnecessary to recall where these routes are: in the family, at school, in business. Hence the context is thought of as taken-for-granted. Yet context is not just space: it is linked to specific modes of action. This is why when we just talk of 'actors', detached from contexts, it is only logical that the regime of truth (growth and entrepreneurship) implicitly makes us consider rational actors to be those who optimize the means-end relation. As a final consequence of rational action theory is that the other modes of action are then disregarded. We are here speaking of actors out of context. Without an explicit theory od action, the social dynamic is reduced to the rational action. The dominant discourse (the '*pensée unique*') is a text without a context: it is a profession of faith. And, consequently, CSS are described as heretics, irrational beings, or even a threat to social progress.

We have seen that the GC on CSS (UNCRC 2017) reflects the three components of humanism: the liberal, the socialist, and the evolutionary. All three are trapped in the entrepreneurial mode of action: of securing growth, measured through individual performance indicators. It is thanks to this hidden regime of truth that the

[2] French expression meaning «unique thought» (homogeneous dominant discourse).

Committee on the Rights of the Child achieves consensual texts like the GC on CSS. Although the committee also adopts some 'socialist views' ("the State should..."), a General Comment, even on the most marginalized children, never goes as far as advocating redistribution of capital. The GC on CSS is in fact also tainted by the neo-liberal context which exacerbates individual responsibility. It is a tough job to reach a fragile equilibrium of the three kinds of humanism.

The General Comments always start by defining the population of children affected by a specific issue. In that regard, they are in keeping with a 'technocratic' conceptualisation of the problems. We encircle the 'pockets of resistance' that have a social functioning perceived as normal:

> The realities in which children in street situations live do not fit traditional definitions or conceptualizations of childhood. They have a unique relationship to public spaces compared with other children (UNCRC 2017, par. 36).

Even though this statement is not the object of negative judgement by the authors of the GC on CSS, the treatment usually reserved for any deviant use of the street comes out in the rest of the comment about the need to guarantee the right to peaceful assembly:

> State restrictions on article 15 in relation to public spaces may therefore have a disproportionate impact on children in street situations. States should ensure that their access to political and public space in which to associate and peacefully assemble is not denied in a discriminatory way (Ibid.).

Yet the definition of CSS (groups a and b) remains confined to a technocratic logic that deals with 'data', corresponding to legal-rational domination (Weber 2013). All of the data is treated according to an approach focused on the behaviours or statuses (and expressed in terms of numbers) and not in terms of social dynamics. There are only actors and the social dynamic that connects them is missing: we talk about CSS, the states participating in the Convention, NGOs, economic actors (businesses), and so on. And when we mention the connections between these actors, we talk about the ideal connections that should develop for the rights of the CSS (the beneficiaries of public policies) to be respected, but never of the real and actual connections between these actors. We are therefore not talking about the real social dynamic, but only about the one we, ideally, would like to see realised. This 'wishful thinking' thus places a considerable weight on the shoulders of the state, and a highly unrealistic one in comparison with the state's true capacity to conduct the actions it is supposed to conduct in order to make this ideal vision a reality. In the neo-liberal context of budget cuts, it is highly unlikely that the state could meet such expectations. Moreover, it is the states that face a social dynamic that produces CSS most that have the fewest means to change this dynamic, since they are precisely the ones that are drowning under the debts that the neo-liberal context is only increasing. We are then in a sort of schizophrenia in which we believe that the ideal debtors of children's rights are states, when these are, primarily and concretely, debtors of the development banks that are born of financial power, and whose primary objective is the protection of the elites' accumulation of wealth.

The individualisation of social problems, corresponding with the neo-liberal perspective, leads to the processes concerning these problems being made invisible: there are only out-of-context actors, out-of-system actors. When one identifies problems in terms of behaviours or individual statuses, then the indicators used are indicators of status: counts of the number of CSS, percentage of offenses, cartography, consumption, and so on, and not indicators of processes focused on life paths and social contexts. Such an 'individualisation' of the social generates a psychologisation of the social problems and a top-down interventionism. However, what characterises a General Comment is that it is issued by the Committee on the Rights of the Child as recommendations or guidelines for the states are party to the CRC. These states then have to translate these guidelines into public policies. Thanks to a GC that is a compromise between liberal, socialist, and evolutionary humanism, we can view the analysis of public policies in a critical way (see Fig. 10.3 in Chap. 10). If, as we have seen, human rights are the expression of the social negotiation that distributes responsibilities between actors and institutions, then the position of the different actors can be usefully visualised through this triangle. With the CSS that one claims one wants to place 'at the centre of the intervention', by favouring the child's active participation one must necessarily make the child leave the relatively passive position of 'final beneficiary'. It is about seeing how the GC on CSS positions the final beneficiaries and the target populations. The beneficiaries are the CSS, but they are not passive, and it is a matter of seeing how their own visions can participate in the remodeling of public policies.

In Chap. 10, we have seen that the typical images of the delinquent child, the child victim, and the failing child stem from the three branches of humanism: liberal, socialist, and evolutionary. We can now reassess the two typical icons evoked in Chap. 1 (the delinquent child and the child victim) and see that the third representation (the failing child) is becoming more prevalent today, with the neo-liberal insistence on individual responsibility. All three representations are common sense issues that we have to critically address before we can come back to the child as a social actor, the real child, and not the represented icon. We have done this throughout this book, and this leads us to conclude that granting CSS with access to their rights begins with an understanding of social interactions. Hence, sociology is of primary importance here. We have to understand how the child positions him- or herself as a subject faced with the objectification of which he or she is the object. More generally, it is a matter of understanding how a subject (here the CSS) reconstructs the 'objects' that surround him or her, including the image of self (as object) in the eyes of others. It is by considering this subjective reconstruction, informing the child's personal strategies, that a dialogue can be established with the child's active participation to seek for solutions or alternatives to current problematic situations.

We have seen that a linear vision of institutions construed as constraining people is a false representation of social dynamics. This also applies to the Convention on the Rights of the Child: neither the implementation of the provisions contained in the Convention on the Rights of the Child nor their assimilation or use by children themselves can thus be depicted as linear, or progressively linear, processes. This is what makes the assumption of the linearity of evolving capacities (art. 5 UNCRC) problematic: there is never a linear evolution of a child's agency. As underlined in Chap. 9, the child's capacity to influence its environment is evolving: it takes specific forms or modes of expression because it is the ever changing outcome of a recursive social dynamics.

The cumulative and recursive nature of action is of central importance in the theory of situated agency (Chap. 9). It highlights a fundamental issue regarding life on the streets as compared to other, more stable, spaces. More complex strategies and hence routines depend on cumulative experience that favours the construction of more abstract 'objects', such as solidarity, respect, or justice. Objects must be desirable in order to become relevant in interactions. Yet children's rights may still be an 'object' that is too abstract to be desirable by CSS, as these rights do not seem relevant for street life. Their formal shape is probably too distant from the unstable realities experienced in the streets to be properly understood and taken as a basis for a renewed mode of moral action. This point is quite important, as helps us understand the difficulties of a 'children's rights approach' with CSS. It will not suffice to disseminate the GC on CSS to turn the streets into rights-based places, because the "substantial" approach to CSS, which still pervades the GC on CSS,[3] is still framed by a deterministic, and not an interactional, approach: it does not overcome the subject-object dichotomy. It still thinks in actionist terms, with individuals considered as builders of their environment (and therefore it advocates for child participation), and in deterministic terms, considering actors as objects 'acted upon' by some sort of overarching force (and therefore it advocates for the rights of the child to become this overarching force). A supposed alliance between the rights activists and CSS is expected.

But reality is much more complex. For rights-based social practices to constrain people they must also enable them in ways that are felt relevant by these people. In one word, they must be felt practical. The constraints coming from an 'outside world' are transformed by the 'insiders', in the first instance according to the degree of acceptance. New norms are worked out from the inside. They do not just trickle down. This tells us that there is no object acting upon subjects without a minimum subjective consent or elaboration. This begins with the perception of the 'outside' world, and perception is also socially oriented, as we have seen through the notion of 'thinking horizons' (in Chap. 9). Consequently, opportunities are also the outcome of social preferences, with dominant modes of action switching the ways that specific objectives are built and followed. CSS are found at the crossroads of conflicting socially legitimate claims. We gain here some insights into the view of 'street situations' as negotiations of the symbolic order. Street situations, hence, can be considered a manifestation of anomie, obliging social actors to develop their own autonomy. The degree of elaboration of children's opportunities is therefore also

[3]As seen in Chap. 1, The GC on CSS defines two sub-populations: first "(a) children who depend on the streets to live and/or work, whether alone, with peers or with family", and then "(b) a wider population of children who have formed strong connections with public spaces and for whom the street plays a vital role in their everyday lives and identities" (UNCRC 2017).

linked to the complexity of social configurations. This again underlines the irrelevance of the substantial definitions of 'street children', and the necessity of focusing on 'street situations', as this allows us to highlight social processes that the substantial definitions hide.

The GC on CSS nevertheless focuses on children, starting with a definition of sub-populations (a) and (b) (see Chap. 1). But it also contains recommendations for updated information, and so it can develop into several 'comments on the situations experienced by children in the streets', based on children's voices recollected and analysed with them, under the methodological and theoretical guidance of researchers. As stated in the introduction, an ethical dimension is always present in research, and the present book also intends to pave the way towards more participatory research with CSS. This participation is of vital importance: the non-equivalence (in ontological terms) of social systems and actors justifies the emphasis on individual subjectivities. The way an individual defines his or her experience is, however, not independent of the 'regular social practices' in which he or she has been socialised. This makes the construction of 'objects' by CSS a quite collective phenomenon, in which they play an active role. We have identified several 'objects' reconstructed by children and by us on the basis of empirical observations. The expression CSS has worked as a heuristic device to help us recollect the 'objects' that this concept has led us to decipher. We were in search of an object, but we have actually identified several objects. They are all important, and one might now wonder whether there is an overarching concept that would subsume them all and provide a theory of street life.

## 11.2 Towards a Theory of Street Life

The 'objects' we have highlighted throughout this book enable us to go beyond the current state of play regarding research and intervention in the field of CSS (Aptekar and Stoecklin 2014) and to sketch out a theory of street life. The psycho-social heterogeneity among children experiencing street life (Lucchini 1993) has been stressed for more than two decades now. But what was still missing during all those years, in Lucchini's own words, was a theory of street life.

Some very important and new considerations about Lucchini's 'Child-Street System' can be stressed now. The 'Child-Street System' can also be seen as a 'structure', in Giddensian terms, and in fact the 'Child-Street System' already has several features that suggest a parallel with this Giddensian notion of 'structure'. It has the dual character of being both a medium for social practices and an outcome of them. The feature of time-space structuration is also present, notably with the notion of the 'street career', used in a biographical perspective. Clearly, the 'Child-Street System' resembles "a virtual order of differences produced and reproduced in social interaction as its medium and outcome" (Giddens 1979, p. 3). It resembles, but it is not yet, a 'structure', as some features are still lacking, and this is perhaps what makes the 'Child-Street System' a model and not yet a theory. To make it a 'structure', in Giddensian terms, would require that this model integrates a theory binding together the three dimensions of signification, domination, legitimation. The dimensions of the 'Child-Street System' in fact emerge from, and reinforce, these three elements of 'structure', which are constructed through social practices.

The distinction made between 'system' and 'structure' (Stoecklin 2017) is what also makes the CSS approach more complete than it was until now. The 'Child-Street System' (Chap. 2) is defined as a systemic model: all the dimensions are interdependent and therefore any change in one aspect affects the child's overall experience. This systematic character is precisely why the model is called a 'system', defined as "a system of relations between the child and the street" (Lucchini 1993). But, at the same time, the naming of the model according to its systemic aspect is probably also what prevented its conceiver from seeing it as a 'structure' in Giddensian terms.

Street life, captured in the diversity of 'street situations', is an ever-changing combination of constraints on the child and what the child makes of these as a social actor. Having both constraining and enabling features, street life (or 'street situations') can thus be seen as having, or even being, a 'structure'. However, there was a piece missing for the CSS perspective to become a real theory: the dynamics linking together signification, domination, and legitimation. The dynamics beyond the 'street career' are not only bound to the child's own subjective sense. Signification is linked to domination and to legitimation.

Street situations (as 'structures') evolve through the interplay between actors and social systems. These structures evolve according to the mutual double structuration between the actors' subjectivity and the "reproduced relations between actors or collectivities, organised as regular social practices" (Giddens 1984, p. 25). Yet, as has been highlighted (Stoecklin 2017), only actors are capable of meaning-making, because systems have no ontology. It is not possible to say that the social comes from the social, because it is not reproducing itself independently of human agency. To say that experience comes from experience precisely acknowledges that only humans have ontology and therefore mediate practices. Therefore, the 'regular social practices' that circulate in Giddens' theory are merely 'subjective representations' of practices, and hence the systems that are supposed to stabilise them. In other words, practices do not have an existence independent of their representations.

The 'Child-Street System', as heuristic device of understanding, enables us to conceive of the phenomenon of CSS as a 'set of relations' in which many individual and institutional actors are stakeholders. The context is recursively implicated in the practices, and our scientific analyses are no exceptions: understanding the configurations within which the life of these children fall also defines the possibilities of translating the sociological knowledge we offer into actions. The political, economic, social, and personal factors that define the qualitative aspects of life on the street can be clarified through international comparisons.

Riccardo Lucchini has laid the foundations of a 'theory of the child in a street situation' that reinstates the child's capacities as an actor while showing the limits of his or her agency, and which, consequently, is a major contribution to the development of guidelines and policies likely to optimise the implementation of children's rights in the street-space and around the child. In particular, the understanding of the social and symbolic skills that the child develops in order to improve his or her own condition on the street is at the core of this recognition of the child as an actor who participates in social change. We consider that the sociological study of CSS also constitutes a personal commitment alongside those who want to contribute to reducing the violence against these children.

Thanks to the heuristic property of the expression 'children in street situations', we have then amassed objects, 'social facts', that remain invisible when we cling onto substantialist definitions. The common sense expression 'street child' precisely invisibilises what we need to show: it focuses the light on the child and thus keep us from considering the broader context that participates in the structuration of life on the street. With the heuristic device formed by a less common expression ('children in street situations'), we have then shed light on life on the street as an intersubjective reality, and collected the experiences that the wide degree of openness of the concept, it suggesting the plurality of situations, is likely to embrace.

By studying the representations of the subjects that are 'children in street situations', we have examined what they interpret and rebuild in their own way. We would still need to compare these interpretations and reconstructions to those made by other actors concerning these same objects. In other words, it is a matter of comparing the selections and reconstructions of social objects. We then realise that the concept 'children in street situations' cannot find a specific substantial object to which it would apply, as a name would apply to a specific thing. This is not surprising, since the aim of the heuristic approach, going back and forth between concepts and objects, is not to 'stop' reality through definitions that are supposed to be definitive, but rather to co-build intersubjective space in a less chaotic manner, in order to find a better 'reality congruence' (Elias 1991). This is a constructivist epistemological position that highlights the social connections formed by intersubjective representations that sediment in particular ways. These particular ways can be identified through modes of action. This is the decisive step that we take towards theorisation.

Indeed, the theory of action is enhanced by considering that the modes of action (entrepreneurial, relational, moral, identitary, and motivational) form a structure that filters the interpretations that actors make concerning their social practices. This is what we can call a 'structure of pertinences'. It is a symbolic filter that works in a bi-directional way. Figure 11.1 (below) allows us to visualise this bi-directional filter as it structures social actors (subjects) and the social systems (objects) they build.

Objects are constructed through a language that enables fictional reductions of reality (eidetic reductions), hence constructing 'objects' seen as the existing in the 'environment'. The *thinking horizons* (ARVIM), are "reductions of these reductions", or "second degree reductions" (Stoecklin 2018a) that are pragmatic because they allow for social interactions to be oriented in conventionalized ways, through standardized questions such as "what do you do?", "who do you know?", "what do you think?", "who are you?", "what do you want?". They can be viewed as potential objectives (goals) of the subjects who decipher and categorize the attitudes and answers of others during interactions in order to adapt their behaviours accordingly.

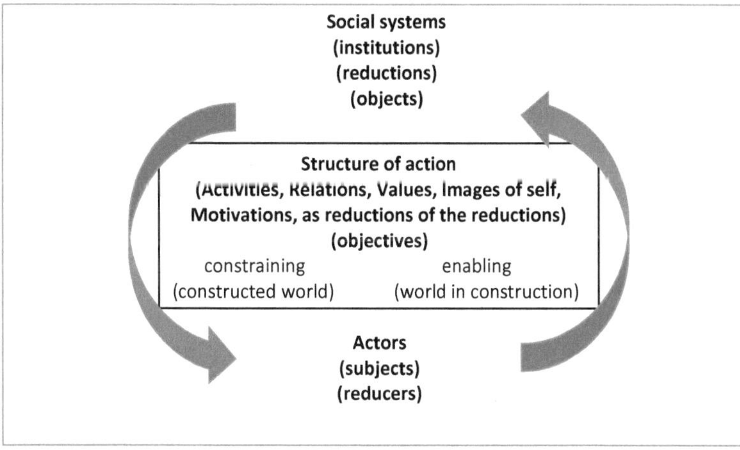


**Fig. 11.1** The structuration process. (Inspired by Giddens (1984). The arrows representing social practices)

This specifies Max Weber's definition of social action by detailing what the symbolic space mediating reciprocal actions is made of: for an action to be social, the subjective meaning that "takes account of the behavior of others and is thereby oriented in its course" must precisely decipher the relevant "directions to look at" (Blumer 1969), or 'thinking horizons' (activities, relations, values, images of self, motivations) that are relevant in the experienced situation.

The social nature of an action therefore lies in the reduction of the 'objects' that potentially enter into the course of the dialogue to one or more 'thinking horizon(s)', by which reality needs to be reduced in order to be invested with subjective meaning and hence intersubjective cooperation around these objects. (This is keeping in mind that even conflicting views on these objects also need a form of cooperation to take place: arguments can be opposed only if there is a minimal agreement that 'this' is a dispute; actors have at least to agree that they disagree.) Social actors (or subjects) are hence the 'reducers' who use 'thinking horizons' to invest reality with subjective meaning, and this is best done by trying to achieve the minimal intersubjective cooperation required to make reality correspond to their goals (objectives). This is how social practices (represented by the arrows) are constrained and enabled by the objectives of the actors, through the structure of 'thinking horizons'.

This is a dual structure, as it filters both the worlds constructed and those under construction. The filter is bi-directional. It corresponds with the structure of pertinences, with a configuration of common objectives seen as pertinent. On one hand, this symbolic structure filters the objects already constructed (the worlds constructed). On the other hand, the filter also works the other way, by enabling the construction of new worlds. Because humans can imagine non-existing things, they can also 'invent' them, make them real (Elias). Consequently, we can say that their objectives become objects. It is then the ability to transform objectives into objects that characterises humans. This works through thought and language, which constitute the "symbolic capital" depicted by Pierre Bourdieu:

> I call symbolic capital any kind of capital (economic, cultural, academic, or social) when it is perceived according to the categories of perception, the principles of vision and division, the systems of classification, the classificatory schemes, the cognitive schemata, which are, at least in part, the product of the embodiment of the objective structures of the field in consideration, that is, of the structure of the distribution of capital in the field being considered (Bourdieu 1998, p. 85).

Symbolic capital is not distributed equally among humans, it depends on social positions. The effective capability to transform objectives into objects varies between individuals, not only because of the individual's social position, as Bourdieu underlines, but also, and this is my suggestion, because of the dominant modes of action that are prevalent in his or her context. We can say that the ability to interpret built worlds comes down to a recreation of these worlds elsewhere. This operation of transposition can be seen as an operation of 'exfiltration', while the ability to ensure that worlds under construction are recognised is an operation of 'infiltration'. We can then understand that the ability to interpret and reconstruct (the act of exfiltrating) constructed worlds and the ability to ensure that worlds under construction are recognised (the act of infiltrating) depends on the position of the actors in symbolic fields.

This enables us to subsume what Bourdieu calls in turn 'categories of perception', 'principles of vision and division', 'systems of classification', 'classificatory schemes', and 'cognitive schemes': the 'thinking horizons' work precisely like such filters that are partly "the product of the embodiment of the objective structures of the field in consideration, that is, of the structure of the distribution of capital in the field being considered" (Bourdieu 1998, p. 85). If we admit that symbolic capital encompasses the other forms of capital (economic, social, and cultural), then we notice that the 'thinking horizons' that are dominant in a field enable the naturalisation of constructed worlds, because these 'thinking horizons' are invisible, and thus also render the process of social legitimisation that they 'exfiltrate' invisible: they transpose or export their 'classificatory schemes' in diverse fields. In other words, the 'thinking horizons' make it possible to 'exfiltrate' the distribution of the capital (economic, social, and cultural), and to recreate it in more than one field. Currently, the most powerful 'thinking horizon' is the one making 'activities' be seen in terms of performance, privileging an instrumental relation between means and ends, and thus the entrepreneurial mode of action, the evaluative measure of any action. This 'system of classification' of individuals is naturalised.

Bourdieu (1998) insists on the incorporation of a constructed world (constrained social practices). However, the example of 'children in street situations' shows that the subjective elaboration of a world under construction (enabling social practices) is just as important. CSS did not go to managerial schools in order to pass off their entrepreneurial mode of action as appropriate on the street and thus legitimate. It is indeed the individual's social position in the field that allows him or her to feel more or less attuned with the mode of action that is prevalent in this field. This feeling of syntony comes from the harmony between the collective mode of action and the personal mode of action. This allows to understand reproduction in terms of syntony between infiltration (internalisation) and exfiltration (exteriorisation). It is especially visible among the dominants of the field: the leaders in peer groups succeed in making their world under construction recognised (infiltration) because it is itself inspired by a constructed world (especially through the 'badasses' or 'kingpins' seen on screen) and because they interpret it as natural, and thus they exfiltrate and recreate in their environment.

Constructed objects thus result from (and are enabled by) 'thinking horizons', which form a structure of pertinences. As we have seen (in Chap. 9), agency is shaped by the structure of pertinences. There is not only the incorporation of an existing world (Bourdieu), but also the individual subjectivity that expresses itself through the 'thinking horizons'. These work as a bi-directional filter: from institutions to individuals and from individuals to institutions. They represent pertinent goals that channel individual energies and institutional injunctions. That is why we can say that agency and structure are one single thing when we see this thing as a structure of pertinences: objects are not only products of objectives, they are also producers of objectives. The recursivity of action can then be seen in these cyclical connections between objects and objectives. These are not 'inside' individuals (not any more than motivations are): they are situated in the intersubjective space of the symbolic world that connects the actors between them, and that sediments into specific institutions (objects).

There is no pure subjectivity, or purely subjective meaning-making. The influence of domination and legitimation over signification should not be underestimated, but this influence includes, in the last instance, the actor's own symbolic contribution, in terms of projections, to his or her environment. All individual symbolic contributions turn into 'regular social practices' once filtered (upwards and downwards in diagram x) through the 'structure'. This is precisely where the notion of 'translations' comes in. And this helped me to formulate the present theory of action, the theory of agency as the transformability of both objects and subjects. This is maybe the paradigmatic view that was missing for a theory of street life:

> With Giddens' notion of structure, made up of the interdependent dimensions signification, domination, legitimation, a 'theory of street life', that Riccardo Lucchini mentioned as 'missing' for so long, may now be formulated: street life is structured along meanings that are (re)produced by dominant modes of action and their attached sanctions. Hence, there is no way to exit street life that would not, at the same time, be a way out of the dominant modes of action and their attached sanctions. As long as the latter do not change, street life will remain what it is – full of violence, but also freedom – and social integration remains both comforting and alienating (Stoecklin 2018b, p. 584).

The simultaneously comforting and alienating sides of social integration are very much linked to the human need for recognition.

## 11.3 The Need for Recognition

CSS experience ambiguous emotional attachments. Their in-group relations are ambivalent, caught in between affection and defiance. Their recognition by others, and hence self-esteem, navigates between combinations of the three dimensions of recognition identified by Axel Honneth: love, rights, and solidarity (Honneth 1995).

By *love*, Honneth refers to "primary relationships insofar as they – on the model of friendships, parent-child relationships, as well as erotic relationships between lovers – are constituted by strong emotional attachments among a small number of people" (Honneth 1995, p. 95). Recognition is here "supported by an affective confidence in the continuity of shared concern" (Honneth 1995, p. 107). To some extent, CSS may reconstitute family-like relationships in their peer groups, and also erotic and sexual relations with partners, although these also tend to be constrained, which is not really *love*.

Honneth refers to rights when it comes to the interpersonal relations resting on reciprocal legal obligations. This is obviously not the case with CSS. Following Marshall (1963), we must consider the "classes of people to whom basic human rights are extended" and the "extension of the types of rights to which they are entitled" (Thomas and Stoecklin 2018). Even though the GC on CSS extends "the status of a responsible person" to them, the capacity of subjects to "reciprocally recognize each other with regard to their status as morally responsible" (Honneth 1995, p. 110) still depends on "the essential indeterminacy as to what constitutes the status of a responsible person" that is a precondition to the "structural openness on the part of modern law to a gradual increase in inclusivity and precision" (Ibid.). Yet cultural contexts are diversely locating this "essential indeterminacy" and are hence ready to include stigmatized 'street children' among those seen as responsible persons, leading to amendments of existing national laws and to new laws. Such structural openness is not solely to be found in the GC on CSS: it must also sustain the constitutions and laws of state parties. It is therefore in the local application of laws that the GC on CSS has to make a difference before it may eventually transform CSS into citizens. In other words, the GC on CSS might strongly benefit CSS in behaving as subjects of rights, but it is not self-sufficient. It will be particularly interesting to see whether and how art. 15 (the right of association), strongly advocated for in the GC on CSS, will be applied and respected. So far, for CSS, although the UNCRC and the GC on CSS are made to guarantee such extensions, the concrete conditions of life in the streets are not conducive to such realizations, because there is almost no room for them to claim their rights. Claiming rights is a learnt ability. No one is born with it. Consequently, children learn the forms of social respect that are prevalent in their environment. The notion of self-respect in terms of rights hardly develops for people who always experience backlash regarding their civil rights, as "the endurance of legal under-privileging necessarily leads to a crippling feeling of social shame, from which one can be liberated only through active protest and resistance' (Honneth 1995, p. 121; see also Fanon 1961).

*Solidarity* is defined as "the forms of social regard in which subjects are recognized according to the socially defined worth of their concrete characteristics" (Honneth 1995, p. 121). This kind of recognition is very important in the sedimentation of peer groups of CSS, as "worth" is very much attached to actors' concrete activities and their consequences, and not to their intentions. This "esteem" is for Honneth linked to the historically variable "cultural self-understanding of a society" (Honneth 1995, p. 122), and we may assume that children's focus on concrete outcomes reflects a street subculture characterized by a rather low "degree of pluralization of the socially defined value-horizon" (Ibid.).

By linking recognition theory (Honneth) and the 'actor's system' (Stoecklin), we can suggest that CSS experience recognition in terms of solidarity (esteem) and love (affection) more than in terms of rights, as instrumental-rational action (efficiency in the relation between means and outcomes) imposes on them as the most pragmatic mode of action in the street environment. The primary object of esteem constructed by CSS is thus the 'law of the group', as an emotional substitute, which they need to both respect and exceed (by personally surpassing themselves).

The discourse around children's rights, based on an 'abstract individual', is not really understandable (audible) for children who have experienced the street as their main environment. This is because this environment reduces the pluralization of "the socially defined value-horizon" (Honneth 1995, p. 122) primarily to the entrepreneurial mode of action, which does not consider rights to be the most efficient way to realize selfish goals:

> (…) the modern and abstract individualism underlying the principles of children's rights cannot be understood in an environment cultivating collective diffuse sets of rules closer to traditional and charismatic authority rather than to legal or rational authority (Weber, 2013; Stoecklin 2018b, p. 577).

This is why, as suggested in Chap. 10, the exit from the street is more than a simple change of place: it requires the ability to pass from one kind of authority to another, and this should be analysed as disciplining endeavour (Foucault 2012). This disciplining process is invisible in the 'saving children' narrative, which requires CSS to give up the traditional and/or charismatic form of authority they are familiar with and to adapt to legal and rational authority. Meanwhile, the routines associated with rational-legal domination are not prominent in the street environment, and consequently CSS cannot learn them here. Changing place therefore equates to changing the habitus, requiring a subjectivation that is only possible if long-term strategies are applied by intervening organisations: mainly NGOs. Yet the latter are under pressure from funders to achieve rapid results. This tension is also an explanation of children's "paradoxical overadaptation" (Samusocial international 2014)[4] to the street environment, although it is in the long run detrimental for them: adaptation to another environment seems too difficult for them in the short run.

## 11.4 Rights Acting Children

The theory of situated agency therefore provides a framework for understanding more generally the institutionalisation of children's rights as the dual structuration of subjects (children) and objects (rights) occurring in given contexts. This makes 'rights acting children' emerge as an interdisciplinary concept: it

[4] Translation from the French "suradaptation paradoxale".

> embodies the idea that certain forms of agency are adapted to specific contexts puts in perspective the socio-historical view of children as rights holders. The rights-based form of 'moral agency' is only one form amongst others that may, or may not, play a significant role in diverse contexts. Children who experience the street as their predominant environment are in a position where this kind of moral agency is far from reach (Stoecklin 2018b, p. 577).

Our observations concerning CSS provide us with a magnifying glass that enables us to see more clearly that it is the same thing for every child: their rights are only truly respected in the social configurations that are themselves already based on a legal-rational habitus, and that embody the 'disciplinary' logic of modernity (Foucault 2012). This reminds us of the necessary similarity between the principle and the nature of the government, dear to Montesquieu. The author of *The Spirit of the Laws* shows that each type of government is based on a social substratum that translates into a dominant sentiment. Hence the republic needs virtue and the monarchy is based on honor, while despotism needs fear. When the nature and principle of the democratic government become disjointed, the void tends to be filled by the principles of honor and/or fear, emerging from the other two types of governments. Legal sentiment can persist, relative to the reality of governance elsewhere, which is sometimes closer to multinational corporations than parliaments.

The habitus (Bourdieu) of a child subject of rights is more easily formed in certain contexts than in others. The street represents a space that, in an intercultural way, represents a context in which such a habitus cannot really be established for the figure of the abstract individual, where the subject of rights (be it child or adult for that matter) cannot find a social substratum to join. This is not necessarily a matter of development: nothing allows us to claim that the street is 'late' compared to other spaces that have, in the meantime, become legally ordered. It is even possible that the street prefigures the evolution of democracies towards a stronger charismatic power, despotic even, under the attack of the entrepreneurial mode of action, which only has the instrumental efficiency as a rudder. When 'the end justifies the means', we are indeed closer to a logic of force to the detriment of legal order, as is the case on the street.

That is why we refuse the substantialism that describes a population (the children) through specific characteristics, because these are not immanent: they do not come from the street situations. What characterises 'children in street situations' is not specific to the street, but comes from configurations far wider than what is directly observable in the microcosm of the street. We can thus also see life on the street as a symptom, among others, of economic globalisation. Through the observation of the strategies of CSS we discover a mode of action that is typical of the market economy, namely the focus on the means-end relation (the entrepreneurial mode of action) that subordinates other modes of action (relational, moral, identitary, and motivational). There is, therefore, no strict contradiction between the globalised world of Wall Street and the world of the street, but rather a continuity. People also take drugs in the most powerful business communities, they also wallow in almost feudal prerogatives, they also discriminate against victims according to inexperience, gender, and subculture, and the notion of human rights is as dubious as on the street...

We have highlighted (in Chap. 2) the importance of the duality of mediations between the personal and the social, which can be defined as a recursive set of "generative rules and resources" (Giddens 1984 p. 127). For Giddens, rules are made of normative rules and codes of signification, and resources are authoritative and allocative, and this cannot be equated with stable models (Parsons), or with a 'system of expectations' translated into institutions guiding actors in social interactions. For Giddens, structural functionalism fails to account for the necessary skills required for actors to be able to create the links between the elements constitutive of their actions. In other words, reflexivity is the central engine of social systems, it is not a by-product of a social system that would require reflexivity to function. The homology between collective consciousness and individual consciousness (Durkheim, Parsons), explained by the internalization of pre-existing norms, is a substantialist view, giving ontology to 'society'. This teleological reasoning assumes that society rests on a minimal integration of its parts, and hence every part that is put under observation must play a function: if it is there, it is because it plays a role in the maintenance of society. We hence end up with tautologies such as "x is functional because it is there, and if x is there it's because it is functional"… The world is not a harmonious system built up by complementary functions. The tensions between modes of action offers a more realistic vision, and 'functions' have different meanings according to different modes of action.

This is illustrated by the notion of '*Funçào*' (exposed in Chap. 7), which is much closer to feudal relationships than to the 'function' of abstract legal-rational provisions. It characterises the relationship between two children based on an exchange of protection for favours (for example finding food, getting money, washing clothes), usually for an older child. Reciprocally, these favours create obligations, which may be considered as 'protection rights'. But these are attached to a concrete person, not to an abstract individual. Different children hence define different prerogatives (which are not universal 'rights') that are seen as valid only among themselves, and that can, to some extent, be 'traded' or 'exchanged'. It is therefore necessary to avoid romantic visions of CSS. They are not romantics, and such a vision in fact does not help them at all. One object (of the group) may be the victim child: we have highlighted how the victim of the group is constantly supervised to avoid escape. The instrumentalisation of other children does not lead to collective emancipation. There is nothing romantic in it: it reproduces hierarchies and inequalities, including sexual abuse. Emancipation here is limited to the individual freeing him- or herself from the group, and does not correspond to a social movement of CSS emancipating themselves as a collective group. This is very different from the attempts made in movements of working children. Emancipation occurs when the victim is able to meet challenges, which reconfigures the boundaries of inclusion and exclusion. Challenges clarify these boundaries, and hence they are a functional object for negotiation. A challenge may in fact replace the function of hierarchical relations. As such, rational-legal domination, bound to hierarchical relations and pervading children's rights, remains alien to CSS: their organisation is much less formal, and is linked to ever changing circumstances. An abstract and formal rule of law is not functional in this context.

With these considerations, we come back to some elements examined in Chap. 7. Several points remain insufficiently researched, notably the notion of justice amongst CSS, and therefore their sense of responsibility. This requires a clarification of the tensions between cultural relativism and moral universalism, as the rights of the child are caught in between. The question of solidarity among CSS has thus yet to be further observed. Their behaviours display a moral sense that is 'contextual', with strong feelings of injustice linked to direct experience. Meanwhile, as has been highlighted, CSS have a tendency to judge others based on the consequences of their actions and not on their intentions. Acts therefore tend to be judged as intrinsically good or bad. The definition of the general good is not the principal criteria of judgement here. In survival contexts, the desirability of an act is linked to its practicality, and not necessarily to a moral standard. There needs to be a desire for objects like the common good for children's rights to enter in the structure or pertinences of CSS. This is not really happening so far. Nevertheless, as CSS choose the victims of their attacks, they are not just using the instrumental-rational type of action. Morality is also to be found within this choice. While pragmatism is predominant, it nevertheless combines with judgments on equity stemming from cooperation. This is not the kind of universal solidarity that presides over the Convention of the Rights of the Child: CSS do not base their own behaviours on the ideal of the 'abstract individual'. Things seem attached to specific people, and therefore the notion of rights attached to an abstract individual is alien to their daily preoccupations. The challenge of a rights-based approach is foremost of turning CSS into actors who are able and willing to use the notion of the abstract individual, and to identify with it. This is something that is taken for granted, but which in fact is not evident. That children may present themselves as victims does not mean that they necessarily perceive themselves as deprived rights-holders. To view experience in terms of rights requires many 'translations' (Hanson and Nieuwenhuys 2013, Stoecklin 2018a, b).

Research must highlight the translations within the 'children's rights agenda' – constituted of the UN Convention on the Rights of the Child (UNCRC 1989), the General Comments, the public policies of GOs and the operational strategies of NGOs – required regarding CSS. As part of the guidance to state parties, the GC on CSS is both a recognition that these children face specific deprivations and a means to curb the discriminations that deny them access to their rights. Observation of the factors transforming these norms into concrete realisations is therefore of primary importance for the sociology of children and childhood. This will allow to find out how the children's rights agenda is converted into participatory capability for CSS in different contexts and, conversely, how their participatory capability feeds back on the implementation of children's rights. It therefore assumes that there is no one-sided determination, but a recursive process. It will be particularly interesting to see how this can happen in the first place where state parties will allow it to take place, namely the care centres sheltering CSS. The findings here will allow us to reconstruct in analytical terms the whole system of translations of children's rights into practices that are more or less conducive to enhancing the participatory capability of CSS.

States party to the UNCRC are committed to integrating all of the components of this binding treaty into their public policy regarding children: not only protection and provision but also participation. The rights that are classified under 'participation rights' are the following: the right to be heard (art. 12), the right to freedom of expression (art. 13), the right to freedom of thought, conscience and religion (art. 14), the right to freedom of association and peaceful assembly (art. 15), the right to privacy (art. 16), the right to have access to information (art. 17), and the right to participate freely in cultural life and the arts (art. 31). All these rights will be the focus of this research, looking at how institutions deal with their implementation.

The reduction of behaviours to only a particular mode of action or, on the contrary, their expansion through all five modes of action will be the qualitative measure of their participatory capability: multiple modes of action testify that more possibilities of participation are at hand. These configurations (Elias 1991) of stabilised interactions in specific social systems will highlight the dynamics among the conversion factors (political, economical, cultural, organisational, personal) in the model of the capability approach. This approach ties the micro, meso, and macro levels together. Programs can be aimed at working with all or some of the three levels, namely the target groups that cause the problem (families, neighbourhoods, gangs, and so on), the recipients who experience the negative effects of the problem (CSS), and the political-administrative authorities who develop and implement a given policy (the state).

The choices (adaptive preferences) made by children reflect their positionings, as some other options – that researchers may identify through the comparisons with other the accounts of other actors (staff of institutions) and through observations – have not been chosen by the children (their capability set). The reasons behind children's choices and non-choices thus reveal another level of power structure, namely the modes of action (and their combinations) that are constitutive of agency and vulnerability. It is this level of analysis that the researchers should reach, not falling into the trap of reifying actor's discourses, but considering these discourses as indicative of the social dynamics that forge social practices. Hence, we can consider that the five modes of action (entrepreneurial, relational, moral, identitary, and motivational) are practical ways of converting entitlements into certain levels of real freedom. These modes of action reflect a structure of social orders (or social pertinences) that mediate social practices. How children's rights are interpreted and enacted within institutions shall therefore be the focus of further observation.

## References


Aptekar, L., & Stoecklin, D. (2014). *Street children and homeless youth: A cross-cultural perspective*. Dordrecht/Heidelberg/New York/London: Springer.

Blumer, H. (1969). *Symbolic interactionism: Perspective and method*. Englewood Cliffs: Prentice Hall.

Bourdieu, P. (1984). *Questions de sociologie*. Paris: Editions de Minuit.

Bourdieu, P. (1998). *Practical reason: On the theory of action*. Stanford: Stanford University Press.

Cheng, F. (2009a). The efficiency of Chinese welfare policy for street children: A perspective of the street children. *Journal of Social Sciences, 4*, 11.

Cheng, F. (2009b). Failure of the traditional childcare model and the causes of street children: An ethnographic study of the street children in the Shanghai Railway Station neighborhood. *Society, 5*, 8.

Cusson, M. (1981). *Délinquants, pourquoi?* Paris: Colin.

Elias, N. (1991). *The symbol theory*. London: Sage.

Fanon, F. (1961). *The wretched of the earth*. Harmondsworth: Penguin.

Foucault, M. (2012). *Du gouvernement des vivants – Cours au Collège de France. 1979–1980* (Edition établie par M. Senellart, sous la direction de F. Ewald et A. Fontana). Paris: EHESS – Gallimard-Seuil.

Giddens, A. (1979). *Central problems in social theory. Action, structure and contradiction in social analysis*. London: The Macmillan Press.

Giddens, A. (1984). *The constitution of society: Outline of the theory of structuration*. Berkeley: University of California Press.

Hanson, K., & Nieuwenhuys, O. (2013). *Reconceptualizing children's rights in international development. Living rights, social justice, translations*. Cambridge: Cambridge University Press.

Harari, Y. N. (2014). *Sapiens. A brief history of humankind*. London: Vintage.

Honneth, A. (1995). *The struggle for recognition: The moral grammar of social conflicts*. Cambridge: Polity Press.

Houchon, G. (1990). Pratiques et réseau: éloge de l'ambiguïté. *Déviance et société, 14*(2), 213–222.

Jacquard, A. (1997). *La légende de demain*. Paris: Flammarion.

Lucchini, R. (1993). *Enfant de la rue. Identité, sociabilité, drogue*. Genève/Paris: Droz.

Marshall, T. (1963). Citizenship and social class. In T. Marshall (Ed.), *Sociology at the crossroads and other essays*. London: Heinemann.

Mead, G. H. (1963). *L'esprit, le soi et la société*. Paris: PUF (translation from the 1934 original version in English).

Quennerstedt, A. (2013). Children's rights research moving into the future – Challenges on the way forward. *The International Journal of Children's Rights, 21*, 233–247.

Rizzini, I. (1996). Street children. An excluded generation in Latin America. *Childhood: A Journal of Global Child Research, 3*(2), 215–233. https://doi.org/10.1177/0907568296003002008.

Rizzini, I. (2010). *Direitos humanos de crianças e adolescentes: 20 anos do Estatuto*. Brasília: Secretaria de Direitos Humanos.

Rizzini, I., & Bush, M. (2013). Affirming the young democracy: Youth engagement in Rio de Janeiro. In M. de los Ángeles Torres, I. Rizzini, & N. del Rio (Eds.), *Citizens in the present*. Chicago: University of Illinois Press.

Rizzini, I., & Strickland, D. (2014). Growing up in contexts of vulnerability: The challenges in changing paradigms and practices for children's and adolescent's rights in Brazil and Mexico. In D. Stoecklin & J.-M. Bonvin (Eds.), *Children's rights and the capability approach. Challenges and prospects* (Children's well-being: Indicators and research 8) (pp. 253–272). Dordrecht/Heidelberg/New York/London: Springer.

Rizzini, I., Princeswal, M., Caldeira, P., & Bush, M. (2012). *A efetivação de políticas públicas no Brasil. O caso das políticas para crianças e adolescentes em situação de rua*. Rio de Janeiro: CIESPI-PUC-Rio.

Samusocial International. (2014). *La Suradaptation paradoxale. Une notion clé dans l'abord clinique et psychopathologique des enfants et jeunes de la rue. Cahier thématique*. Paris: Agence française de développement.

Stoecklin, D. (2014). Transformation of children's lives through their rights. A new approach to agency. In L. Chisholm & V. Deliyanni-Kouimtzis (Eds.), *Changing landscapes of childhood and youth in Europe* (pp. 328–349). Cambridge: Cambridge Scholars Publishing.

Stoecklin, D. (2017). The general comment on children in street situations: Insights into the institutionalisation of children's rights. *The International Journal of Children's Rights, 25*(4), 817–869.

Stoecklin, D. (2018a). Freely expressed views: methodological challenges for the right of the child to be heard. *Child Indicators Research: The official Journal of the International Society for Child Indicators*, Springer. Article first published online: February 5, 2018. https://doi.org/10.1007/s12187-018-9527-6.

Stoecklin, D. (2018b). Institutionalisation of children's rights: Transformability and situated agency. *The International Journal of Children's Rights, 26*(3), 548–587.

Stoecklin, D., & Bonvin, J.-M. (2014a). The capability approach and children's rights. In C. S. Hart, M. Biggeri, & B. Babic (Eds.), *Agency and participation in childhood and youth. International applications of the capability approach in schools and beyond* (pp. 63–82). London/New Delhi/New York/Sidney: Bloomsbury.

Stoecklin, D., & Bonvin, J.-M. (2014b). Cross-fertilizing children's rights and the capability approach. The example of the right to be heard in organized leisure. In D. Stoecklin & J.-M. Bonvin (Eds.), *Children's rights and the capability approach. Challenges and prospects* (Children's well-being: Indicators and research 8) (pp. 131–152). Dordrecht/Heidelberg/New York/London: Springer.

Stoecklin, D., & Fattore, T. (2018). Children's multidimensional agency: Insights into the structuration of choice. *Childhood: A Journal of Global Child Research, 25*(1), 47–62. Article first published online: November 29, 2017; Issue published: February 1, 2018. https://doi.org/10.1177/0907568217743557

Strauss, A., & Corbin, J. (1990). *Basics of qualitative research. Grounded theory, procedures and techniques*. London: Sage.

Thomas, N., & Stoecklin, D. (2018). Recognition and capability: A new way to understand how children can achieve their rights? In C. Baraldi & T. Cockburn (Eds.), *Theorising childhood. Citizenship, rights, and participation* (Studies in childhood and youth) (pp. 73–94. Palgrave Macmillan. (ISBN 978-3-319-72672-4. https://doi.org/10.1007/978-3-319-72673-1).

UNCRC. (1989). *Convention on the rights of the child* (UN, 1989). https://www.ohchr.org/en/professionalinterest/pages/crc.aspx. Accessed 27 Oct 2018

UNCRC. (2017). *General Comment No. 21 (2017) on Children in Street Situations*. CRC/C/GC/21. https://www.crcasia.org/wp-content/uploads/2016/04/G1717034.pdf. Accessed 27 Oct 2018.

Weber, M. (1978). In G. Roth & C. Wittich (Eds.), *Economy and society: An outline of interpretive sociology*. Berkeley: University of California Press.

Weber, M. (2013). *La domination*. Paris: La Découverte.

# Name Index





R. Lucchini, D. Stoecklin, *Children in Street Situations*, Children's Well-Being: Indicators and Research 21, https://doi.org/10.1007/978-3-030-19040-8

# Thematic Index





R. Lucchini, D. Stoecklin, *Children in Street Situations*, Children's Well-Being: Indicators and Research 21, https://doi.org/10.1007/978-3-030-19040-8

**D**

MIX
Papier aus verantwortungsvollen Quellen
Paper from responsible sources
FSC® C105338

If you have any concerns about our products,
you can contact us on
**ProductSafety@springernature.com**

In case Publisher is established outside the EU,
the EU authorized representative is:
**Springer Nature Customer Service Center GmbH**
**Europaplatz 3, 69115 Heidelberg, Germany**

Printed by Libri Plureos GmbH
in Hamburg, Germany